KEYBOARD EQUIVALENTS FOR HYPERCARD MENU OPTIONS

Menu	Keys	Option
File	Command-O	Open Stack
	Command-P	Print Card
	Command-Q	Quit HyperCard
Edit	Command-Z	Undo
	Command-X	Cut
	Command-C	Copy
	Command-V	Paste Text
	Command-B	Background
Go	Command-~ (tilde)	Back
	Command-H	Home
	Command-?	Help
	Command-R	Recent
	Command-1	First
	Command-2	Prev
	Command-3	Next
	Command-4	Last
	Command-F	Find
	Command-M	Message
Objects	Command- + (plus)	Bring Closer
	Command- – (minus)	Send Farther
Paint	Command-A	Select All
	Command-K	Keep
	Command-S	Select

Understanding HyperCard

Understanding HyperCard™

Greg Harvey

San Francisco • Paris • Düsseldorf • London

Cover design by Thomas Ingalls + Associates
Cover photography by Michael Lamotte
Book design by Karin Lundstrom

For Hans Andrew Jutus

Acknowledgments

Supporting every author are a great many people whose hard work and dedication contribute so much to the quality of the final work. I wish to take this opportunity to express a heartfelt thanks to all of the people who worked behind the scenes and helped bring this book into being.

At SYBEX:

Dianne King, acquisitions editor
Barbara Gordon, managing editor
Dave Clark, in-house coordinator
Jeff Green, technical editor
Karin Lundstrom, book designer and layout artist
Jocelyn Reynolds and Adam Zeff, word processors
Cheryl Vega, typesetter
Lynne Bourgault, proofreader

And elsewhere:

Tanya Kucak, editor
Elinor Lindheimer, indexer
Moira Cullen, Higher Education Evangelist at Apple Computer
Frances Yiu and Brad Wallonick at Computer Attic
Shane Gearing, my best friend
Chauncey, man's best friend

Also, I wish to express my thanks to the following companies for furnishing me with copies of their excellent software and hardware for this project:

Abaton Technology for the Abaton Scan 300
Ashton-Tate for dBASE Mac
Acius for the 4th Dimension
Adobe Systems for Adobe Illustrator and PageMaker
Great Wave for Concertware +
Living VideoText for MORE 1.1
Microsoft for Excel and Microsoft Word
Select Micro Systems for MapMaker

TABLE OF CONTENTS

CHAPTER   8   Adding Graphics to Your Stack   251

PART   III   Opening up the Possibilities with HyperTalk

CHAPTER   9   Getting Acquainted with HyperTalk   293

Introduction

This book offers a hands-on introduction to using HyperCard versions 1.0 and 1.1. It covers all aspects of using the program, and it contains many exercises that you can perform while on-line with the program. The material and exercises that you find throughout presuppose no prior experience with HyperCard or any programming language and little familiarity with the Macintosh. You should be able to complete all of the exercises even if HyperCard is the first software program that you have used on the Macintosh.

Part I gives you an overview of HyperCard: what it is and what it does. These chapters provide information on the basic workings of the program. Here, you will learn how to find, edit, and print information in existing stacks.

Part II gives you an introduction to producing your own HyperCard applications. As a result of working through the material in these chapters, you should be able to create your own stacks in HyperCard. It will acquaint you with the components of a HyperCard stack, how to link information in a stack, and how to use the built-in graphics program to add graphic images to your applications.

Part III introduces you to scripting with HyperTalk, the English-like programming language used by HyperCard, whose use vastly extends the power and versatility of the program. Each chapter in this section of the book builds on the one before, giving you a structured view of HyperTalk and its many uses.

The appendices to the book include a complete reference to the commands, functions, properties, and constants used in HyperTalk. Appendix A gives you an alphabetical listing of all HyperTalk commands. Appendix B gives you an alphabetical listing of the functions, arranged in two groups: general and mathematical. Appendix C lists the properties and constants used by the program. The properties are arranged according to the objects they modify, followed by a list of the constants.

It is my sincere hope that this book will provide you with a solid working knowledge of HyperCard and enable you to be immediately productive with it.

Conventions Used in This Book

Throughout this book, you will find notes in the left margin that annotate the general text. There are three types of notes used: general notes (the pointing finger icon), tips (the check mark icon), and warnings (the bull's-eye icon). The notes in the first few chapters are generally designed to help users who are new to the Macintosh. Notes that occur in the later chapters are designed more for users who already have some experience with HyperCard. Many give you alternate ways to accomplish a given task or relate the ideas introduced to another part of the program. They can be used by new users when reviewing the material in a particular chapter. You will also find special information on version 1.1 of HyperCard in the marginal notes.

When you come upon an exercise in the text, all of the steps that you are to perform are sequentially numbered and indicated in boldface type. Explanatory material that accompanies the steps is not shown in boldface type. Whenever possible, Command-key alternatives are indicated along with the mouse-based methods.

P A R T I

Getting Acquainted with HyperCard

HYPERCARD IS NOT A PROGRAM THAT IS EASILY categorized. On one level, you can approach HyperCard as an information retrieval system that you use primarily to look up specific data in applications developed by others. On another level, you can approach it as a development system that allows you to create your own information-based applications. When using either approach, there is a common metaphor that HyperCard uses, that of a file *card* and a group of related cards combined into a *stack*.

Most often, each electronic file card in a particular HyperCard stack follows the same presentation, thereby standardizing the layout of the information it contains. This is analogous to any paper card file you use, whether it be the card catalog at the library, a rolodex file at the office, or a stack of 3×5 cards for a research paper. When using HyperCard, each screen of information on your Macintosh represents a single card in a particular stack of cards. Regardless of the way in which the information (including text and graphics) is presented on the screen, the basic unit that you view and work with at all times is one card out of a stack of related cards.

As you will see, there are several methods for quickly locating a particular card or specific information in a HyperCard stack. One of the benefits of using HyperCard is the speed with which it can locate information. You will find this aspect especially welcome if you use HyperCard primarily as a research tool where you look up information in stacks created by other people.

HyperCard versus Database Management Programs

If an electronic file card layout and quick search/retrieval were the only major features that HyperCard offered you, you might well wonder what sets HyperCard apart from other file managers and database management software available for the Macintosh: Omnis 3, dBASE Mac, and the 4th Dimension, to name a few.

As you may know from experience with one of these programs, database managers allow you to design input forms into which you enter the data you wish to store. Once you design the basic form, you use it not only to enter data but also to edit specific data items as required. Each item of data in an input form is stored in a specific location referred to as a *field*. Collectively, all of the fields in the input form make up a single *record* of the database. In HyperCard, a single card is analogous to a database record. It, too, can contain fields that hold text-based information.

HyperCard allows you to design a card form for your stack, similar in many ways to a database input form. On this card form, you can arrange fields for storing each item of text data that you wish to maintain in the card file (stack). However, as stated earlier, HyperCard restricts the layout of the input form to the basic file card format. Despite this limitation, you still have a great deal of freedom when designing card forms, because the HyperCard "form" can consist of almost any layout that your Macintosh can display in a single screen view.

Database programs make you declare the type of data entry that a field can contain. At the most basic level, these programs differentiate between fields that contain character strings (text) and those that contain numbers. The basis of this division is that number fields can be calculated, where character fields cannot. Depending upon the program in question, it may further differentiate number-type fields into those that contain special numbers representing dates and times and the logical values of true or false (1 and 0), and those that carry standard values.

When setting up fields in HyperCard, you do not have to declare the type of data that they can carry beforehand. This is because HyperCard stores *all* field entries of the card as *text* (character strings).

As you will see later in this book in the section on authoring in HyperCard, text fields are created as boxes that you size. By increasing the size of the field, you increase the number of lines it contains as well as the overall line length. If you need to create a field that will contain more lines than will fit on a single card, you can make it a scrolling field. This type of field contains a window with a vertical scroll bar. By clicking on the gray area in the scroll bar or dragging the scroll box, you can bring hidden text into view. Besides being able to size a text field, you make its lines visible and/or its outline visible on the card.

It does not matter whether you enter *500* or *Five Hundred* in the field, for both are treated as text. Although this presents somewhat of a problem when you wish to perform calculations between fields in a card (see Chapter 14), it eliminates this step of designating the field type and makes it much easier and faster to locate information in the HyperCard stack.

It is also important to note that a card created in HyperCard is not restricted to displaying only text fields in a card. HyperCard contains its own painting program (a definite improvement on MacPaint) with which you can design graphics that can be displayed along with text fields or alone. You can also incorporate graphics generated with graphics programs such as MacDraw or MacPaint, the Adobe Illustrator, GraphicWorks, and the like. Whereas most database managers for the Macintosh allow you to use graphics in designing the input form as well as entries in specific database fields, the ease with which you can generate and include graphics in cards sets HyperCard apart from the database programs on the Macintosh. Moreover, with HyperCard you can generate sounds in cards, including musical notes that were created in HyperCard or with a stand-alone program such as ConcertWare + or MusicWorks, or speech generated with a program such as MacinTalk.

Relating Information

Database management programs such as dBASE Mac, 4th Dimension, and Omnis 3 provide you with the means for relating data kept in separate tables or files. These systems are referred to as *relational* database systems. They allow you to link information kept in separate tables by designating certain fields as key. The reason for relating fields is twofold: it eliminates the need to duplicate data entries in the database, and it allows you to create reports using selected information from any related table.

HyperCard also allows you to link information stored in different cards, whether in the same stack (file) or another stack. However, when you create links in HyperCard, they are *direct* links, quite unlike those created in a relational database system. Whereas a link in a relational database system points indirectly to information stored in

The difference between the links created by HyperCard and standard relational database systems is quite significant: it makes HyperCard more versatile when it comes to browsing through the information contained in stacks and less versatile when it comes to reporting on the information in them.

a separate file so that it can be used selectively in reports, a Hyper-Card link takes you right to the new card and displays whatever information that card contains.

As a result of the direct links that HyperCard maintains, it is ideally suited to different types of applications than those to which relational database management systems are put. In fact, it is this ability to establish links between any card in the same or a different stack that makes HyperCard so flexible when it comes to creating information storage and retrieval systems. To understand how this is so, let's consider how linking works in HyperCard.

Figure 1.1 illustrates typical links that can be set up between cards. In HyperCard, you use buttons to activate the links between cards. When you click on a particular button, the script associated with that button is activated. Quite often, the button script simply instructs HyperCard to take you to a new card. This card can be in the same stack or a different stack. Figure 1.1 shows both of these movements: clicking on Button 1 takes you to the first card in a second stack, and clicking on Button 2 takes you to the third card in the same stack.

Because HyperCard makes it so easy to move to cards in the same or a different stack (which can use a totally different format), it allows you to relate information in a free-form manner, similar to the manner in which we think. For example, suppose you wanted to create a

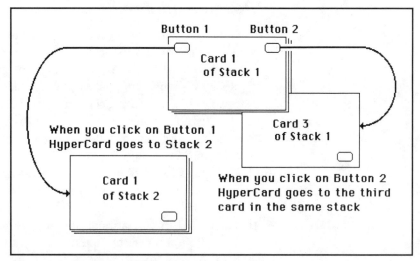

Figure 1.1: Diagram of typical links in HyperCard

teaching application in HyperCard that outlines the history of Western Architecture. In designing the tour of architectural history, you would probably find it advantageous to set up several stacks, each of which uses a slightly different card format (Figure 1.2).

The basic design of the primary stack would contain several text fields used to explain the salient features of the prevalent style of architecture of the times. Along with the text fields, the card could have two graphic elements, one representing a timeline and another a map of the Western hemisphere. The timeline would contain a series of buttons that would send the user to a related card in the same stack that discusses the architectural style prevalent during the time selected.

The map, on the other hand, would contain a series of buttons that would send the user to the appropriate card in a different stack, which illustrates a famous example of the architecture constructed in the particular region selected. This stack would be graphics-based, including pictures and diagrams of architectural forms such as the column, arch, and flying buttress as well as famous building examples such as the Pyramids of Giza, the Parthenon in Athens, the Colosseum in Rome, Chartres Cathedral in France, and so on.

Beyond the links established by the timeline and map in the basic card format, you could establish further links at any point in the discursive text that would take the user to a new, related topic. For

The links between cards can be used to create a web of interdependencies that provide the reader with a wealth of related information, from vital to trivial, on the topic at hand.

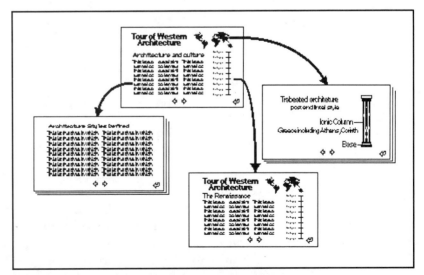

Figure 1.2: Structure of a hypothetical application

All of the different card stacks and informational links required by an application are called *stackware*.

example, you could annotate a discussion on Greek temples with a button that would take the reader to a card in a new stack that discusses the religious rites of the time. In this way, you can link any two items of information that reside on different cards in the tour of Western Architecture.

Once you are finished building the stacks and entering the information into all of the cards, you will have created a network of information whose data can be accessed in several different ways. Through the timeline and its associated buttons, the user can browse straight through the history of architecture card by card, or jump directly to a specific card (or group of cards) detailing a style of architecture prevalent at a given time. Anywhere along the way, the user can detour to annotations in the form of note cards that spotlight the economy, religion, engineering techniques, and famous architects of the region and time. It is also possible to take a different type of architectural tour with this application, since the user can click the buttons associated with the map to browse through a graphics-based stack or go directly to a specific card that contains pictures and diagrams of architectural monuments and components used in different regions at various periods in history.

Notice that this stackware contains both text-based and graphics-based information, as is required to adequately cover the subject matter of architecture. Given the planned design of this hypothetical application, you will have made it possible for the user to obtain this information according to changing needs. Users can look up information in a linear fashion according to the timeline of architectural history, or in a nonlinear fashion according to the examples of a particular region. The important point is that information can be accessed as the user's needs require at the time.

Modifying Existing HyperCard Applications

The architecture tour example should give you some idea of the versatility of HyperCard. Although you could create the architecture tour application with a database management program, it would require a great deal more work than with HyperCard. This is because, for the most part, database managers are not equipped to allow you to relate information as you go. Therefore, you would have to work out all of the details (especially informational links) before you began any work on the application itself. If, in the course of using your application, you found that substantial changes were required to its structure, you would have to proceed with care to ensure that none of your data were adversely affected.

This is in contrast to HyperCard, where it is easy to make changes to the structure of an application at any time in its life to meet new informational requirements. As you will see, HyperCard makes it easy to borrow elements from existing applications, modify the design of cards, and link information in different cards. And you can learn to perform all of these operations quickly. None of them require any in-depth knowledge of the workings of HyperCard (not to mention data systems design). All that is necessary is a little practice with the basic features of the program.

The great promise of HyperCard is that it will enable professionals of all kinds to build the information-based applications that meet their unique needs without requiring them to submit to the rigorous structure demanded by database management programs. In practical terms, this means that the real limitations to designing Hyper-Card applications reside in its fixed card format and the limits of your imagination.

The tour of Western Architecture example illustrates the major strengths of HyperCard:

- HyperCard allows you to build a flexible information retrieval system that does not constrain the user into one way of looking at the information it contains.

- The system can include text and nontext information (both graphics and sound).

- Applications can be designed and executed quickly, and do not require a background in or previous exposure to programming.

- Applications can be easily modified to meet new requirements.

- Applications can be designed for any subject matter, whether for business, academic, or home requirements.

HyperCard and Database Managers Revisited

The foregoing discussion is not meant to imply that there is no longer any place for database management programs on the Macintosh now that HyperCard has arrived. For in fact, database managers are better suited to certain tasks, primarily those involving the creation of sophisticated reports and selecting of subsets of data according to complex criteria. These two related tasks are the real strength of all database management programs.

Although you can create simple reports in HyperCard, it is not really designed to do reporting on the level possible with a relational database. You would find it much less work to create a report format including data from related files and calculations with a database manager than you would with HyperCard. This is all the more true considering that most reports include only a portion of the data selected according the search criteria applied to the entire database. Although you can set up such criteria to locate specific information in a HyperCard stack, it requires the use of HyperTalk (the programming language included in HyperCard) and is generally more difficult to accomplish than with the query facilities built into a database manager.

HyperCard excels as a browsing tool (prompting some reviewers to dub it a browserbase) rather than a reporting tool. It is best used for applications that require information to be organized and presented on-line. Within this framework, its only limitation is that the information must be presented within a single-screen card form. The contents of the information, whether text, graphics, or sound-based, and how it is interconnected, are left entirely up to you.

The HyperCard Command key is denoted by an apple (🍎) or cloverleaf (⌘) symbol on the keyboard.

How HyperCard Is Organized

The HyperCard program is organized into five distinct user levels, referred to as User Preferences:

- Browsing
- Typing
- Painting

To set a new user level, you need to get to the User Preferences card in the Home stack. This is the last card in the stack that contains the Home Card. To get to it, you can press Command-H to get to the Home Card and then Command-4 to get to the User Preferences card. Once there, you can set a new level by clicking the appropriate radio button. When you change the level, new menu options will sometimes appear on the Menu bar.

• Authoring

• Scripting

In practice, the five user levels naturally combine into three modes of working in HyperCard:

• Browsing/Typing

• Painting/Authoring

• Scripting

To use HyperCard in Browsing/Typing mode, you set the User Preference level to Typing. To use HyperCard in Painting/Authoring mode, you set the User Preference level to Authoring. To program in HyperCard with HyperTalk, you set the User Preference level to Scripting.

The Browsing and Typing Levels

When you set the User Preference level to Browsing, you can use HyperCard to perform only its browsing operations, which include viewing cards in the stack, locating specific information in cards, and jumping to linked cards. You keep the level set to Browsing if you are using stackware that does not require any updating, such as the tour of Western Architecture, whose information is intended to be absorbed in the same way as as when reading a book.

However, you need to set the User Preference level to Typing if you are using a stack that does require routine editing, such as the Address stack supplied with HyperCard. Typing mode allows you to perform all of HyperCard's editing functions, which include adding and deleting cards in the stack, filling out fields in new cards, and changing data in existing cards.

When the level is set to Typing, you can not only perform all of these editing functions, but also all of the browsing functions. The Typing level, then, is used whenever you need not only to find information in a stack but also to be able to modify the information it contains.

Chapters 2 through 4 in Part I will acquaint you with using Hyper-Card in Browsing/Typing mode. Chapter 2 contains a complete description of using HyperCard at the Browsing level. In Chapter 3, you will learn how easy it is to modify information in a HyperCard stack using the Typing level. Finally, Chapter 4 teaches you how to obtain printed copies of cards as well as set up simple reports from the information in a stack.

The Painting and Authoring Levels

When you set the User Preference level to Painting, you can use HyperCard's built-in painting program to add, delete, and modify graphic elements in the cards in the stack. If you have used MacPaint or SuperPaint, you will find HyperCard's painting tools quite familiar.

You will need to set the User Preference level to Painting only when you are designing new card forms or making modifications to existing ones. Normally, however, you set the User Preference level to Authoring when creating new stacks, because at the Authoring level, you can use the painting tools as well as set up links between cards (a function that is not available when the level is set just at Painting).

HyperCard uses the term *authoring* to mean designing and implementing an application of any kind that involves designing card forms and linking stacks. If you are an instructor, you may think of authoring in the more specialized sense of CAI (computer-aided instruction) or CBT (computer-based training), where the application is most often a lesson delivered by the computer. Although you certainly can use HyperCard to create such applications, this cannot be done from the Authoring level alone. To create real CAI or CBT lessons with HyperCard requires knowledge and use of HyperTalk in the Scripting level (described in the next section).

Part II of this book is devoted to using HyperCard in Authoring mode. Chapter 5 introduces you to all of the components of a stack, preparing you to create stacks of your own. In Chapter 6, you will trace the steps that you typically follow in creating your own stacks. After learning how to create a stack, you will then learn how to relate information in different cards in Chapter 7. In Chapter 8, you will learn how to use the painting program to add graphic elements to the basic design of a card as well as to specific cards in a stack.

The Scripting Level

When you set the User Preference level to Scripting, you have complete access to HyperTalk, an English-like programming language included in the product. Note that you do not have to learn how to use HyperTalk in order to create your own stackware in HyperCard. However, the applications you create solely from the Authoring level will be limited, for without HyperTalk you can do no more than set up direct links between cards.

Although the first applications you create in HyperCard may not require any "programming" beyond linking information stored in different cards, you will undoubtedly soon come up with applications that can benefit from the use of simple HyperTalk scripts.

Even if you have never had any exposure to programming languages, you should have no trouble mastering the basics of HyperTalk. The language uses a syntax close to that of English, making it easy to read and, therefore, to understand. If you are a programmer, or have had some exposure to programming languages (either on the Macintosh or some other computer), you will also find HyperTalk easy to learn.

You should be advised, however, that you may find HyperTalk to be quite unlike the languages you know. This is because HyperTalk does not create "programs" as they are commonly understood in traditional programming. When using computer languages such as C, Pascal, or BASIC, you enter a complete series of command statements (using the syntax peculiar to the language used), executed in sequence when the program is run, that control the entire working of the application.

In HyperCard, you use HyperTalk to create short scripts, executed only when links established in the stack are activated (or when you enter a command statement directly), that control just the working of a small part of the application. This means that you do not use HyperTalk to create a monolithic program to run your stackware. Rather, you use it just to set up limited actions between components of the stack.

As a result of the way scripting is used in HyperCard, you will find it much easier not only to design procedures but also to debug the scripts you create in HyperTalk. So too, this system of limited control makes it a great deal easier to add new features to the application or modify existing ones.

Part III of this book is devoted entirely to teaching you how to use HyperTalk. Chapter 9 gives you an overview of HyperTalk and its capabilities. Then, Chapters 10 through 14 introduce you step-by-step to using HyperTalk in the Stackware you create. As you will learn in these chapters, HyperTalk can be used to direct navigation within stacks; control the actions the program takes, depending upon the outcome of the input you give it or an existing condition; control the screen display; and perform calculations. In Chapter 15, you will see how HyperTalk enables you to use HyperCard with other Macintosh applications. Also, you have a complete reference of all HyperTalk commands and functions in Appendices A and B.

The HyperCard Disks and Startup Procedures

HyperCard requires at least 1 megabyte of memory to run (the program alone, not counting the memory needed for the System files, requires 750K). This restricts the program to the Mac 512KE, Mac Plus, Mac SE, and Mac II.

The program comes on four 800K diskettes:

- **Disk 1: HyperCard Startup**, which contains the System file, HyperCard Application file, ImageWriter printer driver, and a folder containing sample HyperCard stacks.

- **Disk 2: HyperCard and Stacks**, which contains a backup copy of the HyperCard Application file, and two folders containing sample stacks.

- **Disk 3: HyperCard Help**, which contains a folder with three stacks that make up the on-line help for HyperCard.

- **Disk 4: HyperCard Ideas**, which contains a folder with five stacks that provide you with stack, card, and button ideas you can incorporate into the stackware that you create.

If you start HyperCard with the Startup disk (Disk 1), you will go straight into HyperCard, as this disk does not include a copy of the Finder. This was necessary to provide enough room for the example stacks included on the disk. You can use the Startup disk to run HyperCard if you have only a single disk drive.

If you have a hard disk, you can copy all of the example stacks into the folder that you create for the HyperCard Application file (you only need to copy this once from either Disk 1 or 2). Later, after you have experimented with the stacks supplied with the program, you can decide which ones to delete from the desktop. While the program is still new to you, you should probably keep the Help folder on the hard disk, as it contains a wealth of information on using HyperCard. This includes valuable information on using HyperTalk, which is in short supply in the HyperCard manual (see Using HyperCard's Help Stack, which follows).

Figure 1.3 shows you the icons used for the HyperCard Application file and those used to designate stacks created with it. To start HyperCard, use the mouse to move the pointer to the Application icon and double-click the mouse button. Even if you are running HyperCard on a Mac II, it will take a while for the HyperCard program to load.

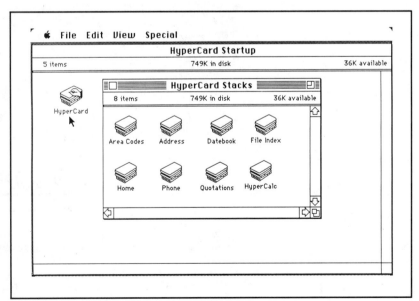

Figure 1.3: Startup screen showing the HyperCard and Stack icons

Using HyperCard's Help Stack

As part of your introduction to HyperCard, you will want to explore the on-line help. To do this, you open the Help stack (this stack is located on Disk 3, the HyperCard Help disk). You can open this stack from the Home Card by starting HyperCard, moving the hand with the pointing finger (referred to as the Browse tool) to the Help icon (the second one from the left on the first row), and clicking the mouse. You can also access Help when using HyperCard by pressing the Command key and typing **?** (the question mark), or by selecting Help from the Go menu. Figure 1.4 shows you the first card in the Help stack.

From this Help card, you can begin exploring HyperCard's on-line help by using the mouse to move the Browse tool to the check box to the left of Introduction and clicking the mouse. This takes you to a special Help stack that orients you to HyperCard and demonstrates many of its capabilities. It will give you more ideas on applications for

You can go straight to the introduction by clicking on the Intro icon at the top left corner of the Home Card.

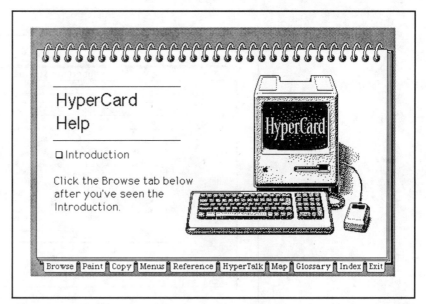

Figure 1.4: The first card of the HyperCard Help stack

You can refer to the on-line help at any time and from any stack while using HyperCard, as long as either the disk containing the Help stack is in one of your drives or the Help stack is in the same folder as the Hyper-Card program and the stacks you are using on a hard disk.

HyperCard as well as allow you to experiment with HyperCard buttons. Once you have finished with the introduction, you can return to the Help stack either by pressing Command-? at any time or by clicking on the button marked *Help cards* once you reach the card entitled *What Next?*.

From the first card in the Help stack, you get help on a particular part of HyperCard by moving the Browse tool to the appropriate tab at the bottom of the card and clicking the mouse (bottom of Figure 1.4). For example, to see a map of the Help stacks and to find out where you are, you can click on the Map tab. This will take you to the card shown in Figure 1.5.

From the Map card, you can go directly to a new help section either by clicking on the appropriate stack on the card itself or by clicking on the appropriate tab at the bottom of the stack. As you can see from this map, the HyperCard Help stack contains information on all aspects of using the program, including a reference on Hyper-Talk divided into four sections.

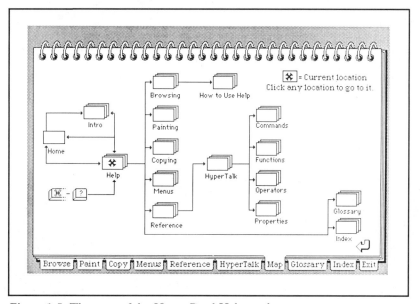

Figure 1.5: The map of the HyperCard Help stack

Summary

This chapter has provided an overview of HyperCard and what you can accomplish with it. If you are like most people, you are probably anxious to get started. In Chapter 2, you will work with the program extensively, exploring HyperCard's menu system and becoming familiar with commands and techniques for finding information in your card stacks. All of the practice in the next several chapters is meant to prepare you for the ultimate adventure, that of creating your own applications with HyperCard.

Finding the Information You Want in a HyperCard Stack

CHAPTER 2

IN THIS CHAPTER YOU WILL LEARN HOW TO SELECT the stack you wish to work with, locate particular cards within the stack, and find specific information entered on cards. As a prerequisite to using these techniques, you must first learn how to set the User Preference level, use the HyperCard menus, and become familiar with the general layout of HyperCard.

A Tour of HyperCard

The first step in becoming familiar with the program is a quick tour of HyperCard. This tour will give you an overview of how the program works, pointing out particular features of interest as well as any potential problem areas.

If you are at your Macintosh, you will now want to start the computer and get HyperCard running before you begin the tour of HyperCard. If you are unsure how to do this, refer to the instructions outlined in Chapter 1 in the section on The HyperCard Disks and Startup Procedures.

The Home Card

As soon as HyperCard is loaded into the computer's memory, the Home Card is displayed on your screen (Figure 2.1). This is the place from which you normally begin a session with HyperCard (if you do not see the Home Card shown in Figure 2.1, you need to copy this stack onto your startup disk).

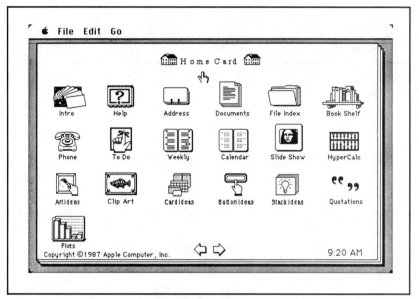

Figure 2.1: HyperCard's Home Card

The Home Card is really the first card in a stack named Home. The Home stack is automatically opened when HyperCard is loaded (later on, you will learn how you can have a different stack opened on startup, if you wish).

There are several interesting things to notice about the Home Card. First, find the pointing-finger icon on your screen (located under the title Home Card in Figure 2.1). This icon is called the Browse tool, and it represents the most common pointing icon used in HyperCard. Notice that when you move the mouse, the browsing pointer moves on the screen. The Browse tool lets you point to and select different areas on the card.

Next, notice the general appearance of the Home Card. It has a boundary that gives it the general appearance of an index card, reinforcing the card concept that is so central to HyperCard. At the top of the card, *Home* appears enclosed in two house icons. Below this title, the card contains several icons, each representing a stack that you can open from the Home Card. Notice that the name of the stack is displayed beneath each icon, starting with Intro through Plots. These stacks are part of the 19 sample stacks supplied with HyperCard.

If you started the program from the Startup disk, not all of the stacks shown here will be available (many of them are on Disk 2: HyperCard and Stacks). To open a stack from the Home Card, it must have an icon displayed on the Home Card. However, you can create an icon for a new stack that you have built and add it to the Home Card (you paste it on the last line of the Home Card, after the Plots stack). Doing this makes it easier to open the stack, since you do not have to access the File menu. You will learn how to do this for the stack that you create in Part II.

Beneath the stack icons, notice the two arrows, pointing to the right and left. You use them to go to the next and previous card in the Home stack. By locating the Browse tool on one of the arrows and clicking the mouse, you move to a new card in the direction of the arrow. Each of these arrows is a *button*, and each button has its own HyperTalk script that instructs it to go to either the next or the previous card in the stack whenever the Browse tool is located over it and the mouse button is clicked.

A button represents a special Hyper-Card component (officially referred to as an *object*). It is with the use of buttons that you create links between two cards in a stack.

Going to Other Cards in the Home Card Stack

The Home Card is not the only card in the Home stack. There are, in fact, five cards total. Let's continue the tour of HyperCard by moving to the next card in this stack.

1. **Move the mouse until the Browse tool (the hand with the pointing finger) is located on the right-arrow button, and click the mouse.**

If you click and nothing happens, it means that the Browse tool is not yet located on the button (the borders outlining the shape of the button are invisible). Just move the Browse tool closer to the arrow and click again.

When you find the button and activate it by clicking the mouse, HyperCard takes you directly to the next card, entitled *Look for Stacks in*. This card is used to tell HyperCard where to look for the stacks that you might wish to access from the Home Card. As you can see, Apple has already listed the location (by path name) of all the example stacks that come with HyperCard. When you create your own folders that contain stacks you have built, you will want to add

To organize files on the desktop, the Finder uses a hierarchical file system (HFS) that allows you to nest folders and files within one another. The path created by this hierarchical organization is noted by using colons to separate the folder and file names, as in the following:

HD-20:HyperCard: HyperCard Stacks:

When entering the path name, you can omit the disk name (volume) as long as the folder and files are located in the current volume and you begin the path name with a colon. This means that the above path name can be abbreviated to

:HyperCard Stacks:

as long as this folder resides in the HyperCard folder on the 20-megabyte hard disk. When you open a new stack in a different folder, HyperCard finds its location by referring to its path name on its *Look for Stacks in* card. If it cannot locate the stack from this card, HyperCard will prompt you to indicate its location in a standard file dialog box. As you indicate the volume and folders that contain the stack you want to use, HyperCard will write out the appropriate path name for you and add it to the *Look for Stacks in* card.

HyperCard always considers the last card in the stack as the previous card if you are on the first card, and considers the first card in the stack as the next card

their names to this card (you will learn how to do this in Part II).

If your Macintosh has an external monitor (for the SE and Mac II models), you will see a Title bar located at the top of the Home Card window. It displays the path where the Home stack is located. If you started HyperCard with the Startup disk, the path name in the Title bar will read

HyperCard Startup:HyperCard Stacks:Home

If your Macintosh has only the 9-inch built-in screen, this Title bar is not visible because the card takes up the entire screen. When you use HyperCard on the standard Macintosh, the card uses all of the screen: only the Menu bar is visible. Nevertheless, if you started the program using the HyperCard and Stacks disk, this is still the path name of the Home stack even though you can't see it listed on your screen.

Notice that at the bottom, the Look for Stacks in card has the same right- and left-arrow buttons as the Home Card.

2. Go to the next card by moving the Browse tool to the right-arrow button and clicking the mouse.

This card is entitled *Look for Applications in*. You can open different application programs such as Excel or WordPerfect directly from HyperCard. When you quit the program, you will return immediately to the card that was displayed before you gave this command.

Now try going in the other direction.

3. Go back to the *Look for Stacks in* card by moving the Browse tool to the left-arrow button and clicking the mouse.

4. Now, return to the Home Card by moving the Browse tool to the left-arrow button and clicking the mouse again.

By now, you understand that you can use the right- and left-arrow buttons in the Home stack to flip through the cards, either from the beginning to the end or from the end to the beginning of a stack. But what happens if you activate the left-arrow button when you are at the first card in the stack? Since you are now at the Home Card, try it.

if you are on the last card. This means that you can flip through all of the cards in any stack continuously in either direction.

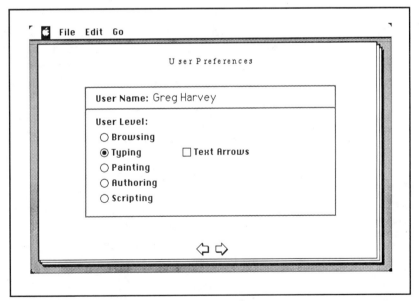 A radio button is a special type of button that allows only one of the listed selections to be active at one time. The currently selected option is always indicated by the black dot in the center of the button.

5. Move the Browse tool to the left-arrow button and click the mouse.

You will see the User Preferences card on your screen (Figure 2.2). This is the fifth and last card in the Home stack.

As mentioned in Chapter 1, the User Preferences card is used to set the user (or working) level in HyperCard. Currently, it should be set to Typing (the factory default when you begin using HyperCard). Notice that you change the user level by clicking on the appropriate *radio button*.

The Browsing Menu Options

At this point in your tour of HyperCard, it's time to turn attention to the HyperCard menus. Because the user level is presently set to Typing, only three menus are available: File, Edit, and Go. There are, however, more pull-down menus in HyperCard that appear only when you raise the user level. When you begin designing a new

Figure 2.2: The User Preferences card in the Home stack

Go	
▶ Back	⌘~
Home	⌘H
Help	⌘?
Recent	⌘R
First	⌘1
Preu	⌘2
Next	⌘3
Last	⌘4
Find...	⌘F
Message	⌘M

stack, you will become familiar with them. For now, you need only be concerned with the options on the Go menu.

View the options on the Go menu, if you have HyperCard on-line.

1. Use the mouse to move the Browse tool to Go on the Menu bar.

When you do, the cursor will change from the Browse tool to the standard Arrow pointer.

2. With the pointer on Go, click the mouse.

The menu options shown at left will appear.

Going to Specific Cards in a Stack

Most of the options on the Go menu are used to take you to a particular card in a stack. As you will learn shortly, you can also use commands found here to view cards in different stacks, find information entered on a card, and enter HyperTalk commands directly.

For now, discussion will focus on the commands that help you find specific cards in a stack. Notice that the second set of options on the Go menu will take you to the first, previous, next, and last card in the stack you are working with. Besides being able to execute these commands from this menu, you can accomplish the same moves by pressing the Command key in combination with a number between 1 and 4. Try using this method to flip through the cards.

1. Press Command-1 to go to the Home Card.

2. Press Command-3 to flip through the rest of the cards in this stack.

Stop when you reach the User Preferences card.

If your keyboard has arrow keys, you can use the → key to move to the next card and the ← key to move to the previous card.

The first set of options on the Go menu can also be used to perform the following:

In version 1.1, the → and ← arrow keys work the same way as in version 1.0, as long as the Text Arrows check box is not checked in the User Preferences card. With the Text Arrows option on, you can go to the next or previous card by pressing Option-→ or Option-←.

- Back (Command- ~) takes you back one card; you can retrace your visits to all of the cards you viewed during your session with HyperCard, regardless of the stack they are in, by continuing to issue the Back command.

- Home (Command-H) takes you to the Home Card of the Home stack, regardless of which stack you are in.
- Help (Command-?) takes you to the first card of the Help stack.
- Recent (Command-R) shows you miniatures of the cards you recently viewed, allowing you to go back to any one of them.

Note that if you have the regular or extended keyboard designed for the Macintosh SE and II, you can use the Esc key or Command- ~ (tilde) to go back and view the previous card for each time you press the key.

Using the Recent Command to Locate a Card

The Recent command on the Go menu (alternatively accessed by pressing Command-R) maintains miniature "snapshots" of the last 42 *unique* cards that you viewed, regardless of which stack they are in. This gives you a quick way to return to a particular card that you viewed previously. All you have to do to go to a particular card is to move the pointer to the miniature of the card and click the mouse. Try going to the Home Card using the Recent command.

1. **Select Recent from the Go menu, or press Command-R and view all of the different cards that you visited (Figure 2.3).**

2. **Move the Arrow pointer to the miniature of the Home Card and click the mouse.**

You will find the Recent command to be most helpful when building your own stacks. It comes in handy when you want to return quickly to a card that you previously viewed in another stack so you can copy one of its elements to the stack you are constructing.

Using the Message Box

The last set of options on the Go menu are Find and Message. The Find command (alternately, Command-F) is used when you want to locate specific information in a card, *or* a specific card in a stack. You will explore this important option shortly. Right now, let's examine the purpose of the Message box in HyperCard.

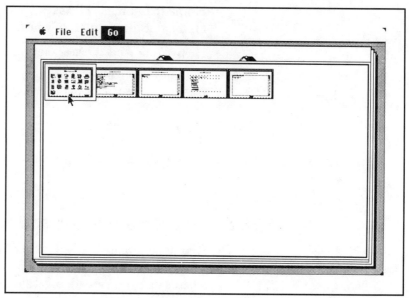

Figure 2.3: Using the Recent command

To bring up the Message box on your screen, either select Message from the Go menu or press Command-M. When you do, the program displays a window at the bottom of your screen (shown in Figure 2.4). This window contains a gray bar (where you would normally expect the title to be displayed) that has a Close box in the upper left corner. You can move the Message box to new areas of the screen by clicking on this area and dragging until it is properly located in its new position.

You use the Message box to enter HyperTalk commands directly into HyperCard. HyperCard attempts to execute the command entered into the Message box as soon as you press Return or Enter. This lets you make use of most commands in the HyperTalk vocabulary.

In version 1.1, if the Text Arrows option is checked, you can use the ← and → keys in the Message box to move the cursor one character at a time in either direction.

To enter a HyperTalk command once the Message box has been opened, you merely start typing. You can enter only a single line of text in this box, and HyperCard can process only a single command at a time. As soon as you begin typing, you will see your text being entered in the Message box. If you make a mistake, you can use the Backspace (Delete) key. As you type, you will see a flashing text insertion pointer letting you know where the next character will be entered.

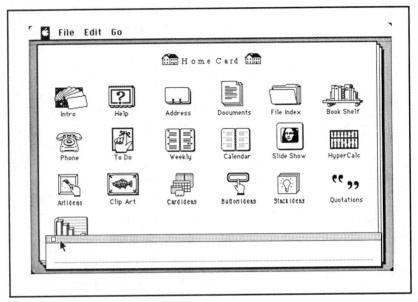

Figure 2.4: The Message box

The Browse tool changes to an I-Beam cursor whenever it is in the text area inside the Message box.

You can also edit the contents of the Message box by positioning the I-Beam cursor where you want it in the text and clicking the mouse. When you click the mouse, the I-Beam changes into the flashing text insertion pointer. You can then insert new text by typing. If you wish to delete some text, click and drag across the text until all the characters you want to remove are highlighted, and then press the Backspace (Delete) key.

To clear the text in the Message box, you can press the Clear key on the numeric pad (on the Macintosh Plus, SE, and II keyboards). However, if you wish to replace the existing text with a new command, you can simply begin typing it in, regardless of where the Browse tool is located on the screen. Existing text will automatically be replaced by the new characters that you enter.

To close the Message box, you have several alternatives: you can click the Close box or enter the Message command either from the Go menu or by pressing Command-M. Sometimes, after Hyper-Card executes the command you have entered in the Message box, the Message box is automatically closed.

Even when this happens, the Message box retains the text of the command you just used. If the Message box remains open after executing the command, you will still see the command in the text area. To reissue this command, you have only to press Return or Enter a second time (the Message box must be open to do this).

Entering Go Commands in the Message Box

You should now be familiar with the working of the Message box. Now you can start using your first HyperTalk command to locate specific cards in a stack. To do this, you use the *Go* command, which is one of the most basic and useful words in its vocabulary. For example, instead of using the Last option on the Go menu to go to the User Preferences card, you can do the same thing by entering

　　go last

in the Message box and pressing Return or Enter. Try doing that now.

1. **Choose Message from the Go menu, or press Command-M to get the Message box on the screen.**

2. **Type** *go last* **and press Return (or Enter).**

Now go back to the Home Card.

3. **Type** *go first* **and press Return (or Enter).**

   (You could also get there by typing *go back* or *go home*.)

You can also use the Go command to get to a particular card in a stack by following Go with the number of the card. Try going to the second card in the Home stack in this way.

4. **Type** *go to card 2* **and press Return (or Enter).**

You should note that HyperTalk will accept the ordinal numbers *first* through *tenth* (it doesn't know eleventh and up). However, you can always get to a specific card (assuming that you know its numerical position in the stack) by typing *go to card* followed by the cardinal number (1, 2, 3, and so on). Also, the use of prepositions such as *to* are optional in HyperTalk commands. You could just as well have entered

　　go card 2

to get to the *Look for Stacks in* card.

Although HyperTalk is fairly forgiving of the use of conversational English, there is one pitfall you need to avoid if you prefer to enter commands in complete sentences. This involves the use of the definite article *the* in command statements. For example, to move to the first card in the stack, you could enter

go first

or

go to first

or even

go to first card

However, you *cannot* do this by entering

go to the first card

If you do, HyperCard will give you a dialog box asking you where the stack called *the first card* is located on your disk.

By the way, you can always return to the Home Card from any place in HyperCard by entering the command

go home

in the Message box. Later on, you will learn how you can use the Go command to get to a specific card in a stack by using its name or ID number. For now, let's see how it can be used to open another stack.

Opening a New Stack

Up to now in your tour of HyperCard, you have not journeyed outside the confines of the Home stack. Although the Home Card represents the base of operations in HyperCard, you need to extend the tour and take a look at one of the example stacks that you have on disk. Since you have been working with the Go command in the Message box, let's use it to open a new stack.

To use Go to open a stack, you must already know its name. The stack you will explore is called Address.

1. Type *go to address* **and press Return (or Enter).**

This takes you to the first card in the Address stack (shown in Figure 2.5).

An alternate method for opening a new stack is to select the Open Stack option from the File menu or press Command-O, as shown at left. Then you need to select the name of the stack you wish to open by moving the pointer to it and either clicking the Open button in the dialog box or double-clicking on the name (Figure 2.6). Try opening the Address stack using the Open option.

2. Type *go home* **and press Return (or Enter).**

This takes you back to the Home Card.

3. Press Command-O.

Address is already selected (indicated by the highlighting).

4. Double-click the mouse on the word *Address* **or move the pointer to the Open button and click one time.**

Because the Address stack has its own icon button on the Home Card, you have yet a third method for opening this stack: move the pointer to the Address icon and click the mouse (Figure 2.7). You cannot use this method, however, when the stack you wish to open does not have its own icon button on the Home Card.

Note that you can always open a stack from the desktop by double-clicking on its icon, as shown in Figure 2.8. You do not have to start HyperCard before you can use a stack as long as the HyperCard program is also located in one of the disk drives or on a hard disk.

Finding Information in Cards

The Address stack provides you with a ready-made rolodex file in which you can store the names, addresses, and telephone numbers of business associates and friends. Presently, it contains fictitious records that you can use to practice locating specific information

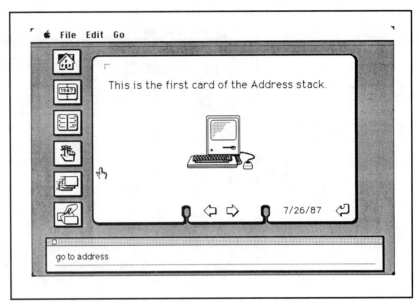

Figure 2.5: The first card of the Address stack

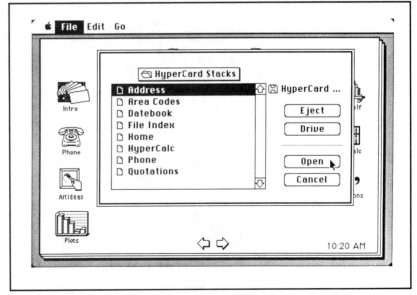

Figure 2.6: Selecting the Address stack from the File dialog box

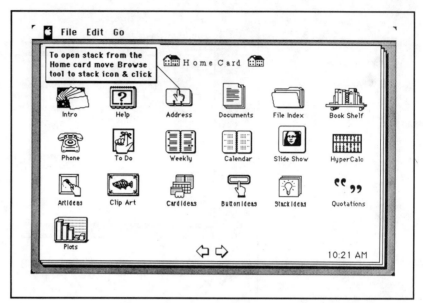

Figure 2.7: Opening a stack from the Home Card

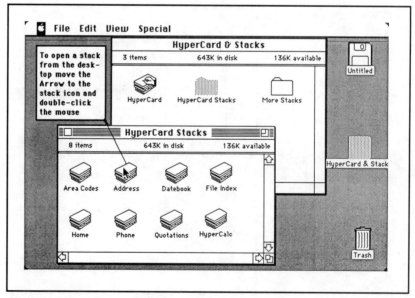

Figure 2.8: Opening a stack from the desktop

entered into cards. In the next chapter, you will learn how you can edit the data in this stack so that you can add the names and addresses of real people you know and work with.

Notice that the first card in the Address stack does not contain an actual address card (Figure 2.5). It merely tells you that it is the first card in the Address stack. The rolodex card (where the greeting, Macintosh icon, and date of entry are entered) houses the name, address, phone number, and date fields along with three buttons: next (right arrow), previous (left arrow), and return (bent arrow). To the left, outside the rolodex card, you can see six icons (buttons) that perform different actions when selected.

Look at the second card in the Address stack (click on the next arrow). This card shows you the name, street address, and phone number of Steve Aaron. Notice, however, that even though the information in the rolodex card has changed, all of the icon buttons remain the same as on the opening card with the exception of the telephone icon, immediately to the left of the telephone number. You can use this button to have HyperCard autodial the phone number through a modem. It is not part of the opening card because this card does not contain a phone number to dial.

As you now know, you can use a variety of methods to browse through a card stack and locate the card you want. However, browsing is inefficient when you want to look up a specific card in a large stack and you don't know its position in the stack (as is most often the case). As long as you know some piece of information that has been entered on the card you wish to locate, you can use the Find command to get to it.

Using the Find Command

When a field entry consists of text (as opposed to numbers), it often includes spaces between words. This is the case with the Find example using the name of Steve Aaron in the second Address card. Enclosing the text in a

You can use the Find command by making the Message box visible (Command-M or select the Message option from the Go menu) and typing *find* followed by the text to look up enclosed in a pair of double quotation marks (""). For example, to find Sue Thompson's card in the stack, enter

    find "sue thompson"

CH. 2

pair of quotes ensures that HyperCard will match all of the characters entered within them, including any spaces between words.

You will often find it advantageous to set off (or delimit) text with quotation marks when entering HyperTalk commands to ensure that HyperCard treats the text as a single unit and does not confuse it with any of the words in the Hyper-Talk vocabulary.

HyperCard retains the search string, so you can have the program search again for the same text by pressing Return or Enter. You can use this feature to locate subsequent occurrences of the search string. If you have used the Message box to execute some other HyperTalk command, however, you must press Command-F or choose Find from the Go menu before the program can search again.

in the Message box (if you do this and press Return or Enter, you will find that she is not listed in this stack).

Although you can always type in the HyperTalk command Find in the Message box, as illustrated in the previous example, it is far easier to use the Find option on the Go menu (Command-F).

When you use either method to access the Find command, you will discover that HyperCard automatically opens the Message box window (if it is still closed), enters the command *find* and a pair of double quotation marks, and locates the flashing text insertion pointer between the quotes. Then all you have to do is type in the text you want HyperCard to search for in the stack and press Return or Enter.

When you use the Find command, HyperCard searches all fields of each card in the stack you are in. When it locates the first match, it displays the card and shows the search string enclosed in a box. It is important to note that the program searches from your current position in the stack to its end. If you are at the first card when you initiate the search, HyperCard will search the entire stack. If you are not, it will search from the current card. This may mean that a match exists in the previous cards that is not located on the first pass.

When entering commands in the Message box, you can always replace the current search string with new text by reissuing the Find command (Command-F). This will highlight the current search string, and you can just begin typing in the new text. As long as the existing text between the pair of quotation marks is highlighted, it will be automatically replaced with the new text that you enter. You can also clear the current search string by pressing the Delete key or the Clear key if your keyboard has this key on a numeric pad.

As with any searching function, the more specific you can be when entering the search string, the faster you will locate the information you want to see. However, HyperCard will eventually take you to the correct card even if you give it little to go on. For example, if you were trying to find Sue Thompson's card but you had forgotten her last name, you could simply enter

    find "sue"

Of course, if your stack has cards that contain the name *Sue* on them and they come before Sue Thompson's card, you will have to repeat the Find procedure several times.

If, further, you have forgotten whether you entered Susan or Sue as the first name and still didn't know her last name, you could find the card by entering

find "su"

This avenue might require more repetitions of the Find procedure because HyperCard would match such field entries as Sullivan entered as a last name or Surrey entered as a street name or Susanville as the city, as well as Susan, Sue, and Suzanne entered as the first name. This is all the more likely if you simply enter "s" as the find string.

Therefore, whenever possible, make the search string as specific as necessary to make it unique enough to go directly to the card you are looking for. In stacks that you create and work with, this is easier to do because you will be familiar with the types of entries they contain. For instance, to find the address card for Sybex (to call my publisher), I just enter "sy" as the search string. Because no other card has a field entry containing the characters *sy*, it takes me directly to the proper card. There is no need to spend time typing *syb* or even *sybex*. However, I would not enter "s" as the search string, as it would detour the search to earlier cards that have entries starting with the letter s.

HyperCard always matches the characters in the search string against whole words in the card fields unless specifically told otherwise.

If the characters in the search string match the initial characters of any word in a card, the program considers it a match and displays the card, enclosing the entire match word in a box. This means you cannot use the Find command to match a search string against characters embedded within a word. For example, if you wanted to view all of the cards where the title *consultant* is entered, you could not do so by entering

find "su"

as the search string. HyperCard will only match the characters *su* against entries that begin with *su* (as in Susan). It will not consider the *su* in *consultant* as a match. To find these cards, enter characters that match the initial letters of this entry, as in c, co, con, cons, consu, and so on. See the section on Extending Searches to Include Characters within Words in a Card, later in this chapter, for information on how to work around this limitation.

Practice Searching for Cards in the Address Stack

To see how easy it is to use the Find command in HyperCard, let's use it to locate several different cards.

1. **Press Command-F.**

   This brings up the Message box, with *find* already entered and the flashing text insertion pointer properly located between the quotation marks.

2. **Type *ge* and press Return or Enter (Figure 2.9).**

You should see Liz Georges' card on your screen. Notice her last name is enclosed in a box, indicating that HyperCard matched the search characters *ge* with the entry *Georges* on this card (Figure 2.10).

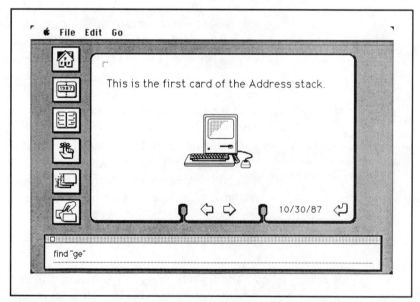

Figure 2.9: Using the Find command to find cards that contain *ge*

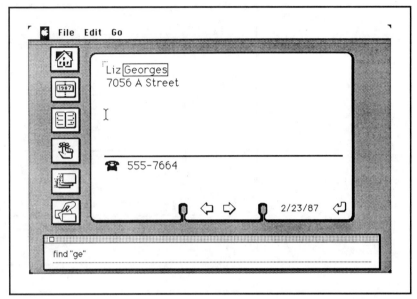

Figure 2.10: The first match for the search string "ge"

Now, see if there are any more matches for this string in the Address stack.

3. Press Return (or Enter).

HyperCard retains the search string *ge* so you need not reenter it.

You should now see Beverley Richie's card on your screen. Notice that HyperCard went to her card because it found a match for the search string in *Gettysburg* (indicated by the box around it in Figure 2.11).

See if there are any more matches for this string.

4. Press Return (or Enter).

HyperCard returns to Liz Georges' card, indicating that there are no matches in other cards in the Address stack.

Try the Find command using a new search string.

5. Press Command-F or select Find on the Go menu.

This highlights the retained search string *ge*.

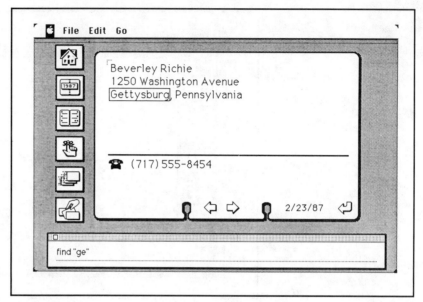

Figure 2.11: The second match for the search string "ge"

6. Type *ca*.

This immediately replaces *ge* with *ca* as the search string within the pair of quotation marks.

7. Press Return (or Enter).

This causes HyperCard to search for the occurrence of *ca* in entries in subsequent cards.

HyperCard now displays Edith Lyons' card with *Camino* (in the street name Camino Alto) enclosed in a box.

Continue to press Return or Enter to flip through the rest of the matching cards in the Address stack. The next card to appear will be Edmund Reid's, selected because of *California* in the address. The card following Reid's will be Throckmorton Scribblemonger's, selected because of *CA* in the address. Continue to view selected cards until HyperCard stops at the first card in the Address stack. Notice that the word *card* is enclosed in a box.

Inserting Text Found in the Card into the Search String

To get some more practice with the Find command, you will now use a new search string. HyperCard will allow you to insert a text entry found in the card you are viewing into the Message box or into a Find command search string. This eliminates the need to retype information that you wish to search next, if it is found on the current card.

1. **Click on the next card button (the right-arrow button at the bottom of the first card).**

   This takes you to Steve Aaron's card.

2. **Press Command-F (or select Find on the Go menu).**

   This highlights the search string *ca* so that it can be replaced.

3. **Position the I-Beam cursor immediately before the D of *Drive* in the 2260 Oak Creek Drive street address.**

4. **Hold down the Command key.**

   The I-Beam cursor changes to the Browse tool.

5. **Click the mouse and let up on the Command key.**

   Drive should now replace the search string *ca* for the Find command (Figure 2.12).

6. **Press Return (or Enter) twice.**

   Pressing this key a second time takes you to the next card that contains *Drive* in its text, which in this example is located in the street address (Foxborough Drive) of Maria Deguara's card.

Extending Searches to Include Characters within Words in a Card

Up to now, all of the practice searches have located cards by matching the search strings against whole words in the card. If the initial characters of the card entry match the string entered into the Find command, the card is displayed.

You can change this so that HyperCard will match an entry if the search string is contained within a word. To do this, enter the Find

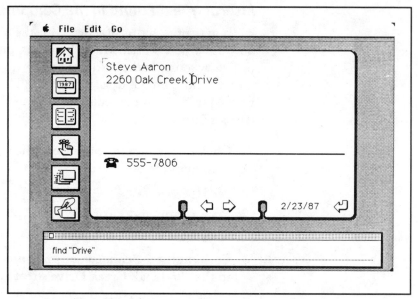

Figure 2.12: Inserting text from a card into the search string

command in the Message box, this time adding the parameter *characters* (or *chars*) before you enter the search string enclosed in quotes. Remember that you cannot find the occurrences of the word *consultant* in the cards in the stack just by entering

> find "su"

However, you can find the word *consultant* if you let HyperCard know that the characters *su* are to be found somewhere within the word. To do this, enter

> find characters "su"

To demonstrate how this works, try it now by taking the following steps.

1. Press Command-F (or select Find on the Go menu).

This highlights the search string *Drive* for replacement.

2. **Type *ex* as the search string and press Return (or Enter).**

   HyperCard sounds the bell and displays an error dialog box telling you that it can't find "ex" in the Address stack (Figure 2.13).

3. **Click the Cancel button on the dialog box.**

4. **Type *find chars "ex"* (be sure that you enclose *ex* in double quotation marks).**

   As soon as you begin to type this Find command, HyperCard blanks out the previous one.

5. **Press Return (or Enter).**

   HyperCard displays Edith Lyons' card. Notice that the letters *ex* of *Texas* are the only characters enclosed in the selection box (Figure 2.14).

You can use the *characters* parameter whenever you need to have HyperCard search for characters embedded within a word.

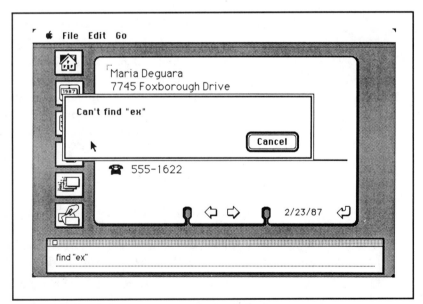

Figure 2.13: HyperCard's error message dialog box

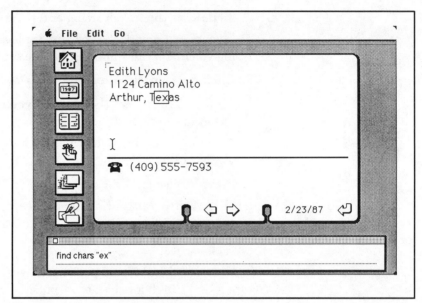

Figure 2.14: Finding characters embedded in text entries

Limiting Searches to Entire Words in a Card

You can also tighten up your searches so that the search string entered with a Find command must match an entire word (as opposed to the first part of a word). To do this, precede the search string with *word* as the parameter when entering the Find command in the Message box. For example, if you know that you entered *ST* for Street on a card you wish to view, you can avoid having to view those cards where you entered *Street* by using this Find command:

        find word "st"

To see how this works, try the following search in the Address stack.

1. **Press Command-F (or select Find on the Go menu), type** *mount* **as the search string, and press Return or Enter.**

   This takes you to Roger Benrey on Mount Vernon Drive.

2. **Press Return or Enter to repeat the search.**

   This takes you to Richard Boyd's card, matching on *Mountain* in Black Mountain Road.

3. **Type** *find word "mount"* **(make sure that mount is enclosed in double quotes) and press Return (or Enter).**

   This takes you back to Roger Benrey, matching on *Mount* in Mount Vernon Drive.

4. **Press Return or Enter to repeat the search.**

   Roger Benrey's card remains displayed. HyperCard no longer considers the *mount* in Mountain (of Black Mountain Road in Richard Boyd's card) to be a match when the *word* parameter is added to the Find command.

Limiting Searches to Particular Fields in a Card

Before leaving the the Find command and concluding your initial tour of HyperCard, let's use one more searching technique. This involves restricting the search to specific fields of a card. As mentioned in the last chapter, text entries in a card are entered into fields that are designed into the basic card form. Since you did not design this stack, you do not know how many fields it contains. Nevertheless, you can always tell how many fields a card contains by pressing the Tab key.

1. **Press Tab.**

   This highlights the first field, which contains the name and street address of the card (Roger Benrey on Mount Vernon Drive).

2. **Press Tab a second time.**

   This highlights the second field, which contains his telephone number.

3. **Press Tab a third time.**

   This highlights the third field, which contains the date the card was entered.

4. **Press Tab one last time.**

   This returns you to the first field. There are only three fields in the cards of the Address stack.

5. **Move the cursor off the rolodex card. When it changes from the I-Beam to the Browse tool, click the mouse.**

   This removes the highlighting from the first field, thereby deselecting it.

If you start typing when a field is highlighted, HyperCard clears the current entry, making room for you to replace it with new text.

To restrict a search to a particular field, you can refer to it by number (later on, you will learn that you can also refer to it by name or ID number). To see how this works, try the following exercise.

6. **Type** *find chars "31" in field 1* **and press Return or Enter.**

   This takes you to Throckmorton Scribblemonger's card. Notice that the 31 in the zip code 94131 in the first field is enclosed in the box (Figure 2.15).

7. **Use the mouse to position the I-Beam cursor right before the 1 of field 1 in the Message box.**

8. **Click the mouse and drag until 1 is highlighted.**

9. **Type 2.**

   This replaces 1 so that the Find command reads *find chars 31 in field 2*.

10. **Press Return (or Enter).**

    This brings you to Joshua Carlson's card. Note that the 31 in the phone number 555–3109 is enclosed in the box.

11. **Select the 2 of field 2 in the Message box (just as you did in steps 7 and 8).**

12. **Type 3 and press Return (or Enter).**

    HyperCard sounds the bell and displays an error dialog box indicating that 31 is not found in field 3 (the date entered field).

13. **Click on the Cancel button in the dialog box.**

14. **Select the search characters 31 for editing. Be careful to position the I-Beam after the first quotation marks and before the 3 before you click. Drag the mouse until both 3 and 1 are highlighted and then type 26 over them.**

    The Find command should now read *find chars "26" in field 3*.

15. **Press Return (or Enter) to have HyperCard search for the occurrence of 26 in the third field.**

    HyperCard will display Amy McGinnis' card entered on 5/26/87.

This concludes your initial tour of HyperCard. If you wish, you can quit HyperCard at this time. You do this either by selecting Quit

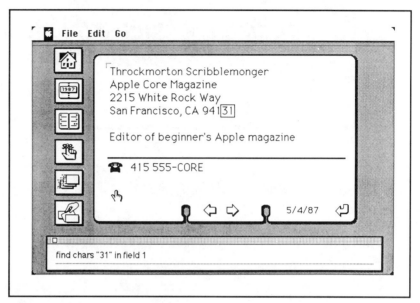

Figure 2.15: Searching for characters in a specific field

HyperCard from the File menu or by pressing Command-Q (the standard way to quit all Macintosh software). Note that when you quit HyperCard, you do not have to return first to the Home Card.

Summary

During this tour, you have been exposed to the many ways that HyperCard allows you to browse through stacks: from going directly to a card by specifying its position (first, last, card 20, and so on) to specifying search strings (find "carl", find chars "inc", find word "smith", find "va" in field 4, and so on). You have also learned how to open a new stack from the Home Card (go to Address, go to Datebook, and so on) and become familiar with the makeup of the special Home stack. With this tour under your belt, you should be able to find your way around any stack that you purchase or download. You can practice your new skills by browsing through some of the other example stacks supplied with HyperCard.

In the next chapter, you will learn how to edit information in cards. This includes not only being able to modify the information entered into specific fields, but also being able to add new cards and delete the ones that have become obsolete.

Adding and Editing Information
in a HyperCard Stack

_____

IN THIS CHAPTER, YOU WILL LEARN HOW TO MAKE editing changes to the information in a card stack. You will apply these skills to stacks that require routine updating to keep them current, such as the Address stack. However, many of the stacks that you will use, especially third-party Stackware that you purchase, do not require this type of maintenance. The information in these types of card stacks will be updated solely by the author of the Stackware.

You can apply the following editing tasks to stacks that require routine maintenance:

- Add new information to specific fields in a card.

- Replace incorrect or outdated information with new information in particular fields of the card.

- Delete incorrect or outdated information entered in the card fields.

- Add new cards to the stack and fill in the fields that each contains.

- Delete outdated cards from the stack.

As you edit the information in a card, HyperCard automatically saves it for you. Because the program is always updating your disk as you make additions or changes to the open stack, there is no "save" command that you must use.

Since the address stack contains only fictitious information, you can use it to practice all of these tasks. This will enable you to work with the Address stack until it contains information that you can use (real names, addresses, and telephone numbers). In the next section, you will learn how to add, replace, and delete text entered into fields of an existing card.

Editing Data in a Card

If you quit HyperCard at the end of the last exercise in Chapter 2, you should now start it again. After HyperCard is loaded into the computer's memory, click on the Address stack icon on the Home Card. This will bring you to the first card in the Address stack. Because this card acts like the home card of this stack, there are no changes required to the information here, although you can to customize this card by adding new graphics or changing the greeting text.

Go to the next card (that of Steve Aaron) by clicking on the right-arrow button at the bottom of the card. Assume that you need to make two changes to Steve's card: add the city, state, and zip code below the street address, and add the area code to the telephone number.

Identifying the Locations of Fields in a Card

Before you can make these changes to this card, you must know where the fields are in the card. In the final lesson of the last chapter, you discovered that there are three fields in the Address card stack (by pressing the Tab key to highlight each field). However, even though you know that there are three fields and you know their relative location on the card, the extent of each one is not obvious. This is because the author of this stack chose to make the fields invisible.

Later on, you will learn that when designing your own stacks, you can specify that the number and location of lines in a field be displayed at all times in the card. You will also learn that you can display the extent of existing fields, even when this is normally invisible, by selecting the Field tool (you cannot do this now because the user level is set to Typing, and the Tools menu is not available until you set the level to Painting).

When the location and extent of the fields in a card are not visible and you do not have access to the Tools menu, you must use the mouse to explore the card, watching when the Browse tool changes to the I-Beam cursor. Wherever the I-Beam cursor is available you can make editing changes, for you are located within a text field of the card.

Following standard Macintosh editing practices, at the place where you click the mouse the I-Beam inserts the flashing text insertion

In version 1.1, with the Text Arrows option on, you can use the ↑ and ↓ keys to move the flashing text insertion pointer from line to line, and use the → and ← keys to move it from character to character.

pointer. If you then begin typing, HyperCard will insert new characters from the pointer on. If you hold down the mouse button and drag the I-Beam cursor, HyperCard will select text (shown by highlighting) as you move the mouse to the right. Once text is selected, you can cut, copy, or delete the text, just as you do in any standard application such as MacWrite or Microsoft Word.

Before you complete Steve Aaron's address in the first field of his card, you should use the mouse to explore the size of this field.

1. **Place the Browse tool on the corner piece on the card.**

   The Browse tool will change to the I-Beam cursor (Figure 3.1).

2. **Move the mouse down in a straight line from the corner piece (the I-Beam may change into the Browse tool if you stray too far to the right as you move down).**

3. **Stop moving the I-Beam down the card when it changes back to the Browse tool (this will happen when the cursor reaches the line dividing the address from the phone number).**

   This shows you the height of the field.

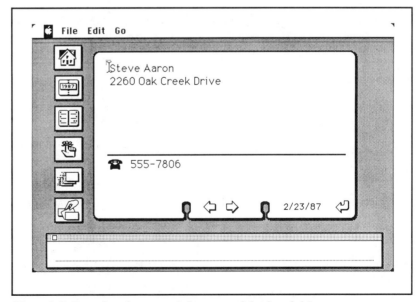

Figure 3.1: Locating the upper left corner of the first field

4. **Move the mouse up until the Browse tool changes back to the I-Beam cursor.**

5. **Move the mouse to the right until you reach the limit of the field on the right (you will know this when the I-Beam changes to the Browse tool).**

This shows you the width of the field.

6. **Continue to trace the outline of this field by moving the mouse up and then to the left until you reach the corner piece again.**

Now that you have identified the boundaries of the first field, notice the spacing of the first two lines of text (containing the name and street address). From this, you can tell that the first field can accommodate several more lines of text.

Adding Text to a Field

To add a new line that contains the city, state, and zip code beneath the street address, you must locate the third line of the field.

1. **Use the mouse to move the Browse tool into the midst of the first field.**

The Browse tool will change into the I-Beam when you are in the confines of the field.

2. **Move the I-Beam cursor beneath the line containing the street address.**

The cursor can be anywhere below this line—it does not have to be in line with the 2260 of the street address.

3. **Click the mouse.**

This inserts the flashing text insertion pointer. Notice that it is automatically located at the beginning of the third line of the card.

4. **Type *Sonoma, CA 95468* as the third line of the address for this card and press Return or Enter (Figure 3.2).**

If you make a mistake when typing, use the Backspace (Delete) key to delete the incorrect characters.

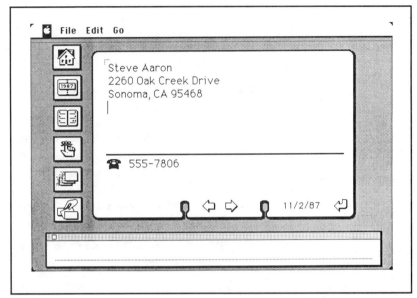

Figure 3.2: Adding the third line of the address to the card

Notice that by pressing Return (or Enter), you have located the flashing text insertion pointer at the beginning of the next line in this field. If you needed to add another line to this field, you could do so at this time.

Inserting Text into a Field

Next, you need to add the area code to the telephone number in the second field. To do this, you do not have to add an extra line to the field. Instead, you just need to insert this text before the existing telephone number.

1. **Use the mouse to move the I-Beam cursor so that it is immediately before the first 5 of the 555 prefix.**

   When it changes from the Browse tool to the I-Beam on this line, you are in the correct position.

2. **Click the mouse.**

   This places the flashing text insertion pointer right before the telephone prefix.

3. **Type** *(707).*

The area code will be inserted before the rest of the phone number (Figure 3.3).

Replacing Text in a Field

This completes the changes for Steve Aaron's card. Go to the next card (by clicking on the right-arrow button), that of Katie Aichler, where you will learn how to replace text in a field. You will enter a new street address for her and add the city, state, and zip code for it.

1. **Locate the I-Beam cursor immediately before the 9 of 9424 Middlefield Road.**

2. **Click the mouse and drag to the right until the entire street address is selected (Figure 3.4).**

3. **Type** *2311 Milvia Street* **and press Return (or Enter).**

As soon as you type *2*, the old street address is blanked out (you could accomplish the same thing by pressing the Backspace/Delete key).

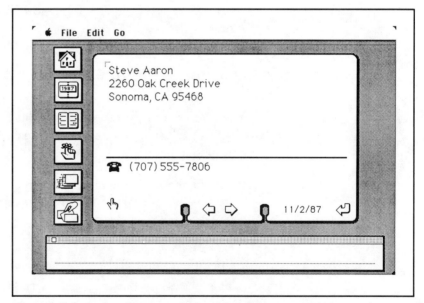

Figure 3.3: Inserting the area code into the telephone number

4. **Type *Berkeley, CA 94704* to complete Katie Aichler's new address (Figure 3.5).**

Deleting Text in a Field

Unlike the previous exercise, where you replaced one piece of information with another, there may be times when you need to delete existing text without replacing it. To do this, you simply select the text and then press the Backspace (Delete) key.

If you want to delete just a single word, you can select it by locating the I-Beam cursor somewhere on it and double-clicking the mouse. If you just want to delete several characters in a word, you need to locate the I-Beam cursor before the first character you want to remove, and click and drag the cursor over these characters to select them. To delete several words or an entire line, you do the same thing except that you need to drag the cursor over a longer distance to select all of the text you want removed. To delete several lines or an entire line and part of the line below it, locate the I-Beam at the beginning of the first line and drag down before moving to the right to select the text to be removed.

In version 1.1, with the Text Arrows option on, you can use the arrow keys to position the flashing text insertion pointer after the characters to be deleted. You can then use the Backspace (Delete) key to delete them.

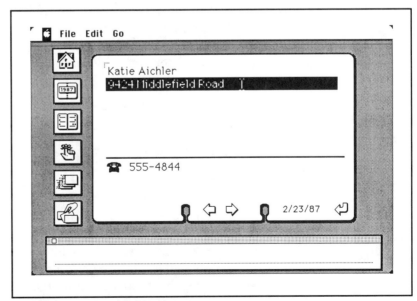

Figure 3.4: Selecting the street address to replace it with a new one

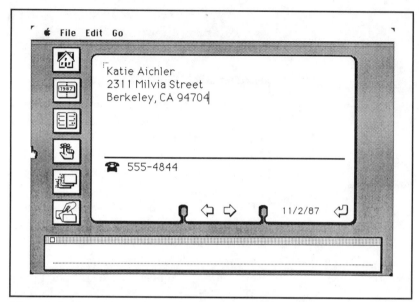

Figure 3.5: The new address completed for this card

If you delete any text in error, invoke the Undo command by selecting Undo from the Edit menu or by pressing Command-Z. This will restore all of the text removed during the very last deletion. Be sure that you do not perform another deletion or cut some text (see the section on Cutting and Pasting Information in Cards below) before you restore text deleted in error, or you will not be able to bring it back using the Undo command.

Performing Other Kinds of Edits in Cards

Thus far, all of the editing changes that you have practiced have involved entering new information from the keyboard, whether you were adding or replacing existing text. You can also make editing changes to cards by cutting and pasting information between cards in the same or a different stack or, in the case of numerical data, calculate a result in the Message box and insert it into the text of the card. You will next learn about both of these methods, starting with the more common cutting and pasting of text entries between cards.

Cutting and Pasting Information in Cards

You can copy or move information within or between cards. Before you can perform either of these operations, you must select the text to be copied or moved (just as you select text when you intend to delete it). Then, to copy the selected text, choose the Copy option on the Edit menu or press Command-C. To move the text, choose the Cut option on the Edit menu or press Command-X.

After either copying or cutting the selected text, you move the I-Beam cursor to the beginning of the place where you want the text to appear, click the mouse, and choose the Paste option on the Edit menu or press Command-V.

To see how easy it is to copy or move text between cards, even when they are located in different stacks, perform the following exercise.

1. **Move the pointer to the Home button icon on the card (the first icon on the left, as shown in Figure 3.6) and click the mouse.**

   This takes you to the Home Card.

2. **Move the pointer to the stack icon called File Index (the fifth from the left in the first row, as shown in Figure 3.7) and click the mouse to open this stack.**

3. **Move the pointer to the left-arrow icon and click the mouse to go to the previous card (in this case, the last one in this stack).**

4. **Move the I-Beam cursor immediately before the C in *Call*, then click the mouse and drag to select all of the text on this card (Figure 3.8).**

5. **Press Command-C or select Copy from the Edit menu to copy the selected text.**

6. **Move the pointer to the bent-arrow icon (in the far right of the card) and click the mouse.**

   This returns you to the Home Card.

7. **Move the pointer to the stack icon called Weekly and click the mouse to open this stack.**

8. **Move the I-Beam cursor to the first line of the entry in the upper left of the datebook and click the mouse (the date of the entry will depend upon when you do this exercise).**

9. **Press Command-V or select Paste from the Edit menu to paste the text copied from the last card in the File Index stack into this page of the Datebook stack (Figure 3.9; remember the date shown here will not match the ones shown on your screen, since the datebook is designed to take you to the current week).**

As you will see when you begin to author your own stacks in HyperCard, there are many situations where cutting and pasting information from one stack to another saves time. You can use this method not only to copy data between fields (as you did in this exercise) but also to copy graphics and buttons that you wish to reuse.

Inserting Calculations Performed in the Message Box into a Card

In Chapter 2, you saw how you can use the Message box to enter Go and Find commands when you need to locate specific cards in a stack. You can also use the Message box to perform calculations whose result can be entered directly into a particular field of a card.

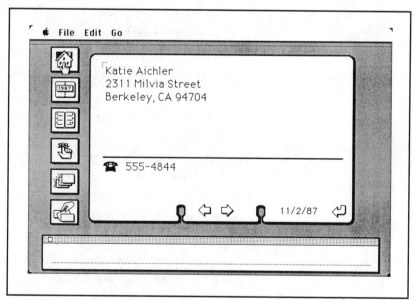

Figure 3.6: Using the Home icon to return to the Home Card

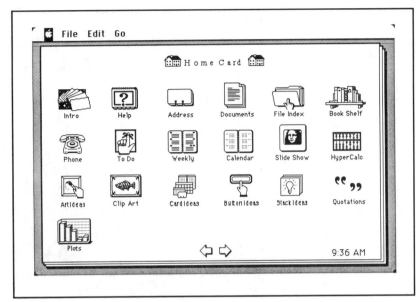

Figure 3.7: Opening the File Index stack from the Home Card

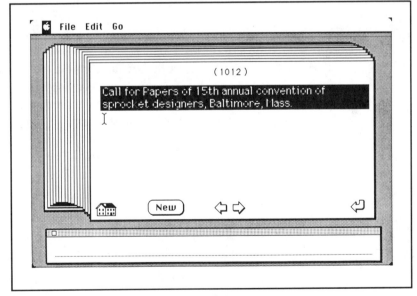

Figure 3.8: Selecting the text to be copied

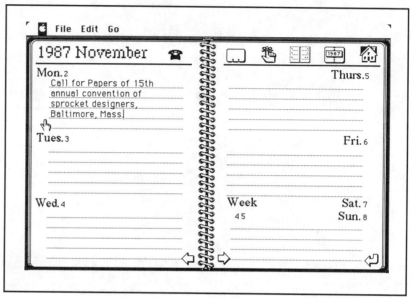

Figure 3.9: Inserting the copied text into a card in the Datebook stack

To have HyperCard perform a calculation in the Message box, you enter a formula in it and press Return (or Enter). HyperCard will then replace the formula with the calculated result, which can be inserted into a field of your choice in one of the cards in the current stack. To insert the result in a field, you first select it in the Message box and cut (Command-X) or copy it (Command-C). Then move the I-Beam cursor to the appropriate field, click, and paste it in place with Command-V just as you did in the previous exercise.

When creating your formula, you must use the mathematical operators and/or built-in functions recognized by HyperCard. The mathematical operators are as follows:

Function	Operator
Addition	+
Subtraction	–
Multiplication	*
Division	/
Exponentiation	^

For example, to calculate the difference between $4,567.85 and $279.96, enter the following formula into the Message box:

    4567.85 − 279.96

When you press Return or Enter, the result 4287.89 will replace the formula in the Message box. If you then want to insert this result into a particular field of the current card, you can either type it into the field or copy it. To copy the result from the Message box to a field, you select the text in the Message box, press Command-C (or choose Copy on the Edit menu) to copy it into the buffer, move the I-Beam cursor to the correct place in the field where you want it copied to, click, and press Command-V (or select Paste on the Edit menu) to insert it into place.

The Order of Calculation in Formulas

When you use the Message box to calculate formulas, you must be aware of the order of calculation that HyperCard uses. It follows the standard algebraic order of calculation, as follows:

1. Functions
2. Exponents
3. Multiplication and division
4. Addition and subtraction

Multiplication and division have equal status in the calculation order. This means that only their position in the formula determines which is calculated first. In all such cases, the formula is evaluated from left to right, the same as you read a line of text.

Note that addition and subtraction also have equal status in the calculation order, although any functions, exponents, or multiplication or division entered in the formula will be calculated before addition or subtraction (even when they are entered to the right of the addition or subtraction). To alter the order of calculation in some part of the formula, you must enclose the operation with lower status in parentheses.

To illustrate how this is done and its effect on the result, consider the following formula:

6 + 5 * 2

Because muliplication is evaluated before addition, HyperCard will first multiply the last two numbers and then add the first number to this result, giving you 16 as the answer (5 * 2 = 10 and 10 + 6 = 16).

If you want the sum of the first two numbers to be multiplied by the third, you must alter the order of calculation by placing the first operation within parentheses, as follows:

(6 + 5) * 2

In this case, HyperCard sums the first two numbers before multiplying the result by 2, giving you 22 as the answer (6 + 5 = 11 and 11 * 2 = 22).

Using Functions in Formulas

You can also enter special *functions* (built-in formulas) in formulas you create. HyperTalk includes a variety of mathematical as well as date and time functions that can be used in the Message box (refer to Appendix B for a complete list of HyperTalk functions). Many HyperTalk functions require only that you enter the name of the function and press Return or Enter. For example, you can enter the current date into the Message box by typing

the date

and pressing Return or Enter. If today's date were February 15, 1989, the Message box would then contain

02/15/89

If you want the day of the week and name of the month spelled out as well as all four digits of the year, you can enter

the long date

All four of the date and time functions—the date, the long date, the time, and the long time—must always be prefaced with *the* to avoid an error message.

into the Message box. Assuming that the current date is still 02/15/89, HyperCard will return

Wednesday, February 15, 1989

in the Message box. Similar results can be obtained when you enter *the time* or *the long time* function into the Message box.

All of the mathematical functions with the exception of pi require more information than just the correct function name to be calculated. For instance, to find the square root of a number, you must enter *sqrt* followed by the number whose root you wish calculated enclosed in a pair of parentheses. To have HyperCard find the square root of 121, enter

sqrt(121)

in the Message box. When you press Return or Enter, the result of 11 is returned.

Whenever parenthetical information must be tacked on to the end of a function name, this indicates to the program what data that function is to operate on. This information is known as the *argument* of the function.

Simple functions such as the square root function require only one argument (that of the number whose root is to be calculated), but other mathematical functions require multiple arguments. For example, to find the average of a group of numbers, you enter *average* followed by a listing of all the numbers in the group as the functional arguments. When a function requires multiple arguments, you separate each one by entering a comma. To find the average of the numbers 23, 42, and 70, you enter

average(23,42,70)

in the Message box. HyperCard will return the result of 45 when you press Return or Enter.

You can mix the mathematical functions with regular mathematical operators when entering formulas into the Message box. For example, if you wanted to add 25 to the square root of 144, you could

When entering HyperTalk functions that take arguments, you can insert a space between the function name and its arguments, if you wish. You can also enter spaces within a list of arguments when the function requires multiple arguments, without adversely affecting the calculated result.

do so by entering

25 + sqrt(144)

HyperCard would return the result of 37 in the Message box when you press Return or Enter.

Adding New Cards to a Stack

In addition to modifying information in the fields of existing cards in a stack, you will also need to add new cards to the stack you are working with. To add a new card, choose the New Card option on the Edit menu or press Command-N.

When you use the New Card option, HyperCard always inserts a blank card after the card that is currently displayed on your screen. If you want the new card to be the last card in the stack, you open the stack, use the Last option on the Go menu, and then choose the New Card option on the Edit menu (or press Command-N). If you want to insert the new card between two existing cards in the stack, go to the first card and issue the New Card command once it is displayed on your screen.

When you add a new card to a stack, you can begin filling in its text fields by locating the Browse tool at the beginning of the first field (where it changes to the I-Beam cursor), clicking the mouse (where the I-Beam cursor changes into the flashing text insertion pointer), and typing in the entry. Once you have finished entering your text in this field, you have only to press the Tab key to proceed to the next text field in the card.

Adding a New Card to the Address Stack

When you add a new card to the Address stack, you do not have to manually locate the Browse tool at the beginning of the first field to begin filling out the card. This is done automatically for you whenever a new card is added to this stack through a HyperTalk script that has been attached to the background of the basic address card form. Also, once you finish adding text to the first field and press the Tab key to move to the second field to enter the person's phone number, the date entry in the third field is automatically updated with the current date. This, too, is the result of a HyperTalk script that has been added to the background of the address card. Later on in Part II, you will learn about these HyperTalk scripts in some detail, as they both might prove useful in the stacks that you will be creating for yourself.

To see how this works and to get practice in adding cards to a stack, perform the following exercise.

1. **Move the Browse tool to the rolodex card icon (between the telephone and reminder icon, as shown in Figure 3.10) and click the mouse.**

   This returns you to the first card in the Address stack.

2. **Select the Last option from the Edit menu (or press Command-4).**

   This takes you to the last card in the Address stack, that of Fred Yoshioka.

3. **Select New Card from the Edit menu or press Command-N.**

   A blank card will appear on the screen.

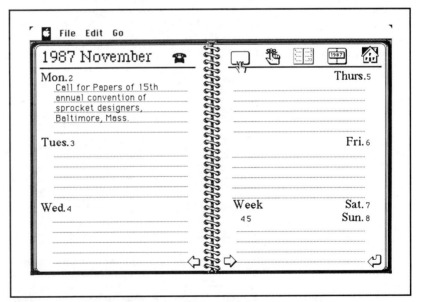

Figure 3.10: Returning to the Address stack from the Datebook stack

4. **Enter the name and address information for Hans Andrew, as shown in Figure 3.11.**

5. **Press Tab to move to the second field to enter the telephone number.**

As soon as you do, the current date will appear in the third field.

6. **Enter *555–2345* as the telephone number in the second field.**

This completes the data entry for this new address card.

Deleting Cards from a Stack

When you need to delete a card from the stack you are working in, you simply go to the card in question and, once it is displayed on your screen, use the Delete Card option on the Edit menu or press Command-Delete (or Command-Clear, if you have a numeric pad).

The Delete Card option on the Edit menu allows you to delete only one card (the current card) at a time. To delete several cards, you must repeat this command. Later on in Part III, when you learn

If you ever delete a card in error, you cannot restore it to the stack by using the Undo option from the Edit menu (or Command-Z) in version 1.0. In version 1.1, you can use this option to restore a card that was previously deleted.

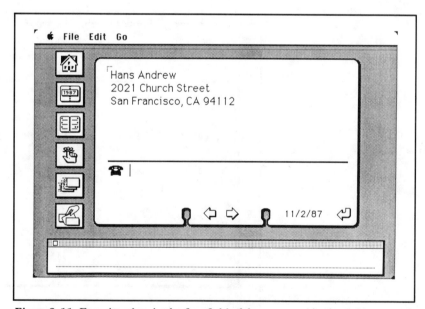

Figure 3.11: Entering data in the first field of the new card in the Address stack

more about using HyperTalk, you will find out how you can set up a script that will automatically delete all cards in a stack that meet a certain condition (such as delete all cards where the date of entry is prior to January 1, 1984).

Summary

You have now learned about all of the major editing procedures that you will use in HyperCard to maintain and add to the stacks that you use. These include adding, replacing, and deleting text in fields of a card, copying and moving text between fields and cards as well as from the Message box into fields, and finally, adding and deleting cards in a stack.

With your new editing skills, you can now modify the example Address stack so that it contains the names and addresses of real people that you know. In editing the Address stack, you can either use the existing cards, editing the fields as required, or simply begin by deleting all of the sample cards and then add and fill out new cards for each of the people you want in it.

In the next chapter, you will learn how to print the information in a stack. As you will learn, you can print all of the information in a particular card or from all of the cards in the stack, as well as set up simple reports that contain information from some or all of the fields in a card.

Printing Cards and Reports

CHAPTER *4*

HYPERCARD ALLOWS YOU TO PRINT THE CURRENT card or all of the cards in the open stack, or even create a simple report that prints just some of the fields from each card in a stack. In this chapter, you will explore all of these methods for obtaining hard copies of the information contained in a stack.

Before printing with HyperCard, make sure that you have selected the correct printer from the Chooser (on the Apple menu). When you select the Chooser, it displays the icons for the various devices that are available to you (according to the resources of the current startup device). To select the appropriate printer from the Chooser, click on either the ImageWriter or LaserWriter icon. If the printer is connected directly to your computer, icons representing the Modem and Printer port appear. Select the appropriate port by clicking on its icon.

If the printer you want to use is connected to the AppleTalk network, you must make sure that it is activated. The radio buttons for activating or deactivating the network are either on the Chooser or the Control Panel (also available from the Apple menu), depending upon the version of the Finder you use with your Macintosh. After you click on the device (printer) you want to use, the names of all the devices connected to the network appear. Click on the appropriate name (if you have only one ImageWriter or LaserWriter, there will be no aliases used in the select box). After selecting the name of the device you want, type your name in the User Name box (Apple-Talk can then let others on the network know who is using the shared printer).

In addition to using the Chooser to configure your printer, you can use the Installer (this program is found in the Utilities folder on your System Tools disk). The Installer allows you to configure your HyperCard startup disks with the printer you are using. When you open the Installer, you will see a list of the printing resources that you can install on the startup disk. Select the appropriate drive that contains the startup disk to be updated followed by the name of the printer resource to be installed, and then click on the Install button. After you have installed your printer, it will be available for printing cards whenever you use HyperCard.

Page Setup

```
┌─────────────────────┐
│ File                │
├─────────────────────┤
│ ▸New Stack...       │
│  Open Stack...   ⌘O │
│  Save a Copy...     │
├·····················┤
│  Page Setup...      │
│  Print Card      ⌘P │
│  Print Stack...     │
│  Print Report...    │
├·····················┤
│  Quit HyperCard  ⌘Q │
└─────────────────────┘
```

HyperCard's File menu is shown at left. Notice that the Page Setup option is the first one of the four printing options on this menu. The Page Setup option allows you to select the page size and orientation to be used as well as select some special printing effects. What these effects are depends upon the type of printer you have configured with the Chooser.

Always be sure that the page layout options you want to use are in effect before you select the Print Card, Print Stack, or Print Report option that you wish to use.

Printing with the ImageWriter

If you are using the ImageWriter, the dialog box shown in Figure 4.1 will appear when you select the Page Setup option from the File menu. From this dialog box, you can change the page size from the default of US Letter ($8^1/_2 \times 11$ single-sheet paper) to US Legal ($8^1/_2 \times 14$ single-sheet paper) or Computer Paper ($8^1/_2 \times 11$ fanfold paper). Note that A4 Letter and International Fanfold are paper sizes that conform to international (non–US) standards. To change the paper size, just click on the appropriate radio button.

You can also change the orientation of the printing from the normal view (also referred to as *portrait mode*) to a 90-degree shift to the right (also known as *landscape mode*). To change from portrait to landscape mode, click on the icon that shows the figure turned on its side.

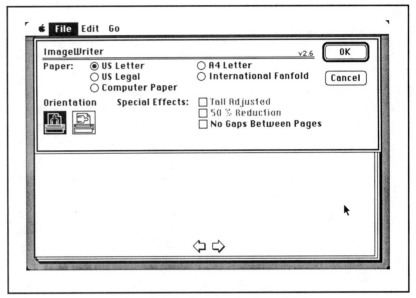

Figure 4.1: The Page Setup dialog box for the ImageWriter

When printing from HyperCard, the only special printing effect that is available is to print pages with no gaps between them. You will want to use this option only when you have also selected the Computer Paper option. Note that you cannot use the 50% Reduction or Tall Adjusted options with HyperCard.

Printing with the LaserWriter

If you have selected the LaserWriter with the Chooser, the dialog box shown in Figure 4.2 will appear when you select the Page Setup option. Just as with the ImageWriter, you can select the appropriate paper size and orientation. However, there are more printer effects available when using the LaserWriter.

The Font Substitution option is already selected. This instructs the LaserWriter to substitute built-in laser fonts for nonstandard fonts that are used in a card. When this effect is checked, the printer will do its best to substitute built-in fonts that look as much as possible like those that appear on your screen. If you leave this option unchecked, the LaserWriter will treat the text in a card as graphic images.

Using the Font Substitution option may save you some time, since graphics always take longer to print. Of course, leaving the Font Substitution option checked will have no effect if your cards use only built-in laser fonts such as Helvetica, Times, and Courier.

Depending upon the number and type of fonts used in the stack, you may want to leave this option unselected when you print it.

The Smoothing option affects graphic images in the cards that you print. When you check this box, jagged lines that appear in the screen version of the card are smoothed out in printing (the LaserWriter can show much greater resolution than the Macintosh screen). The trade-off is that using Smoothing slows down the printing quite a bit. You will want to use this option only when your cards contain graphic images whose lines must appear as smooth as possible and when it is not important how long it takes to print them out.

The last printing effect, Faster Bitmap Printing, is already selected. This option reduces the overall printing time by increasing the speed at which the printer driver sends data to the printer. It is recommended that you keep this option in effect when using the LaserWriter. However, you may have to turn off this effect if you are printing with a Postscript device, other than the LaserWriter, that requires slower printing, and when using the Invert option (discussed in the following section).

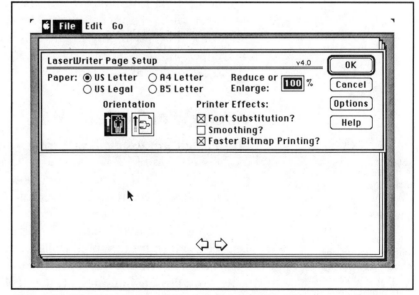

Figure 4.2: The Page Setup dialog box for the LaserWriter

Using the LaserWriter Options

When printing cards or reports in HyperCard, you cannot reduce or enlarge the image as is possible when printing with the Laser-Writer in other applications. As a result, any changes made to the percentage in the Reduce or Enlarge box on the Page Setup dialog screen will be ignored when you select the cards to be printed.

You can flip the image, invert it (reverse black and white), further reduce distortions to the printed image, or even enlarge the image area by selecting the Options button in the Page Setup dialog box. When you do, you will see the options shown in Figure 4.3.

The image of the dog on the sample minipage changes to illustrate the effect of selecting either the Flip Horizontal, Flip Vertical, or Invert option. You can combine these options or use them alone. For example, Figure 4.4 shows you the effect of inverting (reversing) the image. Figure 4.5 shows you the effect of flipping the image both hor-izontally (left to right) and vertically (upside down). When you use either of the flipping options, you should make sure that the Faster

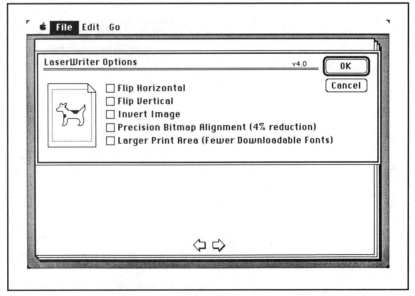

Figure 4.3: The LaserWriter Options dialog box

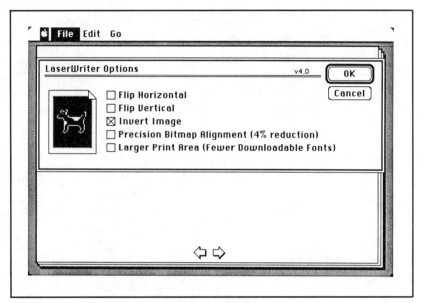

Figure 4.4: Inverting the image to be printed

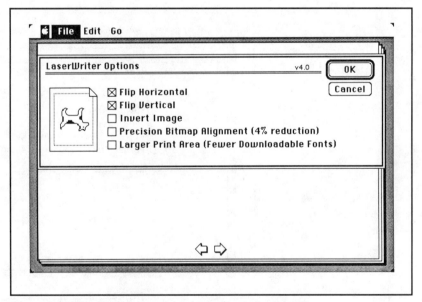

Figure 4.5: Flipping the image horizontally and vertically

Bitmap Printing option that appears in the Page Setup dialog box is turned on (checked). When you use the Invert option, you must make sure that this faster laser-printing option is turned off (unchecked). Be aware that inverting the printed image appreciably slows down the printing not only because the Faster Bitmap Printing must be turned off, but also because reversing the image most often calls for printing of a much larger area in black.

You can use the Precision Bitmap Alignment option along with Smoothing to further reduce the distortions that occur in Macintosh screen images. When you use this option, the overall size of the image is reduced by 4 percent. This results in a slightly smaller printed image.

The last option in this dialog box, Larger Print Area, prints the card closer to the edges of the paper. Although doing this increases the print area, it also uses more of the LaserWriter's internal memory, thus allowing you to use fewer downloadable fonts. If you wish to reduce the margins in printing cards and have not used fonts that have to be downloaded, you can use this option with no problem.

HyperCard will remember the printing options that you select, from either the Page Setup or Options dialog box. Always remember to select the Page Setup option from the File menu and adjust the settings before printing a new stack or cards that require printing effects different from those that are in effect.

Printing Cards

HyperCard allows you to print either the current card on the screen or all of the cards in the current stack. Although you can vary the number of cards printed per page as well as their layout when printing a stack, you cannot select just certain cards for printing. When you need to print only a select group of cards from a stack, you have two choices: either you can go to each card in the stack and print it individually, or you can copy each card you want printed to a new stack and then print that entire stack.

To copy cards into a new stack, you must have the user level set to at least the Painting level. At this level, the options Copy Card and Cut Card become available on the Edit menu. To create a new stack for printing, begin by going to a representative card in the stack whose cards you want to copy. Select the New Stack option from the File menu. A dialog box will appear. Type in a new name and click New. The first card of a new stack will now appear on the screen. Go back to the stack you wish to copy from and visit the first card you wish to copy. When you have the card on the screen, select the Copy Card (Command-C) option, return to the newly created stack, and use the Paste (Command-V) command on the Edit menu to insert it in the new stack. Then, return to the stack that contains the rest of the cards to be copied and repeat this procedure. Once you have copied all of the cards you wish to print, select the Print Stack option from the File menu.

Many stacks, such as the Address stack that is supplied with HyperCard, have a sort button that allows you to sort the cards in the stack before printing (its icon shows a hand selecting a card from the stack). Even if the stack you are using does not include such a sort button, you can sort the cards in your stack by using the HyperTalk Sort command. This command allows you to sort a stack by keywords in a particular text field. You will learn how to use this command in Chapter 11.

Printing the Current Card

When you want to print the card currently on your screen, simply select the Print Card option from the File menu or press Command-P. This starts the printing without requiring any further option selection. HyperCard will print the card full-size at the top of the page. It leaves a margin of about one-half inch at the top and three-fourths inch on the left and right. To stop the printing of the current card, press the Command key and a period.

Printing the Current Stack

To print all of the cards in the stack you have open in sequential order, select the Print Stack option on the File menu. When you select this option, the Print Stack dialog box shown in Figure 4.6

The dialog box for the ImageWriter is similar, except that the *Fast laser printing* option is replaced by the *Darker printing* option. This option produces a higher quality printout but slows down printing. The default setting is for normal printing (that is, *Darker printing* is not selected).

appears if you have a LaserWriter. The default settings are one copy of the stack, fast laser printing, continuous-feed paper (as the manual-feed option is turned off), and full-size cards using the standard format.

To obtain more than one copy of the cards in the stack, you need to enter a new number in the Copies box on this screen. This number can be between 1 and 99. When using the LaserWriter, keep the *Fast laser printing* option turned on unless you are printing the cards in landscape mode (turned 90 degrees on their side). If you do turn off this option, the stack printing will slow down quite a bit.

Selecting the Page Layout

When you select the Print Stack option, HyperCard shows you the layout of the printed cards by displaying miniatures of the current card on a page (Figure 4.6). The default is to print two full-size cards per page in what is referred to as the standard format. This format evenly spaces the cards on the page, giving you almost an inch for the

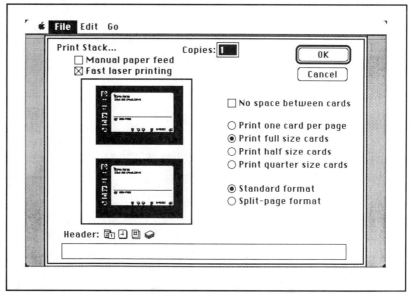

Figure 4.6: The Print Stack dialog box showing the default settings

left margin and an inch between the bottom of the first card and the top of the second card. The left margin is sufficient to allow you to add holes for a ring binder.

If you wish to bind the printed cards in a minibinder as indicated in Figure 4.7, then change the format selection to Split-page format. This arrangement allows you to fold the pages down the middle and punch holes in the top and bottom margins so that they can be stored in minibinders. In this layout, the left and right margins are almost equal and the distance between the cards is somewhat less than in the standard format.

Besides printing just two full-size cards per page, you can print 8 half-size cards by selecting *Print half size cards* (Figure 4.8), or you can print 32 quarter-size cards by selecting *Print quarter size cards* (Figure 4.9). Also, if

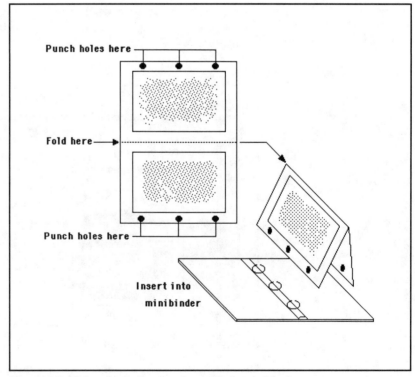

Figure 4.7: Using the Split-page format in a minibinder

you want to have just one full-size card printed on a page, select the *Print one card per page* option. When you use this option, the single card is always printed at the top of the page just as it is when using the Print Card option. With any of these layouts, you can use either the Standard or Split-page format. Figures 4.10, 4.11, and 4.12 show you the difference in size between printing 2, 8, and 32 cards per page using these options. Note that when you have 32 cards printed on a page, they are so small that their text is practically illegible.

Adding a Header to the Printout

You can create a header that appears in the top margin of each page of the printout by entering it in the Header box. To create a header, click in this box. This will place the flashing text insertion pointer at the beginning of the line. Then type in the text of the header just as you enter any text in HyperCard. If you wish to add the current time or date, the page number, or the stack name, simply

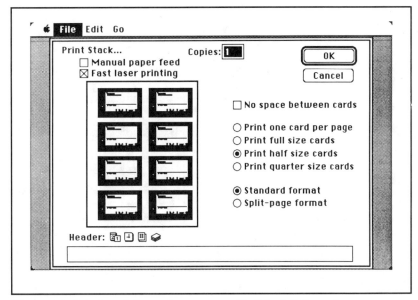

Figure 4.8: Printing eight cards per page with *Print half size cards*

select the appropriate icon by clicking on it. Figure 4.13 shows you a sample header that uses the stack, date, and page number icons. Figure 4.14 shows how this header looks when printed.

To delete a header, choose the Print Stack option again, move the Arrow pointer to the beginning of the header text in the Header box, and click the mouse. Then drag over the text to select and press the Backspace (Delete) key. To edit the text of a header, move the Arrow pointer right before the text you want to change and click the mouse. This places the flashing text insertion cursor immediately ahead of the text. To insert new text, just begin typing. To delete existing text, drag the mouse to select it and press the Backspace (Delete) key.

Once you have made all of the changes to the settings in the Print Stack dialog box that you want, click on the OK button to begin printing the stack. If you are using the LaserWriter, HyperCard will print the stack in reverse order (from end to beginning) so that the pages are in the correct order in the output tray. If you need to stop the printing before the entire stack has been printed, press the Command key and the period.

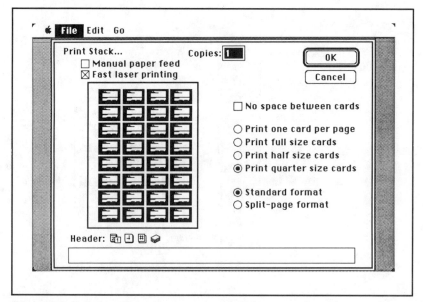

Figure 4.9: Printing 32 cards per page with *Print quarter size cards*

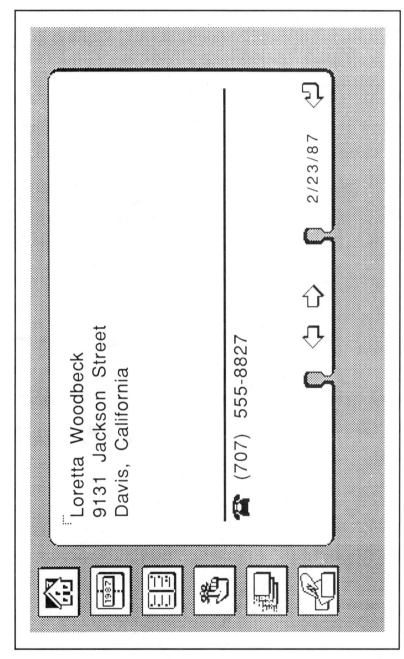

Figure 4.10: Actual printout size of a card from Address stack with two cards per page

Figure 4.11: Actual printout size of a card from Address stack with eight cards per page

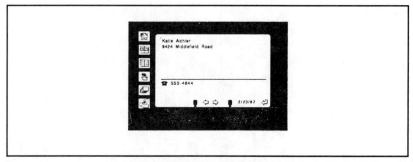

Figure 4.12: Actual printout size of a card from Address stack with 32 cards per page

Printing Reports

HyperCard allows you to create and print simple reports using the information contained in stacks. To do this, select the Print Report option from the File menu (Figure 4.15). By using the *Arrange fields in* option, you can print reports in one of three formats: mailing labels, columns, or rows. When setting up the report, you can use either all of the fields on a card or just some of them. When selecting

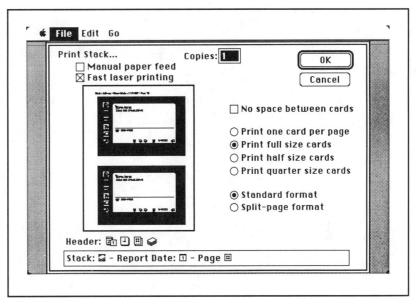

Figure 4.13: Creating a header

fields, the order in which they are selected determines the order in which they appear in the report. Various options are available depending upon the type of report format chosen.

It is important to note that HyperCard does not allow you to create reports based on more than a single stack. If you need to print information from multiple stacks, you must create a new stack that contains all of the combined data and then set up a report format for this new stack. This procedure is similar to the one outlined for printing only selected cards in a stack by copying them to a new stack, except that you must copy the cards from multiple stacks (refer back to the section on Printing Cards for more information on creating a new stack by copying existing cards).

HyperCard distinguishes between two basic types of fields: background fields and card fields. When you author a stack, you create an underlying design containing the placement of text fields and graphics that are used. Those fields that are created in the card's background appear in every card in the stack. For instance, the Address stack has three background fields: name and address, telephone, and date.

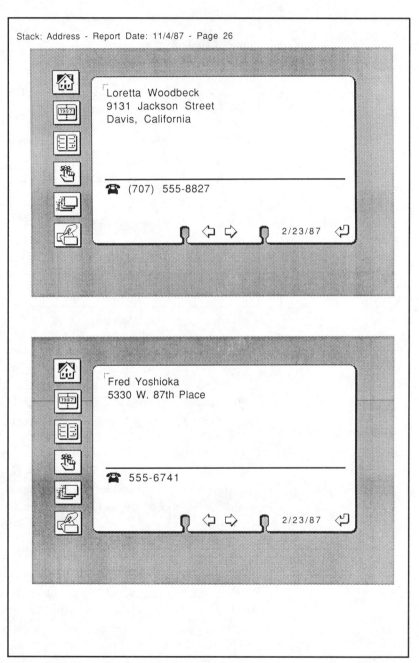

Figure 4.14: Sample printed page with header

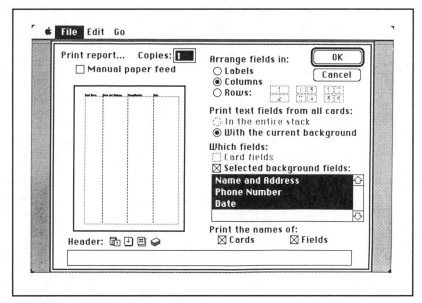

Figure 4.15: HyperCard's Print Report dialog box

Although many stacks require only a single background design, a stack can have more than one background. If this is the case, the background fields may differ depending upon the card that you are looking at. In addition, you can add text fields to individual cards. Such fields are not part of the background and therefore belong only to the current card and do not appear in any other card in the stack.

When setting up reports, you can specify that all text fields in the stack be used (both background and card fields), just certain background fields be used, or that all fields with the current background (the background used by the card that is current when you create the report) be used. You can see what combinations are available and how they are created in Table 4.1.

When you select the *With the current background* radio button, Hyper-Card will show you the names of all of the fields in the card. The order in which you select these fields determines the order in which they will be printed in the report. To select a field, you simply click on its name. To select several fields, keep the Shift key depressed as you click on the field names. You will want to do this whenever you set up a report that prints text fields that share the current background, except in the rare instances when you just want to include a single

From *Print text field from all cards,* select:	From *Which Fields*, select:	To produce:
In the entire stack	Card fields	Report using all card fields in the entire stack
In the entire stack	Background fields	Report using all background fields in the entire stack
In the entire stack	Card fields and Back-ground fields	Report using all cards and all background fields in the entire stack
With current background	Card fields	Report using all card fields that share current background
With current background	Card fields and Selected background fields	Report using all card fields and selected background fields that share the current background
With current background	Selected background fields	Report using selected background fields that share the current background

Table 4.1: Specifying which fields are to be included in the report

If you are using an ImageWriter, an additional option box for *Darker printing* will appear beneath the one for the *Manual paper feed* (not shown in Figure 4.15, as this was made with the LaserWriter selected as the printer device). Check this box if your printer has an old ribbon and you need a darker print-out, or just to produce a higher quality printout.

field. You can deselect a field by clicking on its field name a second time. Likewise, you can deselect several fields by holding down the Shift key as you click on each field name.

You can set the number of copies of the report to be printed by entering a number between 1 and 99 in the Copies box. If you are using single sheets that must be fed by hand, you check the *Manual paper feed* box (don't use this option if paper is fed from the paper tray on the LaserWriter). If you select this option, HyperCard will pause after printing each page of the report to allow you to feed another sheet.

You can add a single-line header to your reports just as you can when printing cards in a stack. To create a header for the report, click on the header box and enter the text. If you want to add the current date, stack name, or page number, click on the appropriate icon. Be sure to add a space after the icon selected if you want a space to appear between the text that it adds and the header text that you type in.

Once you set up a report format using these options, HyperCard will remember them until you choose the Print Reports option from the File menu and modify their settings.

Mailing Labels

Perhaps the most popular report format is the one that prints information from text fields on mailing labels. When printing mailing labels with the LaserWriter, you must use special labels made for photocopiers or especially for the LaserWriter. When printing mailing labels on the ImageWriter, you need to use labels on $8^1/_2 \times 11$ tractor-feed paper.

To set up the labels report format, you must click on the Labels radio button under the heading *Arrange fields in*. When you do, the layout box and options will change to those shown in Figure 4.16. The layout of the mailing labels is shown in the minipage window in the dialog box. HyperCard will print a label for each card in the current stack that shares the current background. The printing order of the fields on the card is determined by the order in which you select them from the scrolling window to the right of the minipage window.

Field entries printed in the mailing label are automatically centered on each line. If the text of the field is too long to fit on one line, it is automatically wrapped to the next line of the label. Should there be too many lines of text for a single mailing label, HyperCard will print only those lines that do fit.

The dimensions of the labels, the top and left margins, and the space between the labels are displayed at the bottom of the dialog box. To change the number of labels, margin settings, and spacing between labels, drag on the lower right corner of the first label (marked with a black square) or on the last label (the one in the lower right corner) in the minipage window. You drag on the square in the lower corner of the first label primarily to change the number of labels per page as well as the top and left margins. You drag on the label in the lower right corner of the minipage primarily to change the spacing between labels. As you drag on either of these places, the dimensions at the bottom of the dialog box will change accordingly. Note that you can see these measurements either in inches (the default) or centimeters by activating the appropriate radio button.

After you have sized the labels, set the margins and spacing between them, and selected all the other printing options you want in effect, you can print the mailing labels by clicking on the OK button. If you do not want your changes to take effect and continue with the printing of the mailing labels, select the Cancel button instead. Once you have started the printing, you can abort it at any time by pressing the Command key and period, just as you do when printing cards.

Printing a Columnar Report

By selecting the Columns radio button under the *Arrange fields in* heading, you can have HyperCard print the text from selected fields in columns across the page. Note that this is the default report format

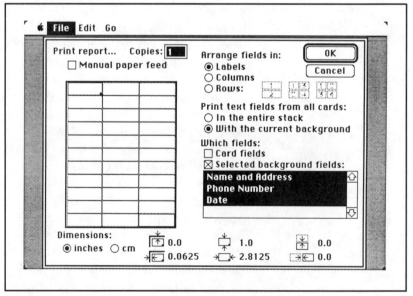

Figure 4.16: Setting up a report to print mailing labels

that first appears when you select the Print Reports option on the File menu (Figure 4.15). When the Columns radio button is selected, HyperCard automatically selects *With the current background* beneath the *Print text fields from all cards* heading and *Selected background fields* beneath the *Which fields* heading. These are the only selections available when printing a columnar report.

When selecting the fields to be included in this type of report, again, the order in which you select the fields determines the order in which they appear across the page (from left to right). HyperCard will not allow you to select more fields than will fit across the page. You can size the width of each column in the report by dragging on the vertical dotted lines shown in the minipage window (see Figure 4.17).

When you set up a columnar report, two more option boxes appear in the lower right corner of the dialog box beneath the heading *Print the names of* and above the header box. To have the names of the fields printed above each column, leave the Fields box checked. When the report is printed, the field name automatically appears left-justified with the column's edge and is underlined. To have the name

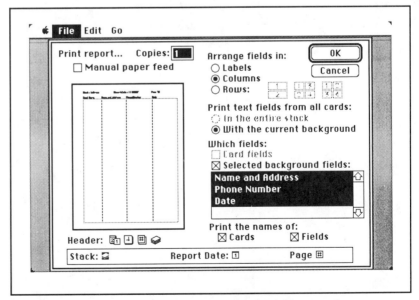

Figure 4.17: Setting up a columnar report for the Address stack

of the card appear as the first column of the report, leave the Cards box checked. The card name is analogous to the card number.

Figure 4.18 shows you the first half-page of the columnar report printed according to the specifications shown in Figure 4.17. Notice that the card names printed in the first column are really the card numbers, and that the field names for the Address stack appear underlined and left-justified with each column. By using the report view displayed in the minipage window, and by adjusting the spacing of the headers in the Header box, it was possible to justify the various parts of the header so that the stack name is left-justified with the first column, the report date is centered, and the page number is right-justified with the last column of the report.

After you have sized the columns and set the options you wish to use in the report, you can print it by clicking on the OK button. If you do not want to continue with the printing of the report, select the Cancel button. Once the printing has begun, you can abort it at any time by pressing the Command key and period.

Stack: Address	Report Date: 11/5/87		Page 1
Card Name	Name and Address	Phone Number	Date
first	This is the first card of the Address stack.		7/26/87
Card 2	Steve Aaron 2260 Oak Creek Drive	555-7806	2/23/87
Card 3	Katie Aichler 9424 Middlefield Road	555-4844	2/23/87
Card 4	Martha Belion 8495 Jefferson St	555-0934	2/23/87
Card 5	Marti Belisle 3703 Maude Ave	555-8203	5/26/87
Card 6	Roger Benrey 9541 Mount Vernon Dr	555-3005	2/23/87
Card 7	Loween Blank 6686 Martin Ave Prairie, Texas	(214) 555-5456	2/23/87
• • •	• • •	• • •	• • •

Figure 4.18: The first half-page of the columnar report for the Address stack

Printing a Report Arranged by Rows

The last type of report format that you can use is to arrange the field information by rows. This is done by clicking on the radio button marked Rows under the *Arrange fields in* heading (Figure 4.19). When you use the row format, HyperCard prints each selected field vertically down the page for each card used. There are three row layouts from which to choose.

The default row layout (shown in Figure 4.19) prints the selected fields from each card used in the report as a block, one over the other (shown by the boxes marked 1 and 2 on top of each other). If you select either of the two remaining row layouts, HyperCard prints the blocks of information from two cards side by side. When you select the second (middle) layout option (boxes marked 1 above 2 and 3 above 4), these blocks are arranged so that information from individual cards follows down the first column before commencing at the beginning of the second column (much like newspaper columns). When you select the third layout option (boxes marked 1 above 3 and 2 above 4), this arrangement is changed so that the blocks from

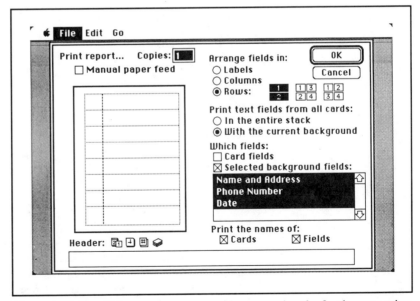

Figure 4.19: Specifying a report arranged by rows using the first layout option

individual cards alternate between the left and right column down the page. Figures 4.20 and 4.21 contrast these arrangements by showing the first half-page of a row report for the address stack.

Just as when specifying a columnar report, you can change the size of the line length that contains the information from each field selected by dragging on the vertical dotted lines in the minipage window. So, too, you can specify that the field names and names of the cards be printed as part of a row report. In a row report, the field names are printed to the left of the field information on each row of the report, and the card name is printed above each block of field information.

You print a row report after specifying all of its layout options by clicking on the OK button just as you do to print any other report in HyperCard. Likewise, you can abort the printing by pressing the Command key and period.

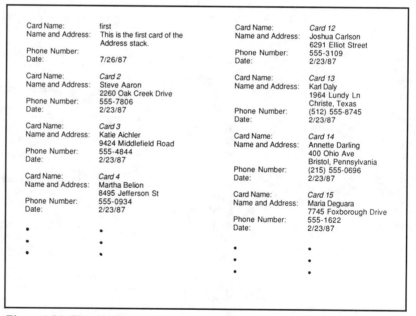

Card Name:	first	Card Name:	Card 12
Name and Address:	This is the first card of the Address stack.	Name and Address:	Joshua Carlson 6291 Elliot Street
Phone Number:		Phone Number:	555-3109
Date:	7/26/87	Date:	2/23/87
Card Name:	Card 2	Card Name:	Card 13
Name and Address:	Steve Aaron 2260 Oak Creek Drive	Name and Address:	Karl Daly 1964 Lundy Ln
Phone Number:	555-7806		Christe, Texas
Date:	2/23/87	Phone Number:	(512) 555-8745
		Date:	2/23/87
Card Name:	Card 3		
Name and Address:	Katie Aichler 9424 Middlefield Road	Card Name:	Card 14
Phone Number:	555-4844	Name and Address:	Annette Darling 400 Ohio Ave
Date:	2/23/87		Bristol, Pennsylvania
		Phone Number:	(215) 555-0696
Card Name:	Card 4	Date:	2/23/87
Name and Address:	Martha Belion 8495 Jefferson St		
Phone Number:	555-0934	Card Name:	Card 15
Date:	2/23/87	Name and Address:	Maria Deguara 7745 Foxborough Drive
		Phone Number:	555-1622
		Date:	2/23/87

Figure 4.20: First half-page of a row report that prints card information down one column before beginning the next

Summary

In this chapter, you've explored all of HyperCard's printing options. If you have not yet tried printing with HyperCard, you will probably want to experiment with its printing capabilities before you create your own stacks and need to produce reports from the data they contain.

To get printing practice, you can use the Address stack supplied with HyperCard (especially if you have now customized it so that it contains the names and addresses of people you know). You should begin by opening this stack and then accessing the Page Setup option to make sure that your printer is properly configured. Once you have verified the information in this dialog box, try printing the first card in the stack (Command-P). If this prints all right, try using the Print Stack option. If you don't want to use a lot of paper, you can try

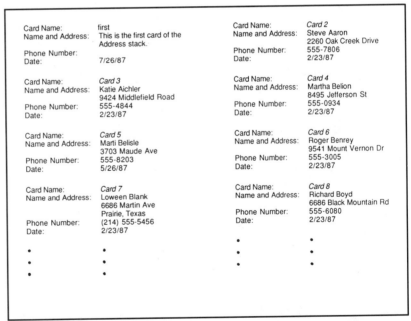

Figure 4.21: First half-page of a row report that alternates card information left and right down the page

printing the stack with half-size cards (or even quarter-size cards if you don't mind them being tiny). After printing all of the cards in the stack, try printing mailing labels using the Print Report option. Finally, see how the information looks printed in a columnar format, and then in one of the three row layouts.

This concludes Part I, which has presented all of the fundamental features of HyperCard. These are features such as browsing, editing, and printing that every HyperCard user needs to be familiar with, even if your only intention is to use other people's stackware. In the following chapters, however, you will move from the basic to the intermediate level in HyperCard. In Part II, you will learn how to design and create stacks of your own. The next chapter will introduce you to the underlying structure of a HyperCard stack.

P A R T II

Authoring Your Own HyperCard Stacks

The Parts of a HyperCard Stack

CHAPTER 5

Although Hyper-Card often refers to the background of a stack, it does not refer specifically to the foreground, preferring to use the terms *background* and *card* (meaning the card level) instead. I have introduced the term *foreground* as a description of the individual card level because it makes it easier to conceptualize the structure of a stack. When you stand at the foreground level, all items, both those in the background and in the foreground, are visible to you (as when browsing through cards in a completed stack). However, when you stand at the background level, only those items in the background are seen; items in the foreground are not yet visible to you (as when viewing a card in the Background mode).

BEFORE YOU BEGIN CREATING YOUR OWN STACKS, you should have a good understanding of the components of a stack and how they are structured in HyperCard. As you have seen, a stack represents a group of cards that are related to each other. This is really just another way of saying that the cards in a stack share a common structure.

At the most basic level, a stack has a background and foreground. The background includes those text fields, graphic images, and buttons that are shared by various cards in a stack. Many stacks have only one background that is shared by all of the cards in it. However, it is possible, and sometimes desirable, for a stack to have multiple backgrounds. In such a case, some of the cards may use one background while others use a different background structure.

In the foreground of a stack, at the card level, are the components that belong only to specific cards within it. These components can also include text fields, graphic images, and buttons. However, even if a card does not have any of these text fields, graphics, or buttons, it usually still has unique field entries that belong to each individual card in the foreground (although the fields themselves are still part of the background).

When creating a new stack, you must design the background (or backgrounds) that the cards will use. As you will see, this can be done either by designing a new background or by copying one from an existing stack. After you have designed the background, you can proceed to add cards to the stack and enter information into them. You may also add text fields and their entries, graphics, and buttons that belong to the individual card you are adding to the stack.

The Background of a Stack

The best way to understand the concept of the background of a stack is to examine various backgrounds of existing stacks. To do this, let's begin by examining the background of the Address stack that you practiced with in Part I.

The purpose of this stack is to keep a person's name, address, and telephone number, as well as the date that these data items are entered or updated in the card. In addition, you can use it to automatically dial the telephone number that has been entered into the card (if you have a modem connected to your Macintosh). The Address stack also contains buttons that enable you to go directly to various parts of a related stack named Datebook (which has three different backgrounds), to sort the cards in the Address stack, and to return to the Home Card in the Home stack.

Before you can examine the background of the Address stack, you must reset the user level from the User Preferences card in the Home stack. To do this, start HyperCard and, from the Home Card, take these steps:

1. **Click on the left-arrow button at the bottom of the card or press Command-4.**

   This takes you to the User Preferences card, currently set at the Typing level.

2. **Click on the radio button marked Authoring (Figure 5.1).**

When the user level is set to Authoring (or Scripting), two new menus appear on the HyperCard menu: Tools and Objects. In addition, new options become available on the File and Edit menus, as shown at left. The full File menu includes options for compacting, protecting, and deleting a stack. The full Edit menu includes options for cutting and copying a card as well as for selecting a new text style (currently unavailable) and accessing the background of the card.

At the Authoring level, a new option called Power Keys (to the right of Painting) appears on the User Preferences card. As power keys are only useful when you are using HyperCard's painting program, it does not matter at this point if its box is checked or unchecked (you will not use the painting program for a while).

File

New Stack...	
Open Stack...	⌘O
Save a Copy...	
Compact Stack	
Protect Stack...	
Delete Stack...	
Page Setup...	
Print Card	⌘P
Print Stack...	
Print Report...	
Quit HyperCard	⌘Q

Edit

Undo	⌘Z
Cut	⌘X
Copy	⌘C
Paste	⌘U
Clear	
New Card	⌘N
Delete Card	
Cut Card	
Copy Card	
Text Style...	⌘T
Background	⌘B

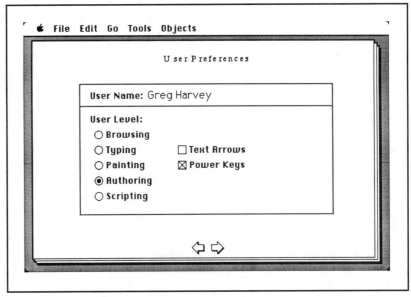

Figure 5.1: Setting the user level to Authoring

Now that the user level is set at Authoring, you should open the Address stack.

3. Click on the right-arrow button on the User Preferences card or press Command-H.

This takes you to the Home Card.

4. Move the Browse tool to the Address Stack icon and click.

5. Press Command-M.

This removes the Message box from the screen (you will not need it to examine the background of this stack).

6. Click on the right-arrow button at the bottom of the first card.

This takes you to Steve Aaron's card.

To look at the fields and buttons that are a part of the background of the Address stack, you will have to use the Tools menu. The Tools menu is a special kind of tear-off menu. When you click on Tools on the HyperCard menu and then drag downward until the Arrow pointer is below the last icons on the menu, you will see a flashing dotted outline of the menu box. When you release the mouse button, you create a miniwindow that contains all of the Tools options where the dotted outline was located (Figure 5.2).

This window can be then be positioned (and repositioned) anywhere you want on the screen by clicking and dragging on the gray border of the window (the same as with the Message box). Tearing off the Tools menu in this way makes it possible to access its various options without having to pull down the menu each time to click on the desired option. To make the Tools menu disappear, click on the box in the upper left corner of the miniwindow.

Try tearing off the Tools menu and positioning it in the upper right corner of the screen.

7. **Click on Tools on the HyperCard menu.**

8. **Drag the Arrow pointer downward until it is located below the last row of icon options.**

   You will see a flashing dotted line outlining the Tools menu box.

9. **Release the mouse button.**

   The Tools menu will now be positioned in the midst of the current card.

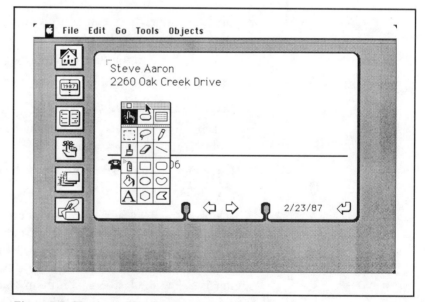

Figure 5.2: Tearing off the Tools menu

10. Move the Arrow pointer to the gray border of the miniwin-dow, and drag the miniwindow until it is located in the upper right corner of the screen (refer to Figure 5.3).

Notice that all of the options on the Tools menu are represented by icons. Presently, you are only interested in the first three icons: those above the dashed dividing line in the miniwindow. You will learn about the others when you use the painting program to create graphics for cards in your stack.

The first of these icons is the Browse tool, which you have already become familiar with when you learned how to browse through the cards in a stack. The second icon, to its right, is the Button tool. When you click on this icon, you can view the existing buttons in a card or change the attributes of buttons in a card or the background. The third icon, to the right of the Button tool, is the Field tool. When you click on this icon, you can view the existing fields in a card or change the attributes of fields in the card or the background. See what happens when you click on these tools.

11. Move the Arrow pointer to the Field tool and click.

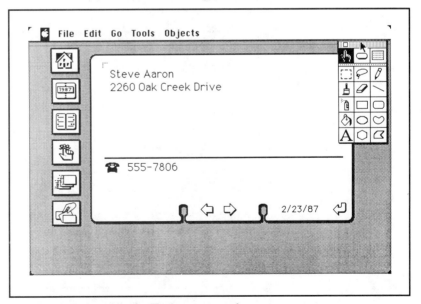

Figure 5.3: Relocating the Tools menu on the screen

You will see the borders of each field as well as the number of lines it contains (Figure 5.4).

12. Move the Arrow pointer to the Button tool and click.

You will now see the borders of the buttons in this card appear and the field borders disappear (Figure 5.5).

13. Move the Arrow pointer back to the Field tool and click again.

Background and Card Text Fields

When the Browse tool is selected, you are looking in the foreground, that is, at the individual card. At this level, you cannot tell which fields and buttons belong only to the card and which belong to the background. To access the current background of this card, you must select the Background option from the full Edit menu (Figure 5.6).

1. Click on the Background option of the Edit menu or press Command-B.

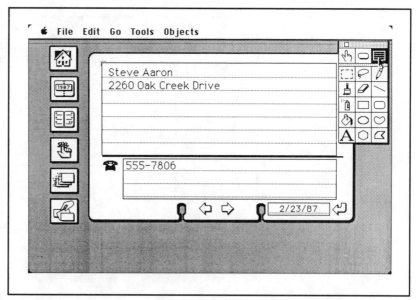

Figure 5.4: Viewing the existing fields in the card by selecting the Field tool

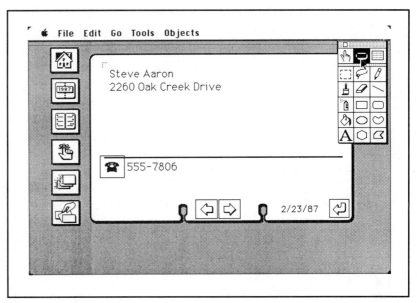

Figure 5.5: Viewing the existing buttons in the card by selecting the Button
tool

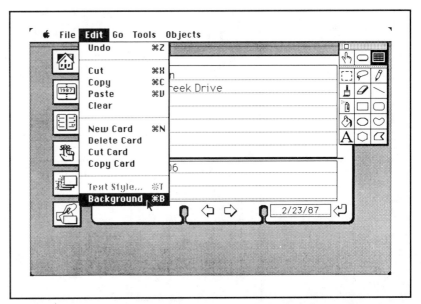

Figure 5.6: The Background option on the full Edit menu

To let you know that you are looking at the background of this card, the HyperCard menu is striped (Figure 5.7). Also, you will see that the Background option on the Edit menu is checked when you next access it. To return to the card level, you select the Background option on the Edit menu or press Command-B a second time. You also return automatically to the card level *whenever* you select the Browse tool. When you use the Background option to return to the card level, this does not also deselect the Field or Button tool as does using the Browse tool.

Notice that the text entered into Steve Aaron's card has disappeared from view (it still exists in the foreground, at the card level). However, all three fields (as indicated by their borders) are still visible. You now know that these fields are part of the background. If any of them were card fields, it would have disappeared along with its text when you used the Background option.

Examining the Field Name, Number, and ID

When the Field tool is selected, you can get information about the existing fields as well as make changes to them. You should now get

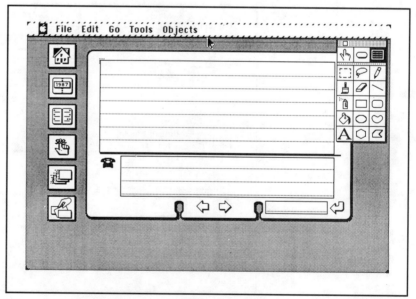

Figure 5.7: Viewing the background of the current card (indicated by the striped menu)

familiar with how you obtain information about individual fields in a card.

1. **Move the Arrow pointer somewhere within the boundary of the first field (the largest field at the top of the card where the name and address is entered).**

2. **Click the mouse.**

    This selects the field indicated by the moving dotted line around its border. When a field is selected, you can move, resize, or copy it.

3. **Move the Arrow pointer to the Objects menu, drag down until the Field Info option is highlighted, and then let up on the mouse button (Figure 5.8).**

    You will now see the Field Information dialog box for the first field as shown in Figure 5.9 (you can also access this dialog box by double-clicking anywhere within the borders of the field).

    The Field Information dialog box identifies the field by name and number and displays its current attributes. As you can see, it begins by listing the field's name, which represents an optional name of

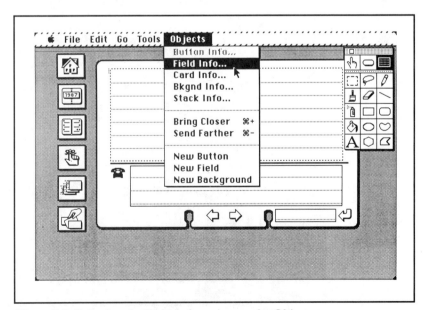

Figure 5.8: Selecting the Field Info option on the Objects menu

Strictly speaking, the field number may not always reflect the order in which the field was created. This is because both background and card fields are layered. This makes it possible to overlap fields for certain effects in a stack. As you will learn later on, there are two options on the Objects menu (*Bring closer* and *Send farther*) that allow you to reposition the field. Using these commands will alter the field number regardless of the order in which they were created (the higher the field number, the closer the field is in the overlay scheme).

your choice that you enter when creating the field. Below that, it lists the type of field (background or card) and the field number. Most often, the field number reflects the order in which it was created.

If this were a card field instead of a background field, it would indicate this and indicate the order in which this field were created. The numbering of background fields is done independently of that for card fields. The number given to a field depends upon its position in the card. As you will learn later, this position and, consequently, its number can be altered. This means that the field number is a relative identification that is subject to change when you make certain modifications to the stack.

In addition to a name and field number, the field is given an ID number. This is a sequential number that is assigned to the field when it is created. However, unlike the field number, the field ID remains attached to the field as long as it exists. If the field is deleted, the ID number is retired from the stack and is never reused. This means that the field ID is an absolute reference to the field. It remains the same even after you modify the field name and the field number.

You can reference a field by either its name, field number, or field ID. Remember that in Chapter 2 you used the Find command in the

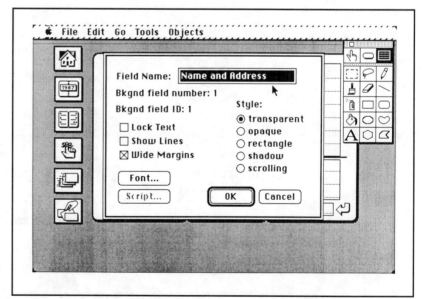

Figure 5.9: The Name and Address Field Information dialog box

Message box to locate the occurrence of certain characters in a particular field by referring to the field by its field number. For example, you entered

> find chars "ex" in field 1

in the Message box to restrict the search to the first field of the card. You could just as well locate these characters by entering

> find chars "ex" in field ID 1

or by entering

> find chars "ex" in field "Name and Address"

Notice that when you refer to a field by field number, you do not have to enter *field number,* as just entering *field* alone will suffice. However, when referring to a field by its ID, you must enter *field ID* before its number. Remember that the field number and field ID are not necessarily the same number, as they happen to be in this example. When referring to the field by name, you must enclose the name in quotation marks and it must follow the word *field.* Also, although you can ascertain the field number by tabbing through the fields, you must use the Field tool and access the Field Information dialog box to find out its field ID and field name.

This system of referring to a field by name, number, and ID carries over to other components of a HyperCard stack. You will find that a similar system is used for referring to buttons in a background or card, as well as backgrounds and cards in a stack.

Examining the Attributes of a Field

Below the field identifiers in the Field Information dialog box, you can see the current attributes of the field (Figure 5.9). Notice that the current style of the field is transparent. The transparent style is the default of HyperCard. A transparent field allows the background to show through the field. Its opposite is the opaque style. If you want the borders of the field to be displayed on the card, you can choose between rectangle (a simple box), shadow (giving it a three-dimensional look), or scrolling (a simple box with a vertical scroll bar that works like any scrolling Macintosh window).

In addition to selecting the style of the field from this dialog box, you can lock the text (preventing the data entered into the field from being changed), show the lines inside the field boundaries (whether or not the boundaries are visible on the screen), and set up wide margins (allowing less data to be entered in the field because of its wider left and right margins).

Although you can select only one style for the card (only one radio button can be selected at a time), you can combine the Lock Text, Show Lines, and Wide Margins attributes with it by checking some or all of them. You will find that the Wide Margins option works best with either the rectangle or shadow style of field. Also, the Show Lines option can be used effectively with any style. When it is used with either the transparent or opaque styles (neither of which display the field borders), you will see only the lines where you can enter the field data.

Changing the Font

There are two more buttons on the Field Information dialog box: Font and Script. The Script button is ghosted because you can add a HyperTalk script to a field only when you are using HyperCard at the Scripting user level. However, you can change the font of the text that is entered into a field by selecting the Font button. Figure 5.10 shows you the Text Style dialog box that is displayed when you click on the Font button.

Currently, the Name and Address field uses the 14-point Geneva font and the text entered into it is left-aligned. To change the font and/or point size, click on the name of the font and then the point size. Any change to either one is reflected in the sample box below. When you make a change to the point size, the line height is automatically adjusted so that there is always 2 points or more between each line of text. You can increase or decrease the spacing between lines by editing the number of the point size in the Line Height box. If you want to accommodate as many text lines in a field as possible, you can decrease the line height point size to that of the point size of the text (HyperCard will not allow you to set a smaller point size for the line height than you use for the point size of the font).

In addition to adjusting the font, point size, and line height, you can change the style of the text by checking one or more of the Style options. These allow you to add enhancements to the text such as boldfacing, italics, underlining, outlining, shadowed, condensed, or extended. You can also change the alignment of the text in the field by selecting one of the Align options. You can have the text either left-aligned, centered, or right-aligned in a field. Once you have made all of the desired changes in the Text Style dialog box, you set them by clicking on the OK button (or by pressing Return or Enter). If the field of the current card already contains text, it will reflect these changes as soon as you select the Browse tool. If the field does not yet contain text, you will see the font changes as soon as you begin entering text in the field.

HyperCard gives you several shortcuts for changing the text style of a field. Table 5.1 outlines these Command key combinations. Try using some of them to change the text style for the Name and Address field.

1. **Click the Cancel button on the Field Information dialog box or press Return (or Enter).**

   This takes you back to the current background.

2. **Press Command-T.**

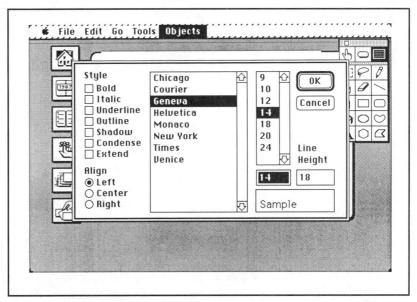

Figure 5.10: The Text Style dialog box for the Name and Address field

This takes you directly to the Text Style dialog box. Because the Name and Address field is still selected, any changes you make here will affect the text in this field.

3. **Change the point size of the text to 18 points by clicking on the 18.**

4. **Click on the OK button or press Return (or Enter).**

5. **Select the Background option on the Edit menu or press Command-B.**

You will now be able to see the text for this field and the effect of enlarging the font from 14 to 18 points (Figure 5.11).

6. **With the Arrow pointer somewhere within the borders of the Name and Address field, click the mouse.**

This selects the field again (shown by the moving dotted line around the borders).

7. **Press Command-< (left angle bracket).**

The text size is reduced back to 14 points (the next lowest size).

Key Combinations	Function
Command-T	Displays Text Style dialog box
Command->	Selects the next larger text size in the font
Command-<	Selects the next smaller text size in the font
Command-Shift->	Selects the next font in the system
Command-Shift-<	Selects the previous font in the system
Command-Option->	Increases the number of points between lines
Command-Option-<	Decreases the number of points between lines

Table 5.1: Keyboard shortcuts for changing the text style of a field

8. **Press Command-Shift-> (right angle bracket).**

   The font changes to Helvetica (the next font in the system) 12 point (Helvetica is available only in 10 and 12 point sizes).

9. **Hold down Command-Shift and press the < (left angle bracket) key three times.**

   The font changes to Chicago (available only in 12 points, with a default line height of 16 points).

10. **Hold down Command-Option and press the > (right angle bracket) key twice.**

    This increases the line height to 18 points; the first time you type < it increases from 16 to 17 points, and the second time from 17 to 18 points (Figure 5.12).

11. **Press Command-T.**

    This takes you back to the Text Style dialog box.

12. **Click on Geneva.**

    This changes the font back to Geneva so that it will once again match the text in the other fields of the card.

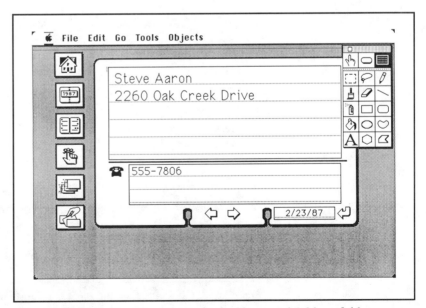

Figure 5.11: Enlarging the text size in the Name and Address field

13. **Click on 14.**

    This changes the point size back to 14 points.

14. **Click on the Center radio button (beneath the Align heading).**

15. **Click on the OK button (or press Return or Enter).**

    The text in the Name and Address field is now centered in the field.

16. **Click on the Browse tool on the Tools menu.**

17. **Click on the right-arrow button at the bottom of the card.**

    This takes you to the second card in the stack. See that this text is also centered in the first field.

18. **Click on the Field tool on the Tools menu.**

19. **Position the Arrow pointer somewhere within the Name and Address field and double-click the mouse.**

    This takes you to the Field Information dialog box.

20. **Click on the Font button. This takes you to the Text Style dialog box.**

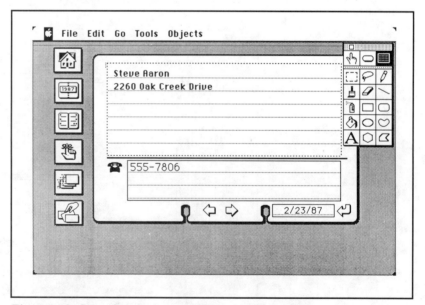

Figure 5.12: Changing the font to Chicago and increasing the line spacing for the Name and Address field

21. **Click on the Left radio button.**

22. **Click on the OK button.**

The text in the first field of the current card is once again left-aligned, and its style matches that of the rest of the text in the card.

Background and Card Buttons

Like text fields, buttons can exist both in the background and at the card level in a stack. Background buttons affect all of the cards in the stack that share the same background. To find out which buttons belong to the background and which belong to the card, take the following steps.

1. **Click on the Button tool.**

Note the buttons that appear at the card level.

2. **Select the Background option on the Edit menu (or press Command-B).**

This returns you to the background (the menu is striped). Look at the buttons that appear in the background.

From comparing the buttons that were visible when you were at the card level with those that are visible in the background, you can see that all of the buttons in the Address stack are background buttons. None of them disappeared when you switched from the card level to the background level.

Getting Information about Buttons

You can obtain information about existing buttons and make changes to them by accessing the Button Information dialog box. To get to this box, you must click on the button you want to know about to select it. Then select the Button Info option on the Objects menu to get to the Button Information dialog box (you can also get there directly by double-clicking on the button).

1. **Move the Arrow pointer to the right-arrow button at the bottom of the card and click the mouse.**

This selects the button.

Card buttons are not only *not* part of the background of the card, but also do not affect other cards in the stack. The links or scripts attached to a card button pertain only to that card. Therefore, the button does not show up when you switch to the background or go to a new card.

In contrast, a background button shows up in all of the cards that share the same background, and the links and scripts attached to it work in the same manner when activated from any card.

2. Move the Arrow pointer to the Objects menu, drag down to the Button Info option, and release the mouse (Figure 5.13).

This takes you to the Button Information dialog box (Figure 5.14). You can also access this dialog box directly by double-clicking on the button.

Notice from Figure 5.14 that the Button Information dialog box is similar to the Field Information dialog box. It lists the button's name, number, and button ID. In this case, the name of the button is Next. It contains a script that takes you to the following card in the same stack whenever you click on it. The next button is listed as the second background button, and it has a button ID of 7. Just as with field numbers, button numbers are relative and can change, while ID numbers are permanent and never change (although they are retired if the button is deleted).

The Button dialog box also allows you to choose from various styles of buttons. Currently, the Next button uses the transparent style (allowing any graphics beneath it to show through). When you select either the transparent or opaque style (which shows as a white rectangle blocking any graphics beneath it from view) for a button,

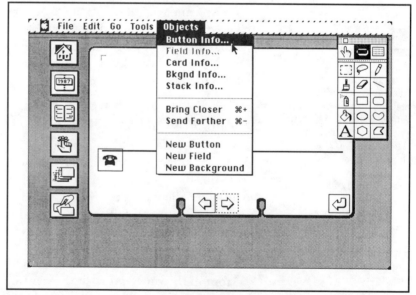

Figure 5.13: Selecting the Button Info option on the Objects menu

its outline is not visible on the card when the stack is used with the Browse tool. It is only when you choose either the rectangle, shadow, round rectangle, check box, or radio button that you see the borders of the button on the card when using the Browse tool and, thereby, can judge its size as well as location.

By checking the *Show name* box on this screen, you can have the optional name that you assign to the button appear on the card. If you want, you can also check the *Auto hilite* box. This highlights a button (as long as it does not use the check box or radio button style) when you click on it. When the button uses the *check box* button style and you select *Auto hilite*, it toggles between being checked and unchecked each time you click on it. When the button uses the *radio button* style and you select *Auto hilite*, it toggles between having a dot in the middle and being blank each time you click on it.

When a button uses any style besides the *check box* or *radio button*, you can also select an icon to represent it on the card. To do this, you click on the Icon button on the Button Information dialog box. As you can see in Figure 5.15, the Next button uses the Next Arrow icon. Notice that this icon has its own icon ID number.

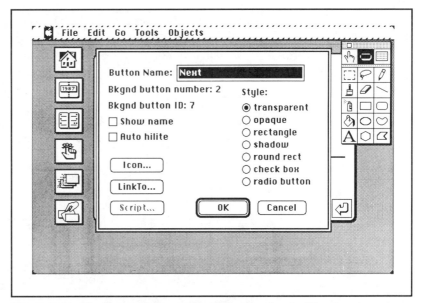

Figure 5.14: The Button Information dialog box for the Next button

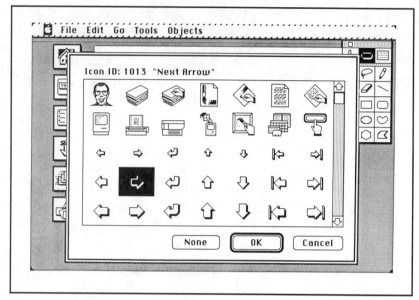

Figure 5.15: Viewing the icon for the Next button

Selecting a Button Icon

To change the icon used for this button, you have only to click on a new icon in this window. There are many more ready-made icons from which to choose than are shown in this figure. To see more of the icons, you need to scroll the window by clicking on the scroll box.

Besides using one of the ready-made icons, you can create icons of your own. By locating these icons on a transparent or opaque button, you can associate your own icon design with any button in a background or card (a technique that you will learn later on when creating your own stack).

To see how easy it is to change button icons, perform the following steps.

1. **Click on the Icon button in the Button Information dialog box.**

2. **Click on the scroll box in the window and drag it until it is about halfway down the window (Figure 5.16).**

3. **Click on the Fleet Next Arrow icon with the ID 22308 (Figure 5.17).**

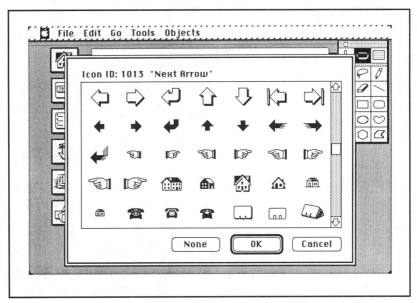

Figure 5.16: Scrolling the Icon window

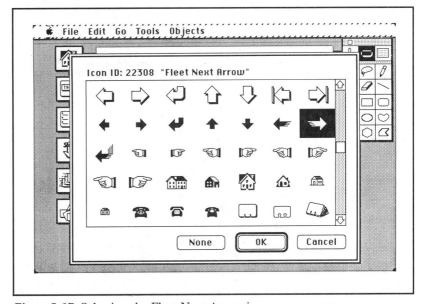

Figure 5.17: Selecting the Fleet Next Arrow icon

4. Click on the the OK button.

5. Click on the Browse tool and click on the new Next button icon to move to the next card (Figure 5.18).

Now change the Next button icon so that it uses the Next Arrow icon once more.

6. Click on the Button tool.

7. Click on the Fleet Next Arrow icon.

   This selects the button.

8. Select the Button Info option on the Objects menu.

9. Click on the Icon button on the Button Information dialog box.

10. Drag the scroll box back up to the top of the window.

11. Click on the Next Arrow (second from the left in the second row from the bottom) with the ID 1013.

12. Click on the OK button.

13. Click on the Browse tool in the Tools menu.

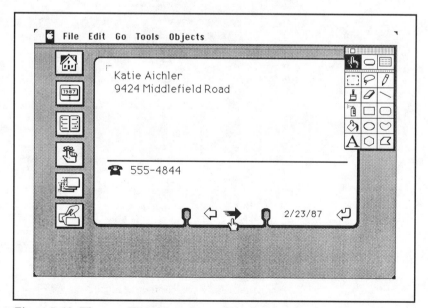

Figure 5.18: The new Fleet Next Arrow icon for the Next button

Buttons That Link Cards in Other Stacks

Besides the readily identifiable buttons on the bottom half of the rolodex card form (which contains name and address, telephone number, and entry date), there are six more buttons in the background of the Address stack. These buttons are stacked vertically and are located to the left of the rolodex card. They all use the shadow type of button. You can tell that all of these buttons exist in the background of the Address stack because they are available no matter what card you view in this stack.

Notice that each of these six buttons on the left uses an icon to disclose its purpose. The first of these buttons uses a house icon to denote the Home Card (the first card in the Home stack). It contains a HyperTalk script that tells HyperCard to go to the Home Card when you click on this button. In other words, this button links the Address stack to the Home Card.

The next three buttons link the Address stack to the Datebook stack. However, depending upon which button you select, you will find yourself in a different part of this stack, each of which uses a different background.

If you click on the third button, the program takes you to the weekly calendar section of the Datebook stack. This part of the stack contains cards that display a daily register, a week at a time, for the period from June 29, 1987, to January 3, 1988. This part of the Datebook stack uses a second backgound design. When you click on this Daily button in the Address stack, HyperCard takes you to the card in the weekly section of the Datebook stack that contains the current date. Again, this is accomplished with a HyperTalk script attached to the button that calculates the current week using the current date and instructs HyperCard to go to the card that contains it.
mine the current week and highlight it in the card by surrounding it with a rectangle.

If you click on the third button, the program takes you to the weekly calendar section of the Datebook stack. This part of the stack contains cards that display a daily register, a week at a time, for the period from June 29, 1987, to January 3, 1987. This part of the Datebook stack uses a second backgound design. When you click on this Daily button in the Address stack, HyperCard takes you to the card in the weekly section of the Datebook stack that contains the current date. Again, this is accomplished with a HyperTalk script attached to the button that calculates the current week using the current date and instructs HyperCard to go to the card that contains it.

If you click on the fourth button, HyperCard takes you to a card in the Datebook stack that contains a to-do register. This card in the Datebook stack uses a third background, which allows you to enter reminder messages. The HyperTalk script for the To Do button is straightforward; it links directly to the card named First Do in the Datebook stack.

To get a feel for how these buttons work, perform these steps.

1. **Click on the Yearly button (the button that displays 1987 below the Home button).**

   Make sure that the Browse tool is selected before you click on this button.

2. **Find the current week on the monthly calendar (it should be surrounded by a rectangle) and click on today's date.**

   This takes you to the appropriate weekly register in the Datebook stack.

3. **Now, click on the Address button (the one that uses the rolodex card icon at the top of the weekly register, immediately to the left of the spiral binding).**

   This returns you to the first card of the Address stack.

4. **Click on the Daily button (the one directly beneath the Yearly button).**

   This takes you right back to the weekly register you just saw in the previous step.

5. **Click on the To Do button at the top of this card (the one that uses the icon of a string tied around the finger).**

   This takes you to the card named First Do in the Datebook stack.

6. **Finally, click on the Address button.**

   This returns you to the first card of the Address stack.

From doing this exercise, you should get a feel for the linking that is possible between cards. Also, you get an idea of how different backgrounds can be used in a single stack. Although the various calendar functions could have been accomplished by placing each in a different stack and providing the necessary links to it, that is not required as long as each section uses a slightly different background and the buttons contain appropriate links to each one.

Buttons That Perform Specific Tasks in the Stack

The last two buttons to the left of the rolodex card form in the Address stack do not have linking functions. Instead, they provide the means for performing tasks within the Address stack. The second-to-the-last button (beneath the To Do button) flips through all of the cards in the stack, one at a time. When you click on this button, HyperCard displays each card in the stack until you click the mouse to stop it at any card, or until it returns to whatever card you were viewing when you selected the button. It accomplishes this by using the HyperTalk Show command (the script simply says *show all cards*).

The last button in this column is used to sort the stack by either the first or last name listed in each card. It accomplishes this by using the HyperTalk Sort command. The button script also employs a special Answer command, which enables it to display the prompt for sorting by either the first or last name. Once you select one of these choices, it then uses the appropriate sorting command.

Buttons such as these can be added to any stack that you create. Because they employ built-in HyperTalk commands, you can easily adapt them to the applications that you will soon be designing.

Card Buttons

There is only one card button in the Address stack. This button is located in the very first card. It performs no linking, nor does it have any HyperTalk script attached to it. Its purpose is simply to mask the background button below it that performs the automatic dialing for all of the other cards in the Address stack. To locate this card button, perform the following steps.

1. **Click on the Button tool in the Tools menu.**

   Make sure that you are at the first card in the Address stack before you do this. Notice the empty rectangle to the left of the Macintosh (Figure 5.19).

2. **Select the Background option on the Edit menu (or press Command-B).**

   This takes you to the background. Notice that the button containing the Old-style Telephone icon is located directly beneath it.

3. **Select the Background option on the Edit menu (or press Command-B) a second time.**

   This returns you to the card level where you can once again see the card button.

4. **Click on this card button.**

   This selects it (shown by the moving dotted line around its borders).

5. **Select the Button Info option on the Objects menu (or double-click on the button).**

   This shows you the Button Information dialog box for this button (Figure 5.20). Note that this is the first card button in this stack.

6. **Click on the Cancel button.**

   This returns you to the first card in the Address stack.

7. **Click on the Browse tool in the Tools menu.**

   The card button disappears from view.

   Note that this card button does not yet have a name. It does, however, have a card button number and ID. It uses the transparent style so that its outline is not visible when you view this stack with the Browse tool. This button is located directly on top of the background button that contains the link to the Phone stack to prevent you from activating this button. Because the first card of the address stack does not contain a phone number, the telephone button has no purpose here. Instead of designing a new background for this first card that did not contain the telephone button, the author chose to mask it with an empty button.

   If you happen to click on this card button, nothing will happen, as the button is not currently linked to another card nor does it contain a HyperTalk script (something you cannot verify unless you set the user level to Scripting). This method of masking an unnecessary background button with an empty card button provides an alternative to creating a new background for just one card.

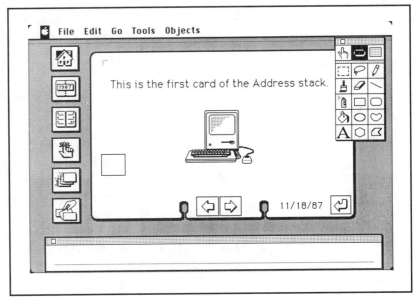

Figure 5.19: Locating the card button in the first card of the Address stack

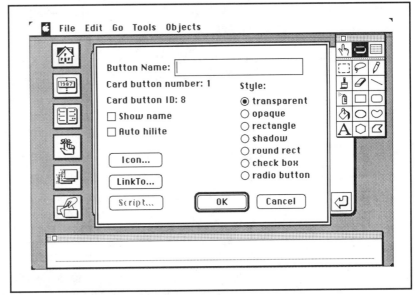

Figure 5.20: The Button Information dialog box for the card button in the Address stack

Background and Card Graphics

The last component of a stack consists of graphic images you create. You can create graphics either with HyperCard's own painting program or with a stand-alone graphics program. If you create graphics with another program such as MacPaint, GraphicWorks, or MapMaker, you can bring in the image through the clipboard. HyperCard will also directly import graphics that are saved as a MacPaint file.

Graphic images can be part of the current background or a part of a particular card. As with fields and buttons, background graphics are visible in all cards in the stack that share that background, and card graphics are visible when looking at the card they are on.

The Address stack makes use of an original graphic image with a picture of the Macintosh in the first card that introduces the stack. This graphic is not part of the background of the Address stack, as it appears only when viewing the first card. In fact, other than the graphic of the card itself, the only background graphics in the Address stack are the thick black line that separates the name and address field from the telephone field and the icons that are associated with the various buttons it contains. To compare the card graphics with the background graphics in the Address stack, follow these steps.

1. **Select the Background option on the Edit menu (or press Command-B).**

   Notice that the text and Macintosh graphic in the first card disappear when you view the background of this stack. In its place you can see the thick dividing line and the Old-style Telephone icon.

2. **Select the Background option on the Edit menu (or press Command-B) again.**

   This returns you to card level, where the picture of the Macintosh replaces the dividing line and telephone icon.

When you are at the card level, the dividing line and telephone icon in the background are not visible because the picture of the Macintosh includes an opaque white area of sufficient size to mask them. As mentioned earlier, this card contains an invisible transparent button that covers the telephone button beneath it (preventing you from inadvertently activating the script attached to the telephone button).

When creating your own stacks, you may find it expedient to use graphics from the Art Ideas and Button Ideas stacks that are supplied with HyperCard. These stacks are located on the HyperCard Ideas disk. You will get an opportunity to explore these stacks in subsequent chapters as you build your own stack.

Getting Information About a Stack

The Objects menu that is available when you set the user level to Authoring or Scripting contains options that allow you to get useful information about either the current card, background, or stack. The dialog boxes that are displayed when you select one of these options give you a synopsis of information about the particular component. Not only can you use these options to get information about the stack but, in the case of the card and background information, you can protect them from being deleted.

Card Information

To get information about the current card in a stack, you select the Card Info option on the Objects menu. Figure 5.21 shows you the Card Information dialog box that appears when you use this option if the first card in the Address stack is the current card.

Like the dialog boxes for fields and buttons, the Card Information dialog box gives the name of the card (first in this case), its card number, and card ID. However, the Card Information dialog box tells you how many cards there are in the stack. It also lists the number of card fields and buttons that the current card contains. For example, the first card of the Address stack has no card fields and only one card button (the empty button that masks the telephone button beneath it in the background).

Below these statistics, you can see a check box that allows you to protect the card from being deleted. To protect the card against deletion, you simply click on this box to check it. If you then try to remove a card that has been protected in this manner (with the Delete Card option on the Edit menu), you will receive a message telling you that you can't delete a protected card (Figure 5.22).

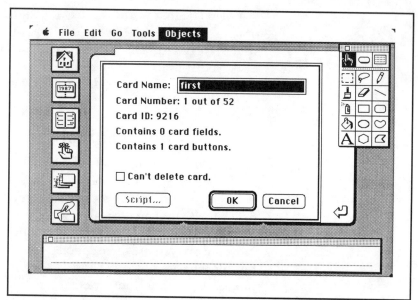

Figure 5.21: The Card Information dialog box for the first card in the
Address stack

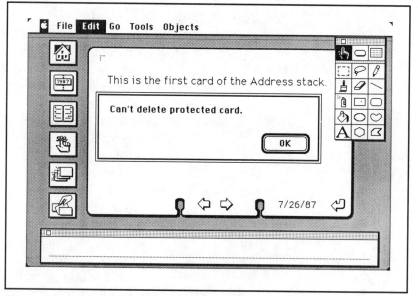

Figure 5.22: Trying to delete a protected card

Background Information

To obtain information about the background of the current card, select the Bkgnd Info option on the Objects menu. You can see the Background Information dialog box for the first card in the Address stack in Figure 5.23. Just as with the Card Information dialog box, you are given the name of the background (File Card in this case) and its background ID. However, unlike the card, the background is not assigned a background number. Instead, this box tells you how many cards share this background. In the case of the Address stack, all 52 cards in the stack use the same background.

As with the card information, the Background Information dialog box lists the number of background fields and buttons used in the stack. It tells you that there are three background fields (you already knew that all three fields in the stack were in the background) and ten background buttons (all of the buttons except for the empty card button in the first card).

You can protect the last card that uses the current background from being deleted by checking the *Can't delete background* box. This

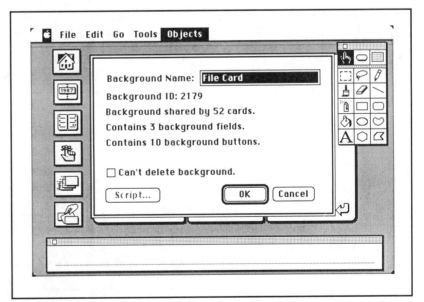

Figure 5.23: The Background Information dialog box for the first card in the Address stack

does not, however, prevent HyperCard from deleting the entire stack, which would necessarily include this card with the protected background (for information on protecting a stack from deletion, see the following section on getting information about a stack).

Stack Information

In addition to getting information about the current card and background, you can get information about the stack you are using by selecting the Stack Info option on the Objects menu. Figure 5.24 shows you the Stack information dialog box that appears when you choose this option for the Address stack. This dialog box tells you the name of the stack, the search path where it is located, the total number of cards it contains, the number of backgrounds in the stack, the size of the stack in kilobytes, and the amount of free space in the stack.

Notice that unlike the Card and Background Information dialog boxes, this dialog box does not allow you to protect the stack from deletion. You can, however, accomplish this by selecting the Protect

Free space is really space that is unavailable within a stack. Free space is created in a stack whenever a card, background, button, or field is deleted. You can eliminate free space by choosing Compact Stack from the File menu.

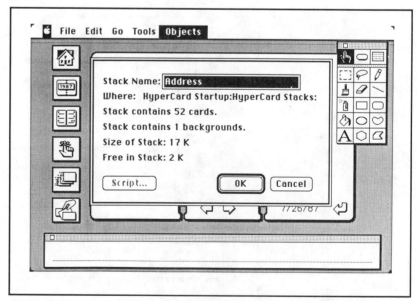

Figure 5.24: The Stack Information dialog box for the Address stack

Stack option on the File menu. Figure 5.25 shows you the dialog box that appears when you choose this option. To prevent a user from deleting a stack with the Delete Stack option on the File menu, you click on the *Can't delete stack* check box in this window. Once the protection is set, you will receive an error message anytime you try to delete this stack.

Password-Protecting a Stack

You can also assign a password, set up private access, and limit the user level from the Protect Stack option on the File menu. To set up or change a password, click on the Set Password button. This takes you to the dialog box shown in Figure 5.26. After you enter the password in the upper box, you must verify it in the box below (click with the I-Beam cursor in the lower box to verify it) before you click on the OK button. To have HyperCard accept your password, the verified version must match the original entry in all ways—case, spelling, and punctuation.

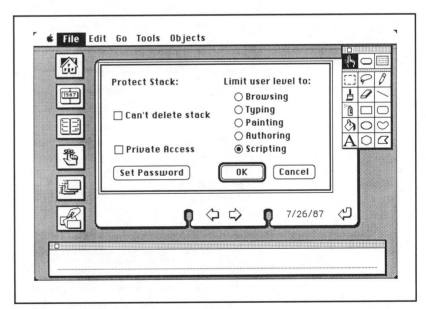

Figure 5.25: The Protect Stack dialog box

After you assign a password to a stack, you cannot access the Protect Stack dialog box (to unprotect the stack, to set a new user level, or to change the private access) without first entering the password correctly. When you select the Protect Stack option on the File menu, the dialog box shown in Figure 5.27 appears. If you cannot reproduce the password here exactly as it was assigned, HyperCard will ignore your request to access the Protect Stack dialog box, and you will be returned to the current card.

To remove a password from the stack, you select the Set Password button in the Protect Stack dialog box (upon successfully entering the password after selecting the Protect Stack option). When the Password dialog box appears, you simply click on the OK button without entering a new password.

In addition to restricting access to the Protect Stack dialog box unless a person knows the password, you can likewise prevent a user from gaining any access to a stack by clicking on the Private Access check box. With private access in effect, you cannot open a stack unless you enter the correct password.

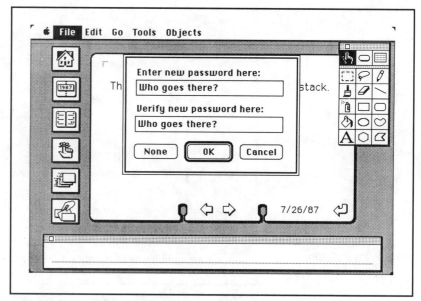

Figure 5.26: Assigning a password to the stack

There is no way to find out the password that you assigned to a stack if you forget it. If you can't reproduce the password correctly, you cannot access the Protect Stack dialog box again. If you can't get to this dialog box, you will not be able to remove the password or change the user level. Further, if you have checked the Private Access box as well, you will not be able to use the stack again. This means that all of the data it contains will be lost to you. To prevent this from happening, either write down the password or keep an unprotected copy of the stack stored in a secure place.

Although this enables you to protect stacks that contain sensitive data from unauthorized access, it also makes it imperative that you do not forget your password. If you do, you will have no way of using the stack again. Therefore, use this feature with care!

You can also limit the user level to any of the five levels by checking the appropriate radio button in the Protect Stack dialog box. If you limit the user level to Browsing or Typing, the Protect Stack option will no longer appear on the File menu. However, this does not mean that once you limit the user level to either one of these that it can never be reset to a higher level. To access the Protect Stack option when Browsing or Typing level is in effect, you must hold down the Command key before you drag through the File menu options. Doing this will give you a full File menu regardless of whether the user level is set from the Protect Stack dialog box or the User Preferences card in the Home stack.

Restricting the user level to Browsing or Typing is useful when you have completed a stack for distribution whose design you do not want changed by your users.

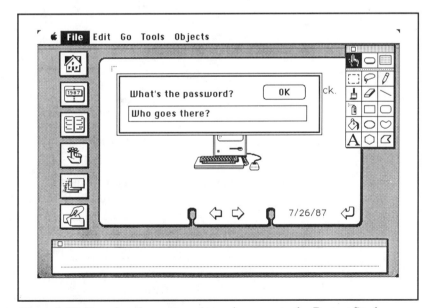

Figure 5.27: Entering the password to gain access to the Protect Stack dialog box

Summary

If you have made it to this point in the chapter, you have exposed yourself to all of the basic components of a HyperCard stack. This detailed examination of the building blocks of a stack, coupled with the working knowledge of HyperCard that you have gained from Part I, put you in a perfect position for going ahead to learn how to create your own HyperCard applications.

If any of the concepts introduced in this chapter are still foggy, don't worry. As you create and refine the sample stack in the upcoming chapters, you will get plenty of practice working with each of the components introduced here. More importantly, this process will give you an opportunity to see how these components are combined and work together to produce the final application.

You are now finished with the ready-made stacks supplied with the HyperCard program. It is time for you to begin work on a new stack of your own. This stack will become an continuing example you can add to and refine as you explore new HyperCard functions. Before getting to work, you might want to review these points about a HyperCard stack covered in this chapter:

- To create a stack, set the user level to the Authoring level. Do this by clicking the Authoring radio button on the User Preferences card, the last card in the Home stack.

- When you set the user level to at least Painting, the Tools and Objects menus appear on the HyperCard menu.

- The Tools menu is a special tear-off menu that can be dragged and located anywhere on the HyperCard screen.

- A stack has a background and a card level. What is in the background is shared by all cards that you add to the stack. What is on the card belongs only to the card (and is not visible in the background).

- To work in the background, select the Background option on the Edit menu (or press Command-B). The menu becomes striped to show you are in the background. To get to the card level, select the Background option a second time (if you switch to the Browse tool, you are automatically placed at the card level).

- A stack can have more than one background. When a stack has several backgrounds, certain cards in the stack will share one background, and others will share different backgrounds.

- HyperCard text fields can exist in the background or in the card. To work with the fields in a card, select the Field tool on the Tools menu. Make sure that you are in the background (the HyperCard menu is striped) when you want to work with background fields.

- You can select the field style and text attributes for a particular field by selecting the Field tool, clicking on the field, and choosing the Field Info option on the Objects menu.

- HyperCard buttons can exist in the background or in the card. To work with the buttons in a card, select the Button tool on the Tools menu. Again, make sure that you are in the background (the HyperCard menu is striped) when you want to work with background buttons.

- You can select the button style and icon for a particular field by selecting the Button tool, clicking on the button, and choosing the Button Info option on the Objects menu.

- Graphic images can also exist in the background or in the card. You can generate graphics with HyperCard's painting program or create them with another graphics program and import them into a stack.

- You can obtain information about the card you are working on by selecting the Card Info option on the Objects menu.

- You can obtain information about the background you are working on by selecting the Bkgnd Info option on the Objects menu.

- You can obtain information about the entire stack you are working on by selecting the Stack Info option on the Objects menu.

Creating a New Stack

CHAPTER 6 _____

Even if your Macintosh is equipped with an external monitor that has sufficient space to display multiple cards, HyperCard cannot yet display more than one card at a time.

When creating a stack on a Macintosh that has a larger monitor, you must keep in mind that the majority of Macintosh users have systems with the 9-inch built-in screen. A card viewed on this screen takes up the entire viewing area (a 512×342 pixel display area).

When HyperCard's Menu bar is displayed on the screen, it takes up part of this card display area (the Menu bar actually overlaps part of the card). When the same card is viewed on a larger external monitor, the Menu bar does not overlap the card at all.

BEFORE YOU BEGIN CREATING A NEW STACK, YOU should be clear on its purpose and spend some time planning its design accordingly. Among the many factors to be considered in planning the design are the following:

- The ways in which you can use the program's card format to best communicate (display and organize) the information.

- Whether the information can be accommodated in a single stack or requires multiple stacks.

- The number and type of text fields required in the stack(s).

- The graphics required in the stack(s).

- Whether the stack(s) include sound as well as graphics and text.

- The links (that is, buttons) needed between cards in the stack(s).

Because, currently, HyperCard can only display a single card on the screen at a time, you must plan your stack so that its information is communicated effectively as a series of individual cards. This means that the user must be able to get sufficient information from each card as well as understand how the card related to the rest of the cards in the stack. In the planning stage, you should visualize the information communicated as *serial*, that is, as a sequence of cards that can be flipped through. This process is somewhat akin to the one used by graphic artists when they create story boards to illustrate the shooting of a movie scene or television advertisement. The entire shooting sequence is broken down into individual units, each of which illustrates part of the story. Together, they illustrate the flow of information and communicate the entire message.

Although this leaves you more area for displaying text and graphics information, it does mean that some of the card information can be obscured when you view the stack on the standard 9-inch screen. As a result, when designing a stack with a larger monitor, you should take care that you do not position vital information in the card that can be obscured by the Menu bar when viewed on a standard Macintosh screen.

When thinking about the cards as units of information, you need to consider whether you can communicate all of the information in a single stack or if multiple stacks will have to be created. This decision turns on the type of information (text, graphic, or sound) that the stack or stacks are to contain as well as how this information is to be linked.

If the stack will allow the user to look at the information in widely diverse ways (graphically as opposed to textually), you will almost always be better off creating multiple stacks. Also, if the information links (buttons) required by one set of cards greatly differs from the rest, you may find it easier to accomplish with multiple stacks, although you can sometimes do this just as well by creating multiple backgrounds in a single stack.

All of these determinations are best made at the outset, before you begin work on the stack, but you will sometimes find that your initial decisions have to be modified as you begin executing your plan. Fortunately, you will find that HyperCard is flexible enough to accommodate many kinds of structural changes and that there are ways to work around almost any obstacle that arises.

However, making this process your own does require some hands-on experience with the planning and execution of a concrete Hyper-Card application. In the following sections, you will learn to design and build an example application from scratch. Going through this exercise from start to finish should be a great help as you begin to design and build your own HyperCard applications. As you go through this process, think about how you can adapt the techniques outlined here to the stacks that you want to create for yourself.

Planning the Design of the Application

The example stack that you will be creating is a tour of the Northern California wineries. The purpose of this stack is twofold: to keep vital statistics about the wineries and the wines produced in the region, and to help you locate particular wineries that you want to visit. To keep the statistics about the wineries and their wine, you will need a simple card form that displays all of the pertinent information in an easy-to-read format. Remembering that with HyperCard you

When designing a HyperCard stack, the first priority is on-screen communication as that concept translates into the visual display and organization of information in the card. This contrasts to designing databases, where the behind-the-scene relationship of the data (structure) is the first priority. Communication in the form of printed reports, data views, and input screens are secondary considerations. Although this represents only a difference in emphasis, it does underscore a basic difference between traditional databases and HyperCard. In Hyper-Card, the on-screen format of the information (card form) is fixed because it functions as a vital carrier of the information it contains; in a database, the format of the data is fluid because the underlying structure functions as the vital carrier of information.

can easily annotate any of the information on this basic card form, you should keep the information on the basic card limited to items that you want to see for each winery included.

The information on the winery cards will be text-based. Graphics, if any, that are added to the card will be purely ornamental. This means that in designing the background of this stack, you will be concerned mainly with organizing the items of information that you want to include into text fields. The size and placement of these text fields will depend upon how much information each card is supposed to convey.

In addition to cards that contain the statistics about wineries and the wines they produce, you will need to create cards that illustrate the location of the wineries. This will require road maps that show where the wineries are as well as illustrate the relative distance between them. That way, by referring to the winery cards and the accompanying maps, you can create a realistic tour itinerary for a visit to the region. Because you can refer to both the types of wines produced and the location of the wineries, you can tailor this tour to your taste in wines and the time you can allot to the tour.

The wine map cards will be graphics-based. Text fields are not required on the maps to help you locate a particular winery, although the winery cards should also contain detailed directions on how to reach the winery from a given point on the map. Because of the limitation of the card size (512 × 342 pixels), you will probably need to create several wine map cards to cover just some of the wineries in the major Californian wine-producing regions of the Sonoma Valley, the Valley of the Moon (home of Jack London), and the world-famous Napa Valley.

Because the winery cards require multiple text fields and the wine map cards require none, you will find it easier to execute this application if you create two separate stacks: one that contains all the winery cards and another that contains the wine maps.

The map cards should be interlinked so that you can easily flip from one map to the other (they should also make it quite clear how they are physically related to each other). Within the wine map stack, the cards can be organized geographically.

All of the cards in the winery stack will be interlinked so that you can browse through the information on each one, either from beginning to end or end to beginning. Within this stack, the cards can be ordered alphabetically by the name of the winery.

The two stacks should be linked so that you can obtain statistics on a particular winery by clicking on its location in one of the wine maps. The wine map stack will be the primary stack for the wine tour application. It will contain an opening card (Figure 6.1) from which you can go to a particular road map for one of the three wine-producing regions (Figures 6.2 to 6.4). From a road map, you can go directly to the winery card for a particular winery by clicking on its location (containing a button) on the map (Figure 6.5).

Keeping in mind that you may not always want to access a winery card from a regional wine map, you should also include an index card (Figure 6.6) as part of the wine map stack. The index card will list all of the wineries for which you have winery cards (arranged alphabetically by winery name within a region). Then, by clicking on the name of a particular winery (containing a button), you can also go directly to its winery card to look up or edit the information on it.

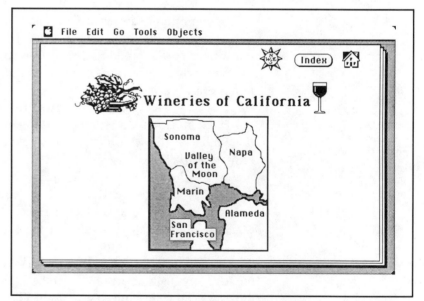

Figure 6.1: The opening card of the wine tour application

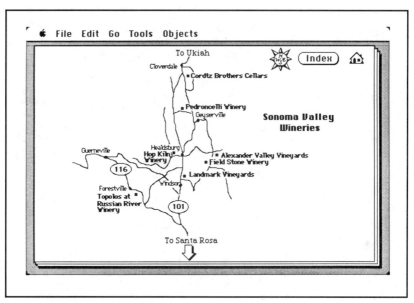

Figure 6.2: The map card for the Sonoma Valley Wineries

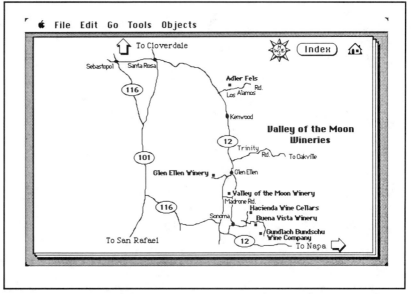

Figure 6.3: The map card for the Valley of the Moon Wineries

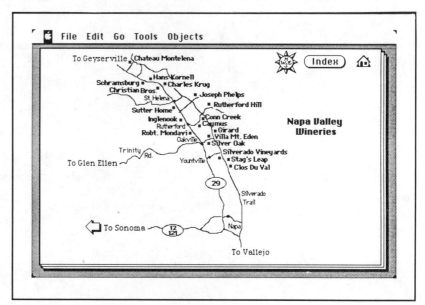

Figure 6.4: The map card for the Napa Valley Wineries

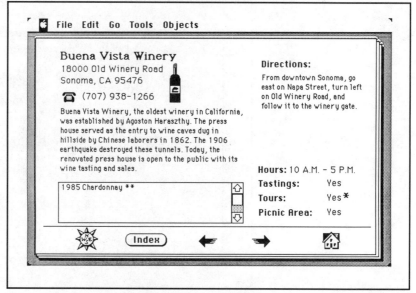

Figure 6.5: Winery card for Buena Vista Winery

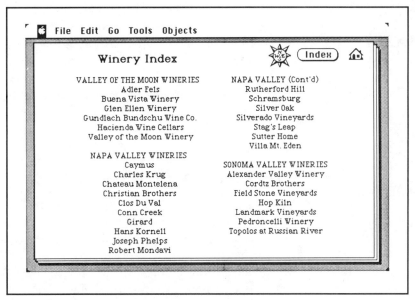

Figure 6.6: The index card for the wine tour

Executing the Design

With this overall design in mind for the wine tour, you can now set about creating this application. The first step is to design the background for the wineries stack. In creating this stack, you will learn how to create a new stack using the background of an existing stack. Once this is done, you can adapt it as required to the new application.

Because the wineries stack is going to contain multiple text fields, you will then have to learn how to create new fields, and size and place them in the background of a card. Because you will want to include some simple graphics along with the text fields for the winery cards, you will also begin to learn how to use HyperCard's painting program. Of course, you will learn much more about using this versatile graphics program when you start building the second stack that is to contain the opening card and the wine maps.

To begin, you should make sure that the user level is set to Authoring. To do this, start HyperCard and from the Home Card go to the User Preferences card (either by selecting the Last option on the Go menu or by pressing Command-4).

If you are using HyperCard on a Macintosh with disk drives, you should prepare a special disk. After initializing the disk (which you can name HyperCard Example disk), copy the HyperCard program, the Home stack, the Phone stack, and the Art Ideas stack. After starting the computer with a disk that contains the System folder, start HyperCard from this new disk. You will have sufficient room to create the two stacks required for the wine tour application on this disk.

Creating the Wineries Stack

To create a new stack, you use the New Stack option on the File menu (Figure 6.7). When you select this option, a dialog box similar to the one shown in Figure 6.8 will appear. Notice from this figure that the box marked *Copy current background* is already checked. This means that HyperCard will use the background of whatever stack is open when you select the New Stack option. This includes not only the buttons and fields in the background but also any graphics, including the basic appearance of the card.

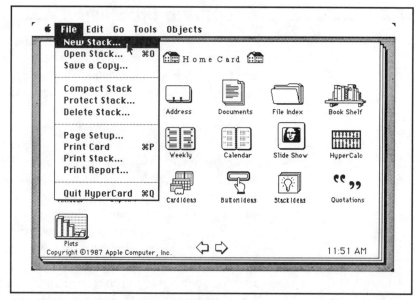

Figure 6.7: Creating a new stack with the New Stack option on the File menu

You can use this feature to avoid having to create the background of a new stack from scratch. Just open the stack that has the background closest to the one you want to use and then select the New Stack option. Leave the *Copy current background* box checked, give the stack a new name, and click on the New Button. Your new stack will then have the same background graphics, buttons, and fields that were present in the previously open stack.

For your new wineries stack, you can use the card background of the Home stack. This background has two buttons, Next and Prev (for *previous*), which you will want to have in the wineries stack. Also, graphically, the background of the Home stack represents the card as one of several by drawing its outline as though it were the first of three cards.

HyperCard provides you with a stack called Card Ideas. To use any of the backgrounds illustrated in this stack, you merely open the Card Ideas stack, go to the card that displays the card format you wish to adapt, and then use the New Stack option with *Copy current background* in effect. HyperCard also provides a stack called Stack Ideas, which works the same way.

1. **Open HyperCard.**

   The Home Card should be displayed on your screen.

2. **Select the New Stack option on the File menu.**

3. **Enter the name of the stack as *Wineries*.**

   Leave the *Copy current background* box checked.

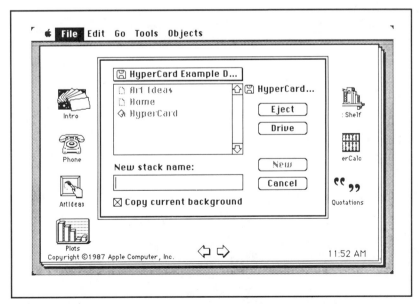

Figure 6.8: The New Stack dialog box

4. Click on the New Button.

The blank card shown in Figure 6.9 should appear on your screen.

Adding Text Fields to the Card Background

The new card that HyperCard created when you gave the command to start a new stack contains only the Next and Prev buttons and displays the overall graphic design for the card used by the Home stack. No other information is displayed at this time. Although the blank appearance of the card may give you the impression that you are in the background of the card, you are at the card level looking at the graphics and buttons that exist in the background.

Because the text fields you now want to create should all exist in the background where they can be shared by all of the winery cards in the stack, you must be sure that you are at the background level before you begin adding the fields. Remember that HyperCard always lets you know that you are in the background by displaying the striped

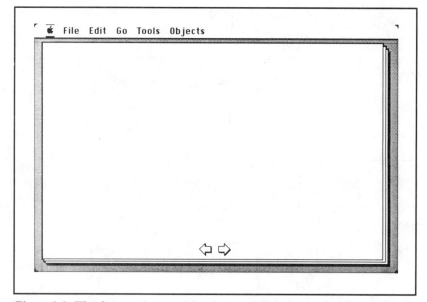

Figure 6.9: The first card created for the new Wineries stack using the background of the Home stack

HyperCard menu. To get to the card background, select the Background option on the Edit menu or press Command-B.

1. Select the Background option on the Edit menu (or press Command-B).

The HyperCard menu will become striped.

Once you are in the background, you can begin adding the necessary text fields. To create a new field, select the New Field option on the Objects menu. This places a field in the middle of the card. As with any selected field, it is bounded by a moving dotted line and shows several text lines within it. The new field can now be moved and sized as you wish. Because it is selected, you can also modify its attributes by selecting the Field Info option on the Objects menu or by double-clicking within its borders.

HyperCard also offers you an alternate method for adding a new field to a card. First, select the Field tool from the Tools menu (remember that this is a tear-off menu that can be located anywhere on the screen). Next, hold down the Command key. When you do this, the cursor changes to the crossbar cursor, marked by a plus sign (+). While continuing to keep the Command key depressed, position the crossbar at the upper left corner of the place where you want the field to be. Then click the mouse and drag the cursor to the right and down. As you do this, HyperCard will show you the boundary of the field you are creating. When the field is sized correctly, release both the Command key and the mouse button. Just as when adding a new field with the New Field option, this newly created field will be selected (shown by the moving dotted line around its borders). You can still resize, relocate, or modify its attributes at this point.

You will get an opportunity to use both methods as you add the necessary background fields to the Wineries stack. Before you do, you need to analyze the number and type of fields you want to have on each winery card. Figure 6.10 shows you the size and location of the text fields in a typical winery card (this was done by selecting the Field tool from the Tools menu). There are ten text fields in the background of this card. The first text field contains the name of the winery, the second the address, and the third the telephone number.

Creating a field that you intended to be part of the card background when you are not yet *in* the background is one of the most common mistakes that you will probably make when creating a stack. If this happens, you can remedy the situation by cutting the field (or button) and pasting it into the background. To do this, select the field by choosing the Field tool on the Tools menu and then clicking on the field in question. Next, choose the Cut Field option on the Edit menu or press Command-X. Then, choose the Background option on the Edit menu or press Command-B (the HyperCard menu will become striped) and, finally, select the Paste option from this menu or press Command-V.

You can also reverse this process if you ever need to make a background field into a card field. Similar procedures can be utilitized to bring a button from the card level to the background and vice versa.

The first field, the Winery Name, is separated from the address so that it can use a bolder and larger font than the Address field does.

The fourth field contains a short description of the winery and the fifth is for wine-tasting notes. All of these fields follow each other in a column on the left side of the card.

In the next column to the right are the last five fields, each of which is accompanied by a heading: Directions, Hours, Tastings, Tours, and Picnic Area. These headings are part of the background graphics of this card. Field names for text fields cannot be displayed as part of the field. To add them as headings in a card, you will have to add them as they are here, as paint text (graphics) in the background.

Of the ten fields, only the Wine Tasting Notes field does not use the transparent style. This information requires a scrolling field so that you can continue to add notes about superior wines and wine tastings as you continue to visit the winery.

Field Layers

As you know from examining the fields in the Address stack, when you add fields to the card background or card, they are given field numbers. Initially, field numbers follow the order in which the

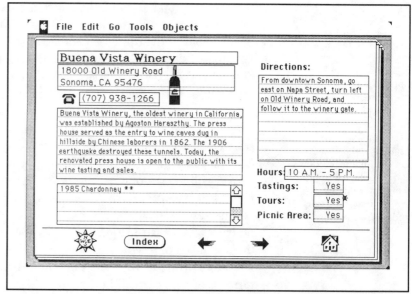

Figure 6.10: Winery card showing the size and location of text fields

fields are added. When you use the Browse tool to add or edit text in a field, you can press the Tab key to move from field to field. The tabbing order follows the field numbers.

In addition to the field number, the field position is marked by a layering system. Each field exists in its own layer relative to the other fields in the same background or card. The layer in which a field exists is the same as the field number. The lower the field number, the farther away the field layer. The higher the field number, the closer the field layer. The field with the highest field number is the topmost (or closest) field. The one with the lowest field number is the farthest away. Because the field number is related to the field layer, the tabbing order necessarily follows the field layer.

The diagram in Figure 6.11 illustrates this relationship. Field 1 is the farthest away (in the back, if you will), and Field 3 is the closest. As you tab through the fields, the flashing text insertion pointer jumps from Field 1 to Field 2 to Field 3.

The overlaying of the fields is important when the style of the new field is opaque (that is, any style other than transparent). In such a case, fields in lower layers that are directly behind a field will not show through the field that is in a layer above them. Of course, the layering of the fields in the background is also important since it

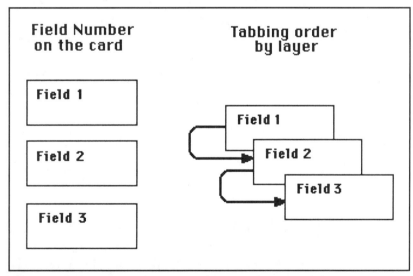

Figure 6.11: Field numbers and tabbing order follow the field layers

The numbering and layering of background fields exists independently of the numbering and layering of card fields. Card fields, even those with the lowest field numbers (and, therefore, the farthest away in the card field layering scheme) are still in front of the closest background field.

affects the tabbing order, the order in which text information will be added to a card.

When you create a new field, it is always placed in a higher (closer) layer than the fields added before it. Also, when you cut and paste a field from the card or background, it is always treated as a new field, that is, given the highest field number and placed in the closest layer.

In such a case, you may need to alter the field's layer. To do this, you select the field to be moved and use either the Bring Closer or the Send Farther option on the Objects menu. Each time you use the Bring Closer option (or press Command-+), the field gets closer to being the topmost layer (as its field number also increases). Each time you use the Send Farther option (or press Command- –), the fields get closer to being the layer the farthest away (as the field number decreases). As you use these commands to change the field layer, you are also altering the tabbing order.

For example, say you were adding addresses to rolodex cards, and you forgot the city/state line for one card. You've since added dozens of entries. If you simply add the line, then tabbing will follow the strict order of entry. But to tab to the new information in its proper place, you need to use the Send Farther option (Command- –).

Adding the First Field for the Wineries Stack

Armed with this information, you are now ready to begin adding the background fields to your new Wineries stack.

1. **Select the New Field option on the Objects menu (Figure 6.12).**

   Make sure that you are still in the background before you select this option (note that the menu is still striped).

A new field will appear in the middle of the card (as shown in Figure 6.13). Notice that this field is large enough to accommodate five lines of text. The first field of the Wineries stack requires only one line. Also, you need to reposition this field in the upper left corner of the card.

Sizing and Positioning Fields in a Card

Once you create a new field and it is still selected (shown by the moving dotted line around its borders), you can resize and relocate it anywhere within the confines of the card.

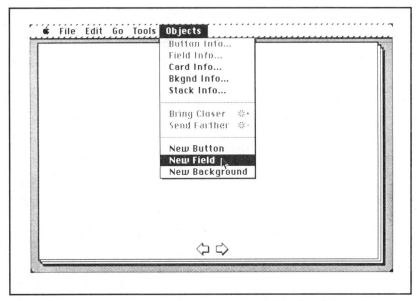

Figure 6.12: Selecting the New Field option to add the first field to the Wineries stack

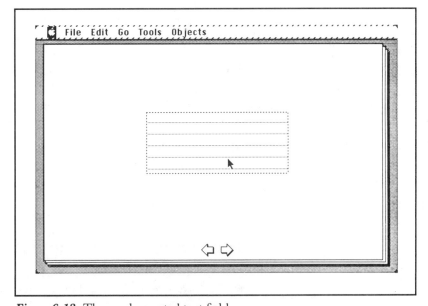

Figure 6.13: The newly created text field

To resize a field, you need to place the Arrow pointer at one of the four corners of the field outline. Then, click the mouse and move as required to either enlarge or reduce the size of the field. As you increase its size, more text lines will appear. Conversely, as you decrease its size, fewer text lines will be visible.

To relocate a field, you simply place the Arrow pointer somewhere within the borders of the field, click the mouse, and move it to its new position in the card. You need to use both techniques on this first field.

1. **Place the Arrow pointer on the lower right corner of the field.**

   Make sure that the very tip of the Arrow is right on the corner.

2. **Click the mouse and drag the Arrow pointer upward (the moving dotted line will become solid) until there is only one text line visible in the field (Figure 6.14).**

3. **Once there is only one text line and the text line is almost touching the bottom of the field, release the mouse button.**

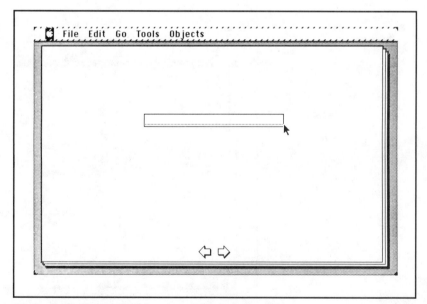

Figure 6.14: Decreasing the size of the first text field

4. **Position the Arrow pointer so that it is somewhere within the field.**

   This allows you to move the field.

5. **Click and drag the mouse (the moving dotted line will become solid) until you have positioned the field in the upper left corner of the card (as shown in Figure 6.15).**

   Don't worry about the exact positioning of this field in relation to the edges of the card.

6. **Position the Arrow pointer on the lower right corner again.**

7. **Click and drag the field to lengthen it until the right edge of the field extends at least as far as the point of the right-arrow button at the bottom of the card (more than halfway across the card; refer to Figure 6.15).**

Now that you have resized and relocated this field, it is time to name it and modify its font.

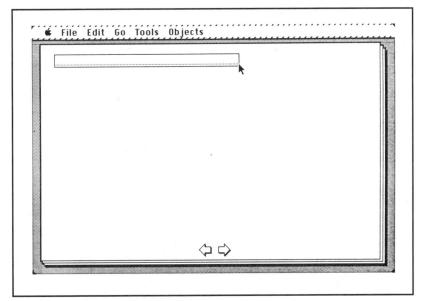

Figure 6.15: Repositioning the first text field in the card

8. **Select the Field Info option on the Objects menu (or double-click on the field).**

   This brings up the Field Information dialog box.

9. **Type *Winery Name* as the field name (Figure 6.16).**

10. **Click on the Font button.**

    This brings up the Text Style dialog box.

    Notice that Left radio button is selected beneath Align in this box. This means that the text will be left-justified in the field. You will want to leave this in effect for the Winery Name field. However, you will want to change the font, text size, and text style to make the name of the winery stand out in the card.

11. **Click on New York.**

    This changes the font from Geneva to New York.

12. **Click on 14.**

    This changes the point size to 14 points and the line height to 18 points.

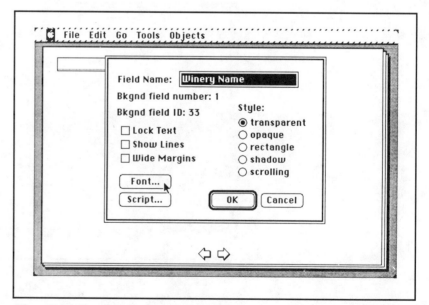

Figure 6.16: Entering the name of the field

13. **Click on the Bold check box beneath Style.**

    The changes to the Text Style dialog box should now match those shown in Figure 6.17.

14. **Click on the OK button.**

15. **Move the Arrow pointer outside the confines of the first field and click the mouse.**

    This establishes the first field (the moving dotted line is replaced by a solid outline).

    Congratulations! You have just added your first field to the Wineries stack. Now that you see how easy it is to create fields, you should have no trouble going on and adding the rest of the fields.

Adding the Winery Address Field

The second field of the stack requires two text lines for the Winery's address. It is located directly beneath the first field. Try creating this field using the second method for adding a field.

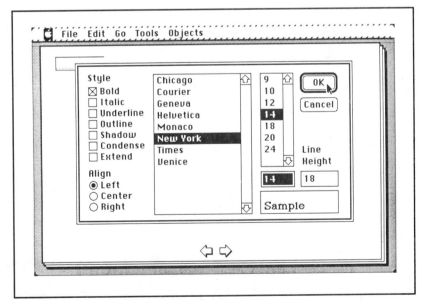

Figure 6.17: Modifying the text style of the Winery Name field

1. **Locate the Arrow pointer on the lower left corner of the first field.**

2. **Hold down the Command key.**

   The cursor should change to the crossbar (+). If it does not, select the Field tool on the Tools menu and try this again.

3. **Click and drag the mouse as far right as the field above and then drag downward until you can see two text lines and the bottom of the field is slightly below it (Figure 6.18).**

4. **Release both the Command key and the mouse button.**

   You will see the outline of the new field shown by a moving dotted line.

Now it is time to name the field and change its font.

5. **Select the Field Info option on the Objects menu (or double-click the mouse).**

6. **Type *Winery Address* as the field name.**

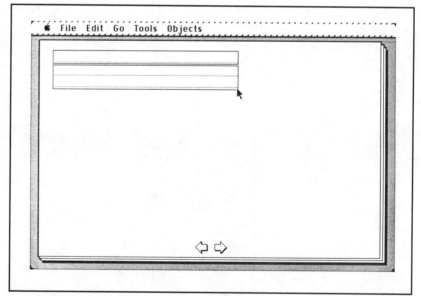

Figure 6.18: Adding the second text field to the card

7. **Click on the Font button.**

   Notice that *Geneva* and *12* are highlighted.

8. **Click on the OK button.**

9. **With the Arrow pointer outside of the second field, click the mouse.**

   This establishes the second background field in the card.

Adding the Winery Telephone Field

The third text field in the stack will contain the winery's telephone number. Later, you will add a button that will automatically dial the phone number that you enter in this field. This button will be located immediately to the left of this field. The telephone number requires only a single line of text. Its font will also be Geneva 12-point, like the Winery Address field. Again, the alignment of the text will remain left-justified.

1. **Select the New Field option on the Objects menu.**

2. **Resize the field so that it contains only one text line.**

   Refer back to the steps on adding the first field, if you need to refresh your memory on how this is done.

3. **Relocate the field so that it is positioned beneath the Winery Address field.**

4. **Set the left edge of this new field in about one-half inch from the Winery Address field above it (Figure 6.19).**

5. **Select the Field Info option on the Objects menu (or double-click on this field).**

6. **Type *Winery Telephone* as the field name.**

7. **Click on the OK button.**

Adding the Winery Information and Wine Tasting Notes Fields

The last two fields on the left side of the card will hold information about the winery and wine-tasting notes. Both fields will require more text than the standard winery name, address, and telephone number fields. To accommodate this, you should reduce the font size to 10-point Geneva. Beyond reducing the size of the text for the two fields, you can make the wine-tasting notes field a scrolling field. That way, you can continue to add your notes and comments on various wines without having to make the field so large that you cannot later locate the necessary buttons on the card.

1. **Select the New Field option from the Objects menu.**

2. **Select the Field Info option from the Objects menu.**

3. **Type *Winery Info* as the field name.**

4. **Click on the Font button.**

5. **Click on 10 (Geneva is already selected).**

6. **Click on the OK button.**

7. **Move the field beneath the Winery Telephone field.**

8. **Position the field so that its left edge is aligned with the left edge of the Address field.**

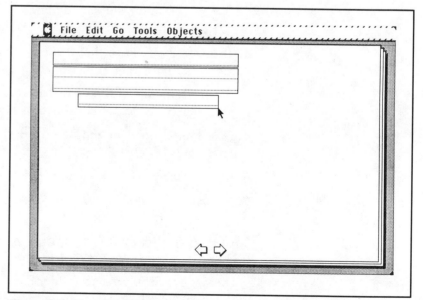

Figure 6.19: Positioning the Winery Telephone field in the card

9. **Click on the lower right corner of the field and drag the Arrow pointer to the right until the right edge of the field is aligned with Winery Address field and then down until you can see seven lines of text.**

   This adds an additional text line (Figure 6.20).

   You will create the wine-tasting notes field in the same way, except that you will need to change the field style from transparent to scrolling and reduce the number of text lines to four. Because the wine-tasting notes field is so similar to the one you just added, you will create it by copying the Winery Info field and making the necessary changes to the copy.

10. **Select the Copy Field option from the Edit menu.**

    Because the Winery Info field is still selected (shown by the moving dotted line around it), this field is copied.

11. **Select the Paste Field option.**

    This places a duplicate of the Winery Info field on top of the original field.

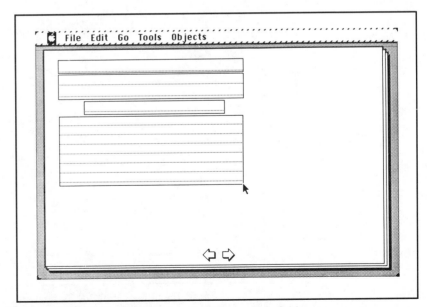

Figure 6.20: Sizing and locating the Winery Info field

12. **Click on the duplicate field and drag it so that it is located beneath the original Winery Info field.**

The original field will appear as you move the duplicate down.

13. **Select the Field Info option on the Objects menu.**

14. **Type** *Wine Tasting Notes* **as the field name.**

This replaces the current name of *Winery Info*.

15. **Click on the scrolling radio button.**

16. **Click on the OK button.**

17. **Click on the lower right corner of the field and drag the Arrow pointer up until you can see only four lines of text (Figure 6.21).**

This leaves room to add required buttons beneath it.

18. **Move the Arrow pointer to somewhere outside the field and click the mouse.**

When you copied the Winery Info field to make the Wine Tasting Notes field, HyperCard duplicated all of the changes that you made

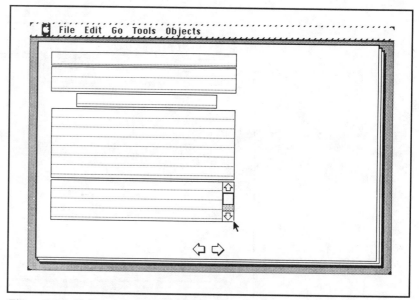

Figure 6.21: Sizing and locating the Wine Tasting Notes field

to the default settings when you created it. For this reason, it was not necessary to use the font button to change the font to Geneva and the point size to 10 points.

You have now finished adding half of the background fields for the Wineries stack. If you want to take a break before going on, you can just select the Quit option from the File menu (or press Command-Q). HyperCard will automatically save your work.

Remember that when you reopen the Wineries stack later on, the Browse tool will be activated and you will be at the card level. This means that you will not see the fields that you have just added to the background. All you need to do to see these fields is select the Field tool from the Tools menu and the Background option from the Edit menu. As soon as you do this, you will see all of the fields that you added.

Adding Graphics to the Background

The last five fields require the addition of headings. These headings will be added to the background of the card as paint text (graphics) rather than standard text characters. Because it will help you to correctly position the last five fields you will soon be creating, you should now add these headings to the background.

To do this, select the Tools menu. Drag this menu down and position it somewhere on the fields to the left (you will be adding the headings to the right side of the card). The painting tools are all located beneath the Browse, Button, and Field tools (if you are familiar with MacPaint, you will recognize most of these tools). To add graphics characters, you use the Paint Text tool, the one with the A in the lower left corner.

1. **Select the Tools menu and drag it to the left side of the card.**

2. **Click on the Paint Text tool (using the A icon).**

As soon as you select this tool, all of the background fields with the exception of the scrolling field (for tasting notes) disappear (Figure 6.22). This is because the Field tool is no longer selected. Whenever you use any of the painting tools, transparent fields (and buttons) will disappear from view. However, notice in Figure 6.22 that

The reason that you can still see the scrolling field for Wine Tasting Notes when the Field tool is not selected is because this style of field uses an outline and vertical scroll bar (notice, however, that the dotted lines indicating the text lines have disappeared because the Show Lines box was not checked). All field styles other than transparent have definite outlines that are visible even when the Field tool is not selected. Only transparent fields will disappear entirely. This means that you must select the Field tool to make the boundary of transparent fields visible.

you are still in the background of the card (you can tell this because the menu is still striped). Selecting a painting tool does not take you out of the background (only selecting the Browse tool does that).

It is important that you add the graphics characters to the background of the card, because you want the headings to appear on each winery card. Note that you can add graphics to the card. However, like card fields and buttons, they belong only to the card and do not appear throughout the stack.

When you select one of the painting tools, as you have just done, the HyperCard menu changes. Notice that the Objects menu disappears and three new menus are added: Paint, Options, and Patterns. In the next chapter, you will look at the many options that become available when you select one of the painting options. At this point, however, you will not need to use any of them.

To select the font, point size, and style of the graphics characters to use, you double-click on the Paint Text tool or select Text Style from the Edit menu (or press Command-I). For the headings, use the Chicago font (available only in 12 point).

The Patterns menu that is used to select different fill patterns (used with the Bucket tool) is also a tear-off menu like the Tools menu. In fact, the Patterns menu is the only other tear-off menu that HyperCard uses. Note that the Patterns menu is also used with the Rectangle, Rounded Rectangle, Oval, Curve, Regular Polygon, and Irregular Polygon tools.

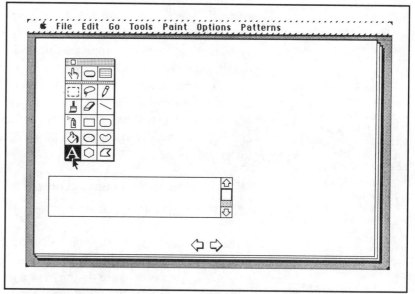

Figure 6.22: Selecting the Paint Text tool

3. **Double-click on the Paint Text tool that is currently selected.**

   This takes you to the Text Style dialog box (identical to the one for setting the text for fields).

4. **Click on Chicago.**

   This selects this font and changes the point size to 12.

5. **Click on the OK button.**

To enter the text for the field headings, you need to locate the I-Beam cursor at the leftmost point you want the text to begin (because the Left Align option is in effect) and click the mouse. he I-Beam cursor then changes to the flashing text insertion pointer, and you can type your text. If you make a mistake, use the Backspace (Delete) key to rub out any unwanted characters.

The first heading is for the Directions field. You will want to locate this heading about one-half inch down from the top of the card and about 2½ inches in from the right edge of the card. Don't worry if you don't locate the heading exactly where you ultimately want it. It is an easy process to relocate graphics in a card.

6. **Locate the I-Beam cursor so that the top of the I-Beam is about one-half inch down from the top of the card and the middle of the cursor is about 2½ inches in from the right edge of the card (refer to Figure 6.23).**

7. **Click the mouse.**

   The I-Beam cursor becomes the flashing text insertion pointer.

8. **Type *Directions:* as the heading.**

The rest of the headings are left-aligned with the Directions heading. The next one for the Hours field is located about a quarter inch above the top of the Wine Tasting Notes field (the scrolling field is still visible on the screen).

9. **Locate the bottom of the I-Beam cursor about a quarter inch up from the top of the Wine Tasting Notes field, left-aligned with the Directions heading above.**

10. **Click the mouse.**

11. Type *Hours:* **as the heading for this field.**

The rest of the field headings are now easy to locate on the card. You want about a quarter inch from the baseline of each line of text to the following line.

12. Locate the I-Beam cursor in line with the first vertical stroke of the H in Hours with its crossbar (marking the baseline of the text) approximately a quarter inch below the baseline of the text above it.

13. Click the mouse.

14. Type *Tastings:* **as the heading.**

15. Repeat steps 12–13 and type *Tours:* **as the next heading.**

16. Repeat steps 12–13 and type *Picnic Area:* **as the last heading.**

Your card should now match the one shown in Figure 6.24.

Repositioning Paint Text in the Card

If you are not satisified with the placement of any of the headings (or any other graphics that you create in the card), you can reposition

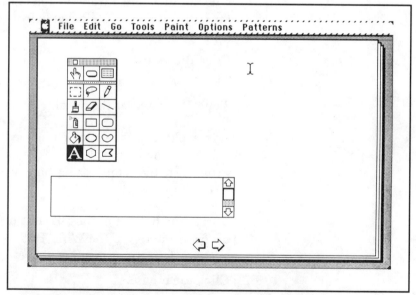

Figure 6.23: Locating the cursor to add the first field heading

Using the Selection tool is similar to choosing the graphic image or text with the Lasso tool. In fact, you will notice that the crossbar changes to the Lasso tool when you release the mouse button and to the Option key when using the Selection tool. The major difference between using the Selection tool with the Option key and using the Lasso tool is that you must outline the image with the tip of the Lasso tool to select it instead of dragging the outline as you do with the Selection tool.

Once paint text is entered and the mouse is clicked elsewhere, you cannot go back to it and use normal Mac text-editing techniques (such as adding characters). This is completely different from text entered in fields, which can always be edited. Paint text can be manipulated only with Paint Text tools.

them easily. You use the Selection tool (the dotted rectangle icon) to select the text and then relocate it with the Arrow pointer.

When you choose the Selection tool, the cursor changes to a crossbar. Position the crossbar at the upper left corner of your text and click and drag the mouse until the rectangle outlined by a moving dotted line surrounds the text. Then release the mouse button. Now move the crossbar within the dotted rectangle until it changes to the Arrow pointer. Once this happens, you can move the text by clicking on the cursor and dragging the text to its new position. To deselect the text, you simply move the crossbar outside of the rectangle and click the mouse.

Anything enclosed within the selection rectangle is moved. This includes any white area included with graphic images or text. When you are working in a close area, the surrounding white space may overlap an existing image. To move just the image or graphics characters, you need to hold down the Option key before you click the mouse. Next, select the image or text as usual. Then release the mouse button *before* you release the Option key. The selected area will include only the graphic image or text; none of the white area originally within the selection rectangle will be selected.

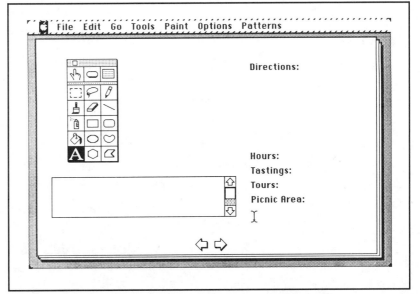

Figure 6.24: The field headings added with the Paint Text tool

If you need to delete any of the headings, you can do so by selecting the Eraser tool (it is located directly beneath the Lasso tool). Once the Eraser tool is selected, the Arrow pointer changes to a square eraser. To delete the graphics characters, you move this Eraser tool to the characters and click and drag. In this way, text added with the Paint Text tool is treated like any other graphic image created with HyperCard's painting program.

Adding the Remaining Text Fields to the Card

Now that you have added the field headings to the card, you can go on and add the remaining text fields to the background. The text field that will hold the directions on how to get to the winery will be located directly beneath the Directions heading. Its attributes will match those of the Winery Info field (transparent field style with 10-point Geneva text). To create this field, you can just copy the Winery Info field.

1. **Click on the Field tool in the Tools menu.**

   All of the fields will now be visible.

2. **Click on the Close box of the Tools menu.**

   You do not need to have it on the card.

3. **Click on the Winery Info field.**

   This selects it for copying.

4. **Select the Copy Field option on the Edit menu (or press Command-C).**

5. **Select the Paste Field option on the Edit menu (or press Command-V).**

6. **Move the Arrow pointer back to the duplicate field (now covering the original Winery Info field).**

7. **Click the mouse and drag the copy of the Winery Info field so that most of it is located right under the Directions heading.**

8. **Reduce the width of the field so that it is narrow enough to fit in the space beneath the Directions heading.**

9. **Adjust the size and position of the field until the left edge of the field is aligned with the first characters of the headings and the right edge is about one-eighth inch in from the edge of the card.**

10. **Lengthen the card so that there are eight text lines.**

11. **Select the Field Info option on the Objects menu.**

12. **Type *Directions* as the field name.**

    This will replace Winery Info as the field name.

13. **Click the OK button.**

    Your card should now match the one shown in Figure 6.25.

The last four fields require only a single text line. The font to be used is Geneva 12-point. This is the same as the Winery Telephone field. You can copy this field to make the Hours field. This time, instead of using the Copy and Paste Field options, you will use a slightly quicker way to copy fields.

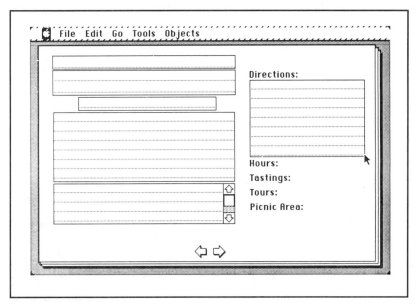

Figure 6.25: Adding the Directions field to the Wineries stack

14. Move the Arrow pointer to the Winery Telephone field and click the mouse.

This deselects the Directions field and selects the Winery Telephone field (shown by the moving dotted line).

15. Hold down the Option key and drag the field until it is located immediately to the right of the Hours heading.

You will see the original Winery Telephone field appear as you drag the copy to its new position (if you don't see this field appear, stop and relocate the field in its original position, then try this step again).

16. Shorten and locate the copy of the field so that its single text line is even with the baseline of the Hours heading, with its left edge immediately following the colon of the Hours heading and its right edge in line with the field above it.

17. Select the Field Info option on the Objects menu.

18. Change the field name to *Hours*.

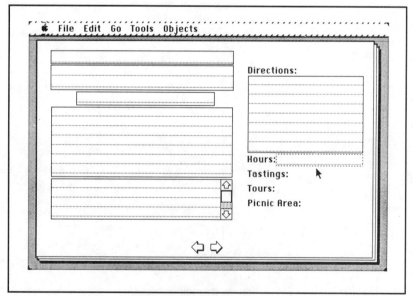

Figure 6.26: Adding the Hours field to the Wineries stack

19. Click on the OK button.

Your card should now match the one shown in Figure 6.26.

The last three fields share identical attributes. They can be created by copying the Hours field you just added. However, besides changing the field name, you will also have to change the alignment from Left to Right. The easiest way to do this is to copy the Hours button to create the Tastings field and then copy this modified field to create the Tours and Picnic Area fields.

The Shift key will constrain movement on either a vertical or horizontal axis, whichever way the user starts dragging.

20. With the Arrow pointer in the Hours field, hold down the Shift key while pressing the Option key, and drag the copy of this field down until it is in line with the Tastings heading.

By holding down the Shift key while pressing the Option key and dragging, the field will be constrained along a vertical axis—no horizontal movement will be possible—and thus perfect columnar alignment will be achieved.

21. Reduce the size of the field until it is about half the size of the field above it.

22. Move the field to the right so that its left edge is beyond the colon in the last heading, Picnic Area (about a quarter inch in from the right edge of the card).

Make sure that the text line in the field matches the baseline of the text of the field heading (Figure 6.27).

23. Select the Field Info option on the Objects menu.

24. Change the field name to Tastings.

25. Click the Font button.

26. Click the Right radio button beneath the Align heading.

27. Click the OK button.

Now you are ready to add the last two fields.

28. Move the Arrow pointer to the Tastings field.

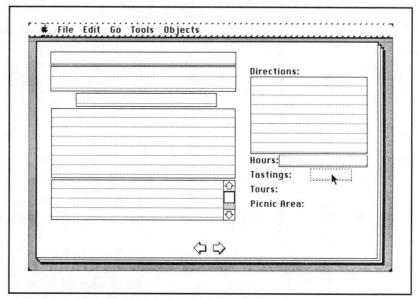

Figure 6.27: Positioning the copied Tastings field

29. **Hold down the Shift key while pressing the Option key, and drag the copy of the field until it is directly below the Tastings field.**

30. **Release the Shift key, the Option key, and the mouse button.**

31. **Again, hold down the Shift key while pressing the Option key, and drag the copy of the field until it is directly below the newly copied Tours field.**

32. **Release the Shift key, the Option key, and the mouse button.**

33. **Select the Field Info option, change the name of the field to *Picnic Area*, and then click on the OK button.**

34. **Move the Arrow pointer to the field directly above and click the mouse.**

35. **Select the Field Info option, change the name of the field to *Tours*, and then click on the OK button.**

36. **Move the Arrow pointer outside of the Tours field and click the mouse.**

    Your card should now match the one shown in Figure 6.28.

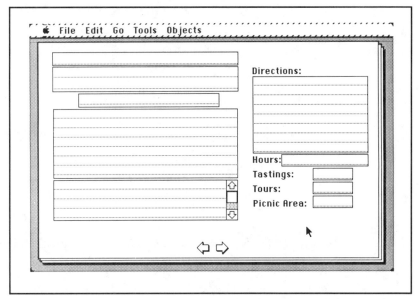

Figure 6.28: The Wineries stack with all of the background fields added

In creating all of the fields required for the Wineries stack, you are well on your way toward completing the wine tour application. The next step is to add some sample wine cards to the stack.

Adding Cards to Your Stack

Before going on to create the Wine Map stack, you can create three sample cards for the Wineries stack. To add information to the first card (containing all of the background fields and paint text), you must leave the background to get to the card level.

If you make a typing mistake when entering field information, use the Backspace (Delete) key to rub out the incorrect characters. If you press Return or Enter instead of the Tab key, use the Browse tool to locate the I-Beam cursor in the field you want to be in, click the mouse, and type in the desired entry. If you discover that you have made an error after you have left a field, use the Browse tool to move to the beginning of the incorrect characters, click and drag to highlight these characters, and type in the correct entry (which will replace the highlighted characters).

1. **Select the Browse tool on the Tools menu.**

   The striping around the HyperCard menu and the field boundaries disappears.

2. **Press the Tab key.**

   This takes the flashing text insertion pointer to the beginning of the first field.

3. **Type *Buena Vista Winery* in this field and press Tab.**

   This takes you to the Winery Address field.

4. **Enter *18000 Old Winery Road* and press Return (you cannot use the Enter key here).**

   This takes you to the second line of the Winery Address field.

5. **Enter *Sonoma, CA 95476* on this line and press Tab.**

   This takes you to the Winery Telephone field.

6. **Type *(707) 555–1266* as the telephone number and press Tab.**

   This takes you to the Winery Info field.

7. **Type**

   > Buena Vista Winery was established by Agoston Haraszthy. It is the oldest winery in California.

   in this field and press Tab.

   The text will automatically wrap to the second line when you reach the end of the first line of the field. When you press Tab, the flashing text insertion pointer will be located at the beginning of the Wine Tasting Notes field (the scrolling field).

8. **Type *1985 Chardonnay* ** in this field and press Tab.**

9. **Enter**

   > From downtown Sonoma, go east on Napa Street, turn left on Old Winery Road, and follow it to the winery gate.

   in the Directions field and press Tab.

10. **Type *10 A.M.–5 P.M.* in the Hours field and press Tab.**

11. Type *Yes* for the last three fields.

Remember to press Tab after entering this text in the Tastings and Tours fields. Your card should match the one shown in Figure 6.29.

12. Select the Card Info option on the Objects menu.

13. Enter *Buena Vista Winery* as the name of the card and click the OK button.

To add more cards to the Wineries stack, you must select the New Card option on the Edit menu (or press Command-N).

14. Select the New Card option on the Edit menu.

The filled-out card for Buena Vista Winery disappears, and you will see a blank card on your screen.

Now your Wineries stack contains two cards. This means that you can use the Next and Prev buttons (shown by the shadowed right- and left-arrow icons at the bottom of the card). Remember that these

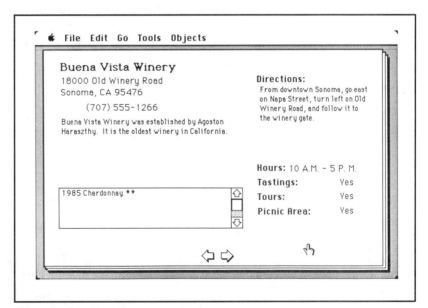

Figure 6.29: The winery card filled out for Buena Vista Winery

buttons were copied from the Home Card, whose background you used for the Wineries stack.

15. Click on the Prev button (the shadowed left arrow).

You will see the card for Buena Vista Winery.

16. Click on the Next button (the shadowed right arrow) at the bottom of the Buena Vista Winery card.

This returns you to the new blank card that you just added to the stack.

16. Fill out all of the information for this card, as shown in Figure 6.30.

17. Select the Card Info option on the Objects menu, enter *Hacienda Winery* as the name of the card, and click the OK button.

18. Select the New Card option on the Edit menu.

The filled-out card for Hacienda Wine Cellars disappears, replaced by a blank card.

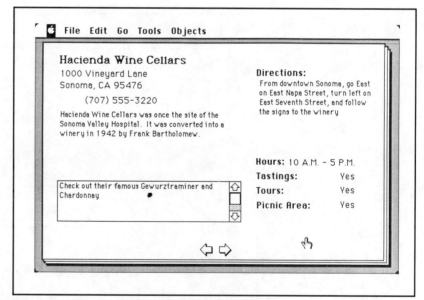

Figure 6.30: The winery card for Hacienda Wine Cellars

19. Fill out all of the information for this card, as shown in Figure 6.31.

20. Select the Card Info option on the Objects menu, enter *Gundlach-Bundschu* as the name of the card, and click the OK button.

Creating the Wine Tour Stack

After you have finished adding these three cards to your Wineries stack, you can practice browsing through them using the Next and Prev buttons. To finish the design of this stack, you will want to add more buttons than these to the card background. However, before you learn how to create the remaining buttons that connect this stack to the appropriate wine map and Index card, and to the Home Card, you will want to create the associated stack that contains the wine maps and Index card.

Remember that this stack, with the maps and Index card, will provide the entry point to the winery cards. Because it is the primary stack of the wine tour application, you should name this stack Wine

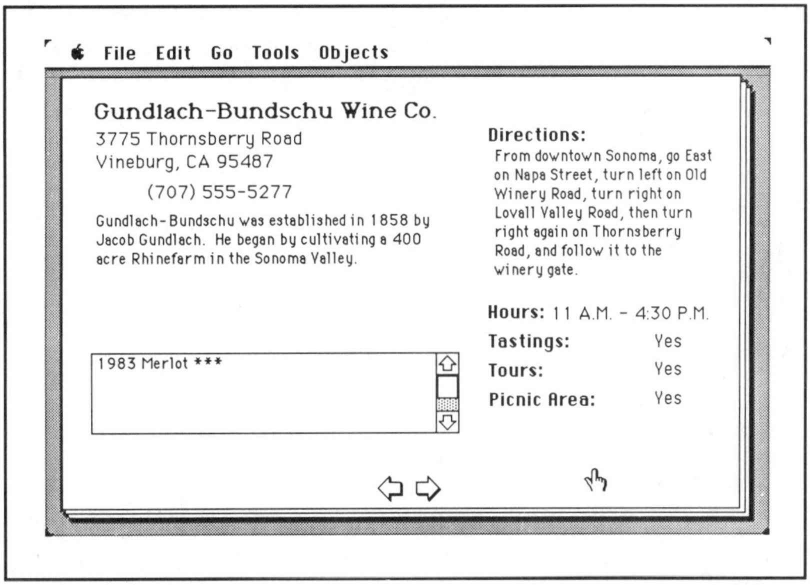

The Wine Tour stack consists almost entirely of background graphics and buttons. With the exception of a single (scrolling) field for the Index card, this stack does not require the use of any text fields. This is a good example of an application that is primarily graphics-based.

Figure 6.31: The winery card for Gundlach-Bundschu Wine Company

Tour, instead of Wine Map. You can use the same background as the Home Card, as this card design gives you a lot of area for drawing the required wine map and contains no background fields.

To copy the background of the Home Card for the new Wine Tour stack, you must first go to this card.

1. **Select the Home option on the Go menu (or press Command-H).**

2. **Select the New Stack option on the File menu.**

3. **Enter *Wine Tour* as the stack name.**

    Leave the *Copy current background* box checked.

4. **Click on the New button.**

Creating the Opening Card for the Wine Tour Stack

The cards in the Wine Tour stack do not have background text fields or graphics that appear throughout the stack. For this reason, you don't want to work in the background as you did when creating the Wineries stack. Make sure that you don't use the Background option (that is, that the HyperCard menu is not striped).

Also, you will not need the Next and Prev buttons, copied from the Home Card, in this stack. You can delete them by taking the following steps.

1. **Select the Button tool from the Tools menu.**

    You don't need to tear off this menu, just pull down the Tools menu and click on the Button tool. The Next and Prev buttons will now be outlined on the screen.

You can delete unwanted fields in a similar way. Just choose the Field tool instead of the Button tool. After clicking on the field to be removed to select it, you will see Clear Field where Clear Button appeared previously. Choose this option to delete a selected field.

2. **Click on the Prev button (the one with the shadowed left arrow).**

    This selects it.

3. **Select the Clear Button option on the Edit menu.**

    The Prev button is deleted.

4. **Repeat steps 2 and 3 using the Next button.**

    The first card of the Wine Tour stack is now completely blank.

The Opening card of the Wine Tour stack will contain a title, surrounded by some borrowed graphics, and a map showing the three primary California wine regions in relation to the San Francisco Bay area (Figure 6.32). To create most of this card, you will use HyperCard's painting program, which you used to add the field headings for the Wineries stack.

5. Tear off the Tools menu and locate it in the upper left corner of the card.

6. Click on the Rectangle tool (beneath the Eraser tool).

The HyperCard menu changes to include the Paint, Options, and Patterns menus.

You will use the Rectangle tool to draw the outline for the wine region map. Before you do, you will want to change the line size to make this border stand out more.

7. Select the Line Size option on the Options menu.

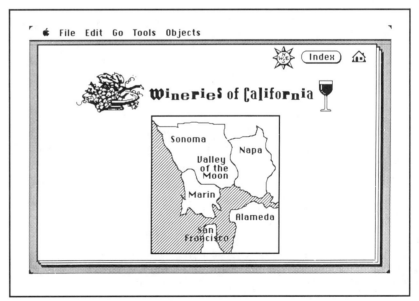

Figure 6.32: The Opening card of the Wine Tour stack

You see a dialog box showing eight line sizes; the first is selected, shown by the rectangle surrounding it.

8. **Click on the second line size choice (Figure 6.33).**

   The crossbar cursor (+) becomes heavier, reflecting this line size selection.

9. **Locate the crossbar approximately 2 inches in from the left edge of the card and 1½ inches down from the top edge.**

   This marks the upper left corner of the rectangle you are about to draw.

10. **Click and drag the crossbar to the right and down until you have drawn a rectangle roughly 2¼ inches across and 2½ inches high (refer to Figure 6.34).**

Now you are ready to draw the map within this space.

11. **Select the Line Size option on the Options menu.**

12. **Click on the first line size choice.**

    The crossbar becomes thinner to reflect this change.

13. **Click on the Pencil tool (immediately below the Field tool).**

Working with Fat Bits When Drawing

The pencil will draw in the opposite color of whatever the color of the pixel was when the mouse was clicked (either black or white). The pencil will *stay the same color* as long as the mouse is down. Thus, if you start drawing in black, the pencil will stay black even if you go over a black surface; it will not erase or change to white pixels. It would erase only if you began drawing with the pencil atop a black pixel.

The Pencil tool allows you to draw lines. As you drag the pencil across the screen, HyperCard puts down individual black pixels that appear on blank portions of the screen as lines emanating from the pencil point. Beware, however, that if the pencil point comes in contact with existing pixels (like those that form the heavy border for the regional map), the Pencil tool will erase them.

To avoid erasing part of the border as you create the outlines of the wine regions and various Bay Area counties, you can use the FatBits option to locate the exact position for placing the pencil point, begin drawing part of the outline, and then exit from Fat Bits. You can also use the Pencil tool when working with Fat Bits to erase a few pixels without having to resort to the Eraser tool, which is rather large when working with Fat Bits.

To work in Fat Bits, you can use the FatBits option on the Options menu. This is not the preferred method, however, because you lose

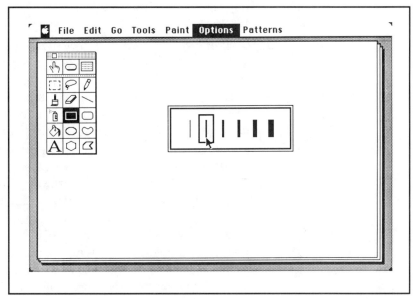

Figure 6.33: Selecting a new line size

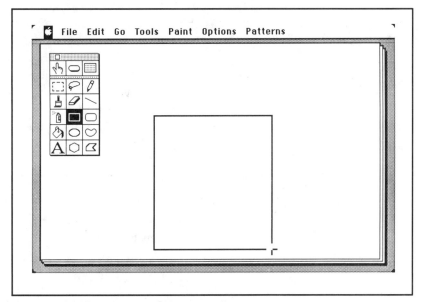

Figure 6.34: Drawing the border for the wine region map

your place in the drawing when you go to select the option from the HyperCard menu. This means that you then have to do a lot of scrolling through parts of the enlarged drawing to find the place you want to work. To avoid this, you can simply locate the point of the Pencil tool in the general area where you want to work in Fat Bits, then hold down the Command key and click the mouse.

When using either method to get into Fat Bits, the general area is enlarged (you can see individual pixels quite clearly), and Hyper-Card automatically creates a window that shows you the area from the normal viewpoint.

To scroll to new parts of the drawing, hold down the Option key. This changes the Pencil tool (or whatever painting tool you are using) to the Grabber tool (using the icon of a hand with all five fingers extended). When you click and drag the mouse, it scrolls the drawing in the direction you are moving.

To shift back to the regular view and out of Fat Bits at any time, you simply hold down the Command key and click the mouse again. You can also accomplish this by locating the Pencil tool (or whatever painting tool you are using) in the window containing the miniature version of the drawing and clicking the mouse.

If you are ever completely unhappy with a change that you just made to the drawing (such as erasing part of the picture or drawing a line in the wrong direction), you can restore the picture to its previous state by choosing Undo from the Edit menu, pressing Command-Z, or pressing the tilde key (~). That way, you don't have to go through several steps to correct the mistake, but can just start over.

With all of these things in mind, you should now add the outlines of the regions to your map.

1. **Move the Pencil tool to the upper left corner of the rectangle.**

2. **Hold down the Command key and click the mouse.**

   Now you can position the pencil point exactly where you want to begin the line in Fat Bits.

3. **Put the point of the Pencil tool in the first white pixel inside the corner of the rectangle.**

4. **Drag the Pencil down and to the right, sloping the coastline down and to the right as it is in Figure 6.35.**

   Watch the line in the miniwindow.

5. **When you near the bottom of the picture plane, release the mouse.**

6. **Hold down the Command key and click the mouse.**

   This takes you out of Fat Bits.

7. **Reposition the Pencil point at the end of the line you just drew, and continue drawing this line until it connects to the right edge of the rectangle.**

   Refer to Figure 6.35 as you draw. If you inadvertently delete any pixels, work in Fat Bits to restore them.

8. **Complete the outline drawing for San Francisco and Alameda counties in the same way.**

   Don't be overly concerned about accuracy in this drawing; just approximate the shapes outlined in Figure 6.35.

Adding a Fill Pattern to the Drawing

Next, you will add a pattern representing the water of the Pacific Ocean and San Francisco Bay. To do this, select a pattern from the Patterns menu and then use the Bucket tool to fill the area outside of

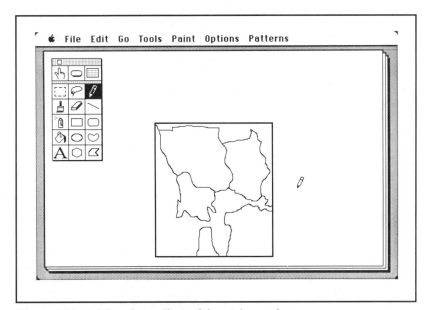

Figure 6.35: Adding the outlines of the region to the map

the regional outlines. To prevent this pattern from getting inside this region, you must make sure that there are no breaks in your outlines and that all these lines connect to the rectangular border. Check this carefully (in Fat Bits, if necessary) before proceeding.

1. **Tear off the Patterns menu (just as you did the Tools menu) and drag it to the right side of the screen.**

2. **Click on the checkered pattern in the Patterns menu that is immediately to the left of the currently selected black pattern.**

   Refer to Figure 6.36.

3. **Click on the Bucket tool (just above the A) in the Tools menu.**

4. **Move the Bucket tool somewhere within the rectangular border and yet still outside of wine regions and Bay Area counties.**

5. **Click the mouse.**

   The area representing the water will now have a checkered pattern (Figure 6.37). If the pattern fills any area within the coastline, press Command-Z or the tilde key (~), repair any breaks in this outline, and repeat steps 3–5.

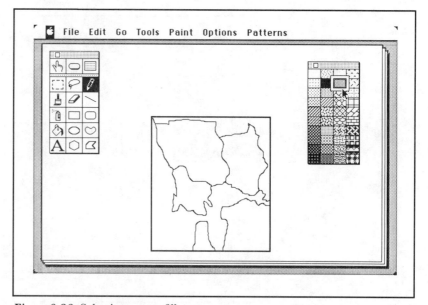

Figure 6.36: Selecting a new fill pattern

Adding the Captions to the Drawing

Next, you can add the captions for each wine-producing region and the Bay Area counties shown in the map.

1. **Click on the Close box in the Patterns menu.**

2. **Double-click on the Paint Text tool in the Tools menu.**

   This takes you to the Text Style dialog box.

3. **Click on Chicago.**

4. **Click on the OK button.**

Instead of trying to correctly locate the captions for each section as you type each one, just type them along either side of the map. Then, you can select and position each one using the Selection tool.

5. **Position the I-Beam cursor to the left of the map area and click the mouse.**

6. **Enter *Sonoma* as the first caption.**

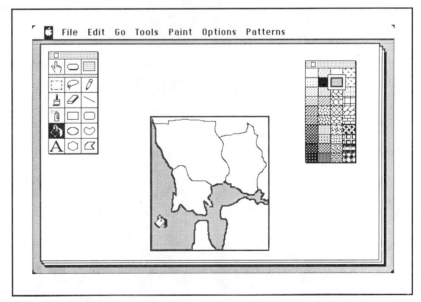

Figure 6.37: Using the new pattern to represent the water in the map

7. **Press Return twice and enter *Marin* as the second caption.**

   (You cannot use Enter here.)

8. **Continue in this way until you have entered all of the other captions, as shown in Figure 6.38.**

Now you are ready to position each caption on the map. Start by locating the Sonoma caption, as indicated by the following steps.

9. **Choose the Selection tool (immediately below the Browse tool) on the Tools menu.**

10. **Place the crossbar cursor in the upper left corner of the word *Sonoma*.**

11. **Hold down the Option key, and then drag the mouse to the right and down until the rectangle made up of a moving dotted line encloses the entire word.**

12. **Release the mouse button and then the Option key.**

    Only the word will be selected.

13. **Move the Lasso tool on the word until it changes back to the Arrow pointer.**

14. **Click and drag the selected word until it is located near the top of the map, as shown in Figure 6.39.**

15. **Release the mouse button.**

16. **Move the Arrow pointer down until it changes to the Lasso tool.**

17. **Click the mouse.**

18. **Following the same procedure you just used to move the Sonoma caption, relocate the rest of the captions (except for San Francisco) to their final positions, as shown in Figure 6.40.**

    If you make a mistake in placing the caption, press Command-Z or the tilde key (~) to restore the caption to its previous position.

If you move only the paint text characters that make up the San Francisco caption, some of them will be lost against the checkered

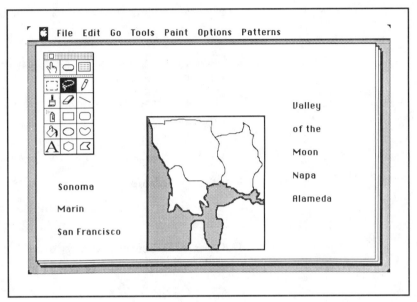

Figure 6.38: Entering the captions for the map

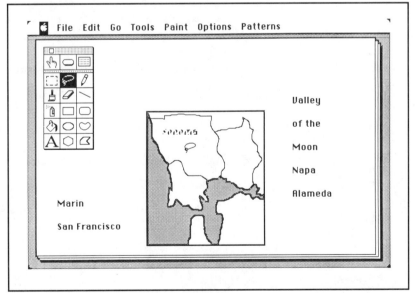

Figure 6.39: Moving the Sonoma caption to its final position in the map

pattern used to denote the water. To avoid this, you can move some of the white background along with the characters.

19. **Move the crossbar cursor so that it is slightly above and to the left of the S in San.**

20. **Click and drag the crossbar until you have drawn a rectangle around San.**

    The white space within this rectangle will be moved along with the characters, because you did not use the Option key.

21. **Release the mouse button.**

22. **Move the rectangle containing the word *San* until it is positioned as shown in Figure 6.40.**

23. **Repeat this procedure, this time selecting *Francisco* and some white space around it.**

24. **Move it into its final position, as shown in Figure 6.40.**

Creating the Title for the Opening Card

The title for the Opening card is *Wineries of California*. You will create this title in the New York font.

1. **Double-click on the Paint Text font.**

    This takes you to the Text Style dialog box.

2. **Click on New York.**

3. **Click on 18.**

4. **Click on the Bold check box under the Style heading.**

5. **Click on the OK button.**

6. **Move the crossbar cursor so that is above the wine region map and far enough left to enter the title and click the mouse.**

7. **Type *Wineries of California*.**

8. **Select the title and position it so that it is centered about one-half inch above the map border.**

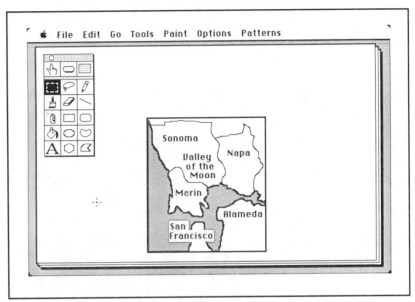

Figure 6.40: The regional map with all of its captions

Borrowing Some Graphic Images for the Opening Card

To complete the Opening card of your Wine Tour stack, you can copy some related graphics from the Art Ideas stack that is supplied with HyperCard.

1. **Click on the Browse tool in the Tools menu.**

   This saves your latest change to this card and allows you to go to the Art Ideas stack.

2. **Click on the Close box in the Tools menu.**

3. **Select the Open Stack option on the File menu (or press Command-O).**

4. **Find the stack called Art Ideas and double-click on it (or click to highlight it and then click on the Open button).**

5. **When the first card of the Art Ideas stack appears, click on the Next button.**

6. **Click on the Restaurants, Food, and Recipes icon or text on this card.**

From this card, you want to copy the bunch of grapes on a plate.

7. **Select the Lasso tool on the Tools menu.**

8. **Locate the Lasso at the top of the image of the grapes on a plate.**

9. **Drag the tip of the Lasso so that you completely outline this image.**

10. **Release the mouse button.**

    Check to make sure that you have not selected part of the other images around it. If you have, move the Lasso outside of the selected image, click the mouse, and try steps 9 and 10 again.

11. **Select the Copy Picture option on the Edit menu (or press Command-C).**

12. **Select the Recent option on the Go menu (or press Command-R).**

13. **Locate the miniature of the Opening card of the Wine Tour stack and click on it.**

    This returns you to the Opening card.

14. **Select the Paste Picture option on the Edit menu (or press Command-V).**

    The selected image of the grapes appears on the card.

15. **Move the Lasso tool to the image of the grapes until it changes to the Arrow pointer.**

16. **Click and drag the image so that it is located to the immediate left of the title *Wineries of California*.**

17. **Move the Arrow pointer until it changes back to the Lasso tool and click the mouse.**

    This establishes the copied graphic image.

As a finishing touch to this card, you can copy the glass of wine on the Restaurants, Food, and Recipes card of the Art Ideas stack.

18. **Select the Recent option on the Go menu.**

19. Click on the miniature of the Restaurants, Food, and Recipes card.

20. Use the Lasso tool to select the glass of wine below the image of the plate of grapes.

21. Select the Copy Picture option on the Edit menu (or press Command-C).

22. Select the Recent option on the Go menu a second time.

23. Click on the miniature of the opening card.

24. Select the Paste Picture option on the Edit menu (or press Command-V).

25. Position the wine glass after the title *Wineries of California*, and click the mouse to establish it.

26. Select the entire title, including the graphics added to it, and center it over the map of the wine regions.

    The text of the title should be about a quarter inch above the top of the map border (refer to Figure 6.41).

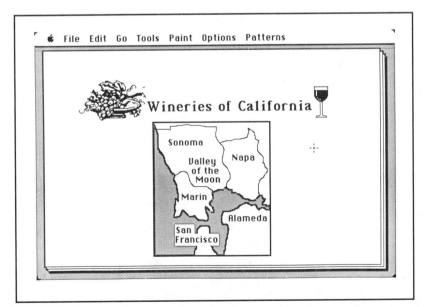

Figure 6.41: The completed Opening card for the Wine Tour stack

27. Select the Browse tool on the Tools menu.

28. Select the Card Info option on the Objects menu, enter *Opening Card* as the name of the card, and click the OK button.

This completes the Opening card for the Wine Tour stack. All that is missing from it are the buttons (which you will be adding in the next chapter). Now it is time to add a second card to this stack: the one that shows the locations of the wineries in the Valley of the Moon region.

Drawing the Winery Location Map

Although there are really three wine-producing regions and, therefore, three winery location maps to be added to the Wine Tour stack, you will have to complete only the one that shows the wineries in the Valley of the Moon. This road map contains the wineries for which you created winery cards in the first stack you created. Once you have drawn this map, you can then go on and create the links between the wineries on the map and the winery cards in this stack.

Figure 6.42 shows you the winery location map card for the wineries in the Valley of the Moon. To draw this map, you must first create a new card.

1. Select the New Card option on the Edit menu.

2. Tear off the Tools menu and drag it to the lower left corner of this card.

Begin the map by drawing the roads with the Pencil tool.

3. Select the Pencil tool on the Tools menu.

4. Draw the roads by referring to Figure 6.43.

The captions for the towns, roads, and winery names will be in 9-point Geneva. To differentiate the wineries from the other place names, you should also add bold to the text style when creating these captions.

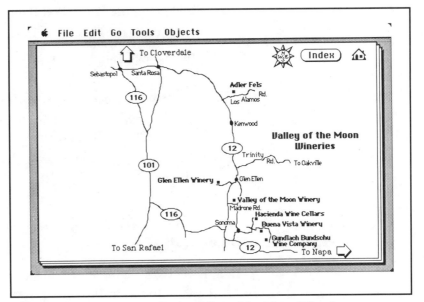

Figure 6.42: The road map for the Valley of the Moon Wineries

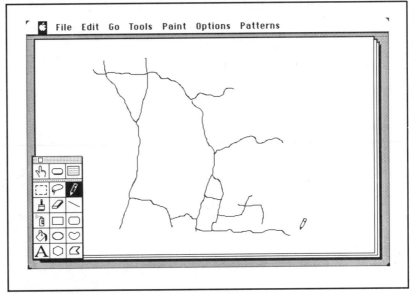

Figure 6.43: Drawing the roads for the winery location map

5. **Double-click on the Paint Text tool.**

   This takes you to the Text Style dialog box.

6. **Click on Geneva and 9 in this box, and then click on the OK button.**

7. **Add the town and road names, as shown in Figure 6.44.**

   Remember that you can enter the text and then select and move it to the proper location in the map.

8. **Double-click on the Paint Text tool and click on the Bold box under Style.**

9. **Click on the OK button.**

10. **Enter the names of the wineries, and position them as shown in Figure 6.45.**

To indicate the location of each town and winery, you can use the Brush painting tool. For the towns, use the smallest round brush shape. For the wineries, use the smallest square brush shape.

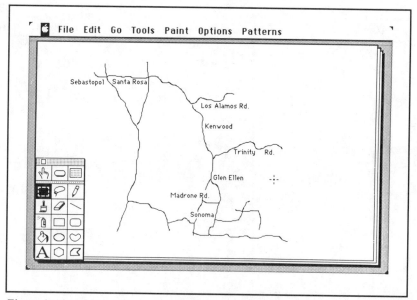

Figure 6.44: Adding the town and road names to the winery location map

11. Select the Brush tool on the Tools menu (located below the Selection tool).

12. Select the Brush Shape option on the Options menu.

13. Click on the smallest round brush shape, even if it is currently selected.

14. Select the Patterns menu and make sure that the solid black fill is currently selected.

    If it is not, click on this pattern.

15. Move the Brush tool to each town location, as indicated on the map shown in Figure 6.46, and click the mouse to add a dot there.

16. Select the Brush Shape option on the Options menu.

17. Click on the smallest square brush shape.

18. Move the Brush tool to each winery location, as indicated on the map shown in Figure 6.46, and click the mouse to add a square there.

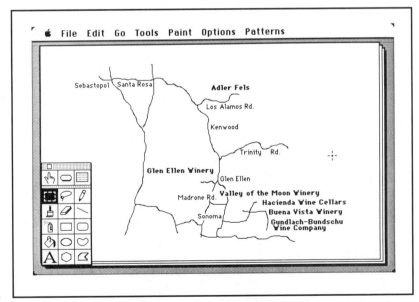

Figure 6.45: Adding the winery names to the map

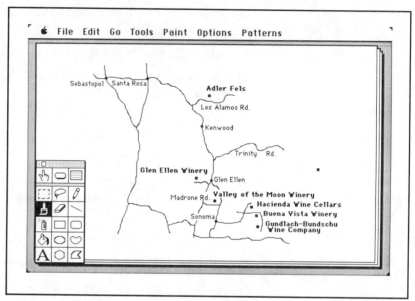

Figure 6.46: Indicating the locations of the towns and wineries on the map

To finish the road map for the wineries, you need only add the references to other map cards, the highway signs, and the title of the card. For the references to adjacent wine regions on other cards, you can use the Paint Text tool with the New York font in 10-point size. For the title of the card, you can use the Chicago font (available only in 12 points). To create the road signs, you can use the Oval tool to draw an elliptical shape in which you can put the highway number.

19. Change the Paint Text font to New York and the point size to 10, and deselect the Bold option.

20. Enter the references as shown in Figure 6.47.

21. Change the paint text font to Chicago.

22. Enter the title for the card as shown in Figure 6.47.

To make the highway signs, you will want to work in the white space available on the left side of this map card.

23. Move the Tools menu to the upper right corner of the card.

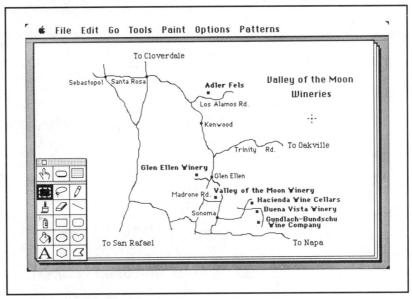

Figure 6.47: Adding the map references and card title to the map

You need to make the ellipses large enough to accommodate three digits in 10-point and bold. Before you create the ellipses, you should change the text style and enter the numbers.

24. Change the Paint Text font to New York, the point size to 10, and the style to Bold.

25. Enter the three highway numbers 101, 116, and 12 in the blank area to the left of the map.

Spread the numbers out sufficiently so that they can be enclosed in ovals.

26. Select the Oval tool (immediately to the right of the Bucket tool).

27. Position the crossbar cursor above and to the left of the first highway number.

28. Drag the crossbar until you have enclosed the highway number in an ellipse.

Remember that you can use Command-Z or the tilde key (~), if you want to reposition the crossbar and start over.

29. **Enclose the remaining highway numbers in ovals using the same technique.**

Both highways 12 and 116 show up twice on the winery road map. You need to copy them before you position the signs in their final positions on the map.

30. **Use the Lasso tool or the Selection tool with the Option key to select the Highway 116 sign.**

Only the oval should be outlined by the moving dotted line.

31. **Move the Lasso tool to the sign until it changes to the Arrow pointer.**

32. **Hold down the Option key and drag the mouse.**

This carries off a copy of the highway sign.

33. **Move this copy to an unused portion of the screen and click the mouse.**

34. **Repeat this copy procedure for the Highway 12 sign.**

35. **Position the five road signs on the map as shown in Figure 6.48.**

You will have to use the Eraser tool to make breaks in the roads to accommodate the signs.

36. **Select the Browse tool on the Tools menu.**

37. **Select the Card Info option on the Objects menu, enter *Valley of the Moon Map* as the name of the card, and click the OK button.**

To complete the Wine Tour stack, you don't have to draw any more maps at this point (although the final version of this stack would require a map for the Sonoma Valley and Napa Valley wineries). It is sufficient to have only the Valley of the Moon Wineries map, since you will be linking locations on only this card to the winery cards that you created for the Wineries stack. However, before you go on to add the buttons and link these cards in the next chapter, you should create the Index card that will also contain links to these cards.

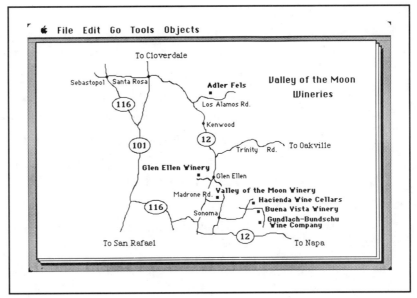

Figure 6.48: The completed Valley of the Moon Wineries map

Creating the Index Card

The Index card will enable you to look at information on a specific winery (stored in the Wineries stack) by its name rather than by location on the map card. To create this card, all you have to do is add a new card to the Wine Tour stack, create the card fields for it, and enter the name of the wineries in these card fields. Then, later, you can add a button to each winery name listed that links it to the associated winery card in the Wineries stack.

To accommodate as many winery names as possible on the Index card, you will set up two fields, side by side, on the new card you add to the Wine Tour stack.

1. **Select the New Card option on the Edit menu (or press Command-N).**

2. **Select the New Field option on the Objects menu.**

   If the Objects menu is not displayed, select the Browse tool from the Tools menu first.

3. Select the **Field Info** option on the **Objects** menu.

4. Click on the **Font** button and change the font to **New York**, the size to **10 point**, and the **Align** option to **Center**.

5. Click on the **OK** button.

6. Move the field so that the upper left corner of the field is three-fourths inch from the left and top edges of the card.

7. Widen the field until it is about 2½ inches wide.

8. Lengthen the field until it is almost touching the bottom of the card (Figure 6.49).

   There should be 18 or 19 text lines in this field.

9. Copy the field and position the copy to the right of the first field so that there is three-fourths inch between the second field and the right edge of the card (Figure 6.50).

   By holding down the Shift key and the Option key while dragging, the field will be constrained along a horizontal axis, thus keeping the fields properly aligned.

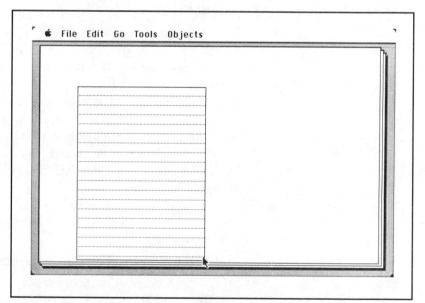

Figure 6.49: Adding the first text field to the Index card

Now you can fill in the names of the wineries found on the Valley of the Moon Wineries map.

10. Select the Browse tool and press the Tab key.

This takes you the first field.

11. Enter the names of the wineries as shown in Figure 6.51.

Next, add a title for this card using the New York font in 14-point bold.

12. Tear off the Tools menu and move it the right side of the card.

13. Double-click on the Paint Text tool.

14. Change the font to New York, the point size to 14, and the style to Bold.

15. Enter Winery Index in this font.

16. Center this title over the entries you made in the first field (Figure 6.52).

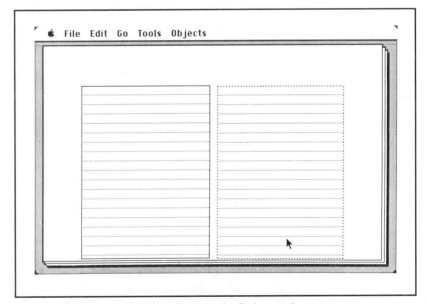

Figure 6.50: Copying the first fields in the Index card

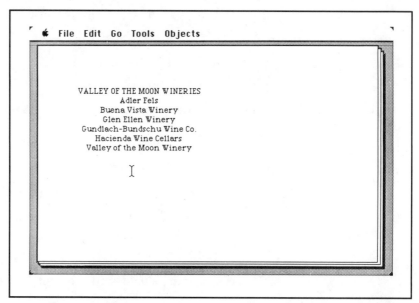

Figure 6.51: Entering the names of the wineries into the Index card

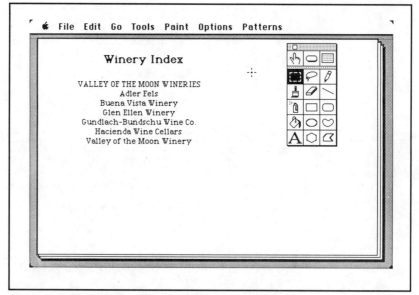

Figure 6.52: Adding the title to the finished Index card

17. **Select the Browse tool and click on the Close box in the Tools menu.**

18. **Select the Card Info option on the Objects menu, enter** *Index* **as the card name, and click on the OK button.**

19. **Use the Next option on the Go menu or the → key on the keyboard to browse through all three cards in the Wine Tour stack.**

If you want to take a break before going on to the next chapter, go ahead and quit HyperCard.

Summary

You should feel quite pleased with yourself! You have now finished creating two stacks: one using a complex layout of text fields and the other using fairly sophisticated graphics. In going through the many steps involved in this process, you have been exposed to both planning and executing a stack idea. You now have experience adding text fields and graphics both in the background and at the card level.

At this point, your stacks still lack one essential element: buttons. Without buttons and the linking they perform, the stacks represent little more than a collection of electronic flash cards. The addition of these buttons will transform the stacks into an information system that can be used intelligently.

The Key to HyperCard—
The Linking Process

CHAPTER **7**

THE LINKS THAT YOU ESTABLISH BETWEEN CARDS IN a stack are activated by particular buttons that you add to the card. As with fields and graphics, these buttons can be placed either in the background of a card or in the card itself.

The linking of one card to another with a button is actually accomplished with a HyperTalk script. When you click on a button the script attached to it is activated, and HyperCard takes you to the appropriate card. Although the linking is accomplished through the use of Hyper-Talk scripts, you don't have to know anything about writing scripts in HyperTalk to create them. As you will soon see, you can link cards either by using a special LinkTo option on the Button Information dialog box or by copying an existing button that already contains the appropriate HyperTalk script.

As you saw when you explored the components of the Address stack in Chapter 5, buttons, like fields, can have various attributes and styles. Unlike fields, buttons can also be represented by various icons. Icons can be used both to indicate the position of the button and to denote its purpose in the card.

Besides buttons that use icons or display their shape and, usually, their name, you can have transparent buttons that neither use an icon nor show their name. Such transparent buttons allow you to associate text in fields or graphics in the card with a button. When the user moves the mouse to this area, the cursor changes from the I-Beam to the Browse tool (indicating the existence of the button). Then, when the user clicks somewhere within the area of the transparent button, the button's script is activated.

Versions 1.0 and 1.1 of HyperCard still lack the ability to directly associate buttons (and their attendant scripts) with specific text in a card. The lack of such "text" buttons is seen by many developers as a serious oversight in HyperCard (other commercially available HyperText programs have this feature). As a result, you should see this feature in an upcoming version.

Although you place transparent buttons close to, or on, the text or graphics to which they are to be associated, the buttons themselves are never directly attached to text or graphics in a card. This means that if you add such a button and later modify the associated text or graphic image (such as moving it to a new place in the card), the button does not automatically move along with it. Because it remains in its original position in the card, if you don't remember to move the button to the new location of the text or graphics, your stack will no longer work correctly. You will need to keep this in mind when you make modifications to the text and graphics in stacks that have transparent buttons associated with them.

Creating the Buttons for the Wine Tour Stack

To get a feel for how buttons are added to stacks and how the links between cards are established, you will start by adding the necessary buttons to the Wine Tour stack. This stack contains just three cards: the Opening card showing the regional wine map, the road map for the wineries in the Valley of the Moon, and the Index card. You will want to link these cards so that you can go directly from the Opening card to the road map or the Index card, as well as return from either card to the Opening card. In addition to the buttons to accomplish these moves, you should also add a button that will take you to the Home Card.

It is customary to add a Home button to each stack that you create. Adding this button makes it easy to return to this central card (and is the point of origin for many HyperCard users). Many different house icons are available for the Home button. The simplest HyperTalk script to accomplish this purpose is simply *go home*.

The buttons to return to the Opening card, to go to the Index card, and to go to the Home Card will all be in the background of the card. Only the button to take you to the Valley of the Moon Wineries map will be card-specific; this button will be a transparent button added only to this card. Let's start by creating the background buttons.

If you quit HyperCard at the end of the last chapter, start it now. Before you open the Wine Tour stack, you should change the user level from Authoring to Scripting on the User Preferences card. Although it is *not* necessary to change the user level to link cards, doing so will allow you to examine the scripts that HyperCard writes for you in HyperTalk. Understanding what takes place behind the scenes when you link a button to a card will prepare you for writing your own HyperTalk scripts later on (even if you don't plan to learn HyperTalk, you will find it beneficial to know a little bit about how buttons work).

1. **With the Home Card on the screen, click on the Prev button (the shadowed left arrow) on the card.**

   This takes you to the User Preferences card.

2. **Click on the Scripting radio button.**

   The *Blind typing* check box will appear to its right when you select this button, and it will be checked (you will learn about blind typing in Part III, as you begin to create your own scripts in HyperTalk).

3. **Select the Open Stack option on the File menu (or press Command-O).**

4. **Click on Wine Tour and then on the Open button (or double-click on Wine Tour).**

5. **With the Opening card of the Wine Tour stack on the screen, select the Background option on the Edit menu (or press Command-B).**

   The HyperCard menu will become striped and the card graphics will disappear (the card appears blank when viewing the background).

The three background buttons that you are about to add will be located in a row in the upper right corner of the card. This area was purposely left blank on each card so that these buttons would appear in the card, unobstructed by any graphics.

Adding the Opening Card Button

To add any type of button to a card, you use the New Button option on the Objects menu. As soon as you select this option, a button named New Button using the round rectangle button style appears centered on the card. You can then modify its attributes and reposition it as required.

1. **Select the New Button option on the Objects menu (shown at left).**

   A button called New Button appears on your screen (Figure 7.1).

2. **Select the Button Info option on the Objects menu (or double-click on the New Button).**

Performing these two steps takes you to the Button Information dialog box shown in Figure 7.2. Notice that the button name, New Button, is highlighted and the default button style is the round rectangle. Also, the *Show name* box is checked, which is why the name *New Button* is displayed on the screen.

This button to return you to the Opening card will use a Compass icon; therefore, it does not need to display its name and its style should be transparent.

3. **Enter *Opening card* as the button name. *New Button* will be replaced as you type.**

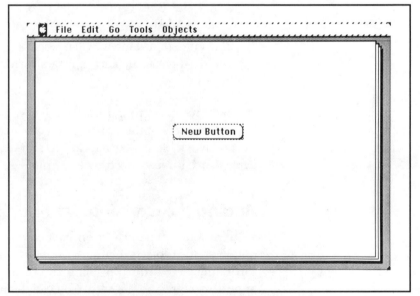

Figure 7.1: The New Button added to the card background

4. **Click on the *Show name* check box.**

   You want this box to be unchecked.

5. **Click on the transparent radio button.**

   The Button Information dialog box on your screen should now match the one in Figure 7.3.

   Next, you need to select the Compass icon that you want displayed with this button.

6. **Click on the Icon button in the Button Information dialog box.**

   This takes you to the scrolling field displaying various icons.

7. **Drag the scroll box all the way down to the bottom of the scroll bar.**

   Notice the Compass icon, displaying the initials of the cardinal directions, in the third row down.

8. **Click on the Compass icon to select it.**

   The icon ID is 9761 (Figure 7.4).

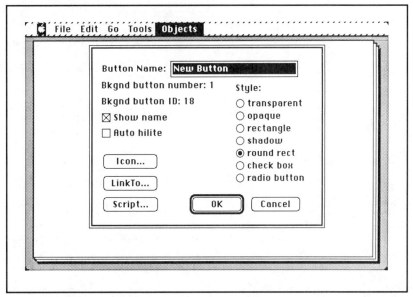

Figure 7.2: The default Button Information dialog box

9. **Click on the OK button.**

   You can now see part of the Compass icon in the transparent button (Figure 7.5).

   Although you have set the attributes for the Opening card button correctly, you cannot see all of the Compass icon yet. You must now resize the button so that it is square and it encloses the icon within it. After you size it, you can position it in the upper right corner of the card.

10. **Position the Arrow pointer so that its tip is on the corner of the button's outline (the moving dotted line).**

11. **Drag the mouse down and to the left until the moving dotted outline is roughly square and completely encloses the Compass icon.**

12. **Position the Arrow pointer somewhere within the moving outline of the button.**

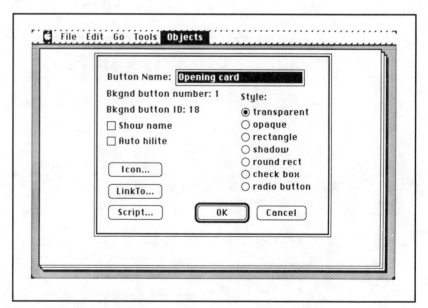

Figure 7.3: The modifications made to the Opening card button

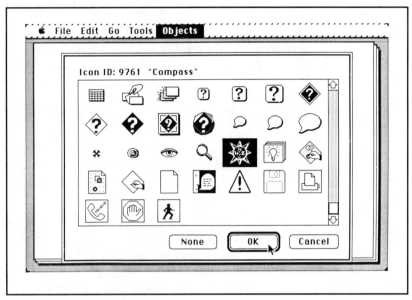

Figure 7.4: Selecting the Compass icon to be used for the Opening card button

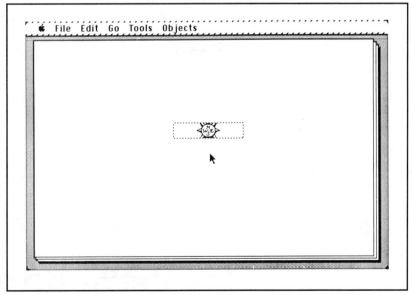

Figure 7.5: The Opening card button after selecting the Compass icon and
changing its attributes

13. Drag the button to the upper right corner of the card.

Position it so the the center of the compass is about 2 inches from the right edge of the card and its top central spike is almost equal with the top of the card (Figure 7.6).

Linking the Opening Card Button to the Opening Card

Now, all that remains to be done with this button is to indicate to which card it is to be linked. This is done with the LinkTo button on the Button Information dialog box. When you use this option, a dialog box appears on your screen. It contains three options: This Card, This Stack, and Cancel.

You indicate which card you want the button linked to by going to the appropriate card and then clicking on the This Card button. That's all there is to interlinking cards. Once you use this option, HyperCard writes the appropriate HyperTalk script for you (you will learn how to examine and read this script shortly).

The Opening card button should be linked, naturally, to the Opening card. Go ahead and establish this link now.

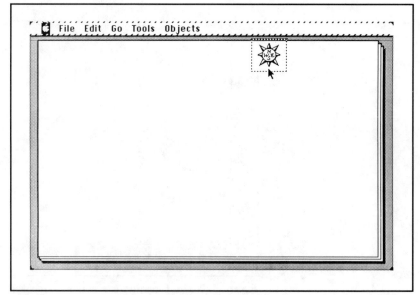

Figure 7.6: Moving the Opening card button to its final position in the card

1. **Select the Button Info option on the Objects menu.**

   Make sure that the button is still selected when you choose this option (shown by the moving dotted outline).

2. **Click on the LinkTo button (beneath the Icon button).**

   This takes you to the dialog box shown in Figure 7.7. Notice that you are no longer in the background (you can see the Opening card graphics, and the HyperCard menu is no longer striped). The program has automatically selected the Browse tool. This allows you to use any HyperCard Go command to get to the card you want to link to. Because you are currently at the proper card, all you have to do now is click on the This Card option in the dialog box.

3. **Click on the This Card option.**

   As soon as you choose this option, HyperCard records the script to link the Opening card button to the Opening card. Once this is saved, the Button tool as well as the Opening card button are selected

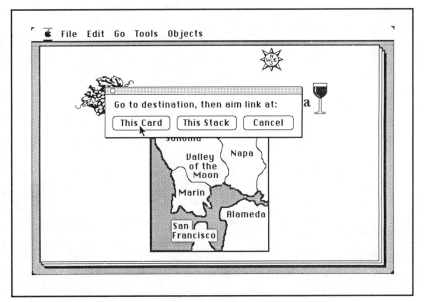

Figure 7.7: The LinkTo dialog box

(marked by the moving dotted line). However, you are no longer in the background (the HyperCard menu is no longer striped).

Testing the Opening Card Button

Before you add the remaining two background buttons to this card, you can test out this button. To do so, you must first select the Browse tool and then go to one of the other cards in this stack.

1. **Select the Browse tool on the Tools menu.**

   The Opening card button is no longer selected.

2. **Select the Next option on the Go menu (or press Command-3).**

   This takes you to the winery road map. Notice the presence of the button (marked by the Compass icon) on this card.

3. **Select the Opening card button by moving the Browse tool to the Compass icon and clicking the mouse.**

   This returns you immediately to the Opening card in the stack.

Adding the Index Button

Now that you have successfully added the Opening card button to the stack, you are ready to add the Index button. This button will take you to the Index card anytime you select it. Rather than use an icon, you will show its name in a round rectangle.

1. **Select the Background option from the Edit menu (or press Command-B).**

   The graphics in the Opening card are no longer visible, and the menu is striped.

2. **Select the New Button option on the Objects menu.**

   A New Button appears in the middle of the card.

3. **Select the Button Info option on the Objects menu (or double-click on the New Button).**

   The Button Information dialog box appears.

4. **Enter *Index* as the button name.**

   As soon as you begin to type, this name replaces *New Button*.

5. **Click on the OK button.**

   You see the word *Index* inside a round rectangle where *New Button* was previously.

   Next, you need to resize the button and move it to its final position in the card (immediately to the right of the Opening card button).

6. **Move the Arrow pointer to the lower right corner of the Index button.**

7. **Drag to the left and up slightly to reduce the size of the button.**

   Stop when the outline of the round rectangle just frames the word *Index* (refer to Figure 7.8).

8. **Move the Arrow pointer somewhere within the button, and drag the button so that it is located to the right of the Opening card button, as shown in Figure 7.8.**

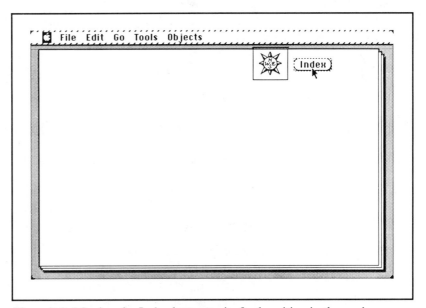

Figure 7.8: Moving the Index button to its final position in the card

Linking the Index Button to the Index Card

Now you are ready to link the Index button to the Index card in your Wine Tour stack. Again, you use the LinkTo option, this time going to the Index card and then clicking on the This Card option in the LinkTo dialog box.

1. **Select the Button Info option on the Objects menu (or double-click on the Index button).**

2. **Click on the LinkTo button. This brings up the LinkTo dialog box and selects the Browse Tool.**

   You can see the Opening card beneath this dialog box.

3. **Select the Last option on the Go menu (or press Command-4).**

   This takes you to the Index card.

4. **Click on the This Card option in the dialog box.**

   This establishes the link and returns you to the Opening card.

Testing the Index Button

You should now test the Index button by taking the following steps.

1. **Select the Browse Tool on the Tools menu.**

2. **Move the Browse tool to the Index button and click the mouse.**

   This takes you to the Index card.

3. **Move the Browse tool to the Opening card button (the Compass icon) and click the mouse.**

   This returns you to the Opening card.

Adding the Home Button

Congratulations! You have now established two complementary buttons. You can now go directly to and from the Opening and Index cards without having to use the Go options. You will now have no trouble adding a Home button to the background of the Wine Tour stack.

1. **Select the Background option on the Edit menu (or press Command-B).**

2. **Select the New Button option on the Objects menu.**

3. **Select the Button Info option on the Objects menu.**

4. **Enter *Home* as the name of the button.**

5. **Click on the *Show name* box to uncheck it.**

   You want to use a house icon instead of displaying the word *Home* in the button.

6. **Click on the transparent radio button under Style.**

7. **Click on the Icon button.**

8. **Drag the scroll button halfway down the scroll bar.**

   You will see a group of house icons near the bottom of the window.

9. **Click on the third house icon from the right.**

   This is icon ID 20098, called White Home (see Figure 7.9).

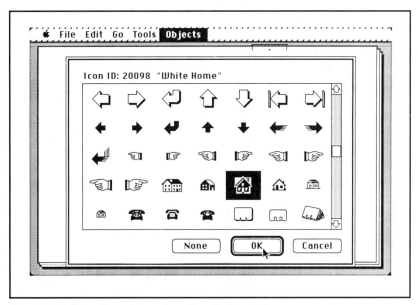

Figure 7.9: Selecting a house icon for the Home button

10. **Click on the OK button.**

11. **Size the button so that its outline is a square that encloses the White Home icon (Figure 7.10).**

12. **Move the button so that it is located to the right of the Index button (Figure 7.10).**

Linking the Home Button to the Home Card

To link the new Home button to the Home Card, you choose the LinkTo option, then go to the Home Card and select the This Card option on the dialog box. To get to the Home Card, you can use the Home option on the Go menu.

1. **Select the Button Info option on the Objects menu.**

2. **Click on the LinkTo button in the Home Button Information dialog box.**

3. **When the dialog box appears on your screen, select the Home option on the Go menu (or press Command-H).**

4. **Click on the This Card option.**

Testing the Home Button

You should now test out the Home button to make sure that it works properly. However, once you get to the Home Card using this button, there will be no complementary button on the Home Card that returns you to the Opening card. You will learn how to add such a button later on, near the end of this chapter.

1. **Select the Browse tool on the Tools menu.**

2. **Click on the Home button.**

    This takes you to the Home Card.

3. **Select the Open Stack option on the File menu (or press Command-O).**

4. **Click on Wine Tour and then click on the Open button (or double-click on Wine Tour).**

    This returns you to the Opening card of the Wine Tour stack.

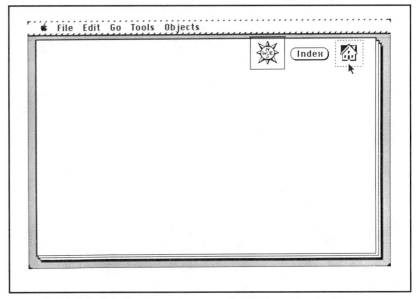

Figure 7.10: Moving the Home button to its final position in the card

Examining the Button Script

Now that you have ascertained that the Home button works correctly, let's look behind the scenes and see how it works. Because you set the user level to Scripting at the beginning of this exercise, you can use the Script option on the Button Information dialog box. This will take you to the window that holds the HyperTalk script for this button.

1. **Select the Button tool on the Tools menu.**

2. **Click on the Home button.**

   This selects it (shown by the moving dotted line).

3. **Click on the Button Info option on the Objects menu.**

   This takes you to the Home Button Information dialog box.

4. **Click on the Script button.**

   This takes you to a new window that displays the HyperTalk script for the Home button (Figure 7.11).

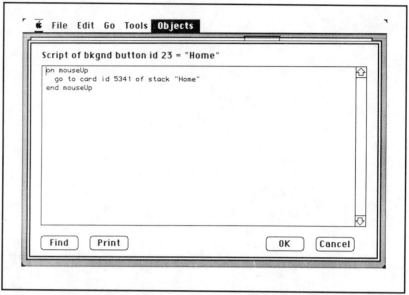

Figure 7.11: The HyperTalk script for the Home button

The script automatically created for this button when you used the LinkTo option reads as follows:

```
on mouseUp
    go to card id 5341 of stack "Home"
end mouseUp
```

The *on mouseUp* command statement means "when the mouse button is released" (when you click the mouse button, it is down; when you release it, it is up). This command statement tells HyperCard when to execute the Go command that follows it. The Go command tells HyperCard to go to the card with the ID number 5341. Further, it refines the Go command by telling HyperCard that this card is located in the stack called "Home".

Remember that card, field, and button IDs are unique and permanent *in the stack that contains them*. The Home Card is the only card in the Home stack that has this identification number, and it retains this ID as long as the Home Card exists (should the Home Card be deleted, this ID number will be retired).

When you establish a link between a button and card in the same stack (as with the Index and Opening buttons), the HyperTalk script created with the LinkTo option does not contain a reference to the stack name. It just contains a Go command that references the card ID. For example, my Index button contains the following HyperTalk script:

```
on mouseUp
    go to card id 4853
end mouseUp
```

(If you examine the Index button script in your stack, you may notice that the ID number given to your Index card is different.)

Because the Home Card is not located in the Wine Tour stack (the stack that contains the Home button), the Go command contains the reference to the stack name (of stack "Home") as well as to the card ID. When the button and the card you are linking it to are in the same stack, this stack reference is not required. It is only necessary when linking cards in different stacks.

Notice that the last line of the Home button script is *end mouseUp*. As soon as the Go command message is sent to HyperCard, the mouseUp condition is terminated with this statement. This allows HyperTalk to send (and the program to receive) a subsequent message (command) when you click and release (on mouseUp) the mouse button, as is the case when you click on one of the buttons in the Home Card after using the Home button in the Opening card to get there. You will become quite accustomed to this pairing of the *on mouseUp* and *end mouseUp* statements as you learn how to write your own HyperTalk scripts later on in Part III.

Now that you have seen what happens behind the scenes when you link a button with a card using the LinkTo option, it is time to move on and add the card buttons to the Wine Tour stack.

5. **Click on the OK or Cancel button in the Home button script window.**

This returns you to the Opening card of the Wine Tour stack.

Adding the Card Button to the Opening Card

There is one card button that you need to add to the Opening card. This will be a transparent button that will be placed over the Valley of the Moon caption in the regional wine map on this card. This button will be linked to the Valley of the Moon Wineries map (the second card in this stack). That way, when you move the Browse tool to the part of the map that contains this caption and click the mouse, the Valley of the Moon Wineries map will appear.

This transparent button will not be in the background as are the Opening card button and the Index and Home buttons. This button belongs only on the Opening card. Because you activated the Browse tool to test out the Home button, you are currently at the card level.

1. **Select the New Button option on the Objects menu.**

   Doing this automatically selects the Button tool, and you see the outlines of the Opening card button and Index button. However, you are not placed in the background (the HyperCard menu is not striped).

2. **Select the Button Info option on the Objects menu.**

3. **Enter *Winery Map* as the button name.**

4. **Click on the *Show name* check box to uncheck it.**

5. **Click on the transparent radio button beneath Style.**

   You do not have to wait until you have properly sized and positioned this button before you link it to the Valley of the Moon Wineries map card.

6. **Click on the LinkTo button.**

7. **Select the Next option on the Go menu (or press Command-3).**

   This takes you to the Valley of the Moon Wineries map.

8. **Click on the This Card button.**

   Now you need to resize the button and move it so that it covers the Valley of the Moon caption.

9. **Place the Arrow pointer on the lower right corner of the button.**

10. **Drag it down and to the left until it has a rectangular shape a little larger than the caption (Figure 7.12).**

11. **Move the button until it encloses the text of this caption (Figure 7.12).**

Testing the Winery Map Button

Test out this new button to make sure that you can get from the Opening card to the Valley of the Moon Wineries map and back.

1. **Select the Browse tool on the Tools menu.**

   The outlines of the Opening card button, Index button, and Winery Map button disappear.

To complete the wine tour application, you would need to create winery road map cards for the Sonoma and Napa Valley wineries. Then, you would add buttons similar to the one you just created for the Valley of the Moon caption. They, in turn, would be located over their captions on the wine region map of the Opening card. Each of these buttons would then be linked to their winery road map card, just as you linked the Winery Map button to its road map card.

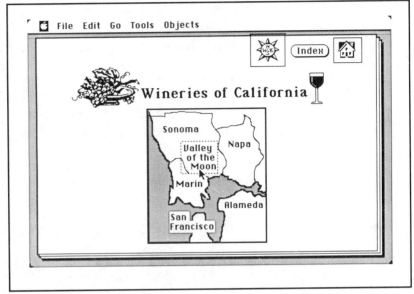

Figure 7.12: Locating the Winery Map button on the Valley of the Moon caption

2. **Move the Browse tool somewhere over the Valley of the Moon caption and click the mouse.**

   If nothing happens, try moving the Browse tool to the center of this caption and click again—you may have been outside this button the first time.

3. **On the Valley of the Moon Wineries map card, click on the Opening card button (the Compass icon).**

   This returns you to the Opening card.

   Try going to the Index card from the Valley of the Moon Wineries map card and returning from there to the Opening card.

4. **Click on the Winery Map button.**

   This returns you to the Valley of the Moon Wineries map.

5. **Once there, click on the Index button.**

   This takes you to the Index card.

6. **Once there, click on the Opening card button (the Compass icon).**

This returns you to the Opening card.

All this button pushing should have given you a real feel for the linking power of HyperCard. With every new button you add to this stack, the application becomes more and more dynamic. The information links that are being established with all these buttons act like two-way streets: you can use them to go quickly and directly to a desired place in the stack and return just as easily to your point of origin.

Adding the Card Buttons to the Road Map Card

Although you have now interlinked all of the cards in the Wine Tour stack, you have not finished adding all of the buttons this stack requires. As you remember, ultimately you want to be able to go from the name of the winery listed either on the road map or the Index card directly to the appropriate winery card in the Wineries stack. This calls for the addition of more transparent buttons on these two cards. Let's start by adding the card buttons to the Valley of the Moon road map.

1. **Click on the Winery Map button.**

This takes you to the Valley of the Moon Wineries road map.

2. **Select the New Button option on the Objects menu.**

3. **Select the Button Info option on the Objects menu (or double-click on the New Button).**

This new button will link to the Hacienda Winery card. It will be transparent and will not show its name.

4. **Enter *Hacienda* as the Button Name.**

5. **Click on the *Show name* check box to uncheck it.**

6. **Click on the transparent radio button under Style.**

7. **Click on the LinkTo button.**

This button will be linked to the Hacienda Winery card in the Wineries stack. To link this button to it, you must open this stack and go to the Hacienda Winery card.

8. **Select the Open Stack option on the File menu (or press Command-O).**

9. **Click on Wineries and then click the Open button (or double-click on Wineries).**

   This takes you to the Buena Vista Winery card (the first in this stack).

10. **Click on the Next button.**

    This takes you to the Hacienda Winery card.

11. **Click on the This Card button in the dialog box.**

Now you must resize the Hacienda button and move it so that it is located over the Hacienda Wine Cellars caption in the Valley of the Moon Wineries map.

12. **Move the button so that its left corner is slightly above and to the left of the Hacienda Wine Cellars caption.**

13. **Resize the button so that it just encloses this caption (Figure 7.13).**

    Be sure that the button encloses the square that marks the winery's location—you want to be able to select its winery card by clicking on this square or any part of its caption.

Go on and add similar buttons for the Buena Vista Winery and the Gundlach-Bundschu Wine Company (if you had created winery cards for the other wineries located on this map, you would also add a button for each one of them).

14. **Select the New Button option on the Objects menu.**

15. **Change its attributes so that the *Show name* box is unchecked, the transparent style is selected, and the button name is *Buena Vista*.**

16. **Click on the LinkTo button.**

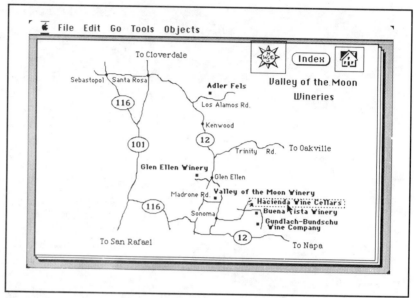

Figure 7.13: Positioning the Hacienda button over its caption in the map

17. Select the Recent option on the Go menu (or press Command-R).

18. Locate the miniature of the Buena Vista Winery card and click on it.

19. Click on the This Card option in the LinkTo dialog box.

20. Size the button so that it will enclose the Buena Vista Winery caption and its square, and position it over this area of the map (Figure 7.14).

21. Repeat steps 14–15. Instead of Buena Vista, enter *Gundlach-Bundschu* as the button name.

22. Repeat steps 16–18.

23. When the Buena Vista Winery card appears on your screen, click on the Next button two times to get to the Gundlach-Bundschu card.

24. Click on the This Card option in the LinkTo dialog box.

25. Size the button so that it will enclose the Gundlach-Bundschu Winery Company caption and its square, and position it over this area of the map (Figure 7.15).

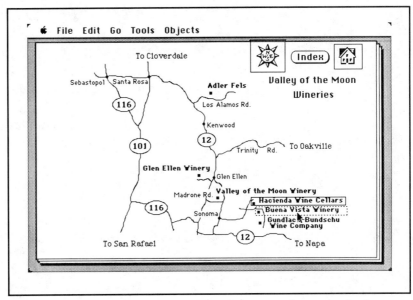

Figure 7.14: Positioning the Buena Vista button over its caption in the map

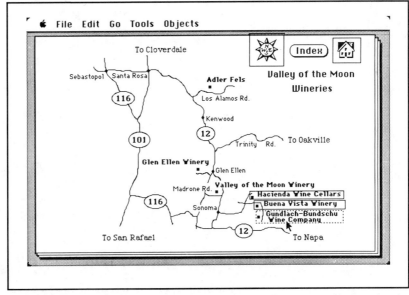

Figure 7.15: Positioning the Gundlach-Bundschu button over its caption in the map

Adding the Card Buttons to the Index Card

The card buttons for the Index card are similar to those that you just added to the Valley of the Moon Wineries map. Like these card buttons, the buttons in the Index card will be transparent, will not show the button name, and will be located over the winery names in the card.

To add these buttons to the Index card, you must first go to this card in the Wine Tour stack.

1. **Select the Browse tool on the Tools menu.**

2. **Click on the Index button.**

   This takes you to the Index card.

3. **Select the New Button option on the Objects menu.**

4. **Select the Button Info option on the Objects menu.**

5. **Change the button's attributes so that the *Show name* box is unchecked, the transparent style is selected, and the button name is *Buena Vista Index*.**

6. **Click on the LinkTo button.**

   You can use the buttons that you set up on the Valley of the Moon Wineries map to get to the Buena Vista Winery card.

7. **Click on the Opening card button (the Compass icon).**

8. **Click on the Winery Map button (somewhere on the caption that reads *Valley of the Moon* on the regional map).**

9. **Click on the Buena Vista button (either on the square to the left of the Buena Vista Winery caption or somewhere on the caption itself).**

10. **When the Buena Vista Winery card appears, click on the This Card button.**

11. **Size and locate the button so that it just encloses the Buena Vista Winery text on the Index card (Figure 7.16).**

In the same way, you will want to go on and add card buttons for the Gundlach-Bundschu Wine Co. and Hacienda Wine Cellars text in the Index card.

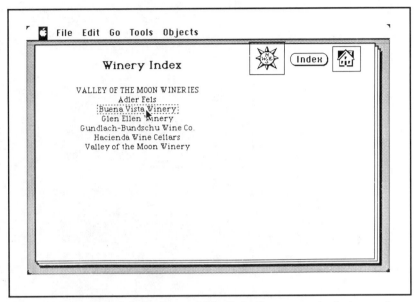

Figure 7.16: Positioning the Buena Vista Index button on the Index card

12. **Repeat the procedure outlined in steps 3–9. Name the button** *Gundlach-Bundschu Index* **instead of Buena Vista Index.**

13. **On the Valley of the Moon Wineries map, click on the Gundlach-Bundschu button (either on the square to the left of the Gundlach-Bundschu Wine Company caption or somewhere on the caption itself).**

14. **When the Gundlach-Bundschu winery card appears, click on the This Card button.**

15. **Size and locate the button so that it just encloses the Gundlach-Bundschu Wine Co. text on the Index card (Figure 7.17).**

16. **Repeat the procedure outlined in steps 3–9. This time, name the button** *Hacienda Index.*

17. **On the Valley of the Moon Wineries map, click on the Hacienda button (either on the square to the left of the Hacienda Wine Cellars caption or somewhere on the caption itself).**

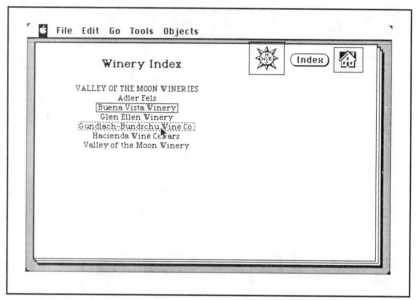

Figure 7.17: Positioning the Gundlach-Bundschu Index button on the Index card

18. **When the Hacienda Winery card appears, click on the This Card button.**

19. **Size and locate the button so that it just encloses the Hacienda Wine Cellars text on the Index card (Figure 7.18).**

Creating the Buttons for the Wineries Stack

You have now completed all of the buttons required in the Wine Tour stack. It is now time to go to the second stack, the Wineries stack, and add all of the buttons it requires. As it stands now, you can get directly from the Wine Tour stack to specific cards in the Wineries stack, but you cannot return directly from these cards to the Wine Tour stack. The background buttons that you will now create for the Wineries stack will make this return trip possible. They will be easy to create, because you can copy them from the Wine Tour stack.

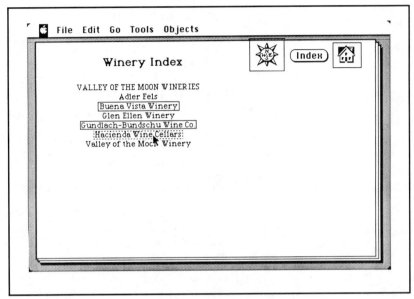

Figure 7.18: Positioning the Hacienda Index button on the Index card

1. **Click on the Browse tool on the Tools menu.**

2. **Click on the Buena Vista Index button on the Index card (somewhere on the text).**

   This takes you to the Buena Vista Winery card, the first card in the Wineries stack.

   You will want to add a Map button, Index button, and Home button to the Next and Prev (previous) buttons. These new buttons will be placed in the background along with the Next and Prev buttons that were added when you copied the background of the Home Card in creating the Wineries stack.

3. **Select the Background option from the Edit menu (or press Command-B).**

   The HyperCard menu will be striped and only the scrolling field and background graphics (the field headings) will be visible.

Adding a Line Separator
between the Buttons and the Fields

Before you add the buttons, you can draw a line to separate the text fields from the buttons at the bottom of the card. Having this line will help you correctly place the new buttons that you add to this background. You draw this line with the Line tool in the painting program.

1. **Select the Tools menu.**

2. **Tear it off and drag it to the upper left corner of the card.**

3. **Click on the Line tool (below the Pencil tool) to select it.**

To draw a line with the Line tool, you move the crossbar cursor to the place where you want the left end of the line to be and drag the crossbar to the right. To keep the line straight, hold down the Shift key as you drag the mouse. This prevents the line from becoming crooked if your hand does not travel smoothly to the right.

4. **Move the crossbar cursor so that it is about one-eighth inch in from the left edge of the card and below the scrolling field.**

5. **Press the Shift key and continue to hold it down.**

6. **Click the mouse and drag to the right until the line extends across the card, about one-eighth inch from the right edge of the card (Figure 7.19).**

7. **Release both the Shift key and the mouse button.**

Assigning New Icons
to the Next and Previous Buttons

Before you copy the buttons from the Wine Tour stack, you can change the arrow icons for the Next and Prev buttons and relocate them at the bottom of the card.

1. **Select the Button tool on the Tools menu.**

2. **Click on the Next button.**

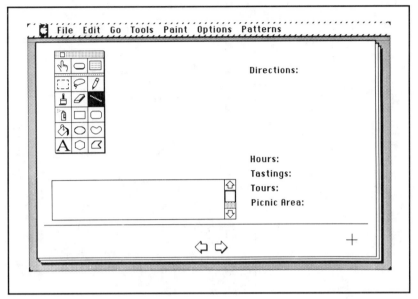

Figure 7.19: Drawing a line separator between the buttons and fields

3. **Click on the Button Info option on the Objects menu.**

4. **Click on the Icon button on the Next Button Information dialog box.**

5. **Drag the scroll button about one-third of the way down the vertical scroll bar.**

   You will see a new group of arrow icons, including a group of pointing hands.

6. **Click on the largest hand pointing right.**

   Its icon ID is 19162 and it is called "Lge Next Hand" (Figure 7.20).

7. **Click on the OK button.**

8. **Enlarge the button so that you can see all of the hand icon, and move it up and to the right of its present position, as shown in Figure 7.21.**

9. **Click on the Prev button to select it.**

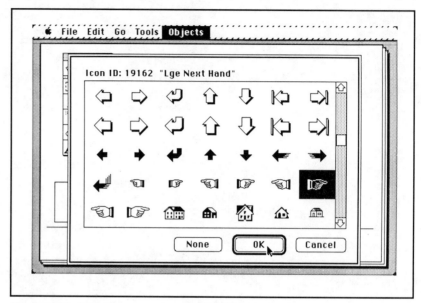

Figure 7.20: Selecting a new icon for the Next button

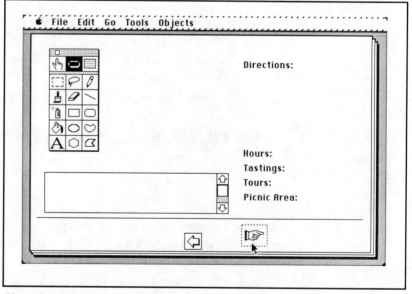

Figure 7.21: Locating the Next button to a new position on the card

10. **Repeat steps 3–5 and click on the largest hand pointing left.**

    Its icon ID is 9120 and it is called "Lge Prev Hand" (Figure 7.22).

11. **Click on the OK button.**

12. **Enlarge this button so that you can see all of the hand icon, and move it up and to the left of its present position, as shown in Figure 7.23.**

Copying the Opening Card Button from the Wine Tour Stack

Now you are ready to copy the Opening card button, Index button, and Home button from the Wine Tour stack to the Wineries stack. To do this, you must first open the Wine Tour stack. Then you select the button you want to copy, copy it, return to the background of the Wineries stack, and paste it in place. To see how this is done, start by copying the Opening card button (using the Compass icon), which will be called simply the Map button in the Wineries stack.

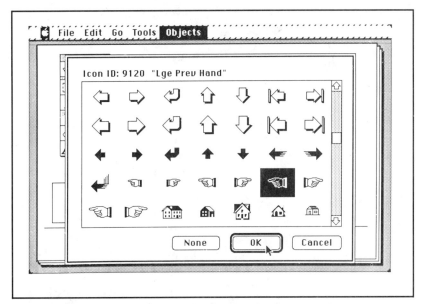

Figure 7.22: Selecting a new icon for the Prev button

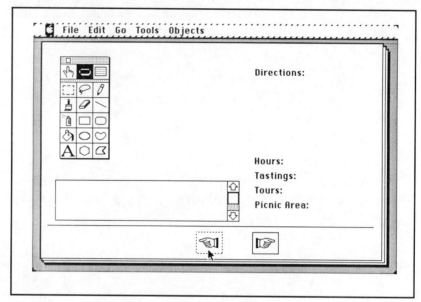

Figure 7.23: Locating the Prev button to a new position on the card

1. **Select the Open Stack option on the File menu.**

2. **Click on Wine Tour and then on the Open button (or double-click on Wine Tour).**

3. **Click on the Opening card button (the Compass icon) to select it.**

4. **Select the Copy Button option on the Edit menu (or press Command-C).**

5. **Select the Recent option on the Go menu (or press Command-R).**

6. **Click on the miniature of the Buena Vista Winery card.**

7. **Select the Background option on the Edit menu (or press Command-B).**

8. **Select the Paste Button option on the Edit menu (or press Command-V).**

   The Opening card button appears in the upper right corner of the card.

9. **Move this button down to the bottom of the card, to the left of the Prev button, as shown in Figure 7.24.**

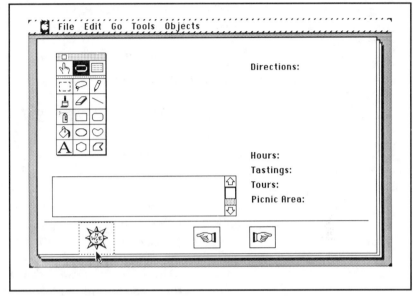

Figure 7.24: Positioning the copied Map button in the background of the Wineries stack

10. **Select the Button Info option on the Objects menu.**

11. **Enter *Map* as the button name. This will replace *Opening card* as the name.**

12. **Click on the OK button.**

Modifying the Map Button Script

Now that you have added the Map button to the stack, you can use it to return to the Wine Tour stack to copy the Index and Home buttons.

1. **Click on the Browse tool in the Tools menu.**

2. **Click on the Map button (the Compass icon).**

Nothing happens! This button does not work when copied to a new stack. Remember that when you originally linked this button to the Opening card, both the button and the card were in the same stack. Now that you have brought the button into a new stack, you must add the stack reference to the button script.

3. **Click on the Button tool in the Tools menu.**

4. **Click on the Map button.**

5. **Select the Button Info option on the Objects menu.**

6. **Click on the Script button.**

The Map button script reads as follows:

```
on mouseUp
   go to card id 2870
end mouseUp
```

(the card ID assigned to your Opening card may have a different number). You must now add the phrase *of stack "Wine Tour"* to the Go command on the second line.

7. **Position the I-Beam cursor immediately following the last digit of the card ID number and click the mouse.**

    The I-Beam cursor is replaced by the flashing text insertion pointer.

8. **Type *of stack "Wine Tour"* as shown in Figure 7.25.**

9. **Click on the OK button.**

Copying the Index and Home Buttons from the Wine Tour Stack

Now that you have edited the button script to include a reference to the stack the card is linked to, try using it to get to the Wine Tour stack. Once there, you can copy the Index button. The copy of this button will also require the addition of the stack reference to its script.

1. **Click on the Browse tool on the Tools menu.**

2. **Click on the Map button (the Compass icon).**

    This time, it should take you directly to the Opening card of the Wine Tour stack.

3. **Click on the Button tool on the Tools menu.**

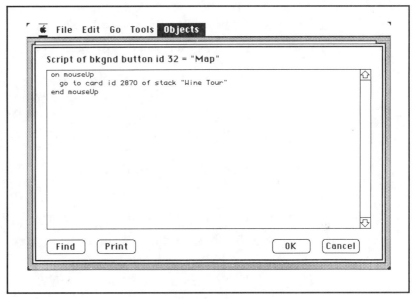

Figure 7.25: The modified button script for the Map button

4. **Click on the Index button to select it (shown by the moving dotted line).**

5. **Select the Copy Button option on the Edit menu (or press Command-C).**

6. **Select the Recent option on the Go menu (or press Command-R).**

7. **Click on the miniature of the Buena Vista Winery card.**

8. **Select the Background option on the Edit menu (or press Command-B).**

9. **Select the Paste Button option on the Edit menu (or press Command-V).**

   The Index button appears in the upper right corner of the card.

10. **Move this button down to the bottom of the card, between the Map and Prev buttons, as shown in Figure 7.26.**

11. **Select the Button Info option on the Objects menu.**

12. **Click on the Script button.**

13. Add *of stack "Wine Tour"* to the Go command on the second line of this button script, just as you did for the Map button.

14. Click on the OK button.

You can copy the Home button from the Index card of the Wine Tour stack. This will give you the opportunity to test the Index button in the Wineries stack to make sure it is working.

15. Click on the Browse tool on the Tools menu.

16. Click on the Index button.

This should take you directly to the Index card.

17. Click on the Button tool on the Tools menu.

18. Click on the Home button to select it (shown by the moving dotted line).

19. Select the Copy Button option on the Edit menu (or press Command-C).

20. Select the Recent option on the Go menu (or press Command-R).

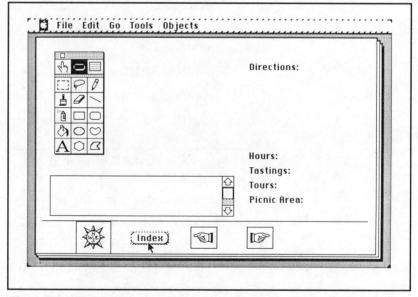

Figure 7.26: Positioning the copied Index button in the background of the Wineries stack

21. **Click on the miniature of the Buena Vista Winery card.**

22. **Select the Background option on the Edit menu (or press Command-B).**

23. **Select the Paste Button option on the Edit menu (or press Command-V).**

   The Home button appears in the upper right corner of the card.

24. **Move this button down to the bottom of the card, to the right of the Next button, as shown in Figure 7.27.**

Copying the Telephone Button from the Address Stack

There is just one more button to be added to the Wineries stack. This button will instruct HyperCard to dial the winery's telephone number (as entered in the Winery Telephone field) through a modem connected to your computer whenever it is clicked. Although the HyperTalk script to perform these actions is quite involved, you need

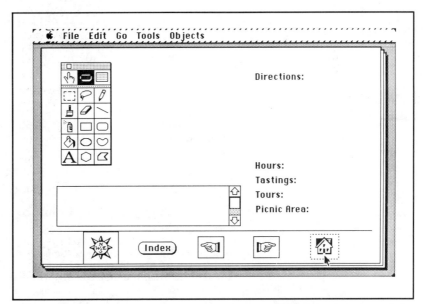

Figure 7.27: Positioning the copied Home button in the background of the Wineries stack

not take the time to learn the HyperTalk commands to use in your stack. You can easily copy such a button from the Address stack.

The telephone button will be located immediately to the left of the Winery Telephone field. Currently, the Tools menu is located in this area. Before you begin the procedure to copy the telephone button from the Address stack, you should move this menu.

> For the telephone button to work in the Wineries stack, it must have access to the Phone stack (one of the example stacks located on the HyperCard Startup disk, along with the Address stack). This means that a copy of the Phone stack should be on the same disk that contains your Wine Tour and Wineries stacks.

1. **Click on the top of the Tools menu and drag it to the right side of the card.**

To copy the button, you must now go to the Address stack.

2. **Select the Open Stack option on the File menu (or press Command-O).**

3. **If the Address stack is already highlighted, click on the Open button (or double-click on Address).**

   If this stack is located on a disk in your other drive, click on the Drive button and select the Address stack from this disk. This takes you to the Opening card of the Address stack.

Remember from your earlier tour of the Address stack that the telephone button is masked by a blank button on the first card. To copy the button, you need to go to the second card (Steve Aaron).

4. **Select the Next option on the Go menu (or press Command-3).**

   This takes you to Steve Aaron's card where you can see the Old-style Telephone icon marking the position of the telephone button.

5. **Click on the telephone button (using the Old-style Telephone icon) to select it (shown by the moving dotted line).**

6. **Select the Copy Button option on the Edit menu (or press Command-C).**

7. **Select the Recent option on the Go menu (or press Command-R).**

8. **Find the miniature of the Buena Vista Winery card and click on it.**

This button is to be pasted in the background of the Wineries stack. Going between stacks takes you out of the background. You must get back into the background before you paste this button.

9. **Select the Background option on the Edit menu (or press Command-B).**

10. **Select the Paste Button option on the Edit menu (or press Command-V).**

    The copied telephone button will appear near the bottom of the screen, over the scrolling field (its original position in the Address stack).

In the Address stack, this button was not given a name. Assigning names to fields, cards, and buttons is not mandatory. However, if you do assign names to these components, you can refer to them by name in HyperTalk scripts that you might add later on.

11. **Select the Button Info option on the Objects menu.**

12. **Enter *Winery Phone* as the button name, and click on the OK button.**

    You will use the same icon and look at its script later on, after it is correctly positioned.

Positioning the button immediately left of the Winery Telephone field will not be easy. You must use trial and error. You cannot see the outline of the Winery Telephone field when using the Button tool, and you cannot move the Winery Phone button when using the Field tool.

The best method is to switch first to the Field tool, and mark the placement of the field and the desired placement for the Winery Phone button. Next, switch to the Button tool, select the button, and drag it as close to its desired position as possible. Then, switch back to the Field tool and see if you need to further refine the button's position. If so, switch back to the Field tool, and select and move the button again. It will probably take a few tries to get it positioned exactly as you want it.

13. **Click on the Field tool. Mark the position of the Winery Telephone field (indented about one-half inch to accommodate the telephone icon).**

14. **Click on the Button tool.**

    The field outlines disappear.

15. **Click on the Winery Phone button to select it.**

16. **Drag it as close to the desired position as you can.**

    Depending upon the size and placement of the Winery Telephone field in your card, the center of the telephone icon should be a little over 1 inch down from the top edge of the card and one-half inch in from the left edge of the card (Figure 7.28).

17. **Click on the Field tool. If the icon is not positioned correctly, repeat steps 13–16.**

Testing the Winery Phone Button

Now that you have positioned the copied telephone button in the background of the Wineries stack, you should try it out.

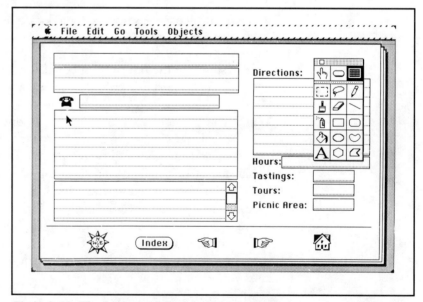

Figure 7.28: The final position of the Winery Phone button in relation to the Winery Telephone field

1. Click on the Browse tool in the Tools menu.

2. Click on the Winery Phone button (on the Old-style Telephone icon).

When you click on this button, you receive a HyperTalk error message inside a dialog box (Figure 7.29) telling you that HyperCard has never heard of a background field named Phone Number. This is the name given to the telephone field in the Address stack. In your stack, this field is called Winery Telephone. To get the button to work, you must edit its script. Notice that the dialog box allows you either to cancel or to go directly to the button script to change it.

3. Click on the Script button in the dialog box.

This brings up the window containing the button script, as shown in Figure 7.30.

The script for this button will probably seem quite complex (you will get a chance to study it in Part III as you learn about Hyper-Talk). For now, you need only concern yourself with the offending

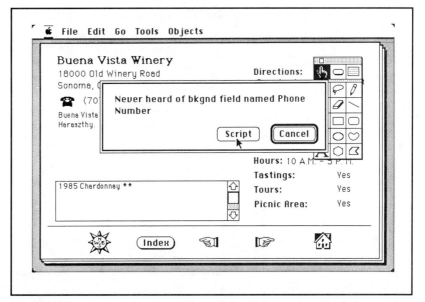

Figure 7.29: The error message dialog box that appears when you test the Winery Phone button

field name, Phone Number, that brought about the error. This reference is located in the third line of the button script, where it says,

if it is empty then get first line of field "Phone Number"

In your stack, this line should read as follows:

if it is empty then get first line of field "Winery Telephone"

Go ahead and edit this line of the script.

4. **Move the I-Beam cursor to the P in Phone (right after the first double quotation mark).**

5. **Click the mouse and drag to the right until *Phone Number* is highlighted.**

   Be sure that the second double quote is not included.

6. **Type *Winery Telephone*.**

   This will replace the current field name reference. Your button script should now match the one shown in Figure 7.31.

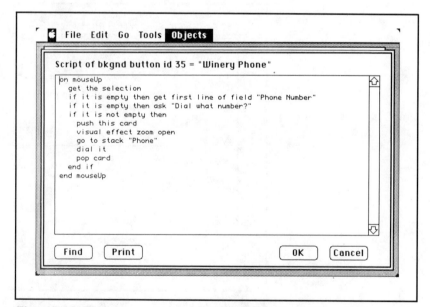

Figure 7.30: The incorrect button script for the Winery Phone button

Even after making all of these changes to the Phone stack, you cannot reach the Buena Vista Winery by using your Winery Phone button. To prevent the folks at this winery from receiving hundreds of test calls and running up your long-distance bill, I have masked the correct prefix of their and the other wineries' telephone numbers (there is no 555 prefix). If you want to try out your modem to see if you can use this button for autodialing, change the phone number in the Winery Telephone field to that of someone you know locally, and then test the button.

7. Click on the OK button.

8. Click on the Close button in the Tools menu.

It will only get in the way of your screen view when trying out the revised telephone button.

9. Click on the Winery Phone button.

This time, the button should take you to the first card in the Phone stack (this sample stack must be on your disk for this button to work). At the bottom of this card, you will see that HyperCard is trying to call 9,1–707 555–1266, and you will hear the speaker simulating the tones for dialing this number.

The Phone stack assumes that your phone system requires 9 to get an outside line and 1 for long-distance dialing. If this is not the case, you need to open the Phone stack and edit the *Dial for an outside line* and the *Dial for long-distance* fields. Also, you should enter the correct local area code for your service in the Local Area Code field.

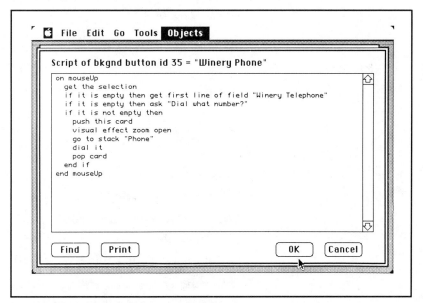

Figure 7.31: The corrected button script for the Winery Phone button

To have the winery phone number dialed through a modem, you must also click either on the *Modem (tone dialing)* or the *Modem (pulse dialing)* radio button. As long as the *Speaker (tone dialing)* radio button is selected, the number is not actually sent through the modem. If you have a touch-tone telephone, select *Modem (tone dialing)*. If you have a rotary-dial telephone, select *Modem (pulse dialing)*.

Testing the Stack Connections

You have now finished adding all of the buttons that link the two stacks of the wine tour application. At this point, it would be wise to test out the links to see that they perform as planned.

By clicking on the Next and Prev buttons, you can go to any card in the Wineries stack. These buttons interlink all of the existing cards (and any future winery cards that you care to add).

1. **Click on the Next button until you have viewed all three cards in the Wineries stack.**

2. **Click on the Prev button until you have done the same thing in the reverse order.**

To return to the Wine Tour stack, you can go either to the regional map of the Opening card or to the Index card.

3. **Click on the Map button.**

To go to a particular winery card, you can click on its location in the road map or its name in the Index card.

4. **Once you are at the Opening card, click on the Winery Map button (on the Valley of the Moon caption).**

5. **From the Valley of the Moon Wineries map, click on the Hacienda button.**

6. **From the Hacienda Winery card, click on the Index button.**

7. **From the Index card, click on the Gundlach-Bundschu Index button (somewhere on the Gundlach-Bundschu Wine Co. text).**

To go to the Home Card, you can click on the Home button in either stack.

8. **From the Gundlach-Bundschu winery card, click on the Home button.**

9. **From the Home button, select the Recent option on the Go menu (or press Command-R) and click on the miniature of the Opening card.**

Modifying the Function of the Map Button

If you were to make any modification to the functioning of any of the buttons, it would be to the Map button in the Wineries stack. Instead of returning you all the time to the Opening card, it would be nicer if it returned you, instead, to your point of origin: the Valley of the Moon Wineries map card. That way, you could immediately select another winery on the map and get information about that winery without having to select the Winery Map button on the Opening card each time.

You cannot accomplish this using the LinkTo option. This option can only add HyperTalk scripts that contain Go commands using the appropriate card IDs. The links that it can set up never vary; they will always take you to the card or stack that you indicate as the destination.

However, you can modify the way the specific winery buttons on the Valley of the Moon Wineries map relate to the Map button with the use of two simple HyperTalk messages: *push card* and *pop card*. The Push and Pop commands work together. Whenever HyperTalk pushes a card, it marks it for quick retrieval. The Pop command then retrieves it later. The Pop command works on the LIFO principle (last in, first out). As long as the card you want to retrieve (pop) was the last one pushed (marked for retrieval), the Pop command will redisplay it.

All this pushing and popping may appear a bit strange in abstract. Let's apply it to two of your buttons to see how it works in practice.

1. **Click on the Winery Map button in the Opening card.**

This takes you to the Valley of the Moon Wineries road map.

You can send a *push card* message by pressing the Command-↓ key on the keyboard. Conversely, you can send a *pop card* message by pressing the Command-↑ key. That way, you can test the effect of pushing and popping cards before you add the commands to your HyperTalk scripts.

When you use the Push and Pop commands, unexpected cards may pop up. This is because other stacks may have previously sent their own push messages. For instance, the Home stack contains a *push card* command as part of its start-up (stack) script. As a result, if the card you wanted to retrieve with *pop card* was not the last pushed, you might end up at the Home Card instead of the card you wanted to retrieve.

2. **Select the Button tool on the Tools menu.**

3. **Click on the Hacienda button to select it.**

4. **Select the Button Info option on the Objects menu and then click on the Script button.**

You need to add the HyperTalk command *push card* so that it precedes the Go command between the *on mouseUp* and *end mouseUp* statements. This command must appear on its own line, immediately following *on mouseUp* and preceding the *go to card id 3234 of stack "Wineries"* statement (the ID number will probably be different in your stack).

5. **Position the I-Beam cursor at the beginning of the second line containing the Go command.**

6. **Press Return. This inserts a blank line.**

   (Do not use the Enter key.)

7. **Press the ↑ key or click the I-Beam cursor at the beginning of the blank line and press the Tab key.**

   The flashing text insertion pointer will be indented on this line (you want to keep the new command indented to show that it is part of the command executed on the *on mouseUp* condition).

8. **Type *push card*.**

   Your modified button script should match the one shown in Figure 7.32.

9. **Click the OK button.**

10. **Select the Browse tool on the Tools menu and click on the Hacienda button.**

This time, HyperTalk instructed the program to push the card before it went to the Hacienda Winery card in the Wineries stack. For every push, you need a pop. You will add this to the Map button. In fact, the HyperTalk command *pop card* will replace the current Go command written with the LinkTo option.

11. **Select the Button tool on the Tools menu.**

12. Click on the Map button to select it.

13. Select the Button Info option on the Objects menu, and then click on the Script button.

To replace the *go to card id 2870 of stack "Wine Tour"* statement with *pop card*, you can select this text and then type over it. (Again, the ID number in your stack will probably be different.)

14. Move the I-Beam cursor so that it is located immediately in front of the *g* in *go*, and drag it across the entire go command on this line (it should be completely highlighted).

15. Type *pop card*.

This text will replace the Go command. Your modifications to this button script should match those shown in Figure 7.33.

16. Click on the OK button.

Try the modified Map button to verify that it now takes you back to the Valley of the Moon Wineries map instead of to the Opening card in the Wine Tour stack.

Although you have changed the function of the Map button in the Wineries stack, there is no need to modify that of the Opening card in the Wine Tour stack. Even though they share the same icon, they should function differently. When you click on the Compass icon in the Wine Tour stack, you always want to return to the Opening card that contains the regional wine map. From there, you can choose to see another road map for either the Sonoma Valley or Napa Valley wineries (the fundamental purpose of the Opening card), supposing that you create these map cards and the necessary links later on.

** File Edit Go Tools Objects**

Script of card button id 1 = "Hacienda"

```
on mouseUp
  push card
  go to card id 3234 of stack "Wineries"
end mouseUp
```

Find   Print   OK   Cancel

Figure 7.32: The *push card* addition to the Hacienda button script

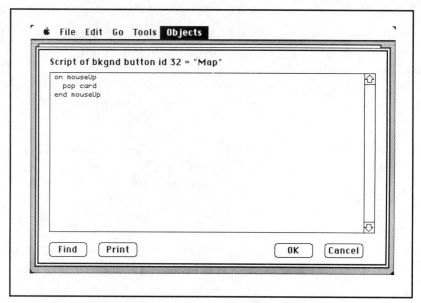

Figure 7.33: The *pop card* script for the Map button

17. Select the Browse tool on the Tools menu.

18. Click on the Map button.

This should return you to the Valley of the Moon Wineries map.

To have the other two winery buttons on this card (the Buena Vista and Gundlach-Bundschu buttons) behave in the same manner, you should edit their button scripts to include the *push card* message. If you don't, then when you click on either of them to get to the appropriate winery card and click on the Map button to return, you will be returned to the Home Card instead of the map of the Valley of the Moon Wineries. This is because the Home stack contains its own *push card* message as part of its stack script (executed when HyperCard is started).

Creating a Wine Tour Stack Button

There is only one more connection that you will probably want to add to your wine tour application. That is a Wine Tour stack button in the Home Card. By adding this button, you can then start Hyper-Card from the Home Card and open the Wine Tour stack simply by clicking on its button.

To add this button, you should first go to the Home Card. You can do this easily by clicking on the Home button in your Wineries stack.

1. Click on the Home button.

This takes you to the Home Card.

You want to add the Wine Tour stack button to the Home Card (not its background). This is where all of the other stack buttons are located (remember that only the Next and Prev buttons were copied when you copied the Home Card's background to create the Wineries and Wine Tour stacks).

2. Select the New Button option on the Objects menu.

3. Click on the Button Info option on the Objects menu.

This button will be a transparent button named Wine Tour, and it will show its name.

4. Enter *Wine Tour* as the button name.

5. Click on the transparent radio button under Style.

Leave the *Show name* box checked.

Next, you need to select an icon to represent this button. There is really no proper icon available to represent the winery tour application, so you can choose the generic stack icon (called simply Stack).

6. Click on the Icon button.

7. Click on the Stack button (the second one on the first line, immediately to the right of Bill Atkinson's button).

The icon ID is 1000 and the icon name is Stack.

8. Click on the OK button.

You can see only part of the Stack icon in the button and none of its name. You need to resize and reposition the icon.

To add a new icon designed especially for the Wine Tour stack requires that you create it and add to the available icons using the Resource Editor (Resedit). Using Resedit is not recommended for the beginning Macintosh user. If you make a mistake, you could damage your System folder and not be able to use it to start your computer again. Regardless of experience level, you should always use Resedit on a *copy* of your System folder. You can obtain a copy of this utility and documentation for it from your local Macintosh user group.

9. Drag the button down toward the bottom of the screen.

10. Resize the button until you can see the name *Wine Tour*, and the button is roughly the same size as the Plots stack button in the Home Card.

11. Drag the button to its final position immediately to the right of the Plots stack button, below the Clip Art stack button (Figure 7.34).

Now you need to link this button with the Opening card of the Wine Tour stack.

12. Select the Button Info option on the Objects menu.

13. Click on the LinkTo button.

14. Select the Open Stack option on the File menu (or press Command-O).

15. Click on Wine Tour and then on the Open button (or double-click on the Wine Tour).

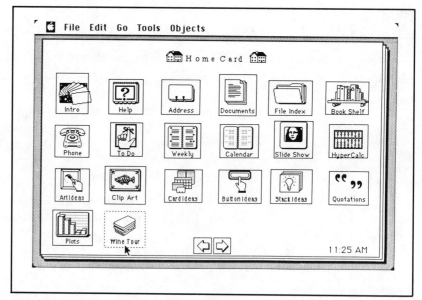

Figure 7.34: The final position of the Wine Tour stack button in the Home Card

16. **When the Opening card of the Wine Tour stack appears, click on the This Card button in the dialog box.**

Now make sure that the Wine Tour stack button operates correctly.

17. **Select the Browse tool on the Tools menu in the Home Card.**

18. **Click on the Wine Tour stack button.**

    This should take you directly to the Opening card of the Wine Tour stack.

19. **Click on the Home button on this card.**

    This returns you to the Home button.

You have now established a complementary link between the Home Card and your completed winery tour application.

Summary

This completes your work on the winery tour. By going through all the exercises in this and the preceding chapter, you have obtained first-hand knowledge of how to use HyperCard to create your own information system. The winery tour example contains all the basic elements you will be using as you go on and create stacks of your own design. You should also have gotten a much clearer idea of the kinds of applications best suited to HyperCard.

In this chapter, you learned how buttons are created and how the links between buttons and cards are established. Moreover, you got a chance to look behind the scenes at the HyperTalk scripts that were generated for each button and had some experience with modifying them to suit the special environment required in the wine tour. By combining this experience with your experience in designing and creating stacks, you are now ready to begin work on the stacks you have in mind.

The next chapter is on using the HyperCard painting program. You've already had first-hand experience with the painting program, which you used to create the Wine Tour and Wineries stacks. The following chapter contains comprehensive information on using all the features of this versatile graphics program.

Adding Graphics to Your Stack

YOU HAVE ALREADY HAD SOME EXPERIENCE WITH HyperCard's painting program: you used it to create the background and card graphics for your Wine Tour and Wineries stacks. In this chapter, you will learn about all the features of this part of the HyperCard program.

The HyperCard painting program is based on MacPaint, an earlier Apple graphics program developed by Bill Atkinson (primary author of HyperCard), which was originally bundled with the Macintosh and is now available as a separate program. The version integrated in HyperCard includes more features than the original MacPaint, although they both work in similar ways. If you already have experience using MacPaint, you will want to investigate the improvements made to this version. If you are new to creating graphics on the Macintosh, you will find the HyperCard painting program an excellent program to begin with. Except for graphics in stacks that either involve animation (such as is possible with Video Works II) or digitized images (such as those produced with scanners or video cameras), you should find the painting program sufficient for almost all your graphics needs in HyperCard.

Overview of HyperCard Graphics

In HyperCard you can use graphics to create the basic design for the card background or to add graphic images and text to the background or card layers of a stack. In your work with the wine tour application, you did not bother to design a new card background for the Wine Tour and Wineries stacks. Instead, you copied the card design of the Home Card. This design simulates three cards superimposed on each other against a gray patterned background.

Although it is always possible to adapt the basic card design from an existing stack (the sample Stack Ideas stack being an excellent source), you can also create it from scratch using the HyperCard painting program. To do this, you simply uncheck the *Copy current background* check box when you use the New Stack option on the File menu to create the new stack.

After you enter the name for the new stack and click on the New Button, the program will create a new card with a blank background. All you will see is the HyperCard menu at the top of the card (if your Macintosh uses an external monitor, the Menu bar is not superimposed on top of this blank card). It is then up to you to create whatever card design, if any, you want the background to have using the painting program (remember to go to the background layer with the Background option on the Edit menu before you start painting).

Even when you copy a background from an existing stack, as you did for the winery tour, you can still use the painting program to add various graphic images or text to the basic card design. Remember that you can create graphics for either the background or card layer. Any graphics added to the background show up in all the cards added to the stack that share that background.

Graphics added to the card layer are in front of those in the background. You can think of card layer graphics as being added to a transparent sheet of plastic that is laid down over the background layer. Card graphics are not only in front of the background; they are also unique to the card they are created on. A graphic image or paint text added to an individual card disappears as soon as you go on to a new card.

Painting versus Drawing Programs

The HyperCard graphics program is referred to as a *painting program* to distinguish it from a slightly different type of graphics program called a drawing program. A painting program, such as MacPaint or the HyperCard painting program, lays down a series of black dots on a white background (actually, these dots are small squares called *pixels*) as you use its tools. With such programs you have control over these individual dots so that you can erase or add to an image, pixel by pixel.

You get the same blank card background when you use the New Background option on the Objects menu. This allows you to create a new background in a stack. However, unlike using the New Stack option with the *Copy current background* box unchecked, it automatically places you in the background when you select it.

■ The square shape of
each pixel accounts
for the jagged edges that
appear in curves, circles,
and some diagonal lines.
On the other hand, it also
accounts for the clarity of
graphic images on the
screen. Images composed
of square pixels do not
appear as fuzzy as those
composed of rounded
pixels.

In drawing programs, such as MacDraw, the pixels are treated as groups of pixels that make up a particular shape or image (referred to as *objects*). When you use a drawing program, you have control over the objects you create; you can move them, shade them, and so on, but you cannot modify them pixel by pixel as with a painting program.

Painting in HyperCard, then, means that you are working with individual pixels. The entire screen is made up of pixels that can be turned on (a black pixel) and off (a white pixel) anywhere on the screen with the painting tools. As you know, a card in HyperCard is limited to the screen size of the 9-inch diagonal screen built into the majority of Macintosh models. This screen has 512 pixels horizontally and 342 pixels vertically. All of your painting is done within this environment.

The density of the pixels on the screen is 72 per inch (referred to most often as 72 dpi—dots per inch). At this density, an individual pixel is almost indistinguishable. This makes it difficult to work with individual pixels (the primary benefit of using a painting program rather than a drawing program).

To compensate for this, the painting program allows you to magnify any part of the screen so that you can easily work with a pixel at a time. Magnified pixels are referred to as *Fat Bits* (you were introduced to Fat Bits when you drew the winery map for your Wine Tour stack). The chief drawback to working with Fat Bits is that at such a large scale, only a small part of the screen is available at any time. At this level, you have to do a lot of scrolling, and it is easy to lose your place in the drawing. Because of this, you will want to restrict your use of Fat Bits to making small refinements to images created at the normal scale.

The Tools Menu

To use the painting program, you must set the HyperCard user level to at least Painting on the User Preferences card in the Home stack (of course, it is always available if you set the user level higher—to either Authoring or Scripting). At the Painting user level (or higher), the Tools menu appears on the HyperCard menu. You already have quite a bit of experience with this menu. As you know, this menu represents a special kind of tear-off menu that can be separated from the Menu bar and dragged anywhere on the HyperCard screen, where it remains visible. This keeps the menu available so that you can quickly select new tools for use.

Figure 8.1 shows you the tools available on this menu. Here, you will see the various names assigned to them. The first three tools on this menu are not part of the painting program. They are referred to as Object tools. When you select a new Object tool, the options on the Objects menu (next to Tools on the Menu bar) change. When the Browse tool is selected, the Button Info, Field Info, Bring Closer, and Send Farther options are not available (they are ghosted). When you select the Button tool and a particular button, the Button Info, Bring Closer, and Send Farther options become available. When you select the Field tool and a particular field, the Field Info, Bring Closer, and Send Farther options become available and the Button Info option is ghosted.

Painting Tools

Below these three Object tools (beneath the dividing line on the menu) is the painting program's palette, which contains all of

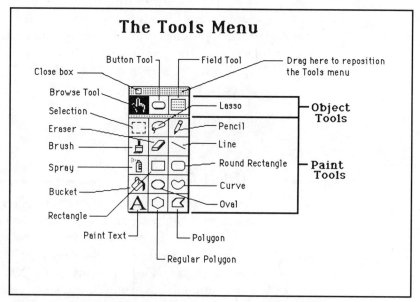

Figure 8.1: The Tools menu with the various tools called out

the Paint tools. Before you can create a graphic image in HyperCard, you must select one of the Paint tools to use. As soon as you select one of the Paint tools, the HyperCard menu changes: the Objects menu disappears and the painting program's Paint, Options, and Patterns menus appear (you will examine these menus and their options later on in this chapter). Depending upon the Paint tool chosen, the cursor will also change its shape and size.

Let's examine the function and use of each of the Paint tools on this palette.

The Selection Tool

The first Paint tool on the palette is the Selection tool. It allows you to select a rectangular portion of the picture. Once an image is selected, you can move it, cut and paste or copy it, stretch or shrink it, or make multiple copies of it.

When you choose the Selection tool, the cursor changes to a dotted crossbar. To select an image, move the crossbar to one of its corners and drag diagonally. As you drag, a moving dotted outline of a rectangle will appear. Anything within this rectangle is selected. This includes the white space that surrounds the image (Figure 8.2). To restrict the selection to the outer perimeter of the image, hold down the Command key and then drag the Selection tool (Figure 8.3). To restrict the selection to just the image itself, hold down the Option key and then drag or press Command-S after dragging to select the image (Figure 8.4). This has the same effect as lassoing the image with the Lasso tool.

You can select the entire picture plane (the entire card) by double-clicking on the Selection tool. This can be useful if you want to cut out the entire picture and paste it in another card (or move it from the card background to the card level or vice versa). If you double-click by accident, you can negate the selection by selecting the Undo option on the Edit menu (or by pressing Command-Z) or by moving the crossbar cursor somewhere within the picture and clicking again.

Moving a Selected Image

To move an image somewhere within the card after selecting it, move the crossbar somewhere within the image until it changes to the Arrow pointer. Then drag the image to its new location. To establish

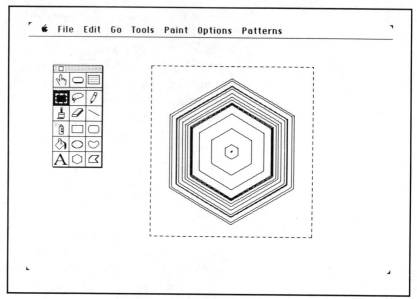

Figure 8.2: Image selected with the Selection tool

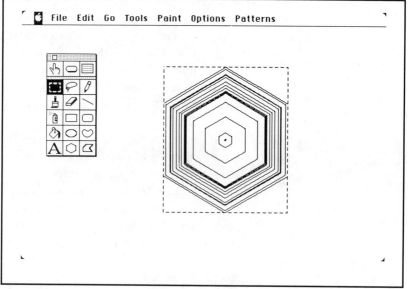

Figure 8.3: The outer perimeter of the image selected with the Command key
and the Selection tool

the image in its new position, move the Arrow pointer outside the selected area (it will change back to the crossbar cursor) and click the mouse. To restore a moved image to its original position, select the Undo option on the Edit menu (or press Command-Z).

The HyperCard painting program also allows you to restrict the movement of an image vertically or horizontally. To do this, press the Shift key before you drag the image either up and down or left and right.

Copying a Selected Image

To copy an image once you have selected it, press the Option key before you drag it. As you drag, it will appear as though you are tearing off a copy from the original. Once you have separated the copy from the original, you can move it in the card as you would any selected image.

The painting program also gives you a highly efficient way to make multiple copies of a selected image. To do this, hold down both the Option key and the Command key, and then drag the image.

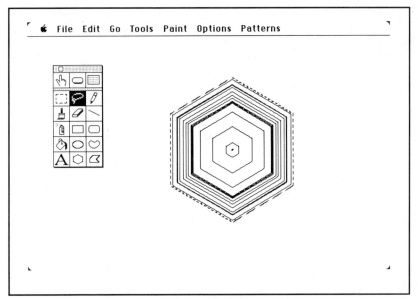

Figure 8.4: The image lassoed with the Option key and the Selection tool

Before making multiple copies, you can control the spacing (density) of the copies by pressing the Option key and a number between 1 and 9. Figure 8.5 shows you multiple copies of a triangle that were made with various Option-number combinations. As you can see from this figure, Option-1 leaves the least space between copies, and Option-9 leaves the most. Other Option-number key combinations give you gradations of spacing within these two limits. The lower the number, the less space between copies.

Stretching or Shrinking a Selected Image

You can stretch or shrink a selected image (thereby modifying its size and shape) by placing the Arrow pointer in one of the corners of the selection rectangle, holding down the Command key, and dragging. Depending upon the direction you drag, you will either expand or shrink the image. To enlarge or decrease the size of the selected image without distorting it, you must drag diagonally, taking care that you stretch or shrink equally in both the horizontal and vertical directions.

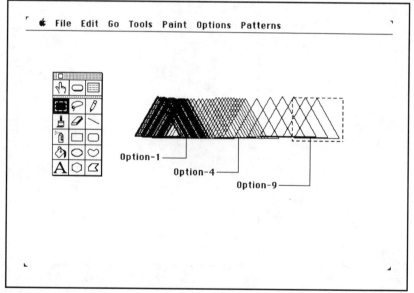

Figure 8.5: Making multiple copies of an image with varied spacing

The Lasso Tool

In particularly tight areas, you can select a specific image with the Lasso tool without having to trace around its outline. As long as the outline of the image is unbroken or it is composed of solid pixels, moving the tip of the lariat to the image, then holding down the Command key and clicking the mouse will select it.

The Lasso tool also allows you to select a particular part of a picture. It works like using the Selection tool with the Option key in that only the image and none of the white space surrounding it is selected. The Lasso tool is used to select irregularly shaped images or to select a specific image that is close to other images you do not want to select.

To select an image with the Lasso tool, you drag the tip of the lariat around the image. As you drag, it will draw a line tracing your movement with the mouse. Once the line touches the beginning, completely enclosing the image, the image will be outlined with a moving dotted line (the image appears to shimmer). Once an image is selected with the Lasso tool, you can perform all the same functions that are possible with the Selection tool (see the previous section for details).

You can select all the objects in a card by double-clicking on the Lasso tool. This is like double-clicking on the Selection tool, except that only the objects and none of the white space between the pictures is selected.

The Pencil Tool

To help you draw a straight line with the Pencil, you can hold the Shift key as you drag the tip of the Pencil. This will draw a straight vertical or horizontal line in the direction you move the mouse (even if you don't move the mouse in a straight line). If you move the mouse up or down, you get a vertical line. If you move to the left or right, you get a horizontal line.

The Pencil tool allows you to draw lines one pixel wide. These can be horizontal or vertical straight lines or free-form lines (because of the square pixel shape, curving lines are not smooth). To draw a line after selecting this tool, drag the pencil tip tracing the outline of the shape you want to draw with the mouse.

The Pencil draws with black pixels if you start using it on a white area and with white pixels if you start using it on a black or shaded area (such as over an existing image). This means that the Pencil tool will appear to erase existing pixels as you trace over them.

As you saw when drawing the winery map, you can use the Pencil tool to toggle in and out of Fat Bits. If you double-click on the Pencil tool, part of the picture will be enlarged so that you can see each pixel clearly (a window containing a normal-size version of the enlarged area will appear in the lower left corner of the screen). If you then double-click on the Pencil tool a second time, you will be returned to the normal view.

You can also control the area that is enlarged in Fat Bits by moving the tip of the Pencil tool to the area you want to be in, holding down the Command key and clicking the mouse button. To return to the normal view, you can then either double-click on the Pencil tool or click somewhere within the window holding the normal-size view.

The Brush Tool

The Brush tool is an excellent choice for creating any type of calligraphy in a card.

The Brush tool simulates painting with brush and ink on the screen. However, instead of painting with ink, you are painting with a specific pixel pattern (referred to as a brush shape). As you saw when you used the Brush tool to create dots and squares to mark the location of roads, towns, and wineries in the winery map, there are quite a few brush shapes and sizes available to paint with.

To select a new brush shape, you either double-click on the Brush tool or select the Brush Shape option on the Options menu. Then, click on the shape you want to paint with. Once you select a new brush shape, the cursor will reflect its shape and size. To paint with the brush, you drag the mouse, moving it in the pattern you wish to paint.

Figure 8.6 shows you the various brush shapes and sizes available, with samples drawn below.

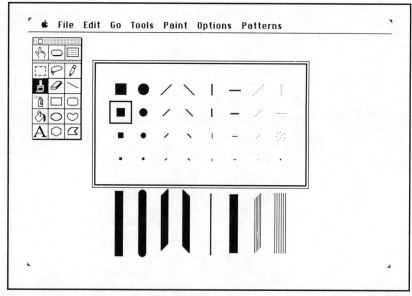

Figure 8.6: Available brush shapes with samples

To draw straight vertical or horizontal lines with the selected brush shape, you hold down the Shift key as you drag, just as you do to draw straight lines with the Pencil tool. You can also use the Brush tool to paint white on black with the selected brush shape. To do this, hold down the Command key as you drag the cursor.

The Eraser Tool

You can use the Eraser tool to remove parts of pictures, images, or shapes in a card. When you select the Eraser tool, the cursor changes to a square. As you drag this square, the pixels beneath it are erased. To erase just a small portion of a drawing, position part of the square over it and click the mouse. If you have trouble erasing just a bit of the image, you can switch to Fat Bits and use the Eraser tool there. The Eraser tool remains normal size even in the enlarged view.

To erase the entire picture that you have created, double-click on the Eraser tool. When you do this, the entire picture is wiped out and the program selects the Paint tool you were using before you selected the Eraser tool. If you do this by mistake, you can restore your artwork by selecting the Undo option on the Edit menu (or by pressing Command-Z).

Because HyperCard graphic images can exist in either the background or the card layer, erasing an image on the card may reveal a graphic that exists in the background beneath it. If you do not want this background image to appear in the card, erase the card graphic by holding down the Command key as you drag the Eraser tool. This removes the card graphic while putting down white pixels that prevent the image underneath from being seen.

The Line Tool

The Line tool allows you to draw straight lines on the horizontal, vertical, or diagonal. You can draw these lines in various thicknesses, choosing from a thickness of one, two, three, four, six, or eight pixels. To change the thickness of the line, double-click on the Line tool or select the Line Size option on the Options menu. Then click on the thickness of line desired in the selection box that appears.

When you select the Line tool, the cursor changes to a crossbar. To use the Line tool, place the crossbar at one end of the line and drag the

CH. 8

mouse in the direction you want to draw the line. When the line is of sufficient length, release the mouse button. To change the angle of the line you have drawn, move the mouse in another direction before you release the button. You can constrain the angle change to 15-degree increments by holding down the Shift key as you drag the mouse.

You can draw a line centered from a particular point by selecting the Draw Centered option on the Options menu before you use the Line tool. When you use this option, the line is drawn out from both sides of the starting point, even though you drag the mouse in just one direction.

You can also draw multiple lines by selecting the Draw Multiple option on the Options menu. As you move the mouse around, multiple lines are drawn (like rays emanating from a common point). You control the closeness of the lines (density) by pressing the Option key and a number between 1 and 9. Just as when making multiple copies of a selected image, the lower the number selected, the closer the spacing.

If you want to draw a line using a pattern other than black, select a new pattern from the Patterns menu and hold down the Option key as you drag the mouse. Even when you select a new pattern, using the Line tool without the Option key depressed will produce a solid black line.

You can combine effects such as Draw Centered and Draw Multiple. You can also constrain multiple lines to 15-degree angles by holding down the Shift key as you drag the mouse.

The Spray Tool

The Spray tool (using the aerosol can icon) simulates painting with a spray gun. Like painting with a spray gun, the more times you go over an area, the more paint it gets and the darker the pattern appears. You control the pattern of pixels put down by the Spray tool by choosing various patterns on the Patterns menu (like choosing different nozzles for a paint sprayer).

When you select the Spray tool, the cursor changes to a round pattern of dots (pixels). As you drag the mouse, the current pattern is painted on the card. To constrain the spray pattern to a straight line, hold down the Shift key as you drag. To use the Spray tool to spray white pixels on a dark background, hold down the Command key as you drag the mouse.

The Rectangle and Round Rectangle Tools

The Rectangle and Round Rectangle tools work in the same way. The difference between the shape drawn by them is that the corners of the rectangle produced by the Rectangle tool are square, and those produced by the Round Rectangle tool are curved. When you select either of these tools, the cursor changes to a crossbar.

To draw a rectangle, position the crossbar at one of its corners and drag the mouse diagonally. If you want to draw a rectangle from the center, select the Draw Centered option on the Options menu before you drag the crossbar cursor.

You can change the thickness of the border for a rectangle by selecting a new line thickness with the Line Size option on the Options menu. You can also use one of the patterns on the Patterns menu to draw the borders of the rectangle. To do this, select the desired pattern on the Patterns menu and hold down the Option key as you drag the crossbar.

Because the rectangle or round rectangle produced with these Paint tools is a closed shape, you can draw them filled with a pattern available on the Patterns menu. To draw a filled rectangle, select the desired pattern, then select the Draw Filled option on the Options menu, and draw your rectangle. You can even use the Draw Filled option to produce a borderless rectangle. To do this, hold down the Option key as you drag the crossbar.

As with the Line tool, you can draw multiple rectangles and round rectangles by selecting the Draw Multiple option on the Options menu before drawing them. To control the spacing between the multiple images, press the Option key and a number between 1 and 9 before drawing the rectangles with the Draw Multiple option selected. Just as before, the lower the number, the closer the spacing.

Figure 8.7 shows examples of the various types of rectangles that you can draw with these two Paint tools.

To draw a square with either the Rectangle or Round Rectangle tool, hold down the Shift key as you drag the crossbar. Regardless of how small or large you make the sides, all of them will remain equal in length.

The Bucket Tool

The Bucket tool is used to fill closed shapes of all types with a selected pattern. It uses a paint can spilling out paint as its icon. When you select the Bucket tool, the cursor changes to this icon. The paint flows from the very tip of this icon, so you must take care to position this tip inside the figure you want filled.

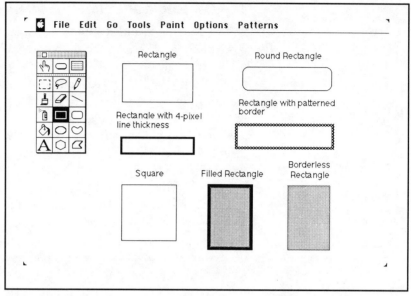

Figure 8.7: Example rectangles of various shapes and types

You cannot use the Bucket tool to replace a previously filled area with a new pattern. To do this, you must choose the new pattern on the Patterns menu, select the filled area with either the Selection tool or the Lasso tool, and then use the Fill option on the Paint menu.

If the figure contains any gaps in its border, the fill pattern will not remain within the image. You can use Fat Bits to check the border of the image to be filled with the Bucket tool. If you use the tool and find that your figure was not closed and the pattern has been added to unwanted areas of the picture, use the Undo option on the Edit menu or press Command-Z right away.

If you double-click on the Bucket tool, the Patterns menu will appear on the screen, detached from the Menu bar (the Patterns menu is a tear-off menu like the Tools menu). To select a new fill pattern, simply click on the square that contains the desired pattern.

Figure 8.8 shows you various shapes filled with the Bucket tool and different patterns selected from the Patterns menu. Notice, in this figure, that you can also fill paint text letters that use the outline style.

The Oval Tool

The Oval tool is used to draw ellipses and circles. When you select it, the cursor changes to a crossbar. Locate the crossbar at one edge of the oval and drag the cursor diagonally. To draw a circle instead of an ellipse, hold down the Shift key as you drag.

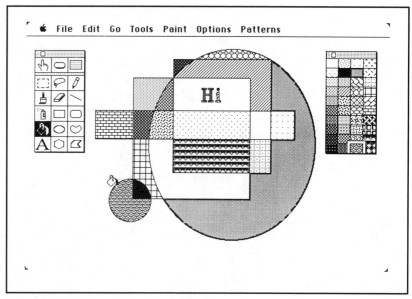

Figure 8.8: Shapes filled with the Bucket tool using various patterns

By using the same key combinations as described for the Rectangle and Round Rectangle tools, you can vary the thickness of the oval's border, use a pattern for the oval's border, draw the oval from the center, draw a filled oval, or draw multiple ovals.

The Curve Tool

The Curve tool is useful for drawing free-form shapes. When you select this tool, the cursor changes to the crossbar. However, unlike when drawing other shapes that use the crossbar cursor, when you drag the crossbar you produce a single line. In this way, the Curve tool acts like the Pencil tool. As you trace the outline with the mouse, the border of the shape is drawn on your screen.

The Curve tool differs from the Pencil tool in that you can vary the thickness of the line drawn, use a pattern as a border, and combine its use with the Draw Filled option on the Options menu. When you draw a shape using the Curve tool with the Draw Filled option selected, the current pattern fills the shape as soon as you connect its starting and ending points. If you do not draw a connecting line to enclose your curved figure, the painting program will automatically draw one for you.

To vary the line thickness of the border, select a new line thickness using the Line Size option on the Options menu before you draw your shape with the Curve tool. To draw a shape with a patterned border, select the pattern and then hold down the Option key as you draw your shape with the Curve tool.

The Paint Text Tool

You are already familiar with the Paint Text tool (which uses the letter A as its icon). You used it to add the field headings for some of the text fields in the Wineries stack. HyperCard treats the text that you add to the background or the card like any other graphic image drawn with the painting program.

Because paint text is treated like any other graphic image produced with the painting program, you cannot use HyperCard's Find option to locate paint text in a particular card as you do to locate text entered into one of the fields with the Browse tool. Limit the use of paint text to card titles and field headings that you will not need to locate with the Find option.

As you know, to add text with the Paint Text tool, you first select the text style you want either by double-clicking on the Paint Text tool, selecting the Text Style option on the Edit menu, or pressing Command-T. This brings up the Text Style dialog box that allows you to select the font, point size, line height, style, and alignment. Once you have selected the text style you want to use, you move the I-Beam cursor to the place where you want the paint text to appear, click the mouse (the I-Beam changes to the flashing text insertion pointer) and begin typing.

Even though paint text is treated like any other part of the picture you create with the painting program, you still do have certain editing features available to you as you are entering the paint text. You can use the Backspace (Delete) key to remove any unwanted characters to the left of the text insertion pointer, and you can press Return to start a new line of text.

To establish what you have typed as part of the card, you must either click the I-Beam cursor in another part of the screen, select another Paint tool, choose the Keep option on the Paint menu, or go to another card in the stack. Until the text is established, you can still change its attributes by returning to the Text Style dialog box and making your desired changes there. As soon as you click on the OK button in the dialog box, the text that you have typed will reflect the changes made there.

Paint text that has been established as part of the card or the card's background cannot be edited like text entered into a HyperCard field. You cannot select text to be edited by dragging the I-Beam cursor over it, nor can you replace text by locating the flashing text insertion pointer and typing over it. Doing this causes the program to literally type over the existing text so that the original characters are hidden from view (not deleted) by the new characters you enter. The only way to edit paint text is to erase it with the Eraser tool and then reenter it with the Paint Text tool.

Once paint text has been established, you can move it to a new part of the card by using the Selection tool or Lasso tool, just as you would with any other image in the card. However, you can quickly select the text you have typed by pressing Command-S as soon as you finish typing it (before you establish it as part of the card or card background).

Changes made to the text style in the Text Style dialog box remain in effect until you either revisit this dialog box and make further modifications there, or quit HyperCard. Whenever you start Hyper-Card, the text style attributes revert to the default settings of plain, 12-point Geneva, left-aligned, with a line height of 16 points.

The Regular Polygon Tool

The Regular Polygon tool allows you to draw various polygons with equal sides. When you select it, the cursor changes to a cross-bar. As you drag the cursor diagonally, the selected polygon is produced from the center, regardless of whether the Draw Centered option is selected.

There are six regular polygons from which to choose: triangle, square, pentagon, hexagon, octagon, and circle. To select a new regular polygon, use the Polygon Sides option on the Options menu or double-click on the Regular Polygon tool. Doing this brings up a dialog box with the six sample polygons (the current selection is highlighted with a rectangle). To select a new shape, click on the desired polygon.

When drawing a polygon, you can rotate the shape by moving the mouse before you release the mouse button. To constrain the rotation to 15-degree increments, hold down the Shift key as you drag the mouse.

When you want to draw a diamond, use the Regular Polygon tool with the square shape selected and rotate it with the mouse. You cannot rotate a square produced with the Rectangle tool into a diamond shape.

Polygons produced with the Regular Polygon tool can be drawn with thicker borders by selecting a thicker line width with the Line Size option on the Options menu. To produce a polygon with a patterned border, choose the desired pattern on the Patterns menu, and then draw the polygon by holding down the Option key as you drag the crossbar with the Regular Polygon tool selected.

You can also draw filled polygons and multiple polygons by using the Draw Filled and Draw Multiple options, respectively, on the Options menu. To vary the spacing between multiple polygons, press the Option key and a number between 1 and 9 (the lower the number, the closer the spacing). To draw a borderless, filled polygon, select the Draw Filled option and hold down the Option key as you drag the crossbar.

Figure 8.9 shows you samples of the six polygons that can be produced with the Regular Polygon tool.

The Polygon Tool

The Polygon Tool is used to produce polygons with unequal (irregular) sides. This tool works very differently from the other Paint tools

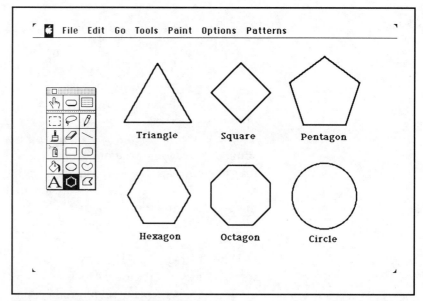

Figure 8.9: Examples of the six polygons that can be produced with the Regular Polygon tool

⊙ If you are drawing a closed polygon, be sure that you don't double-click when you connect the endpoint of the last side to the starting point of the figure. If you do, you will not only end the first polygon but also start a second one. This will also happen if the crossbar is not positioned precisely on the starting point when you click the mouse.

in that you do *not* drag the mouse when drawing with it. Instead, you establish each side of the polygon by clicking the mouse once you have moved the crossbar cursor to the desired position on the screen. As you move the mouse (without dragging it), the Polygon tool draws a line. The end of this line is not positioned until you click and release the mouse button. When you are finished drawing all of the sides of the polygon in this manner, you double-click the mouse to position the last side. However, when you connect the last side to the beginning of the polygon (as is most often the case when creating a closed shape), you only click the mouse a single time to complete the figure.

Just as with regular polygons drawn with the Regular Polygon tool, irregular polygons can be drawn with thicker borders by selecting a thicker line width with the Line Size option on the Options menu.

To constrain the angle of rotation to 15-degree increments when drawing the sides of your polygon, hold down the Shift key when you click the mouse to establish the starting point of the figure. Thereafter, you can release the Shift key and draw the rest of the polygon as you would normally.

To produce an irregular polygon with a patterned border, choose the desired pattern on the Patterns menu, and then draw the polygon by holding down the Option key as you drag the crossbar with the Polygon tool selected.

You can also draw irregular polygons with a fill pattern by using the Draw Filled option on the Options menu. Whenever you use the Polygon tool with the Draw Fill option selected, the program always draws a closed polygon, even if you do not connect the final side to the starting point. If you double-click before you have linked all sides, the program will complete the figure for you and then fill it with the selected pattern.

To draw a borderless filled polygon with the Polygon tool, select the Draw Filled option and hold down the Option key when you click the mouse to establish the starting point of the figure. After you have positioned the starting point, you can release the Option key and proceed drawing the rest of the polygon as you would normally. Just as when drawing a filled irregular polygon with borders, the program will automatically close the figure for you if you double-click before you have linked the end of the last side with the starting point of the figure.

The Painting Program Menus

When you select one of the Paint tools, the Objects menu is replaced with the Paint, Options, and Patterns menus. The options on the Paint, Options, and Patterns menus work in conjunction with the Paint tools on the Tools menu to give you more control over the artwork you add to your stacks.

The Paint Menu

Paint

Select	⌘S
Select All	⌘A
Fill	
Invert	
Pickup	
Darken	
Lighten	
Trace Edges	
Rotate Left	
Rotate Right	
Flip Vertical	
Flip Horizontal	
Opaque	
Transparent	
Keep	⌘K
Revert	

In addition to having power key assignments for all except one option on the Paint menu, four Options menu selections (Grid, Line Size, Draw Centered, and Draw Multiple) and two Patterns menu options (the black and white patterns) have power key assignments (all shown in Table 8.1).

The Paint menu is shown at left. The options on this menu are used to manipulate and make modifications to the graphic images you have created with the various Paint tools. In addition to being able to select Paint menu options by clicking on the desired option on the Paint menu, you can also select any of them (except Keep) by typing a specific letter key as long as the Power Keys option is selected.

To activate the power keys for the painting program, check the Power Keys check box on the User Preferences card in the Home stack or select the Power Keys option on the Options menu (when the Power Keys check box on the User Preferences card has been selected, you see a check mark in front of the Power Keys option on the Options menu). Using power keys can save time in making modifications to your drawings once you become familiar with them. Table 8.1 shows you all the power keys and their functions.

The Select Option

The Select option (power key S or Command-S) lassos the most recently drawn shape. If you have used the Selection tool to select a figure and part of its background, choosing the Select option will lasso it (as though you had pressed the Option key when dragging the Selection tool). If you choose the Selection tool and then use the Select option with no graphic selected in the card, all of the objects in it are lassoed.

The Select All Option

The Select All option (power key A or Command-A) selects the entire picture as shown by the moving dotted line around the edges of the card. This is the same as double-clicking on the Selection tool. If you choose the Select All option in error, either select the Undo option on the Edit menu, press Command-Z, or click the mouse with the crossbar somewhere within the card.

	Key	**Command**
Paint	A	Select All (Command-A)
Menu	D	Darken
	E	Trace Edges
	F	Fill
	H	Flip Horizontal
	I	Invert
	L	Lighten
	O	Opaque
	P	Pickup
	R	Revert
	S	Select (Command-S)
	T	Transparent
	V	Flip Vertical
	[	Rotate Left
	]	Rotate Right
Options	C	Draw Centered (on/off)
Menu	G	Grid (on/off)
	M	Draw Multiple (on/off)
	1, 2, 3, 4, 6, 8	Line Size (number of pixels)
Patterns	B	Black pattern
Menu	W	White pattern

Table 8.1: The power keys for the painting program

The Fill Option

The Fill option (power key F) fills the selected area with whatever pattern is currently selected from the Patterns menu. It works like the Bucket tool except that you must first have selected an area with either the Selection tool or Lasso tool before you use it. You can use the Fill option to insert one fill pattern inside of another to change the fill pattern of a figure.

The Invert Option

The Invert option (power key I) will reverse black to white and white to black in the selected area. Figure 8.10 shows you the effect of using the Invert option on a copy of a bull's-eye design that has been selected with the Lasso tool. Notice that all white pixels have been converted to black and vice versa. While an image is still selected, you can change it back to its original values by selecting the Invert option a second time.

The Pickup Option

The Pickup option (power key P) allows you to pick up the pattern used in one figure so that it will color the selected image. To use the Pickup option, you lasso the image to be colored, drag it so that it is on top of the image containing the pattern you want, select the Pickup option, and drag the selected image off of the patterned image beneath it. The selected image will then be colored with the pattern as the underlying image.

Figure 8.11 illustrates this procedure. To have the wine bottle pick the striped pattern next to it, the bottle is lassoed and then dragged on top of the patterned background. When the Pickup option is selected, the wine bottle becomes striped. Because it is still selected, you can then drag it off the striped pattern.

The Darken and Lighten Options

The Darken (power key D) and Lighten (power key L) options on the Paint menu complement each other. The Darken option adds

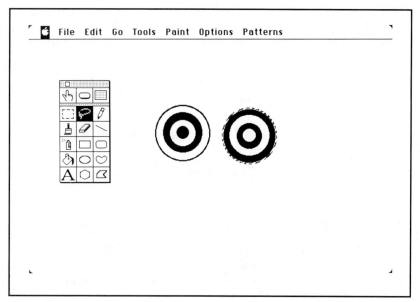

Figure 8.10: Reversing the values in a selected figure with the Invert option

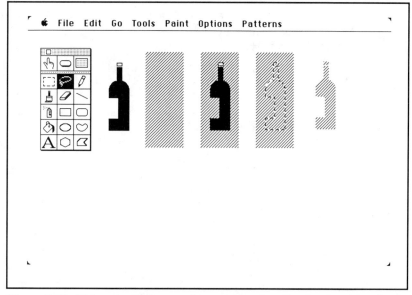

Figure 8.11: Using the Pickup option to color the wine bottle with a background pattern

📝 You can use the Darken and Lighten options to add a mottled effect to black or white images in your card.

random pixels to a selected image, making it a little darker each time you use this option. The Lighten option removes random pixels from the selected image, making it a little lighter each time you use it.

If you use the power keys, you can keep them depressed until the selected image is either dark or light enough for you. If you keep the Darken power key (D) depressed long enough, the image will become totally black. Likewise, if you keep the Lighten power key (L) depressed long enough, the image will become totally white.

The Trace Edges Option

The Trace Edges option (power key E) traces the outline of black areas in a selected image; it transforms the black pixels to white pixels, creating an outline of solid areas. Using the Trace Edges option repeatedly creates multiple outlines of the black areas. You can use this option to transform silhouettes of objects to outline drawings. Figure 8.12 shows you the effect of using the Trace Edges option on a silhouette.

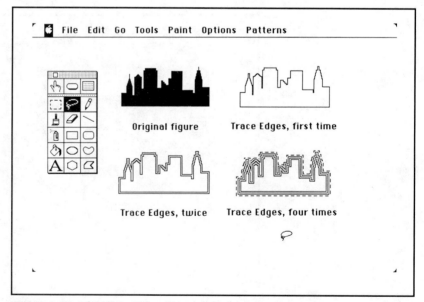

Figure 8.12: Using the Trace Edges option to outline a silhouette

If any part of the selected object moves off the screen (card) when you use either the Rotate Left or Rotate Right option, that part of the image will be permanently lost. You can't retrieve it with the Undo option.

The same warning applies to the Flip Vertical and Flip Horizontal options.

The Rotate Left and Rotate Right Options

The Rotate Left (power key [) and the Rotate Right (power key]) options allow you to rotate a selected object around its center line. The Rotate Left option rotates the object counterclockwise one quarter turn (90 degrees) each time you use it. The Rotate Right option rotates the object clockwise one quarter turn each time you select it. Figure 8.13 shows examples of rotating a selected image with the Rotate Left and Rotate Right options.

The Flip Vertical and Flip Horizontal Options

In addition to being able to rotate a selected image, you can flip the image either vertically or horizontally. To flip an image vertically (turn it upside down), use the Flip Vertical (power key V) option. To flip an object horizontally (turn it over so that it faces the opposite direction), use the Flip Horizontal (power key H) option. When you use either option, the program flips the image around its center line. Figure 8.14 shows examples of using the Flip Vertical and Flip Horizontal options.

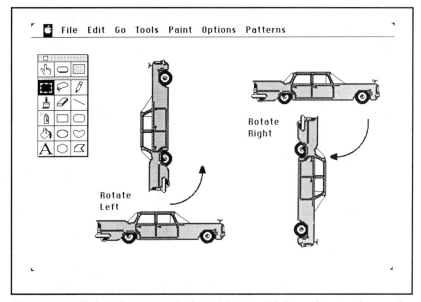

Figure 8.13: Using the Rotate Left and Rotate Right options to change the orientation of selected objects

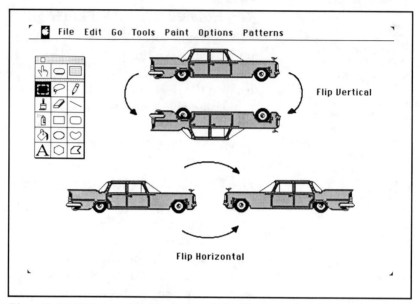

Figure 8.14: Using the Flip Vertical and Flip Horizontal options to change the orientation of selected objects

The Opaque and Transparent Options

As mentioned earlier, graphics added to the card layer of a stack are transparent as far as the graphics placed in the card background are concerned. This means that the background graphics show through and are visible when viewing the card, such as with the Browse tool. Shapes that are drawn on the card layer will then let the background graphics show through in the empty space they enclose. This is illustrated in Figure 8.15, where the cube drawn on the card allows the gray pattern placed in the background to show through. This demonstrates that the card layer is transparent in regard to the background.

You can use the Opaque option (power key O) to make an object in the card level opaque. When an object is made opaque, it blocks out the background beneath it. This is illustrated in Figure 8.16, where the cube was selected and then the Opaque option was used. Notice that you can no longer see the background pattern within the space enclosed by the cube.

You can also use the Transparent option (power key T) to convert an opaque graphic to transparent. In the card layer, this represents a

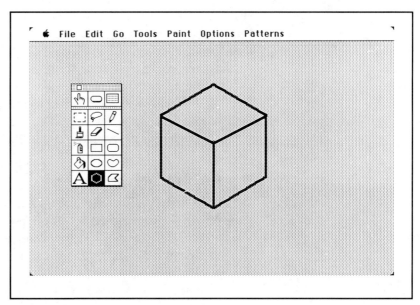

Figure 8.15: Transparent cube drawn on the card allows the pattern in the
background to show through

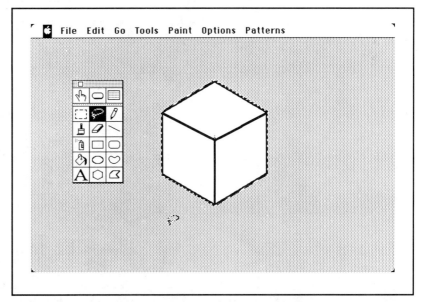

Figure 8.16: The cube made opaque with the Opaque option no longer allows
the background pattern to show through

situation where you want the empty space in the card graphic image to allow the graphics in the background to show through. Figure 8.17 illustrates this situation. There you see the picture of a Macintosh that has been copied from the Art Ideas stack into the card layer. The background of this card contains the same gray pattern as before. Figure 8.18 shows you the same object after it was selected and the Transparent option was selected. The gray background pattern now shows through the empty space in the Macintosh graphic.

The Keep and Revert Options

To save the graphics that you create in a card, you can use the Keep option (Command-K, no power key assignment). Graphics are also automatically saved whenever you select one of the Object tools, go to a new card or stack, or go from the background to the card level (or vice versa).

To return a card to the last saved state, and thus abandon any changes made with the painting program since that time, you can use the Revert option (power key R).

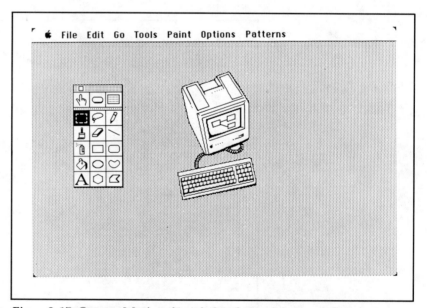

Figure 8.17: Opaque Macintosh copied to the card does not allow the pattern in the background to show through

Options
Grid
FatBits
Power Keys
Line Size...
Brush Shape...
Edit Pattern...
Polygon Sides...
Draw Filled
Draw Centered
Draw Multiple

The Options Menu

The Options menu, shown at left, contains options designed to modify the actions of the various Paint tools on the Tools menu. It also contains the Power Keys option, which allows you to turn on and off the power keys without having to return to the User Preferences card in the Home stack. Most of the options on the Options menu have already been discussed in the context of the Paint tool or tools that they modify. The following discussions recap their use and introduce the Grid option, which has not been discussed previously.

The Grid Option

The Grid option (power key G) constrains the placement of the objects you create with the various Paint tools. After you turn on the Grid option, graphic objects are constrained to an invisible grid composed of lines eight pixels apart vertically and horizontally. You notice the effect of turning on the Grid option in the way that the crossbar cursor behaves. While it is active, it is impossible to locate

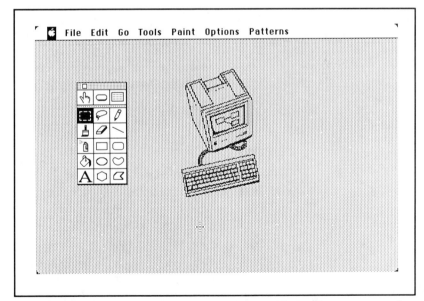

Figure 8.18: The Macintosh made transparent with the Transparent option now allows the background pattern to show through

the crossbar anywhere except on the grid (at the intersection of one of the invisible vertical and horizontal lines on this grid).

Using the Grid option can help you line up objects. However, it can also prevent you from positioning objects exactly where you want them in a card. To turn off the Grid option, you select it a second time (when the Grid option is on, you will see a check mark preceding it on the Options menu).

The FatBits Option

The FatBits option turns on and off Fat Bits, which enlarges part of the picture enough to allow you to work on it a pixel at a time. As you modify the pixels in the enlarged view, you can see the effect in a window (in the lower left corner of the screen) that shows the picture at a normal size. You can move this window to a new part of the screen by dragging on the gray area at the top, or make it disappear by clicking on the Close box.

There are several ways to get in and out of Fat Bits:

- Select the area you want to work on and then select the Fat-Bits option on the Options menu.

- Select the area you want to work on and then press Option-F.

- Select the area you want to work on and then double-click on the Pencil tool.

- Select the Pencil tool, move it to the area where you want to work in Fat Bits, and then press the Command key and click the mouse.

If you do not select an area of the picture before you turn on Fat Bits, the program will enlarge a section of the last area you worked in. To scroll the picture when working in Fat Bits, hold down the Option key (the cursor will change to the Grabber) and move the mouse in the direction you want to move the picture.

To get out of Fat Bits and return to the normal view, use any of the methods for turning on Fat Bits a second time. You can also turn off Fat Bits by moving the tool to the window containing the normal-size version and click on it. When you turn off Fat Bits, this window is automatically closed.

Figure 8.19 shows the effect of using the FatBits option to edit an object, pixel by pixel.

Power Keys and the Power Keys Option

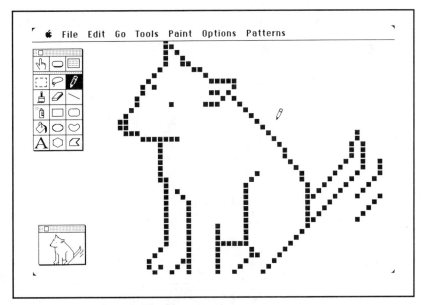 Power keys can save you a lot of time in creating your HyperCard graphics. As you use the various Paint options, experiment with their use. Because almost all of them are mnemonic, they are easy to learn.

Power keys provide keyboard shortcuts for all the Paint menu options except the Keep option (you can use Command-K, however). Power keys can be turned on and off from the User Preferences card in the Home stack. If you turn on power keys by clicking on the check box in this card, they remain on each time you start HyperCard. In such a case, you can use the Power Keys option on the Options menu to turn them off temporarily.

Conversely, you can use the Power Keys option on the Options menu to turn on the power keys temporarily if you have not turned them on in the User Preferences card. However, in this case, the power keys remain in effect only during your current HyperCard work session. When you restart HyperCard and use the painting program, the power keys are no longer turned on.

Refer to Table 8.1 for a complete list of the power keys and the painting program options they activate.

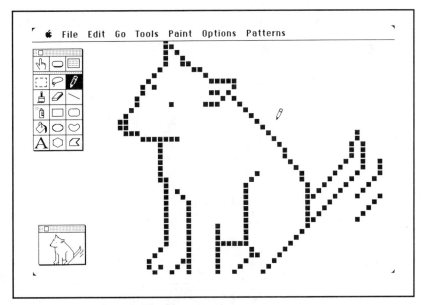

Figure 8.19: Working in Fat Bits

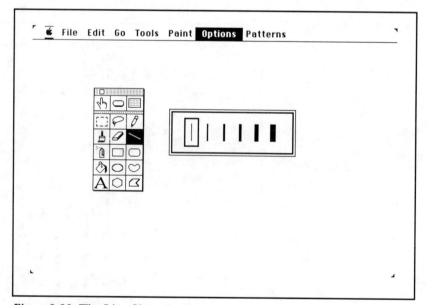

You can bring up the line size selection box by double-clicking on the Line tool as well as by selecting the Line Size option on the Options menu.

The Line Size Option

When you select the Line Size option on the Options menu, a selection box showing you the various line width choices appears on your screen (Figure 8.20). The default choice is the first line thickness, one pixel wide. To select a new line thickness, click on the line that represents that thickness in the selection box. To keep the same line thickness, you must click on the line currently selected (highlighted with a rectangle).

If you have the power keys turned on, you can select new line sizes simply by typing the number that corresponds to the desired thickness in pixels. The choices are 1, 2, 3, 4, 6, and 8 (typing 5 selects 4 pixels, and typing 7 selects 6 pixels).

Selecting a new line size affects the Line, Rectangle, Round Rectangle, Oval, Curve, Regular Polygon, and Polygon tools.

The Brush Shape Option

When you select the Brush Shape option on the Options menu, a selection box showing you the brush shapes and thicknesses available

Figure 8.20: The Line Size selection box

appears on your screen (Figure 8.21). The default choice is the small-est round brush shape. To select a new shape, click on the desired brush shape in the selection box. To keep the same brush shape, you must click on the one that is currently selected (highlighted with a rectangle).

Selecting a new brush shape automatically selects the Brush tool on the Tools menu, if it was not previously selected. Refer to Figure 8.6 to see sample lines created with the various brush shapes of the third largest size.

The Edit Pattern Option

The Edit Pattern option allows you to edit the currently selected pattern on the Patterns menu. When you select this option, it brings up the Pattern Editor, which contains one box that shows you the current pattern and another that allows you to modify it (Figure 8.22). You can also bring up the Pattern Editor by double-clicking on the pattern you wish to modify in the Patterns menu.

To modify the pattern, simply use the mouse to click on and off the pixels that make up the pattern in the box on the left. When you click

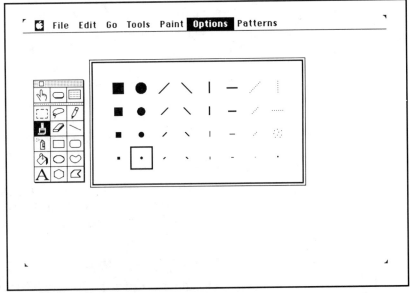

Figure 8.21: The Brush Shape selection box

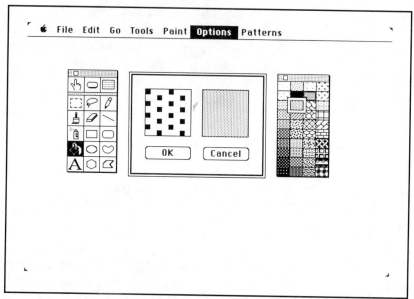

Figure 8.22: The Edit Pattern dialog box

on a black pixel, it turns white, and vice versa. As you make changes to the pixels in a pattern, you see the effect on the overall pattern reflected in the second box on the right. When you have modified the pattern to your satisfaction, click on the OK button. This saves your changes as part of the stack and adds the modified pattern to the Patterns menu. To abandon any changes made to a pattern, click on the Cancel button instead of the OK button in the Pattern Editor. You can edit any of the patterns on the Patterns menu.

You can also use the Edit Pattern option to add a nonstandard pattern to the Patterns menu that you have created on the screen with the Paint tools. To do this, you click on the pattern you want to replace in the Patterns menu, select the Edit Pattern option, click somewhere on the pattern in the screen (the pattern you have created on the screen replaces the selected pattern on the Patterns menu), and then click the OK button on the Pattern Editor.

The Polygon Sides Option

To select a new regular polygon to be drawn with the Regular Polygon tool, you select the Polygon Sides option on the Options menu. This brings up the selection box shown in Figure 8.23 (you can also bring up this selection box by double-clicking on the Regular Polygon tool). To select a new polygon, click on the desired shape. To keep the same shape in effect, you must click on the currently selected shape (highlighted with the rectangle). The square is the default choice.

Selecting a new polygon automatically selects the Regular Polygon tool on the Tools menu, if it was not previously selected. Refer to Figure 8.9 to see sample polygons created with the choices on the Polygon Sides selection box.

The Draw Filled Option

The Draw Filled option uses the currently selected pattern to fill shapes as soon as you have drawn them. The Draw Filled option affects the Rectangle, Round Rectangle, Oval, Curve, Regular Polygon, and Polygon tools. To select the Draw Filled option, select it from the Options menu or double-click on one of the tools affected (except for the Regular Polygon, as doing this brings up the Polygon Sides selection box). When the Draw Filled option is on, a check mark appears before the Draw Filled option on the Options menu

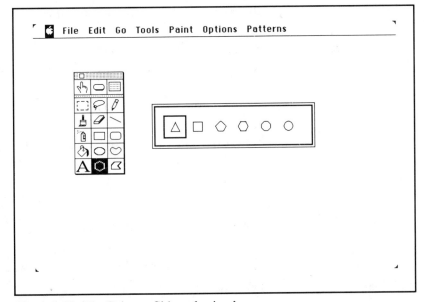

Figure 8.23: The Polygon Sides selection box

and the tools affected appear filled on the Tools menu.

When Draw Filled is on and you use it with the Polygon or Curve tool, the program will automatically finish drawing the last connecting line to enclose the figure if you do not do this yourself before you finish drawing it.

To turn off Draw Filled, either select it a second time on the Options menu or double-click on one of the tools that uses it (other than the Regular Polygon).

The Draw Centered Option

The Draw Centered option (power key C) affects the way you use the Line, Rectangle, Round Rectangle, Oval, Curve, and Polygon tools to draw their respective figures. When Draw Centered is on, instead of drawing the line or shape from one of the edges, you draw it from the center outward (the Line tool draws the line out from both sides of the starting point as you move the crossbar in one direction).

The Regular Polygon tool always draws the polygon from the center outward, whether or not the Draw Centered option is on.

To turn on Draw Centered, select this option on the Options menu (or type C, if the power keys are on). When Draw Centered is on, a check mark appears before the Draw Centered option on the Options menu. To turn it off, select the Draw Centered option or type C (if the power keys are on) a second time.

The Draw Multiple Option

The Draw Multiple option (power key M) draws multiple images with the selected tool as you drag the mouse. The Draw Multiple option affects the Line, Rectangle, Round Rectangle, Oval, and Regular Polygon tools.

To turn on Draw Multiple, select the Draw Multiple option on the Options menu (or type M, if the power keys are on). When Draw Multiple is on, a check mark appears before this option on the Options menu. To turn it off, select the Draw Multiple option or type M (if the power keys are on) a second time.

To control the spacing between the multiple images, you press the Option key and a number between 1 and 9 (the lower the number, the closer the spacing) before you draw with one of the tools.

Importing and Exporting Graphics

You can also press Command-Shift-3 to save the screen image as a MacPaint file. You can save up to ten snapshots of the screen in this manner. These MacPaint files are named sequentially, from Screen 0 to Screen 9. After you have saved the tenth screen file (Screen 9), your Macintosh beeps at you if you try to save any more screens. At that point you must rename some of the screen files or erase some of them before you can save any more screen snapshots.

If the program does not have an option for saving the image as a MacPaint file, try bringing it into HyperCard through the Clipboard (or Scrapbook). To add it to the Clipboard, use the program's commands for selecting the image you want imported, and choose the Copy option on the Edit menu (Command-C). Then open the HyperCard stack you want to import the image into, go to the card where you want it added, and select the Paste option on the Edit menu (Command-V). Remember to select the Background option on the Edit menu, if you want the imported image to be added to the background of the card, before you select the Paste option.

In addition to generating graphics for your stacks with the Hyper-Card painting program, you can also import graphics that have been created with other programs. These can include original images drawn with other graphics programs (such as SuperPaint or GraphicWorks) or digitized images that have been generated by a scanner or video camera attached directly to the Macintosh.

To bring graphics generated with another program into a stack, you can either use the Import Paint option on the File menu or bring them in through the Clipboard or Scrapbook. To use the Import Paint option, the graphics file must have been saved as a MacPaint file.

You can also export the graphics that you generate in the Hyper-Card painting program. When you export HyperCard graphics, you use the Export Paint option on the File menu. Card graphics saved using this option are saved as a MacPaint file, which can be used by any program that can read this file format.

The Import Paint Option

The Import Paint option on the File menu enables you to add images to your stacks that have been saved as MacPaint files. Many graphics programs include an option to save the picture as a Mac-Paint document.

To use the Import Paint option on the File menu, you must have first selected one of the Paint tools. As soon as you choose the Import Paint option on the File menu, HyperCard presents you with the standard file dialog box. From here, you select the MacPaint document you wish to import by clicking on its name and then clicking on the Open button (or by double-clicking on its name). HyperCard then pastes the imported image into the current card, starting from the upper left corner of the card.

If you are in the card's background when you import the image, it is added to the background of the card. If you are at the card layer when you use this option, the image is added to the card only. Once the image has been imported, it is treated like any graphics generated with the HyperCard painting program. This means that you can use any of the Paint tools and painting program menu options to enhance or make changes to it.

Because no image can extend beyond the confines of a single card, you should take care that the image to be imported can be accommodated on a single card before you import it with the Import Paint option. If necessary, reduce the image or crop it before saving it as a MacPaint file. Also be sure that the image is positioned starting in the upper left corner of the window before you save it. If any part of the imported image extends beyond the borders of the card, it will be lost when it is brought into your stack.

Figure 8.24 shows you a photograph that was digitized with an Abaton scanner, saved as a MacPaint file, and then imported into a HyperCard stack using the Import Paint option. Notice that the imported image is positioned starting in the upper left corner of the card.

The Export Paint Option

You can also use the Command-Shift-3 key sequence to save the image of the current card as a MacPaint file. However, when you use this key combination rather than the Export Paint option, the resulting MacPaint file will include the HyperCard Menu bar and the Tools and Patterns tear-off menus if they are on the screen when you use the command. However, menu options on the Hyper-Card menus cannot be captured as part of screen snapshots.

The Export Paint option allows you to save any card in a Hyper-Card stack as a MacPaint file. This option is available only when you have selected one of the Paint tools. When you choose the Export Paint option, the program brings up a standard save dialog box. There, you enter the name of the file you want the card graphics saved under and click on the Save button (or press Return).

When you use the Export Paint option, the image of the full-size card is saved (even if you are working in Fat Bits at the time you use it). If you are in the background of the card, only the graphics seen in the background are saved in the resulting MacPaint file. If you want all of the graphics in the card saved in this file, make sure that you are at the card level before you use it.

The HyperCard Menu bar displayed at the top of the card is not saved as part of the MacPaint file. Also, if the Tools and Patterns tear-off menus are on the screen at the time you use the Export Paint option, they will not be saved as part of the resulting MacPaint file.

The image of the card created when you use the Export Paint option can be used in any program that can import or directly use MacPaint files. Of course, the resulting MacPaint file contains only the graphic image of the card; none of the fields, buttons, or scripts used in the card are transferred to it.

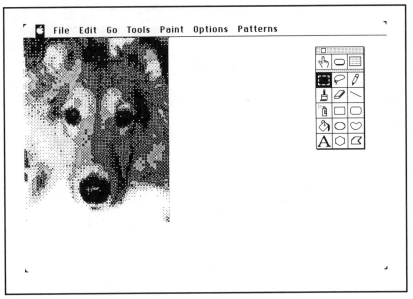

Figure 8.24: Digitized image imported into a HyperCard stack

Summary

HyperCard's painting program equips you with a complete set of graphic tools for use when you build your own stacks. Although graphics may not be an integral part of every stack you create, you will find few occasions when a stack calls for no graphic elements. As you have seen, the painting program is versatile enough to be applied to a wide variety of tasks—anywhere from designing a completely customized background for a stack to adding a simple graphic element to a particular card.

With the painting program, your exploration of authoring Hyper-Card stacks comes to an end. Ahead, in Part III, you will be introduced to HyperTalk and how to use it to create scripts for the buttons, fields, cards, backgrounds, and stacks that you create. HyperTalk scripts give you greater control over HyperCard than is possible when using only the menu commands. Although it is not necessary to use HyperTalk to use HyperCard, knowing its commands and how to apply them will extend the range of what you can do with the program, giving you more possibilities than exist presently.

As you will see, HyperTalk is an easy language to master, even if you have no previous programming experience. It is patterned after English and includes many simple commands that perform sophisticated tasks. Because this is the case, you will soon be writing scripts that accomplish complex and varied tasks.

In the next chapter, you will begin your exploration of HyperTalk. There, you will be introduced to its overall capabilities and basic structure and syntax.

PART III

Opening Up the Possibilities with HyperTalk

Getting Acquainted
with HyperTalk

When you enter a HyperTalk command into the Message box and execute it, the command is acted upon just as it would be if it had been entered as part of a script attached to one of the objects of the stack. You can only execute single HyperTalk commands in this way, and any command entered into the Message box is not saved as part of the stack (it will be lost as soon as you enter a new command in the Message box or end your Hyper-Card work session). Therefore, although you can use the Message box to test the effect of a HyperTalk command, most often you will be using these commands in scripts attached to a particular HyperCard object.

YOU HAVE ALREADY HAD A LITTLE EXPERIENCE with using HyperTalk. In your first encounter, you entered the HyperTalk Go and Find commands directly into the Message box. In your second encounter, you edited a few of the button scripts for the Wineries and Wine Tour stacks.

When you used the Message box, you entered a single HyperTalk command such as *go first* or *find "ex" in field 1* into it, and each command was interpreted and executed as soon as you pressed Return. When you edited the button scripts, you worked with a series of commands such as

```
on mouseUp
    go to card id 4567 in stack "Wineries"
end mouseUp
```

in the script that you edited. Because these scripts were attached to specific buttons, the commands they contained were not interpreted and executed until you clicked on those buttons.

Although your limited experience with HyperTalk has hardly made you an "expert" in its use, it has given you some understanding of what specific commands can do and how they are used. Before you go on and add to this experience, you should become more acquainted with how the HyperTalk language works.

The HyperTalk Language

HyperTalk is a computer language that is unique to HyperCard. This is not to say that it has no similarities to other computer languages, nor does it mean that HyperTalk is unlike the spoken and

HyperTalk's syntax is, in fact, very English-like. Statements in HyperTalk often involve what English would identify as verbs and objects (because you are entering commands, they seldom require subjects), as in *go to first card*. Some HyperTalk scripts will seem terse when compared to written English, as they may dispense with some of the adjectives and prepositions you normally include. However, in such cases, the meaning of the script will still be intelligible even if the expression sounds a little stilted, as in *go Next* instead of *go to the Next card*.

written language that you use to communicate. It does mean, however, that HyperTalk has its own vocabulary and syntax (the way it puts the vocabulary together to make meaningful statements), which you must learn before you can use it effectively.

HyperTalk contrasts with traditional programming languages for the Macintosh in that you do not use HyperTalk to create stand-alone programs. The scripts you write in HyperTalk must be attached to some part of a stack created in HyperCard. You cannot execute these commands without opening the stack and using the objects they are attached to, and you cannot open the stack without the HyperCard program.

Because of this, HyperTalk tends to be more modular because each script is developed for a specific component of the stack. Also, HyperTalk performs many of the complex tasks (such as screen handling) with the use of simple commands, where traditional programming languages would require the development of long and involved programming routines to accomplish the same thing.

The modularity of the language and the inclusion of high-level commands not only cut down significantly on development time, but also reduce the chances of error. And because you are not creating programs that must perform all the tasks required by the application from beginning to end, you will not find learning how to create scripts in HyperTalk to be nearly as demanding as learning how to create a program in a traditional programming language.

HyperTalk Scripts

Scripts are sets of HyperTalk commands that perform a desired action or sequence of actions when certain events happen (the object they are attached to is selected or a particular condition is met). The objects that you can attach a script to include buttons, fields, cards, backgrounds, and the stacks themselves. The HyperTalk commands that you include in a script are determined by what you want to have happen when the object is selected and how you want this action to affect the entire stack (or all stacks in the application).

Recall that the most basic script is one attached to a button in the card or background that takes you to a specific card when you click on it. This script is written automatically for you if you use the

LinkTo option on the Button Information dialog box and then go to the card you want the button linked to.

When you examined one of the button scripts created in this way, you saw that the HyperTalk script consisted of a simple Go command using the ID number of the card, as in

```
go to card id 2870
```

attached to the Opening card button in the Wine Tour stack.

The Script Editor

You can use the Script Editor to add HyperTalk scripts to any object. Simply select the object by choosing its option on the Objects menu (Button Info, Field Info, Card Info, Bkgnd Info, or Stack Info) and then click on the Script button to get to the Script Editor. Remember that the user level on the User Preferences card must be set to Scripting to have the Script button active in the dialog boxes. You can get directly to the script of a button or field in a card by holding down the Shift key and double-clicking on it.

Although you can use the LinkTo option to create simple Hyper-Talk button scripts that link the button to a particular card in a stack, you also learned that it is possible to use the Script Editor to make modifications to a script. By selecting the Script button in the object's dialog box, you get to the Script Editor, a window that allows you to enter and edit the HyperTalk commands that make up that object's script.

Recall the changes you made to the button script for the Hacienda button in the Wine Tour stack and the Map button in the Wineries stack. Originally, the scripts for both these buttons contained simple Go commands created with the LinkTo option. The Hacienda button took you to the Hacienda Winery card in the Wineries stack with the script

```
on mouseUp
    go to card id 3234 of stack "Wineries"
end mouseUp
```

and the Map button took you directly to the Opening card in the Wine Tour stack with the script

```
on mouseUp
    go to card id 2870 of stack "Wine Tour"
end mouseUp
```

By editing their button scripts with the Script Editor, you modified their functioning. First, you changed the script of the Hacienda button in the Wine Tour stack, adding a new command line so that it read as follows:

```
on mouseUp
  push card
  go to card id 3234 of stack "Wineries"
end mouseUp
```

(Remember the *push card* command marks the map card [containing this button] for quick retrieval, before the Go command that takes you to the card with the ID 3234 in the Wineries stack.) Later, you changed the script of the Map button in the Wineries stack so that it read as follows:

```
on mouseUp
  pop card
end mouseUp
```

(Remember that the *pop card* script returns you to the last card that was marked for retrieval with a *push card* command. Assuming that you click on the Hacienda button before you click on this button, HyperCard will return you to the map card that contains the Hacienda button.)

Using the Script Editor

You got a feel for using the Script Editor when you modified the button scripts for these two buttons. Now it is time to further explore its capabilities. Figure 9.1 shows you the edited script for the Hacienda button in the Wine Tour stack. The Script Editor in this figure includes the window with the vertical scroll bar as well as the four buttons (Find, Print, OK, and Cancel) at the bottom of the screen.

To enter new text in the window, position the I-Beam cursor where you want to begin entering text and click the mouse button. Then type the text beginning at the flashing text insertion pointer. If you make a typing mistake, you can use the Backspace (Delete) key to rub out characters to the left of the flashing text insertion pointer.

When editing text in the window, you can select text just as you do when editing a HyperCard field. Once you click and drag over a portion of text to select, you can replace it simply by typing over it or remove it by pressing the Backspace (Delete) key.

In addition to moving the I-Beam cursor and clicking the mouse to position the flashing text insertion pointer in a particular place in the text, you can also use the arrow keys on the keyboard to move it. Press the ← and → keys to move the pointer one space to the left and right on a line. Press the ↑ and ↓ keys to move it up and down a line of text.

When you are working with the Script Editor, none of the Hyper-Card menus, including the Edit menu, are available (the Macintosh beeps at you if you try to select any of them). Although you cannot use the Cut, Copy, and Paste options by selecting them on the Edit menu, you can, nevertheless, still use them by pressing their keyboard equivalents. To cut the text that you have selected, press Command-X. To copy a selected portion of text, press Command-C. Then, to paste the text that has been cut or copied into the Clipboard at the position of the flashing text insertion pointer, press Command-V.

When your scripts are longer than will fit in a single window view, you use the vertical scroll bar to position the cursor at commands you want to edit or add to. To scroll the script up (to go toward the end), drag the Scroll box down or click on the down-arrow button in the

When you click on the OK or Cancel button in the Script Editor to return to the current card, anything that you have copied to the Clipboard (using either Command-X or Command-C) remains in it. This means that you can copy or move a script between objects in the same or a new stack by going to that object, activating the Script Editor, and pressing Command-V to paste it in its new position.

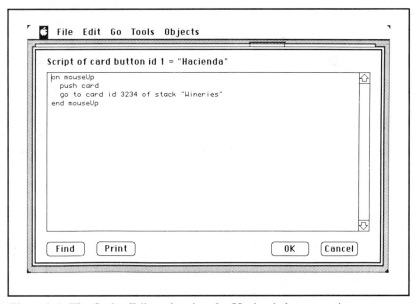

Figure 9.1: The Script Editor showing the Hacienda button script

vertical scroll bar. To scroll the script down (to go toward the beginning), drag the Scroll box up or click on the up-arrow button in the vertical scroll bar.

You can also use the Find button to locate a particular place in the text of a script. When you click on the Find button at the bottom of the screen (or press Command-F), a small box appears on the screen (Figure 9.2). You type in the text you wish to locate and then either click on the OK button or press Return. When HyperCard locates the first occurrence of the text, it highlights it in the script (Figure 9.3). To locate a subsequent occurrence of the search text, press Command-G. If no occurrence of the search text is found, the Macintosh will beep.

You can also enter search text into the Find box by selecting it in the script and then pressing Command-H before you click on the Find button or press Command-F. This places the highlighted text in the Find box for you. When you click on the OK button, HyperCard will attempt to locate a subsequent occurrence of this search text.

You can also print the text of the script from the Script Editor by clicking on the Print button (next to the Find button at the bottom of the screen) or by pressing Command-P. If you have selected part

This technique of entering selected text from the script into the Find box without having to type it does not work if you click on the Find button or press Command-F before you highlight the text and press Command-H. You must select the text and press Command-H before you use the Find button or Command-F.

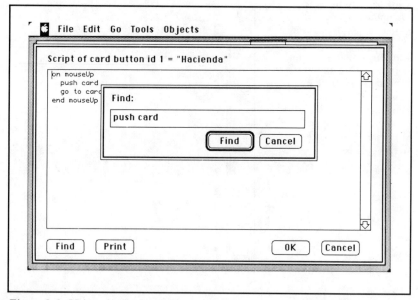

Figure 9.2: Using the Script Editor's Find option to locate specific text in the script

of the text of the script, only that text will be printed when you use this option. If you have not selected any of the text, the entire script will be printed when you use this option. The printout of the script will contain a header showing the current date and time and identifying the object whose script is printed. For example, if you printed the script of the Hacienda button at 9:15 on July 4, 1988, the header would read as follows:

7/4/88 9:15 AM   Script of card button id 1 = "Hacienda"

Below this header the entire text or selected text of the script would be printed.

When you've finished entering the HyperTalk commands that make up the script or editing the existing script, you save it by clicking on the OK button. If you wish to abandon the changes you've made to a script, click on the Cancel button instead.

The Structure of a Script

Even with the simple scripts you have been working with, you may have noticed that the command or commands that are placed

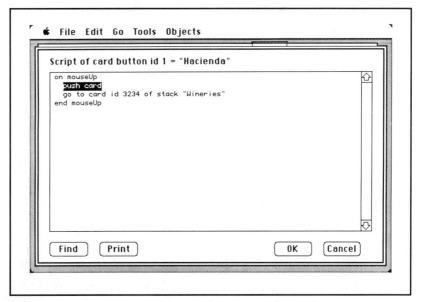

Figure 9.3: The first occurrence of the search text located in the script

A *loop* is simply a group of instructions that are performed as long as a particular condition exists. For example, the commands *push card* and *go to card id 3234 of stack "Wineries"* in the script for the Hacienda button are performed only when (*on*) the mouseUp condition exists (that is, the mouse button is released). Although most HyperTalk loops are begun with *on* followed by the name of the message (as in *on mouseUp*), the If and Repeat commands are also used to begin loops that are placed—or nested—within an *on* loop. All loops are terminated with *end* followed by the name of the message or condition (as in *end mouseUp*, *end if*, or *end repeat*).

between the *on mouseUp* and *end mouseUp* instructions are indented. This represents a common practice in computer programming, whereby all instructions within a loop are indented to the same level. This makes it easy to tell which commands are performed when a particular condition exists.

HyperCard makes it easy to follow this convention. When you enter a command line and press Return, the program automatically indents the next line one tab stop. If you enter an *end* statement, then when you press Return, the program automatically outdents this line so that it is flush left (aligned with the *on* statement that begins the loop). You can also use the Tab key to have HyperCard reformat the script, if need be. The Script Editor's automatic formatting helps ensure that all loops are closed (every *on*, *if*, or *repeat* statement has a complementary *end* statement somewhere later on in the script).

When entering HyperTalk scripts, keep the following rules in mind:

- Each command is entered on its own line terminated by a return (pressing the Return key).

- If a command statement is too long to fit on one line of the Script Editor, press Option-Return to wrap the continuation of the statement to the next line with a soft return. The presence of a soft return at the end of a line is marked by the ⌐ symbol.

- Command statements are always entered in the order in which they are to be executed by HyperTalk.

As you indent successive levels of command statements in more complex scripts, you will have to use the soft return (Option-Return) more often to wrap lines without terminating them. Be careful that you do not press Return unless you mean to terminate a command statement. Although you cannot see a return in the Script Editor window, HyperTalk will treat each return that you enter (by pressing the Return key) as the end of a command statement.

Message Handlers

You have already learned about the formatting conventions used by loops in a HyperTalk script. Now you need to consider how the scripts that you enter with the Script Editor are processed. As you know, scripts are attached to HyperCard objects such as buttons, fields, backgrounds, cards, and even stacks themselves. Any of these objects may receive different messages from HyperCard or from other objects. The part of the script that tells the object what it is to do in response to the message is called the *message handler*.

The message handler has several parts to it. The *on* signals the beginning of the message handler. It is always followed by the name of the message. Following this are the individual command lines containing all the instructions to be sent as part of this message. After the listing of the commands, an *end* statement repeating the name of the message is entered on its own line of the Script Editor. This statement signals the end of the message handler.

For the Hacienda button shown in Figure 9.4, *mouseUp* is the name of the message. The *on mouseUp* statement signals the beginning of the message handler and identifies the name of the message. There are two HyperTalk commands (each on its own line, terminated by a return) that are sent as part of the message when you release the mouse button (*on mouseUp*) after clicking on the Hacienda button. The *end mouseUp* statement that follows then signals the end of the message handler.

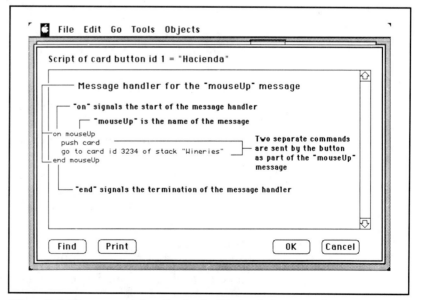

Figure 9.4: The message handler in the Hacienda button script

Message Inheritance

HyperCard uses message handlers to know what part of the script is in control at any one time. A script can contain several message handlers. When the message is sent, HyperCard matches the name of the message with the objects in a stack. When it finds an object that contains a matching message handler, it acts upon the command statements contained within that message.

For example, your Hacienda button contains the *on mouseUp...end mouseUp* message handler. Suppose you have the Browse tool over this button and you click the mouse. As soon as you release the mouse button, a mouseUp message is sent. HyperCard is then able to match this mouseUp message with the *on mouseUp* message handler in the button script. Once this is done, the commands *push card* and *go to card id 3234 of stack "Wineries"* are executed, and the message handler is terminated with the *end mouseUp* statement.

However, if HyperCard does not find a message handler that matches the message sent in the script of one object (there may be no script attached to it or no matching message handlers in it), it will try to find a matching message handler among the other objects in the stack. When HyperCard *passes* a message to new objects, it does so in a definite order or hierarchy. If the program finds an object higher up in the hierarchy whose script contains a matching message handler, the program acts on the commands it contains. If the program sends the message all the way up the hierarchy and finds no matching message handler, nothing happens.

For instance, none of the objects in your Wine Tour and Wineries stacks contain an *on mouseDown* (mouseDown is the opposite of mouseUp) message handler. Therefore, when you press the mouse button down, although this does send a message (the mouse is down) up the hierarchy, nothing happens because HyperCard finds no matching message handler in any of the objects.

The order of message inheritance is illustrated in Figure 9.5. Notice that button scripts, field scripts, menu options, and commands entered into the Message box are on the same level—the bottom level of the hierarchy. Messages are passed from any of these to the card script, to the background script, to the stack script, and so on up the hierarchy, until they finally reach the HyperCard program level.

External resources can be added to a HyperCard stack using a resource utility program (such as Icon Extractor). When you add such resources to a stack, you can put resource commands in a script or enter them in the Message box. The Message Inheritance diagram in Figure 9.5 shows you that if a message is not found in the stack script, the program searches the stack resource, then the Home script, and finally, the Home resource. If the message is not matched in either external resource, HyperCard will give you an error message letting you know that it doesn't understand the command.

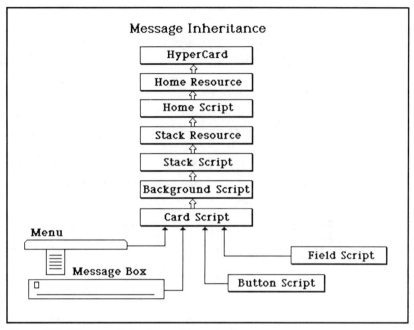

Figure 9.5: Message Inheritance hierarchy

As you can see from this diagram, card scripts are more general than button or field scripts, background scripts are more general than card scripts, and so forth up the hierarchy. This means that if you wanted the same command or group of commands to be acted upon whenever you used any of the buttons in a card, you would attach the script to the card rather than to each button in the card. Later on, you will look more at the best place to attach scripts as you explore the use of specific HyperTalk commands and functions.

How Messages Enter the Hierarchy

Now that you know how messages are inherited, you may wonder what determines the level at which they enter the hierarchy. Quite simply, it is the location of the Browse tool. If the Browse tool is located on a button and you click and release the mouse, the mouseUp message is matched against the message handlers in the script for that button. If no *on mouseUp* message handler is found in that script, the mouseUp message is passed up the hierarchy.

If the Browse tool is located on a field when you click and release the mouse button, the mouseUp message is matched against the message handlers in the script for that field. Again, if no matching *on mouseUp* message handler is found there, this message is passed up the hierarchy. Finally, if the Browse tool is not located on a button or field when you click the mouse and release, the mouseUp message is matched against the message handlers in the script for that card. If none match the *on mouseUp*, it is passed up the hierarchy.

To get a feel for how this works, you can try the following exercise. Start HyperCard and make sure that the user level is set to Scripting on the User Preferences card. Then open your Wineries stack and take the following steps.

1. **Select the Last option on the Go menu (or press Command-4).**

   This takes you to the Gundlach-Bundschu winery card.

2. **Move the Browse tool to the left of the Map button (using the Compass icon) and click the mouse.**

Nothing happens when you locate the Browse tool on the card where there is no button and you click and release the mouse button. This is because the mouseUp message enters the hierarchy at the card level and there is no card script that contains an *on mouseUp* message handler.

3. **Move the Browse tool to the Home button at the bottom of the card and click the mouse.**

   This takes you to the Home Card.

This time, with the Browse tool on a button, the mouseUp message enters the hierarchy at the button level. This message is matched against the script for that button and, when the *on mouseUp* message handler is located, the Go command that takes you to the Home Card is executed.

4. **Select the Back option on the Go menu (or press Command- ~).**

   This returns you to the last card in the Wineries stack.

Now see what happens when you add a script to the Gundlach-Bundschu card, which will take you to the Home Card when you click the mouse in this card.

5. **Select the Card Info option on the Objects menu.**

    This brings you to the Card Information dialog box.

6. **Click on the Script button.**

    This takes you to the Script Editor.

7. **Type *on mouseUp* and press Return.**

    The cursor moves down to the next line and is automatically indented.

8. **Type *go home* and press Return.**

    The cursor moves down to the next line and is automatically indented.

9. **Type *end mouseUp* and press Return.**

    The cursor moves down to the next line, and the *end mouseUp* statement is aligned with the *on mouseUp* statement above it.

10. **Click on the OK button.**

    This returns you to the Gundlach-Bundschu card.

11. **Move the Browse tool so that it is once again located to the left and outside of the Map button, and click the mouse.**

    This takes you back to the Home Card.

    Clicking on this part of the card performs the same action as clicking on the Home button. In fact, clicking on the mouse anywhere in the card, as long as the Browse tool is not located on a field or button, will now execute the command to take you to the Home Card. Where previously clicking the mouse on the card sent a mouseUp message that was ignored and did nothing (because it could not be matched against an *on mouseUp* message handler in the card and on up the hierarchy), clicking on it now executes the *go home* command because the mouseUp message matches the *on mouseUp* message handler that you entered in the card script.

    Before going on, you should now delete the card script from this card so that you can use it without having to worry about suddenly being taken to the Home Card when you meant to click on a field or a button.

12. **Select Back from the Go menu, or press Command-~ .**

    This returns you to the first card of the Wineries stack.

13. **Select the Card Info option on the Objects menu.**

14. **Click on the Script button.**

15. **Drag the I-Beam cursor so that all the text of the card script is selected, and press the Backspace (Delete) key.**

    This deletes the entire script in the Script Editor.

16. **Click on the OK button.**

    This removes the script from this card.

System Messages

HyperCard is constantly sending messages to specific objects in the current card about the current state of affairs. These messages are referred to as *system messages*, as they keep a close watch on the current state of the Macintosh system as a whole. A great many of these system messages inform HyperCard about the state of the mouse. In addition, there are system messages that inform the program about specific keys that have been pressed; when particular HyperCard objects have been created or deleted, entered or exited; when particular menu options have been selected; as well as when the program itself has been started, suspended, resumed, or exited.

Any of the system messages can be used as a message handler in a HyperTalk script. Let's go on and examine these system messages a little more closely.

Mouse System Messages

Perhaps the most common type of system messages concern the state of the mouse. You are already familiar with the most common mouse system message, mouseUp. In addition, there are several more "mouse" states, which generate their own system message. The following mouse-related system messages are possible:

Message	Meaning
mouseDown	The mouse button has been depressed.
mouseStillDown	The mouse button is being held down.
mouseUp	The mouse button has been released.

HyperCard even sends a stream of idle system messages when nothing else is happening on the screen. As soon as something happens, such as your clicking the mouse, a set of mouse-related messages reporting on that condition is sent. As soon as these have been sent, the program returns to sending another stream of idle messages until something else that generates a new system message happens.

mouseEnter	The cursor has entered a field or button.
mouseWithin	The cursor is located within a field or button.
mouseLeave	The cursor has left a field or button.

As you can see, the simple action of clicking on a button in Hyper-Card generates three distinct system messages: mouseDown when you press down the mouse button, mouseStillDown when you hold the button down (even for an instant), and mouseUp when you release the button. In addition, system messages are generated when you use the mouse to enter a button or field, when the cursor is located within a button or field, and when you use the mouse to move the cursor out of a field.

To get a feel for how these system messages work, try the following exercise.

1. **Select the New Stack option on the File menu.**

   This takes you to the new file dialog box.

2. **Enter *Mouse Test* as the name of the stack.**

3. **Click on the *Copy current background* check box to uncheck it.**

4. **Click on the New Button. You will see a new card with a blank background.**

5. **Select New Button on the Objects menu.**

6. **Select Button Info on the Objects menu (or double-click the New Button).**

7. **Type *Beep Button* as the Button Name.**

   This brings up the Button Info dialog box.

8. **Click on the Shadow radio button.**

9. **Click on the Script button.**

   This takes you to the Script Editor.

Notice that HyperCard has already entered the *on mouseUp* and *end mouseUp* statements and has located the flashing text insertion pointer at the beginning of an indented line between them.

10. Enter *Beep*.

This command instructs HyperCard to sound the bell.

11. Click on the OK button.

This returns you to the card where you see the new shadow button.

12. Select the Browse tool on the Tools menu.

Now test the Beep Button.

13. Move the Browse tool on the Beep Button and click the mouse.

When you click and release the mouse button, the mouseUp message matches the *on mouseUp* message handler and the Macintosh beeps at you. Now edit the message handler so that it uses *on mouseStillDown*, instead of *on mouseUp*.

14. Select the Button tool on the Tools menu.

15. Hold down the Shift key and double-click on the button.

This selects the button and takes you directly to the Script Editor.

16. Move the I-Beam cursor to the *U* in mouseUp and drag it to the right until *Up* is highlighted.

17. Type *StillDown*.

The line now reads *on mouseStillDown*.

18. Repeat steps 16–17 for the last line of the script containing the end statement.

It should read *end mouseStillDown* when you are finished.

19. Click on the OK button.

20. Select the Browse tool on the Tools menu.

Click on the Beep Button and hold down the mouse button a little while before releasing it. This time the Macintosh continues to beep all the time the mouse button is depressed (on mouseStillDown). It stops beeping as soon as you release the mouse (on mouseUp). Now the message *on mouseStillDown* activates the Beep command, and the *on mouseUp* message terminates it.

Try modifying the script of the Beep Button so that the Macintosh beeps at you when you move the cursor somewhere within the button.

21. **Select the Button tool on the Tools menu.**

22. **Move the Arrow pointer to the Beep Button, hold down the Shift key, and double-click the mouse.**

23. **Move the I-Beam cursor to the *S* in mouseStillDown and drag the mouse to the right to highlight *StillDown*.**

24. **Type *Enter*.**

    The line now reads *on mouseEnter*.

25. **Repeat steps 23–24 for the last line containing the end statement.**

    It should read *end mouseEnter* when you are finished.

26. **Click on the OK button.**

27. **Select the Browse tool.**

Now when you move the Browse tool anywhere within the boundary of the Beep Button, the Macintosh beeps. The *mouseEnter* message is matched against the *on mouseEnter* message handler entered in the button script as soon as the Browse tool enters the buttons and the Beep command is executed.

On your own, go ahead and see what happens when you change the message handler for the Beep Button script so that it uses the mouseWithin and the mouseLeave messages. To do this, first edit the button script so the message handler reads *on mouseWithin...end mouseWithin*. Then, after testing out the button, change it to *on mouseLeave...end mouseLeave* and test out this script variation.

Keyboard System Messages

HyperCard sends messages to see whether the Tab, Return, or Enter key has been pressed. Remember that pressing these keys within a text field performs certain actions: the Tab key moves the flashing text insertion pointer to the beginning of the next field, the Return key moves it down to the next line within that field, and the Enter key closes the field by adding any new or edited text.

Although you cannot change these field actions by adding a message handler to a field script, you can add such message handlers to other objects in the stack. For example, you could add a card script containing a message handler that tells HyperCard what to do if the Tab key is pressed when the Browse tool is somewhere on the card

You can use specific arrow key messages (arrowKey left, arrowKey right, arrowKey up, and arrowKey down) as commands to press that key in scripts that are activated by other message handlers. For instance, you could add the following stack script:

```
on mouseUp
   arrowKey left
end mouseUp
```

This script causes the program to press the ← key (taking you to the previous card) when the mouse button is released in a card outside of any text field.

(outside any of the text fields). When you add message handlers for these keys, their messages are entered as tabKey, returnKey, and enterKey.

In addition to these keys, you can add message handlers to scripts that check for an arrowKey message, which is sent whenever you press one of the four arrow keys (↑, ↓, →, and ←). Unfortunately, you cannot add message handlers that differentiate between pressing a particular arrow key. This means that you can't add a message handler that will perform a specific HyperTalk command only when the ← key has been pressed, as opposed to the → key.

Object System Messages

System messages are generated when you create or delete a HyperCard object such as a field, button, card, or background. This means that you can add message handlers to scripts that check for the addition or deletion of a particular object in a field. For example, you could add a stack script that performs a particular action when a new card is created for the stack. This script might include the HyperTalk command to add the current date to a particular field in the card, as follows:

```
on newCard
   put the long date into field 3
end newCard
```

Likewise, when a card is deleted, you can have HyperCard perform a specific action such as informing you of the number of cards remaining in the stack in the Message box, as follows:

```
on deleteCard
   put the number of cards – 1 into the message box
end deleteCard
```

When you add message handlers that check for the addition or deletion of objects in a stack, you name the message by adding *new* to the name of the object that is being created and *delete* to the name of the object that is being deleted (field, button, card, background, or stack). When a new field is added, the message is newField. When it is deleted, the message is deleteField. To create the appropriate message handler, you simply preface the message name with *on*, as in *on newField...end newField, on deleteField...end deleteField*, and so on.

System messages are also generated when you open and close an object such as a field, card, or stack (this does not apply to a button). When you go to a new card, field, or stack, an openCard, openField, or openStack system message is generated. So too, when you leave a field (by pressing the Tab key, clicking outside the field, or selecting a new Object tool on the Tools menu) or go to a new card or stack, a closeField, closeCard, or closeStack system message is sent.

The background of the Address stack already contains a script that puts the current date into the Date field as soon as the closeField message is sent.

```
on closeField
    put date into field "date"
end closeField
```

As soon as you enter some text or edit text in one of the fields of an address card and you leave the field (by pressing the Tab key, clicking somewhere outside the field, or selecting another Object tool), the closeField system message is sent. The message handler *on close-Field...end closeField* is then activated and the command to put the date (current date) into the Date field is executed. This is why the date you see in the third field is automatically updated when you add text to or edit any card in the Address stack.

You can also make use of the open and close system messages that are sent when you go to or leave a new card or stack. A common use for openStack and closeStack messages is to turn off the HyperCard menus (referred to as the Menu bar) at the top of the screen when a user opens your stack, and then turn them back on when the user leaves your stack. That way, you can design a stack that makes full use of the Macintosh screen, knowing that the HyperCard menus will not obscure any portion of the cards in the stack. At the same time, you ensure that the user has access to the HyperCard menus when going to a new stack by turning the Menu bar back on when the user leaves your stack.

Before you remove the HyperCard menus from a stack, be sure that operation of the stack does not require the use of any HyperCard menu options. This is the case only if the buttons in the stack allow the user to perform any menu commands required to make full use of the stack (including such functions as browsing the cards, returning to the Home Card, and so on).

The HyperTalk commands to display and hide the HyperCard menus are *show menubar* and *hide menubar*, respectively. To see how this works, you can perform the following exercise. You will add a stack script to your Wine Tour stack that hides the menus when you open it and redisplays them when you leave it.

1. **Select the Open Stack option on the File menu.**

2. **Click on the Wine Tour stack and then the Open button (or double-click on Wine Tour).**

   This brings you to the Opening card of the Wine Tour stack.

3. **Select the Stack Info option on the Objects menu.**

4. **Click on the Script button.**

   This takes you to the Script Editor.

   Notice that there is already quite a lengthy script for the Wine Tour stack. This is the script for the Home Card that was brought into the Wine Tour stack when you copied the background of the Home Card to create this stack. None of the commands in this script are required in the Wine Tour, so you can delete them before adding the script to hide and redisplay the HyperCard Menu bar.

5. **Drag the mouse down the lines of the script, highlighting all of them down to and including *end searchScript*, and press the Backspace (Delete) key.**

   As you continue to drag downward, the script will scroll up in the Script Editor window. When you press the Backspace key, the entire text will be deleted.

   Now you are ready to add the message handler that will hide the Menu bar when the openStack system message is sent.

6. **Type *on openStack* and press Return.**

7. **Type *hide menubar* and press Return.**

8. **Type *end openStack* and press Return.**

   This message handler will hide the HyperCard menus as soon as the Wine Tour stack is opened. Now you need to add the message handler that will redisplay these menus when you close this stack.

Remember that a script can contain multiple message handlers. To make it easier for you to read the script later on, you can skip a line between message handlers (although this is not required to have them work properly).

9. Press Return.

This adds a blank line to the script.

10. Type *on closeStack* and press Return.

11. Type *show menubar* and press Return.

12. Type *end closeStack* and press Return.

Your stack script should now match the one shown in Figure 9.6. After you have checked yours against the one shown in this figure, go on to the next step.

13. Click on the OK button.

Now test out this script to see if works.

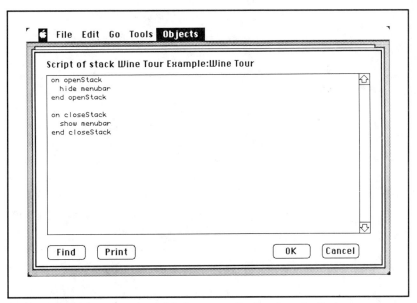

Figure 9.6: The stack script with the *on openStack* and *on closeStack* message handlers

14. Click on the Home button in the upper right corner of the card.

This takes you to the Home Card.

15. Click on the Wine Tour stack button near the bottom of this card.

This takes you to the Opening card of the Wine Tour stack.

This time, the entire Menu bar with all of the HyperCard menus should be hidden. Make sure that they are redisplayed when you leave this stack.

16. Click on the Home button again.

As soon as you click on this button, the Menu bar should reappear at the top of the screen even before the Home Card appears on your screen. When you clicked on the Home button (with its Go command), the closeStack system message was sent and this, in turn, activated the *show menubar* command in the *on closeStack...end closeStack* message handler.

You can always redisplay the HyperCard menus after they have been hidden by pressing Command-Space bar. That way, you have temporary access to any of the menu options when making revisions to a stack that contains a *hide menubar* command in its stack script. To hide the Menu bar once again, press Command-Space bar a second time.

Menu System Messages

The menu options on the HyperCard menus generate their own system messages when they are selected. These messages are sent whether you select an option on the pull-down menu with the mouse or you press a Command-key equivalent (such as Command-H, instead of clicking on the Home option on the Go menu).

The name of the messages begin with *doMenu* followed by the name of the menu option exactly as it appears on its menu. If the option has three periods (ellipsis), they must be included in the message name. For example, selecting the Print Stack option on the File menu generates a *doMenu Print Stack...* message, whereas selecting the Print Card Info option on the File menu (or pressing Command-P) generates a *doMenu Print Card* message.

To see how these system messages are entered, you can experiment with selecting HyperCard menu options from the Message box.

1. Press Command-M.

This brings up the Message box.

Message handlers using the doMenu messages require the use of memory variables to add the name of the option you want checked for. The program will not accept message handlers such as *on doMenu Print Card...end doMenu*. Also, you must use the Hyper-Talk Pass command to allow the other menu option messages not checked to proceed up the message hierarchy. You will learn how to handle these requirements later on when you look at using the HyperTalk doMenu and Pass commands in some detail.

2. **Type *doMenu Open Stack...* (be sure that you type three periods after Stack) and press Return.**

   This brings up the File Selection dialog box.

3. **Click on the Mouse Test stack and the Open button (or double-click on Mouse Test).**

4. **Type *doMenu Card Info* and press Return.**

   You will receive a error message telling you that HyperCard can't find menu item Card Info.

5. **Click on the Cancel button.**

6. **Move the I-Beam cursor after the *o* in Info in the Message box and click the mouse.**

7. **Type ... (be sure that you type three periods after Info) so that it reads *doMenu Card Info...* and press Return.**

   This time, the Card Information dialog box appears.

8. **Click the Cancel button in the dialog box.**

9. **Type *doMenu Find...* (be sure that you type three periods after Find) and press Return.**

   The Find command appears in the Message box, and the flashing text insertion pointer is positioned between a pair of double quotes.

10. **Click on the Close button in the Message box.**

General HyperCard System Messages

HyperCard also sends system messages that report on the status of the program itself. These detect when you start and quit HyperCard (*startUp* and *quit*) as well as when HyperCard has been temporarily suspended and the program resumes control (*suspend* and *resume*).

The startUp message is sent to the first card of the stack that HyperCard opens when you start the program. If you double-click on the HyperCard program icon from the desktop, this message is sent to the Home Card, as the program automatically opens the Home stack when you start it with this icon. If you double-click on the icon for a particular stack, then instead of the HyperCard program icon, the startUp message is sent to the first card of that stack.

If you want a particular action to take place when HyperCard is started, you can add an *on startUp...end startUp* message handler. You add such a message handler to the script for the stack that will be opened when the program is started. For instance, you can create an *on startUp...end startUp* message handler that instructs HyperCard to set new program parameters such as activating the power keys or setting a new user level (different from the settings used on the User Preferences card) or to prompt the user for a password.

Conversely, if you want a particular action to take place prior to exiting from HyperCard, you can add an *on quit...end quit* message handler to the stack script. This could be used to reset program parameters to desired default settings.

The suspend and resume messages come into play only when you use HyperCard's ability to open other Macintosh application programs. HyperCard enables you to run other programs, such as Microsoft Word or the 4th Dimension, from the program itself. When you give the HyperTalk command to open another application program, a suspend message is sent.

When you quit the application, HyperCard resumes control and you are returned to your previous place in the program. Upon quitting the external application, a resume message is sent. You can add message handlers to scripts that perform particular actions when either message is received. To add a message handler to check for the suspend message, you enter an *on suspend...end suspend* message handler. To add one to detect the resume message, you enter an *on resume...end resume* message handler. You will learn how you can open the other Macintosh programs that you use from within HyperCard in Chapter 15, where you will have an opportunity to create a HyperCard Finder stack.

Summary

Even though you now know a great deal more about how Hyper-Talk works, you may still be wondering what you can do with it when you create your stacks. In the next few chapters, you will explore this question in some depth as you learn specific HyperTalk commands. The focus will be not only how the commands function, but also when and how you can put them to use in the stacks you build.

In the next chapter, you will learn about using memory variables in HyperTalk. These allow you to assign names to specific information that the script can process. Not only will you learn how to define them, but you will also see how useful they can be in the scripts that you write.

Specifying the
Correct Information

IN CHAPTER 9, YOU LOOKED AT HOW MESSAGES ARE sent by the system and how message handlers process matching messages. Within a message handler, you place the HyperTalk commands that are to be executed when HyperCard detects that a particular condition exists (the mouse is up, the cursor is within a field, and so on).

Now you are going to examine various ways to enter the information that tells the HyperTalk commands exactly what it is they are to do for you. As part of this, you will learn how you can make scripts more versatile so they can process information that may vary when the script is executed.

Defining the Information to be Processed in a Script

Each HyperTalk command you place within a message handler performs a particular operation based on the information it contains. For example, when you enter the HyperTalk Go command, you have to specify the card it is to go to, as follows:

```
on mouseUp
   go home
end mouseUp
```

Almost all HyperTalk commands require that you enter some qualifying information that tells the command what it is to operate upon. This qualifying information added to a HyperTalk command word is called the *argument* of the command. When you practiced entering doMenu commands in the Message box, you kept changing the argument of the doMenu command by modifying the menu option, as in

    doMenu Open Stack...

and

    doMenu Card Info...

Simply by changing the argument, you got the same command to behave differently.

In addition to HyperTalk commands, the language contains *functions*. Functions differ from commands in that they calculate and return a result that can then be used in processing a command. For instance, in the previous chapter during the discussion on object system messages, you encountered the following example:

    on deleteCard
       put the number of cards – 1 into the message box
    end deleteCard

In the HyperTalk command statement, *the number of cards* is a Hyper-Talk function. It calculates the number of cards in the stack and returns the result. In this particular usage with the Put command, the result minus one is placed into the Message box at the bottom of the card.

Functions, like commands, often require arguments that tell the function what it is to calculate. In the case of *the number of cards* in the Put command, *cards* is the argument of *the number* function. You can use this function to have the program calculate the total of other things in a stack, as in

    the number of fields

or

    the number of words in field 1

By specifying new arguments, you can get different calculated results from the same HyperTalk function.

Conventions Used to Note Arguments

The conventions described in this section follow those used in the HyperCard Help stack. They are strictly adhered to in the appendices of this book, which give you an alphabetical listing of all the Hyper-Talk commands, functions, and properties.

In this chapter, you are primarily concerned with the various techniques for specifying the information that HyperTalk commands and functions operate upon. The most obvious way to specify this information is to enter it directly into the script as part of the command or function statement.

By changing the arguments entered for a command or a function, the program performs a slightly different operation. To help you know what kind of information can be added to a command or function, special typographical conventions describe the general arguments required by the command or arguments of a function. Once you learn this notation system, you can tell when an argument is required as well as what type of information you must enter into it.

Required Arguments

You never enter the angle brackets or the word contained within them in an actual HyperTalk command. Their purpose is to signify that you must substitute an appropriate argument when you enter the command into a script.

All required arguments are enclosed in a pair of angle brackets (as in <file name>). Within these brackets, you will find a term that characterizes the type of information required by the command. For example, you can state the argument for the Go command as

    go <destination>

Because of the angle brackets, you know that an argument describing the destination is required by the Go command in order for it to work (you cannot just enter *go* without telling the program where to go to).

In place of <destination>, you can enter many specific destinations, such as

    go home

or

    go last

or even

    go to card 12 of stack "Stack Ideas"

Optional Command Words

The last example points out another consideration in entering HyperTalk commands. Because its developers wanted to make HyperTalk as English-like as possible, it often allows you to enter prepositions as part of the command statement. Although you may use them, they are not required for the program to execute the command correctly.

The preposition *to* in the *go to card...* command in the previous example is an optional command word. You can add or omit it as you wish when using the Go command. All optional command words are noted by enclosing them in a pair of square brackets (as in [for]). Therefore, the complete notation for the Go command is really

go [to] <destination>

Another example is the Wait command. This command pauses the program for a specified time or until a particular condition is met. It has four generalized forms:

wait [for] <number of ticks>
wait [for] <number> seconds
wait until <true or false expression>
wait while <true or false expression>

When you want the program to wait a specific number of ticks (one-sixtieths of a second) or seconds, the word *for* is optional. You can enter

wait for 5 seconds

or

wait 5 seconds

Either form instructs the program to wait 5 seconds before it continues to execute subsequent commands in a script. However, if you use the Wait command to have the program pause until a particular condition exists, as with *wait until* or *wait while*, the command words *until* and *while* are not optional.

Some commands have optional arguments that, if used, have their own required arguments. The Open command is a good example of

If you entered *wait 5*, the program would pause only 5 ticks, that is, five-sixtieths of a second. You must add the word *seconds* to the command to have it count the waiting period in seconds rather than ticks.

this type of command:

> open [<document> with] <application>

This command can be used to start an application program with or without a particular document. For example, you can have Hyper-Card start Microsoft Word by entering

> **open microsoft word**

However, if you want to start Word with a particular document file, you must enter the document's name and use the preposition *with* in the command:

> **open "Billing Statement" with microsoft word**

If you choose to use an optional parameter of a command that is enclosed in square brackets, you must enter all of the required arguments within them for the command to work properly.

Alternate Arguments

A few HyperTalk commands have alternate arguments that you choose from when using the command. Alternate arguments are separated by vertical bars. For instance, the Put command contains such alternate arguments:

> put <source> before | into | after <destination>

Although you are more familiar with the use of the Put command using *into*, as in

> **put the date into field "Today's Date"**

you can also use it with the preposition *before* or *after* to locate field information in a particular order, as in

> **put field "City" before field "State"**

When you are presented with alternate arguments, you must use one of the words separated by vertical bars when you enter the command into a script, unless the alternate arguments are enclosed in square brackets. For example, the Push command has two arguments that are alternate *and* optional:

    push [this | recent] card

If you use it in its truncated form, as you did for the button script in the Wine Tour stack,

    push card

it means push [this] card.

Arguments of Functions

The notation used to designate the arguments of commands is used in a similar manner to designate the arguments of a function. However, there are really two types of HyperTalk functions: general functions and math functions. Most of the general functions do not require any arguments at all (like *the date* and *the time* functions). Those that do require arguments use the same notation conventions as command arguments. Required information is enclosed in angle brackets, optional words in square brackets, and alternate options are separated by vertical bars.

The *number* function, mentioned earlier, has two forms that illustrate this clearly. You can use this function to have the program calculate the number of cards, buttons, or fields in a stack. When used in this way, the form is

    the number of cards | buttons | fields

You saw an example of this in a script that determined the number of cards remaining after you deleted a card with the Delete Card option on the Edit menu:

```
on deleteCard
   put the number of cards – 1 into the message box
end deleteCard
```

You can also use this function to obtain the count of particular items (components) in a text field. When used in this fashion, the function has a slightly different form:

the number of <components> in <container>

Here, there are no alternate arguments. You must designate the items (<components>) you want counted and the field (<container>) that contains them. For example, you can use this form of the function to find out how many characters are in a particular text field:

the number of chars in field "Address"

Math functions represent a more specialized group of HyperTalk functions. They all require arguments of some type. When noting the arguments of the math functions (and a few of the general functions), there are two alternate ways you can enter it when the function requires only *one* argument. For instance, you can enter the square root function, which calculates the square root of a number, either as

sqrt(<number>)

or

the sqrt of <number>

because it only requires a single number as an argument.

However, when a math function requires multiple arguments, you must enter it in the first way, which encloses the arguments in parentheses. For example, to calculate the average of a list of numbers, the average function follows the general form of

average(<number list>)

Therefore, to find the average of the numbers 12, 20, and 15, you have to enter it as

average(12,20,15)

You can add a space between the function name and the argument enclosed in the pair of parentheses, if you wish. The program will accept

sqrt(49)

or

sqrt (49)

as correct forms.

The *min* and *max* math functions also require number lists as arguments. These are always separated by commas within the parentheses. The other two math functions that require multiple arguments are the *annuity* and *compound* functions. Both require the periodic rate and the number of periods as arguments separated by commas and enclosed in parentheses.

Math functions are not the only HyperTalk functions that have alternate forms. Other functions that require only one argument can also be entered with or without parentheses. For instance, when you use the *number* function with one of the alternate arguments (cards, fields, or buttons), you can enclose the argument in parentheses, as in

```
number(fields)
```

instead of entering

```
the number of fields
```

However, when you want the program to calculate the number of lines in the address field, the number function requires multiple arguments (<components> in <containers>), so you can only enter it as

```
the number of lines in field "Address"
```

Constant versus Variable Information

The message handlers, commands, functions, and their arguments entered directly in the script are constant. Every time the script is executed, the same information is used, resulting in the same use of the command.

Many times, entering the information to be processed directly into the script is not an efficient method because it limits the usefulness of the script to just one operation. However, limiting the script to one operation is okay if you know ahead of time exactly what data will be used or when the script must always perform the same action. For example, it works just fine to use the function *the date* to enter the current date into a field of a card that is always to show today's date (as is the case with the background script for the Address stack, which puts the current date into the *date entered* field of the card).

What if you don't know ahead of time what information a particular command or function will use? A simple example of this is a stack where you set up fields into which you enter all your travel-related expenses for a particular business trip in each card. Undoubtedly, you will want the card to have a field that totals all of the travel

The image of a memory variable as a temporary storage container is a useful one. You can fill the container with information or empty it out. Also, new information can replace old information in the container as called for. Although the container is given a name to identify it, its name is not synonymous with the information it contains. The container name functions only as a descriptor of the kind of information that container may have within it. For example, you might name a memory variable *color*. At any one time, it might contain the information red or blue or yellow, or even be empty of any particular color. *Color* describes the contents of the memory variable without telling what specific color, if any, it contains.

expenses that you enter in the other fields. You will not know what the expense figures will be for any given business trip. Even if you did, creating a script to have HyperCard add those expenses would be of no use when you add a new card to track the expenses for the next business trip. The expenses that the script for the total field must add vary each time the commands in that script are executed.

To take care of these kinds of situations, you can put the information into *memory variables*, which are temporary storage containers that hold the information for processing. They are called memory variables because they reside solely in the memory of the computer. When the commands in a script have been executed, you go to a new stack, or you quit HyperCard, the information in the memory variables is cleared out.

When you return to the object that contains a script using memory variables, it recreates the memory variables and new information is stored in them before they are utilized as the arguments of Hyper-Talk commands or functions. This process is referred to as *initializing* the memory variables. In HyperTalk, you define your own memory variables by initializing them.

Fields are the only information containers that retain their information even after you quit HyperCard. All of the other containers lose their information as soon as you leave the program.

HyperCard Containers

Before going any further, this is a good time to look more closely at the kinds of information containers used by HyperCard and the ways you can refer to individual pieces of information they can contain. Memory variables are only one type of container used to hold information for processing in the program. Text fields, either in the background or card layer of a stack, are also containers of information. The Message box is yet another information container.

All information stored within these different containers is stored as text. Even when you enter only numbers into the Message box or a field, they are stored as text items. This simplifies matters a great deal because the program treats the contents of all containers alike.

When the program calculates a new result with one of the math functions or Hyper-Card commands that performs arithmetic calculations, it transforms any text that it deems should contain a value into a number to perform the calculation. However, it then stores the result of the calculation as text in the appropriate container.

Text Components

When you use the text stored in these containers in a HyperTalk script, you can isolate specific text items by referring to them alone.

This is especially helpful in the case of fields, which often contain many individual pieces of text information.

HyperTalk breaks the text stored in its containers down into several distinct components: characters, words, items, and lines. When you want to extract a particular piece of text, you can do so by referring to its text component by name and the position it has in the container. For example, assume that you had the following text stored on the first line of the first field in the card:

Sandy, Jeff, Andy, and Keri Shewmaker

If you enter

item 2 of field 1

into the Message box and press Return, it will show *Jeff* as the second item. To HyperCard, an item is any piece of text entered between commas. However, when HyperCard extracts an item, it does not include the comma as part of it.

If you replace the contents of the Message box with

word 2 of field 1

and press Return, *Jeff,* will be entered into the Message box. To Hyper-Card, words are any text separated by spaces. When it extracts a word, it includes any punctuation that is not separated by spaces.

You can have HyperCard extract just a single character of text from within a container. For example, if you enter

char 1 of word 5 of field 1

in the Message box, it will return the *K* from Keri when you press Return.

When the field has multiple lines of text, you need to include the line number when extracting information from it. For instance, if the fourth word of the second line of the third field in a card is *Suite*, you could extract it by entering

word 4 of line 2 of field 3

"Lines" in Hyper-card are separated by hard returns. Only when you press Return does HyperCard acknowledge the existence of a new line. Thus, the program would consider a whole paragraph to be one line if you did not press Return at the end of any line.

You can refer to the position of any element you want to extract by last, middle, or the ordinal numbers first through tenth. You can also have the program extract a random piece of information by using the word *any* (as in *any word of first field*). For instance, you could also enter the previous example to extract the word *Suite* by entering

fourth word of second line of third field

When you use the designation *middle*, you can abbreviate it to *mid*. Instead of entering

second char of middle word of last line of third field

you can enter it as

second char of mid word of last line of third field

Be careful not to use the definite article before the first ten ordinal numbers, last, or middle. In other words, you *cannot* enter a statement such as

the fourth word of the first field

It must be entered as

fourth word of first field

to be accepted in a HyperCard command or function.

Joining Text Components

Not only can you extract specific text components, but you can also join them. The technical name for this procedure of joining individual text items is *concatenation*. To have HyperCard concatenate two pieces of text, you use the & (ampersand). If you want the program to include a space between the items you join, you enter && (double ampersand).

You can concatenate any text components. Assume that you had a person's first name entered into field 1 of a card and his last

If you concatenate using only one ampersand (&), there will be no spaces between the text—the words will be literally joined, as in *JimKelly* entered into the third field. If you want more than one space between the text items you join, enter the required number of spaces enclosed in double quotation marks in-between the double ampersand, as in &" "& to have three spaces between the text items.

name entered into field 2. You could have both the first and last name entered into the last field of the card by entering

put word 1 of field 1 && word 1 of field 2 into field 3

If *Jim* were entered into the first field and *Kelly* were entered in the second field, the third field would then contain *Jim Kelly*.

Because you have the power to extract specific text items and join them as you wish, you can control exactly what information is placed into or removed from any of the HyperCard information containers.

Working with Memory Variables

Now that you have a better idea of how you can use HyperTalk to manipulate the text within any of its information containers, it's time to turn your attention back to memory variables. As you recall, memory variables represent a type of temporary storage container for information in HyperTalk. Memory variables are used in the following ways:

- To temporarily store information that is ultimately to be put into fields.

- To store intermediate values to be calculated.

- To store user input so that it can be validated before they are entered in fields.

- To determine what action the script is to take according to what is entered into them.

To create a memory variable in HyperTalk, you assign it a name at the same time you give it a starting value. The program allows you to assign a memory variable any name, so long as it is a single word. Remember that many words are already used by HyperTalk as part of its vocabulary. Although HyperTalk will allow you to use terms in its vocabulary as names for your memory variables, it is not a good idea because it can cause you a great deal of confusion when trying to understand the memory variable's function in the script.

The best way to understand how memory variables work is to get some hands-on experience with them. Although you will almost always use memory variables in the scripts you create, you can practice defining and using them in the Message box.

Let's start by creating a memory variable called *var1* (for variable 1). To create this variable, you need to assign an initial value to this name. This is done with the HyperTalk Put command. In the previous section on the conventions used to note HyperTalk commands, you saw the Put command in an example. Let's review its arguments before going on:

    put <source> before | into | after <destination>

In this case, the <source> argument of the Put command is the initial value that you want to assign to the memory variable. The <destination> argument is a name that you want to assign to the memory variable. When you want to place some information into a HyperTalk storage container, you choose the *into* preposition. Therefore, if you want to assign the starting value of 10 to the memory variable called var1, you enter the Put command as

    put 10 into var1

Try it out by taking these steps:

1. Press Command-M to bring up the Message box (if it is not already on your screen.)

2. Type *put 10 into var1* in the Message box and press Return.

The var1 memory variable is not initialized until you press Return.

When you want to know what value a particular memory variable has at the current time, you can have the program display its contents in the Message box simply by entering its name and pressing Return. Make sure that var1 is currently storing 10 as its contents.

3. Type *var1* and press Return.

As you type, var1 replaces the Put statement. When you press Return, the Message box should contain 10.

The use of the double quotation marks around the word *Hang* is optional in this case because you initialized var2 with a single word (you could have typed *put Hang into var2*). They are required, however, when you put several words into a memory variable (to mark the beginning and end of the text to be placed in the variable), as in

```
put "Hang in there!" into
var2
```

Next, define a second memory variable named var2. Put the word *Hang* into this variable.

4. Type *put "Hang" into var2* **and press Return.**

5. Type *var2* **and press Return.**

The Message box contains *Hang.*

Although HyperCard refers to initializing *values* in memory variables, you now see that it doesn't mean that you can't store text in memory variables. You already know that HyperCard stores the contents of memory variables as text, even in the case of var1, which contains the number 10. You can prove that numbers are stored as text by creating a third memory variable whose contents are the result of concatenating the contents of var1 and var2.

6. Type *put var2 && var1 into var3* **and press Return.**

Remember that the && places a space between the concatenated text.

7. Type *var3* **and press Return.**

The Message box now contains *Hang 10.*

If the 10 in var1 were stored as a number, you would not have been able to join it to the Hang in var2.

The same memory variable can hold new values at various times, that is, can be reinitialized.

8. Type *put "tough" into var1* **and press Return.**

Tough now replaces 10 as the contents of the var1 memory variable.

9. Type *put var2 && var1 into var3* **and press Return.**

This reinitializes the var3 memory variable.

10. Type *var3* **and press Return.**

The contents of the Message box is now *Hang tough.*

This ability to reinitialize the same memory variable has a much more practical application than to display different surfing phrases in the Message box. Let's say you want a stack that required a total field, which would sum all of the travel expenses entered into other expense fields in the card, as mentioned earlier in this chapter. Figure 10.1 shows such a stack. The Total field is automatically calculated by using a memory variable called *sum*. Figure 10.2 shows you the background script that performs this calculation. The script reads as follows:

```
on closeField
    put field "Airline" into sum
    add field "Hotel" to sum
    add field "Meals" to sum
    add field "Misc" to sum
    put sum into field "Total"
end closeField
```

The memory variable *sum* is used as an intermediate storage container where the calculation takes place. The script begins by initializing this memory variable with the contents of the field that holds the cost of the airline tickets as soon as the closeField message is sent. The

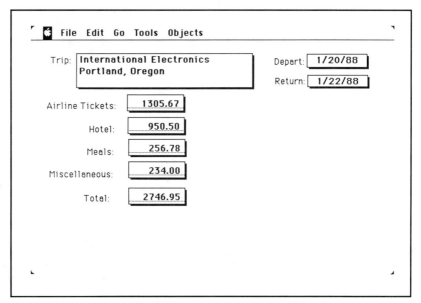

Figure 10.1: Typical card in the Travel Expenses stack

HyperTalk Add command adds the hotel, meals, and miscellaneous expenses to the *sum* variable. The Add command has the form

    add <source> to <destination>

The <source> argument in each Add command is the field that is to be added. The <destination> argument is the memory variable *sum*. Finally, another Put command places the contents of the *sum* memory variable into the Total field.

When you add a new card to the Travel Expenses stack, this background script is activated as soon as you press the Tab key to go to the Airline Tickets expense field, upon completing the description of the trip in the first field of the card. The total of 0 shows up in the Total field at this point, because all of the expense fields are still empty and empty containers have a value of zero as far as HyperTalk calculations are concerned. The *sum* memory variable is initialized with a starting value of 0, which is added to the contents of 0 in all of the expense fields. This results in a total of zero for the *sum* memory variable, which is placed in the Total field.

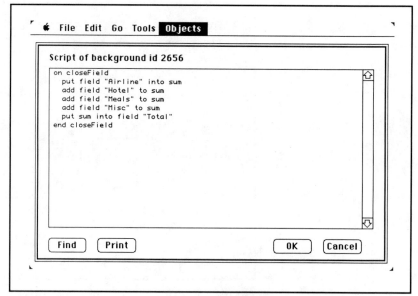

Figure 10.2: Background script for totaling the travel expenses

As soon as you enter a new value into the Airline Tickets expense field and press Tab to move on to the Hotel expense field, the close-Field message is sent again. The *on closeField...end closeField* message handler in the background script is activated once again. This time, the total figure reflects the cost of the airline tickets that you entered into the second field.

This process of updating the Total field each time you enter a new value in the remaining expense fields continues until you reach the Total field itself. At that point, even though the Put and Add commands in the script are reexecuted when you press the Tab key to fill in the Depart and Return date fields, the total no longer changes. However, should you return to one of the expense fields and edit its contents, these commands would update the total as soon as you close the field (by pressing Tab, clicking outside of the field, adding a new card, going to a new stack, or quitting HyperCard).

Local versus Global Memory Variables

When you create a memory variable such as sum in the *on close-Field...end closeField* message handler, its contents are forgotten as soon as the message handler is finished executing the commands within it. This kind of memory variable is referred to as a *local* memory variable. Neither the name nor the contents of a local memory variable are remembered after the end of the handler that uses it.

You can change a local memory variable into a *global* memory variable. The name and contents of global memory variables are remembered after the end of the handler that uses it. This means that their contents can be used in different scripts, even if those scripts are located in different stacks. The program remembers the name and contents of a global memory variable until you start a new application program from HyperCard or quit HyperCard.

All memory variables that you define in the Message box are global variables.

All memory variables that you create in the scripts are local memory variables unless you declare them to be global memory variables. This is done with the Global command. To make a memory variable global, you simply list its name after the Global command. This is referred to as *declaring* the memory variable to be global.

You can declare any number of memory variables to be global memory variables by separating their names with commas after the Global command, as in

global subtotal, ytd, total

To get a feel for how global memory variables are created and work, you can create a new test stack that contains a button, a field, and a card script.

1. Select the New Stack option on the File menu.

2. Click on the *Copy current background* to uncheck it.

3. Enter *Global Test* as the stack name and click on the New Button.

4. Select the Background option on the Edit menu (or press Command-B).

   This takes you to the card background shown by the striped HyperCard menu.

5. Select the Card Info option on the Objects menu.

6. Click on the Script button.

In the card script, you will create a global variable named *beepnumber*. This variable will hold the number of times you want the Macintosh bell to sound when you leave the field or click on the button you will create there.

7. Type *on openCard* and press Return.

8. Type *global beepnumber* and press Return.

9. Type *put 3 into beepnumber* and press Return.

10. Type *end openCard* and press Return.

11. Click on the OK button.

Next, you will add a field to the background of this stack. This will contain a script that uses the *beepnumber* variable to sound the bell when you move the cursor out of the field.

12. Select the New Field option on the Objects menu.

13. Drag the field up to the top of the card.

14. Select the Field Info option on the Objects menu.

15. Click on the shadow radio button.

16. Click on the Script button.

17. Type *on mouseLeave* and press Return.

18. Type *global beepnumber* and press Return.

19. Type *beep beepnumber* and press Return.

20. Type *end mouseLeave* **and press Return.**

21. Click on the OK button.

Finally, add a new button to the card background. This button will contain a script that beeps the number of times stored in the *beepnumber* memory variable when you click on it.

22. Select the New Button option on the Objects menu.

23. Select the Button Info option on the Objects menu.

24. Type *Beep* **as the button name.**

25. Click on the Script button.

26. Type *global beepnumber* **and press Return.**

27. Type *beep beepnumber* **and press Return.**

28. Click on the OK button.

Note that each time you used the *beepnumber* memory variable, be it in the field or button script, you also used the Global command to redeclare it as a global memory variable. This is because it is not sufficient just to declare it once as a global variable prior to initializing it in the card script. If you did not use the Global command in the field and button scripts, HyperCard would tell you that it did not understand the arguments to the Beep command.

To initialize the *beepnumber* memory variable, you must add a new card to your stack. That way, the openCard system message will be detected by the *on openCard...end openCard* message handler and the Global and Put commands will be executed.

29. Select the New Card option on the Edit menu (or press Command-N).

30. Select the Browse tool on the Tools menu.

Now test out the field and button scripts in the new card.

31. Move the Browse tool inside the field and then move it outside of this field.

When the I-Beam cursor changes back to the Browse tool, the Macintosh sounds three beeps.

32. Move the Browse tool to the Beep button and click the mouse.

Again, the Macintosh sounds three beeps.

Because the *beepnumber* memory variable is global, it can be used in two different scripts in this card. It can also be used in scripts in other stacks that you create. Until you start another application or quit HyperCard, the *beepnumber* memory variable will contain the number 3, which can be used as an argument for Beep or any other HyperTalk command.

The It Memory Variable

In HyperTalk, there are a few commands that make use of a special memory variable created by the program. This is the local memory variable named *it*. These commands include Get, Answer, and Ask. In all cases, the information that the program gets either from the system, HyperCard stacks, or the user in response to the use of one of these commands is placed in the memory variable *it*. Because HyperTalk uses this same memory variable for all three commands, its contents will change when these commands are used.

The Get Command and the It Memory Variable

The Get command is used to retrieve information about a specific property of a stack. The information retrieved by the Get command is automatically placed in the *it* memory variable. The form of the Get command is as follows:

    get <expression>

The <expression> argument consists of the name of the property and, except in the cases of global properties, the name of the object whose property it is. Appendix C lists the properties of all five standard HyperCard objects (buttons, fields, cards, backgrounds, and stacks) and a sixth nonstandard property called *window*.

Global properties are those that belong to the program on the whole, such as userLevel or powerKeys. When you use the Get command to retrieve information about a global property, you just

> If you use the *it* memory variable in the scripts that you write, be careful that HyperTalk does not overwrite its contents before your handler is finished using this information. Most of the time, it is easier and safer to have your script put the contents of the *it* memory variable into a new memory variable not used by any of the HyperTalk commands themselves.

specify the property as the command argument, as in

get userLevel

This command checks the user level and places a number between 1 and 5 (with 1 for the Browsing level and 5 for the Scripting level) in the memory variable *it*.

When you use the Get command to retrieve information about some nonglobal property, you must specify the property and the object. For example, to get information about the size of the current stack, you would enter

get the size of this stack

in a script or the Message box. Doing this would place the size of the current stack in bytes into the memory variable *it*.

To get a feel for how the Get command and the *it* memory variable work together, try using them to retrieve various types of information about the Home stack.

1. **Select the Home option on the Go menu (or press Command-H).**

   This takes you to the Home Card.

2. **Press Command-M to bring up the Message box.**

With the first Get command, retrieve the user level—a global property.

3. **Type** *get userLevel* **and press Return.**

   The information about the user level is now stored in the *it* memory variable.

4. **Type** *it* **and press Return.**

   The Message box will hold the number representing the user level—you should see *5* here because the user level should be set to Scripting.

Next, use the Get command to retrieve information about whether the power keys (for the painting program) are active. This, too, is a global HyperCard property.

5. Type *get powerKeys* **and press Return.**

6. Type *it* **and press Return.**

The *it* memory variable will contain either true or false, depending upon whether the painting power keys are currently turned on or off in your program.

You change the status of the power keys by using the HyperTalk Set command. Set requires the same arguments as the Get command. The Get command is used to retrieve information about the current status of HyperCard properties, whereas the Set command is used to make changes to those properties.

Try using the Set command to change the status of the power keys and see how this affects the contents of the *it* memory variable. If the power keys are on (the assumption in the following steps), you want to set them to false to turn them off. If, on the other hand, they are off, you want to set them to true to turn them on. (In other words, you use the opposite of the contents of the Message box.)

7. Type *set powerKeys to false* **and press Return.**

Substitute *true* for *false* if the previous Get command returned false.

8. Type *it* **and press Return.**

The contents of the *it* memory variable has not yet been updated. Although you reset the power keys with the Set command, the information about this property stored in a variable has not yet been updated to reflect this change.

9. Type *get powerKeys* **and press Return a second time.**

10. Type *it* **and press Return again.**

Now the *it* memory variable contains the correct information about the status of the power keys. Keep in mind that the information stored in the *it* memory variable about a particular HyperCard property may not be correct because it is not current. If your script makes a change to the property, you have to reuse the Get command to update this information.

Next, use the Get command to get specific information about the Home stack and the Home Card. Remember that when you are not dealing with a global HyperCard property, you must include the name of the object as part of the command arguments.

11. Type *get name of this stack* **and press Return.**

12. Type *it* **and press Return.**

The Message box contains *stack "Home"*.

Because the name property can belong to a stack, card, background, field, and so on, you have to specify the object as part of the command.

13. Type *get name of this card* **and press Return.**

14. Type *it* **and press Return.**

The Message box contains *card "Home"*.

You can use the Get command to get specific information about particular objects, such as background or card buttons and fields. Use it now it to get information about the text used in the single background field of the Home Card.

Remember that when you refer to a field in scripts, HyperTalk understands that field to be in the background of the card, as in

`get textSize of field 1`

When you are referring to a card field (or button), you need to specifically tell HyperTalk that the field (or button) is at the card layer, as in

`get textSize of card field 1`

15. Type *get textFont of field 1* **and press Return.**

16. Type *it* **and press Return.**

The Message box tells you the font used in this field is Times.

17. Type *get textSize of field 1* **and press Return.**

18. Type *it* **and press Return.**

The Message box tells you that the font size is 18 point.

19. Type *get textAlign of field 1* **and press Return.**

20. Type *it* **and press Return.**

The Message box tells you that the text alignment is centered.

By using the Get command in this way, you can get quite a bit of specific information about any part of the stacks you are working with. In the next chapter, you will learn how you can make the program evaluate the information about particular properties that is returned and stored in the *it* memory variable and perform different operations, depending on what the program finds there.

Storing User Input in the It Memory Variable

The *it* memory variable is also used with the Answer and Ask commands. These commands enable you to prompt the user for a response. The response that is chosen (in the case of the Answer command) or entered (in the case of the Ask command) by the user is stored in the *it* memory variable.

In the following chapter, you will learn how to use these two commands when you are introduced to decision making in scripts using If conditions. As with the Get command, you can have the program evaluate the user's response to the Answer and Ask commands that is stored in the *it* memory variable and perform specific tasks depending upon what information HyperTalk finds there.

The Selection Memory Variable

In addition to the *it* memory variable that HyperTalk maintains and uses, the program also maintains a special memory variable named *selection*. Whenever you select text in a field by clicking and dragging over, this text is placed in the *selection* memory variable. You can create scripts that evaluate the contents of this memory variable and perform particular operations based on what it contains.

In the next chapter, you will examine the script of the telephone button in the Address stack in some detail. This button script evaluates the contents of the *selection* memory variable as part of the decision-making process to determine what telephone number the program is to dial.

Summary

In this chapter, you looked at the ways of defining for HyperTalk what information is to be processed. As you have seen, many HyperTalk commands and functions require arguments that determine exactly what kind of operation is performed. When you enter all of this information directly into a script, it is constant, and each time the script is used, the same actions take place. In some cases, constants must be replaced by variables to make the script more efficient. The use of memory variables makes it possible to process and evaluate information before, during, and after a script has been executed.

In the next chapter, you will examine decision making in Hyper-Talk. There you will learn about the control structures that you can use in the scripts you create. You will examine two control structures there: those that perform operations conditionally and those that perform them repetitively.

CHAPTER 11 _____

NOW THAT YOU ARE FAMILIAR WITH HOW HYPER-
Talk stores information for processing, it is time to look more closely
at the ways it processes this information. A good deal of the time, it is
sufficient to have the commands embedded in a message handler
processed sequentially; however, this is not always the case. As you
will see, HyperTalk affords you many ways for altering the order of
execution. Many of these involve the use of memory variables, which
you learned about in the last chapter.

HyperTalk Control Structures _____

When a HyperTalk message handler finds a matching system message has been sent, it performs all of the commands found in that
handler. Normally, these commands are carried out sequentially
until the program executes an *end* statement that signals the end of the
message handler. There are times, however, when you need to have
HyperCard modify the order in which these commands are executed. HyperTalk provides five control structures for modifying this
order: If, Repeat, Exit, Send, and Pass. In this chapter, you will
learn how the If...Then, Repeat, and Exit control structures are set
up and used, beginning with the most common construction, the
If...Then construction. (See Appendix A for more information about
Send and Pass.)

If Conditions

The If construction is stated and used in HyperTalk as in the
English language. It is not uncommon to say that a certain outcome
will take place depending upon whether a particular condition is met.

For example, you might say, "If I get my raise next month, then I will purchase the BMW." The implication in this sentence is that if you don't get your raise, you won't purchase the car.

The If construction can also express that alternate outcomes will take place depending upon whether a particular condition is met. For instance, you might say, "If I get my raise next month, then I will buy the BMW; otherwise, I will buy the Honda." Of course, you can create even more complex conditions: those that utilize several outcomes as well as those that utilize several conditions.

The crux of the If construction, in HyperTalk as well as in English, is whether the condition raised is found to be true or false. You can create flow diagrams that illustrate what takes place when the condition is true and what takes place when it is false. Figure 11.1 shows you such a diagram; it illustrates the If construction used in the example concerning the purchase of a BMW versus a Honda.

The rectangles in this diagram represent the decision to be made and the possible outcomes. The small solid diamond indicates that a choice is to be made. Arrows are used to connect the decision and outcomes. When the arrows originate in the diamond, they connect mutually

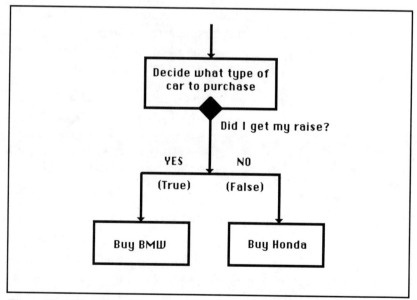

Figure 11.1: The flow diagram of the "raise" If construction

exclusive choices that result from testing the condition (or conditions). The condition to be tested is written next to the diamond.

Such flow diagrams are sometimes useful to clearly delineate what operations are to take place and under what conditions. You can use them to outline decision making that is to take place in the Hyper-Talk scripts you create.

Creating Comparative Expressions

When a decision is to be made depending upon whether a particular condition or set of conditions is true or false in HyperCard, you need to set up a *true or false expression* as part of the If...Then construction. This true or false expression contains operative words that tell the program what is compared to what. There are several operative words and symbols that can be used in HyperTalk true or false expressions. These words and symbols are summarized in Table 11.1. They are referred to as Boolean operators after the nineteenth-century English mathematician George Boole, who formulated the system of algebraic logic that requires their use.

The Boolean operators in Table 11.1 are also used when setting up expressions for the Repeat constructions in HyperTalk. These constructions are introduced later in this chapter.

Notice from this table that you can use either the English word *is* or the equal sign (=) when setting up a true or false expression that tests the equality (sameness) of two elements. The other comparatives, such as greater than or less than, require the use of the mathematical symbols.

When you need to use the *not equal to* operator, you press the < (left angle bracket) followed by the > (right angle bracket). Spaces between any of the compound symbols, such as < >, > =, and < =, are allowed.

When you need to express compound conditions as part of the true or false expression, you use the operator And or Or to join the expressions. When you use the And operator, both expressions must be true before HyperCard will take the action you assign to the true outcome. When you use the Or operator, only one or the other of the expressions must test true for the program to take the action you assign to the true outcome. The Not operator works a lot like the < > operator. It excludes one possibility, and the program takes the actions assigned to the true outcome in all other cases.

From the examples in this table, you can see that you test the content of the various components that are stored in a HyperCard container. This includes any memory variables that you create, as well as the *it* and *selection* memory variables created and used by HyperTalk itself.

Operator	Meaning	Examples
= *or* is	Is equal to or is the same as	If field 1 is empty If field 6 = "CA"
>	Is greater than	If item 4 of the long date > 1988
<	Is less than	If the number of cards < 100
>= *or* > =	Is greater than or equal to	If the length of field 1 > = 35
<= *or* < =	Is less than or equal to	If chars in field 8 < = 1
<> *or* < >	Is unequal to or is not the same as	If field "Phone" <> empty If the number of card buttons <> 2
And	Both conditions must be true	If field 6 = "CA" and field 8 > 25 If it > = 200 and it < = 300
Or	One or the other condition must be true	If field 6 = empty or field 6 = "NY" If field 2 > = 20 or field 3 < = 85432
Not	Test for all conditions except one	If field 6 is not "CA" If item 4 of the long date is not 1986

Table 11.1: The Boolean operators in HyperTalk

Testing if a container is empty is not the same as testing if it contains the value of zero. The statements

    if field 1 = empty

and

    if field 1 = 0

are not equivalent. If field 1 is empty, the first statement will return true and the second will return false as the result of the test. However, if a field contains any value or text—that is, is not empty—then the statements

> if field 1 < > empty

and

> if field 1 < > 0

are equivalent, in that both return *true* as the result of the test.

The If...Then Construction

In HyperTalk, the simplest If condition uses the If...Then construction, as follows:

> if <true or false expression> then <command>

You can also phrase the same command somewhat differently:

> if <true or false expression>
> then <command>

In the first case, the HyperCard command to be executed if the true or false expression is found to be true is placed on the same line. In the second example, the command and the operative word Then are placed on a line of their own, directly beneath the If command and the true or false expression. How you want to enter an If...Then construction is completely up to you. If the true or false expression is lengthy (as is the case with some compound conditions), you may find it better to have the Then clause with the HyperTalk command on its own line.

For example, you can enter a condition to add a new card to the current stack if the *it* memory variable contains the word *yes* either as

> if it = "yes" then doMenu "New Card"

or as

> if it = "yes"
> then doMenu "New Card"

The If...Then constructions you create can have multiple commands that are to be carried out if the true or false expression is found to be true. When you designate multiple commands, you must alter the If...Then form somewhat and add an End If statement to the script, as follows:

```
if <true or false expression> then
<command>
<command>
end if
```

For example, if you wanted multiple HyperCard commands to be carried out when the *it* memory variable contains *yes*, you would enter the If...Then construction in the following way:

```
if it = "yes" then
    doMenu "New Card"
    put the number of cards into the message box
    put the long date into field 5
end if
```

The End If statement tells HyperCard which commands belong to the If...Then construction and which do not. When you want the program to perform multiple commands when a particular condition (or conditions) is found to be true, you must remember to add the End If statement on its own line of the script.

The If...Then...Else Construction

When you want HyperCard to perform one command when the true or false expression is true and another command when it is false, you use the If...Then...Else construction. The Else operative word separates the command or commands that you want performed when the condition is found to be false from the command or commands that you want performed when the condition is true.

When there is only one command to be performed when the condition is true and one command to be performed when it is false, you can use either of the following forms:

    if <true or false expression> then <command> else <command>

or

    if <true or false expression> then <command>
    else <command>

For instance, if you want a new card added when the *it* memory variable contains *yes* and have the program return to the Home Card when *it* contains anything else (or is empty), you could enter

    if it = "yes" then doMenu "New Card" else go home

or

    if it = "yes" then doMenu "New Card"
    else go home

Again, you will have to decide which format is easier to read. If the condition is long, then you will want to use the second form.

Figure 11.2 shows you a flow diagram of this If...Then...Else example. When the handler finds the appropriate system message, the program examines the contents of the *it* memory variable. If HyperCard finds that this variable currently contains *yes*, it adds a new card to the stack using the doMenu "New Card" command; otherwise, it goes to the Home Card. The arrows below the branches to these mutually exclusive choices indicate that the program then continues executing any other commands that are part of the message handler.

When using the If...Then...Else construction, you may find situations where you have multiple HyperTalk commands to be performed when the condition is true and only a single command to be performed when the condition is false. In such cases, you use the following form:

    if <true or false expression> then
        <command>

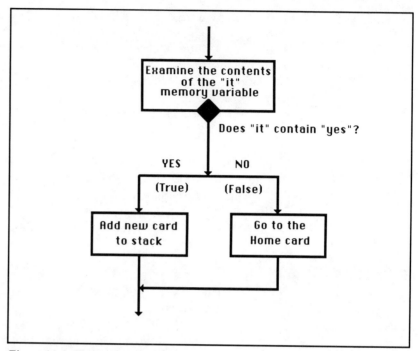

Figure 11.2: Flow diagram of a typical If...Then...Else construction

```
<command>
else <command>
```

Expanding on the previous example somewhat, you would enter the following:

```
if it = "yes" then
  doMenu "New Card"
  put the number of cards into the message box
else go home
```

Notice that the two commands to be performed when *it* does contain *yes* are indented to set them off from the single Else command that is performed when *it* contains something else.

If the If...Then...Else construction has only a single command to be performed when the condition is true and multiple commands to be performed when the condition is false, then you alter the format and terminate the construction with an End If statement. This has the following form:

```
if <true or false expression> then <command>
else
   <command>
   <command>
end if
```

As an example, you could have this script:

```
if it = "yes" then doMenu "New Card"
else
   set userLevel to 1
   go first card
   show cards
end if
```

Notice in this example that indenting the commands beneath Else (those that are performed when *it* does not contain *yes*) sets them off, thereby enhancing the overall legibility of the script.

You will also find times when your script must contain multiple HyperTalk commands that are to be performed both when the condition is true and when it is false. Under these circumstances, you need to include an End If statement and put the If...Then...Else construction into this form:

```
if <true or false expression> then
   <command>
   <command>
else
   <command>
   <command>
end if
```

For example, you could use the following If...Then...Else construction:

```
if it = "yes" then
   doMenu "New Card"
   put the number of cards into the message box
```

```
else
   set userLevel to 1
   go first card
   show cards
end if
```

Nesting If...Then Constructions

You can put an If...Then construction within another If...Then construction in a script. This technique is referred to as *nesting*. When you nest If...Then constructions, the program helps you keep things straight by indenting each new If...Then construction to the next tab stop. By keeping the level of indentation the same for each If...Then construction, you can easily spot if a particular If...Then construction is missing an End If statement.

The following script contains one If...Then...Else construction nested within another:

```
on mouseUp
   get the time
   if it < "12:00 PM" then
      put "Good morning" into the message box
   else
      if it > "12:00 PM" then
         put "Good afternoon" into the message box
      else
         beep 12
         put "Lunch time!" into the message box
      end if
   end if
end mouseUp
```

When the mouseUp message is detected by this handler, the program puts the system time into the *it* memory variable. If *it* is before noon, the good morning greeting is placed in the Message box. If *it* is after noon, the good afternoon greeting is placed in there instead. If *it* contains noon on the dot, the Macintosh beeps 12 times and the message telling you that it's lunch time appears in the Message box.

There are three outcomes to be tested for in this message handler: the time is before noon, after noon, or 12:00 noon exactly. To cover them all, two If...Then...Else constructions are required, one within the other. The first If clause returns the greeting "Good morning" if the time is found to be prior to (less than) 12:00 noon.

If this is not the case, then there are still two possible outcomes: it is noon or it is some time after noon. To test for this, a second If...Then...Else construction is introduced. The If clause of this construction returns the "Good afternoon" greeting if the time is after (greater than) 12:00 noon. If this is not true, then it must be 12:00 noon precisely and the Macintosh sounds 12 beeps and informs you that it's time for lunch. The flow diagram shown in Figure 11.3 illustrates the decision making that takes place when this handler is activated.

Notice the formatting involved with the nested If...Then...Else constructions. The If, Else, and End If clauses for the first (outer) If...Then...Else construction are all indented to the same level. Likewise, these clauses for the second (inner) If...Then...Else construction are all indented to the same level, one more tab stop in. When

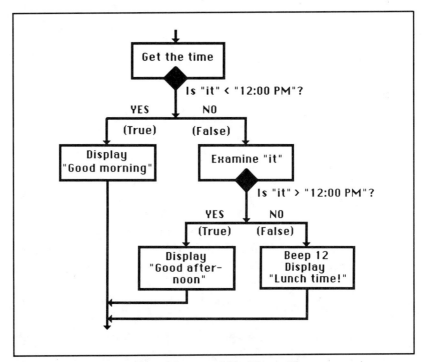

Figure 11.3: Flow diagram of the nested If...Then...Else constructions

nesting If...Then...Else constructions, you must terminate each construction with an End If statement. Note, too, that all of these conditional statements are indented in one tab from the *on mouseUp...end mouseUp* message handler statements, which are kept aligned with each other (flush left in the Script Editor).

Using the If...Then Construction with the Answer Command

In the last chapter, you examined the use of the special *it* memory variable. At that time, you learned that the Get, Answer, and Ask commands all automatically put the information they receive into this container. In the case of the Answer and Ask commands, this information is the result of input entered by the user in response to a question that appears in a special dialog box. It is most common to use the If...Then and If...Then...Else constructions to then have the program examine the user's response stored in the *it* memory variable and perform different commands based on what it finds there.

Let's begin looking at how these commands work by examining the Answer command. The general form of the Answer command is as follows:

answer <question> with [<reply> [or <reply> [or <reply>]]]

When you use the Answer command, you enter a question (enclosed in double quotation marks) along with up to three possible replies. The maximum length of each reply is 13 characters (depending upon the width of the characters in the reply). The text of the <question> and <reply> arguments is displayed in the Chicago font in 12 points (you cannot change the font or point size).

When the message handler that holds the Answer command is activated, the program presents your question along with the responses in a standard dialog box. If you do not specify a <reply> argument, the dialog box displays the text of the <question> argument with an OK button. If you do specify one, two, or three <reply> arguments, these are displayed as buttons. The last button (the one farthest to the right) is prehighlighted to allow you to select it by pressing Return or Enter, instead of having to click on it with the mouse.

When you click on a reply button (or press Return or Enter if it is the last reply), the reply is stored in the *it* memory variable. You can then use an If...Then or If...Then...Else construction to tell HyperCard what action to take as a result of the response chosen.

For example, you could use the Answer command in a Delete button on a card that has the user confirm that the card is to be deleted before removing it from the stack:

```
on mouseUp
    answer "Proceed with deletion of this card?" with "OK" ¬
    or "Cancel"
    if it is "OK" then doMenu "Delete Card"
end mouseUp
```

When the mouseUp message is sent, the dialog box shown in Figure 11.4 appears on the screen. It contains the two reply buttons: OK and Cancel. The Cancel button is prehighlighted. You can click on this button or press Return or Enter to select it. To have the card deleted from the stack, you must click on the OK button.

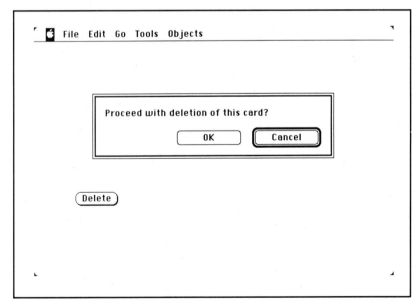

Figure 11.4: The Proceed with Deletion dialog box created with the Answer command

As soon as you choose either of these responses, the reply is stored in the *it* memory variable. If the *it* memory variable contains OK, the If true or false expression is found to be true and the doMenu Delete Card command is carried out. If the *it* memory variable contains Cancel, then the If true or false expression is found to be false and no action is taken.

You can use the Answer command in a wide variety of applications. Let's look at an example of a typical educational application. Figure 11.5 shows a card from a stack that teaches French grammar. This particular card introduces the topic of the French possessive adjectives and pronouns. Each section is accompanied by a Question button. Figure 11.6 shows you the script for the first Question button. It says the following:

```
on mouseUp
    answer "C'est ma chemise. C'est..." with "la mien" or ¬
    "la mienne" or "le mienne"
    if it is "la mienne" then
        answer "Tres bien fait!"
```

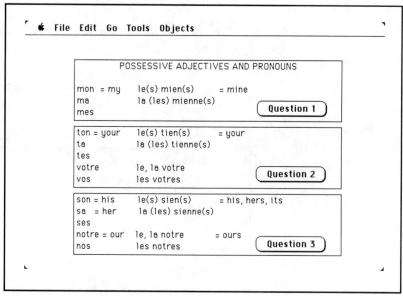

Figure 11.5: French grammar card

```
else
    answer "Non! C'est la mienne."
end if
end mouseUp
```

When the user (the student, in this case) clicks on the Question 1 button, the mouseUp message is detected by the *on mouseUp...end mouseUp* message handler. The Answer command is executed and the dialog box shown in Figure 11.7 appears on the screen. When the student selects one of these three possible responses, the one selected is stored in the *it* memory variable. The If...Then...Else construction is then executed.

If the student has chosen the correct answer of *la mienne*, the true or false expression of the If...Then construction will be true and the second Answer command will be executed. This command displays the reinforcement of *Tres bien fait!* (Very well done!) in a dialog box (Figure 11.8). To continue, the student then clicks on the OK button (or presses Return or Enter) and the dialog box disappears. If the student chooses either of the other two replies, the Answer command in the Else clause

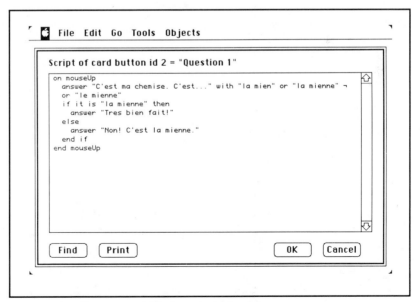

Figure 11.6: The script of the Question 1 button

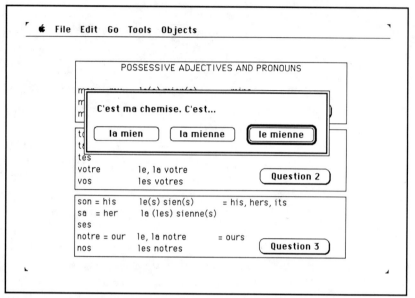

Figure 11.7: The content of Question 1 created with the Answer command

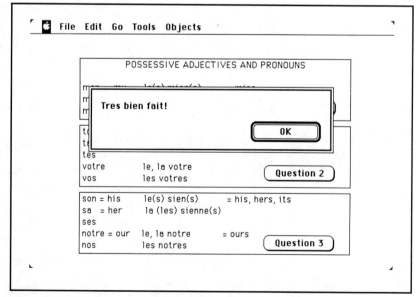

Figure 11.8: Selecting the correct answer to Question 1

will be executed. In that case, a dialog box containing the correct answer is displayed (Figure 11.9). When the student clicks on the OK button (or presses Return or Enter), this dialog box disappears.

Using the If...Then Construction with the Ask Command

The Ask command also stores the user's response in the *it* local memory variable. You can then use an If...Then or If...Then...Else construction to have the program evaluate the contents of *it* and perform accordingly. The Ask command has two forms:

ask <question> [with <default>]
ask password <question>

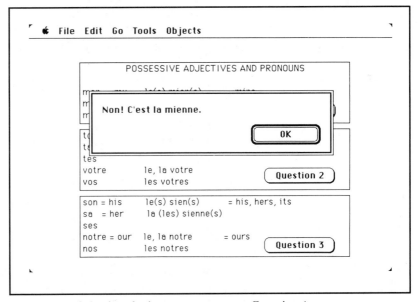

The *ask password* <*question*> form of this command is used to prompt the user to enter a password in the dialog box. The response is automatically encrypted as a number that is stored in the *it* memory variable. When setting up the stack for use, you can then store this number in a field in the stack and have the program compare it to the password that the user enters with this command when he or she uses the stack.

The Ask command differs from the Answer command in that it allows the user to type in a response to the question displayed in the dialog box instead of having him or her choose between alternate replies, as with the Answer command. The <question> argument can be no

Figure 11.9: Selecting the incorrect answer to Question 1

longer than about 40 characters (depending upon the width of the characters). Again, as with the Answer command, the Chicago font in 12-point size is the only text style that the dialog box will display.

If you wish, you can add a default reply that the user can select by clicking on the OK button or by pressing Return or Enter (the OK button is automatically prehighlighted). To enter a reply different from the default, the user simply types it in. As soon as he or she begins typing, the default reply disappears. The dialog box also contains a standard Cancel button that can be selected by clicking on it, if the user does not wish to reply to the question in any way.

When specifying the <default> argument, you can either enter it in the script or specify a HyperCard container that is to supply it. For example, you can ask the user his or her name and have the default supplied from the User Name field in the User Preferences card of the Home stack. The user can then accept the default name or type in a new name that is stored in the *it* memory variable when he or she clicks on the OK button (or presses Return or Enter). The reply stored in the *it* memory variable can then be entered into a particular card field with a Put command.

The script of the User Name field in the User Preferences card already creates a global memory variable called userName, which contains the contents of this field. You can have the contents of this memory variable entered as the default reply to an Ask command by entering the following:

```
on mouseUp
  global userName
  ask "Enter your full name:" with userName
  put it into field 3
end mouseUp
```

Remember that prior to using a global memory variable, you must redeclare it as a global memory variable with the Global command.

Figure 11.10 shows you the dialog box that appears when this script is executed. As the default, it contains my name, which was taken from the userName global memory variable.

My name was placed in the userName global memory variable by the script for the User Name field in the User Preferences card of the Home stack. This script reads as follows:

```
on closeField
  global userName
```

```
        put card field "User Name" into userName
    end closeField
```

The Ask command can be used in a variety of situations where you need further information from the user in order to know what processing is to take place. You can also apply it to educational and training applications. For example, you could create the following button script:

```
on mouseUp
    global userName
    ask "Name the capital of China?"
    if it is "Beijing" then
        ask "Correct!" with "Good going" && userName &"!"
    else
        if it is "Peking" then
            ask "Almost!" with "The modern spelling is "Beijing"
        else
            ask "Sorry!" with "It is Beijing"
```

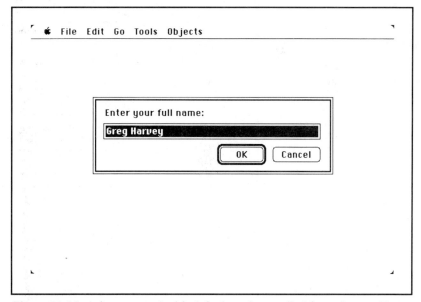

Figure 11.10: Ask command with default reply supplied from the userName global memory variable

```
        end if
      end if
    end mouseUp
```

Figure 11.11 shows you the dialog box that appears when you click on this question button. Because the Ask command does not contain a <default> argument, the dialog box is empty. When you enter a response and click on the OK button (or press Return or Enter), the response is stored in the *it* memory variable. The first If...Then...Else construction then evaluates the contents of this memory variable.

Figure 11.12 shows you what happens when *it* contains the completely correct answer (Beijing). The second Ask command displays a dialog box that confirms the answer is correct and reinforces the user with "Good going" and the user's name. This is done by concatenating the "Good going" with the global memory variable userName and "!".

Figure 11.13 shows you what happens when the almost correct answer of Peking is given. This is done with a third Ask command

When creating an educational stack, store the student's name in a global memory variable that you can use in messages that reinforce and correct him or her repeatedly during the lesson. This can be done by creating a background or stack script with an *on openStack- ...end openStack* message handler. This message handler will then use the Ask command to get the student's name and store it in the *it* memory variable. Be sure that you put the contents of *it* into another memory variable not used by HyperTalk and that you declare it to be global.

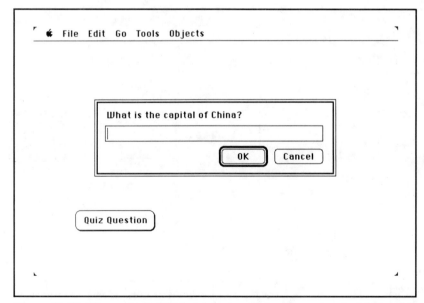

Figure 11.11: The capital of China question dialog box created with the Ask command

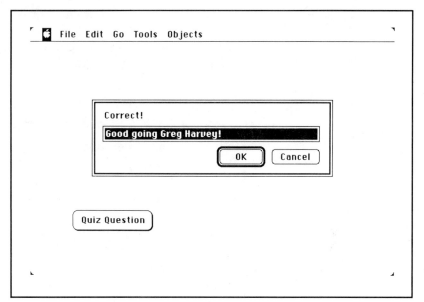

Figure 11.12: Entering the completely correct answer

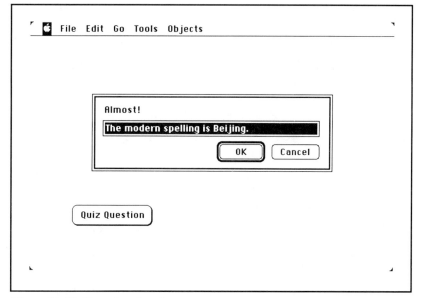

Figure 11.13: Entering the almost correct answer

that is displayed when *it* does not contain Beijing but does contain Peking. Figure 11.14 shows you what happens when a completely incorrect answer is given. This is done with yet a fourth Ask command that is displayed when *it* contains anything other than Beijing or Peking (or is left empty).

The Phone Button Script in the Wineries Stack

To end the discussion of If...Then constructions in HyperTalk, let's examine the script of the Winery Phone button in the Wineries stack. If you remember, you copied this button into your stack from the Address stack. This button script is of particular interest because it incorporates the use of multiple If...Then constructions and the special *selection* memory variable that stores any text that has been selected from a field on the card. The entire Winery Phone button script is as follows:

```
on mouseUp
   get the selection
   if it is empty then get first line of field "Winery Telephone"
```

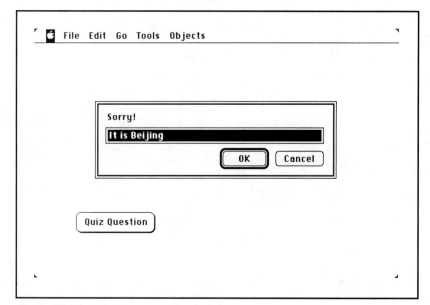

Figure 11.14: Entering a completely wrong answer

```
if it is empty then ask "Dial what number?"
if it is not empty then
    push this card
    visual effect zoom open
    go to stack "Phone"
    dial it
    pop card
end if
end mouseUp
```

When the mouseUp system message is detected by this message handler, the Get command puts anything in the *selection* memory variable into the *it* memory variable (remember that the Get command automatically stores the information that it retrieves in *it*).

This allows you to select an alternate telephone number with the I-Beam cursor before you click on the Winery Phone button. That way, the program will dial the selected phone number instead of the number that has been entered into the first line of the Winery Telephone field. In the address stack, this was done because the field contains two lines: one for entering the business phone and another to enter the home phone. In the Wineries stack, it can be used to dial an alternate phone number entered elsewhere on the card, as in the Wine Tasting Notes field.

Once the program places the contents of the *selection* memory variable into the *it* memory variable, the first If…Then construction evaluates the contents of the *it* memory variable. If no text has been selected, the *selection* variable will be empty and the true or false expression of the If…Then construction will be true. In that case, the program will put the contents of the first line of the Winery Telephone field into the *it* memory variable.

After that, the second If…Then construction is executed. The program examines the contents of *it* a second time. If *it* is empty at this point (because there is no entry in the Winery Telephone field), the Ask command is executed and a dialog box prompting the user to enter the telephone number to be dialed is displayed. Remember that any number entered as a reply here is also automatically entered into the *it* memory variable.

After the user responds to this dialog box, the program executes the third If…Then construction. If the *it* memory variable is not empty, all of the commands below the If...Then command are executed. These instruct the program to push the card for quick retrieval, go to the Phone stack (by using a special visual effect called zoom open; you will learn about the HyperTalk visual effects in Chapter 13), dial the number stored in the *it* memory variable, and then retrieve the winery card where you clicked on the Winery Phone button.

Note that if the *it* memory variable is found to be empty when the third If...Then construction is evaluated, none of these commands are carried out. In other words, nothing happens when you click the Winery Phone button. This will be the case if no text is selected in the card, the Winery Telephone field is empty, and the user enters nothing into the Ask dialog box. Figure 11.15 shows you the flow diagram, illustrating the way this script operates.

The Repeat Commands

In addition to allowing you to control the operations performed by a particular script conditionally, as with the If...Then construction, HyperTalk allows you to control the number of times a particular command or set of commands is repeated. It does this through the use of four different Repeat constructions: Repeat For, Repeat While, Repeat Until, and Repeat With. The commands that you want repeated by the particular Repeat construction are referred to as a *loop*. The business of the Repeat construction is to repeat loops until a particular number of repetitions has been made or a particular condition is met or ceases to exist.

Although each of these Repeat constructions requires slightly different arguments, they do share a common form:

- The particular Repeat command and its arguments, which instruct the program how many times to repeat a loop, are entered on a single line of the script.

- The commands in the loop (that is, the commands to be repeated) are indented and are entered on the lines below the Repeat command (each command on its own line).

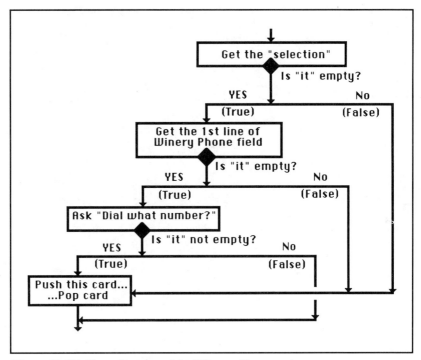

Figure 11.15: Flow diagram of the Winery Phone script

- The loop is terminated with an End Repeat statement entered on a line of its own immediately below the last command in the loop. This statement is outdented so that it is aligned with the Repeat command.

The format of the Repeat constructions is important. By placing the commands in the loop between the Repeat command and the End Repeat command, HyperCard knows exactly what commands are to be repeated and in what order.

In the simplest form, the Repeat construction instructs Hyper-Card to perform the loop a set number of times. In its more complex forms, it instructs the program to continue to repeat the loop until a particular condition is met or while a particular condition is still true. When you use the Repeat construction in this way, you are actually having the program perform a type of decision making somewhat akin to that performed with the If…Then construction.

The Repeat For Construction

The Repeat For construction simply tells HyperCard to repeat the command or commands in the loop for a particular number of times. Its form is as follows:

```
repeat [for] <number> [times]
  <command>
  <command>
end repeat
```

As you can see, the use of the command words *for* and *times* is optional. In other words, you can enter

```
repeat 10
```

or

```
repeat for 10
```

or even

```
repeat for 10 times
```

with the same result: the commands entered on subsequent lines of the Script Editor before the required End Repeat statement are executed 10 times in the order in which they are listed.

For example, you could create a button that would add five cards to the current stack when it is used with this script:

```
on mouseUp
  repeat for 5 times
    doMenu "New Card"
  end repeat
end mouseUp
```

When the mouseUp message is detected by the *on mouseUp...end mouseUp* message handler, the Repeat construction is executed. It instructs HyperCard to perform the doMenu "New Card" command five times, thus adding five new cards to the stack.

When specifying the <number> argument, you do not have to enter a particular value. This argument can be supplied as a result of a calculation (provided the calculation results in a whole number), as in the following:

```
on mouseUp
   repeat for round(the number of cards/4) times
      doMenu "New Card"
   end repeat
end mouseUp
```

In this case, the <number> argument is not a constant number: if the stack contains 20 cards, the loop is repeated four times (20/4 = 5); if the stack contains eight cards, it is repeated only two times (8/4 = 2); and so on. The addition of the *round* function, which rounds a fractional number up to the nearest whole number, prevents the <number> argument from being anything besides a whole number. For instance, if the number of cards is seven when this button is selected, the program will add two cards to the stack, because it rounds up the result of 1.75 (7/4 = 1.75) to 2 and uses this as the <number> argument.

The <number> argument can also be supplied from a Hyper-Card container such as the *it* memory variable or a field, provided that the container holds a whole number. You can make the new card button much more open-ended by modifying the button script as follows:

```
on mouseUp
   ask "How many cards do you want to add?" with 1
   repeat it
      doMenu "New Card"
   end repeat
end mouseUp
```

In this case, the Repeat construction uses the number you enter in the dialog box that appears as a result of the Ask command. This number is stored in the *it* memory variable, which is used as the <number> argument of the Repeat For command.

The Repeat While and Repeat Until Constructions

The Repeat While and Repeat Until constructions both require a true or false expression as their arguments. In this way, they are just like the If…Then and If…Then…Else constructions. The form of the Repeat While construction is as follows:

```
repeat while <true or false expression>
   <command>
   <command>
end repeat
```

In this case, the commands in the loop are repeated while the true or false expression remains true. As soon as the expression is found to be false, the loop is no longer repeated.

The form of the Repeat Until construction is similar:

```
repeat until <true or false expression>
   <command>
   <command>
end repeat
```

However, it works just the opposite of the Repeat While construction. The commands in its loop are repeated only until the true or false expression is found to be true. In other words, the loop is repeated while the expression remains false.

For example, you could create a button script that takes you to the first address card in the current stack whose state field contains the state you specify in an Ask dialog box:

```
on mouseUp
   ask "Enter state code of the card you want to see:"
   if it is not empty then
      repeat while field "State" <> it
         go to next card
      end repeat
   end if
end mouseUp
```

However, you can create the same button script using the Repeat Until construction, as follows:

```
on mouseUp
    ask "Enter state code of the card you want to see:"
    if it is not empty then
        repeat until field "State" = it
            go to next card
        end repeat
    end if
end mouseUp
```

When you use the Repeat While construction, the expression is phrased in the negative:

```
repeat while field "State" < > it
```

When you use the Repeat Until construction, the expression is phrased in the positive:

```
repeat until field "State" = it
```

⊙ Beware of endless loops in your scripts! For example, if you enter a state code in the Ask dialog box that doesn't match any of the state abbreviations entered in the state field of the cards in the stack, HyperCard will repeat the *go to next card* command endlessly. The only way to stop endless loops is by pressing the Command-period key combination.

With the Repeat While construction, the *go to next card* command is repeated while the state code in the state field is not the same as the reply that is stored in the *it* memory variable. As soon as the state code in the card is equal to the contents of the *it* memory variable, the loop is no longer repeated. With the Repeat Until construction, the Go command is repeated until the state code in the state field is the same as the reply that is stored in the *it* memory variable. As soon as this is true, its loop is no longer repeated.

The Repeat With Construction

In the Repeat With construction, you initialize a counter memory variable with a start number and give a stop number, thereby establishing the number of times the loop will be repeated. Each time HyperCard repeats the loop it increases (or decreases) the counter by one until the counter equals the stop number. When you want the program to increase the counter by one each time a loop is executed, you use this form of the command:

```
repeat with <variable> = <start number> to <stop number>
  <command>
  <command>
end repeat
```

When you want the program to decrease the counter by one each time a loop is executed, you use this form of the command:

```
repeat with <variable> = <start number> down to <stop ¬
number>
  <command>
  <command>
end repeat
```

When you increment the counter (using the first form), the start number must be smaller than the stop number. This is just like counting up from one number to another by ones. When you decrement the counter (using the second form), just the opposite is true: the start number must be larger than the stop number. This is just like counting down from one number to another by ones.

As is true with <number> argument for the Repeat For command, the <start number> and <stop number> arguments can be numbers that you enter directly into the script, or they can be supplied by calculations or HyperCard containers that return whole numbers. For example, you can enter the following:

```
on mouseUp
  repeat with counter = 1 to 10
    print this card
    go to next card
  end repeat
end mouseUp
```

In this case, the start and stop numbers for the counter are entered values. When the mouseUp message is sent, the print loop will always be repeated 10 times, printing the next 10 cards. However, you could also have the start and/or stop number supplied from a HyperCard container such as the *it* memory variable, as in the following:

```
on mouseUp
    ask "How many cards to print?" with 1
    if it is not empty then
        repeat with counter = 1 to it
            print this card
            go to next card
        end repeat
    end if
end mouseUp
```

Here, the number of times the print loop is repeated depends upon the number you enter in the dialog box in response to the Ask command.

The Repeat With command provides you with a useful *algorithm* (a set of instructions conceived to solve a specific programming problem) that ensures a particular operation specified in the repeated loop will be applied to all of the cards in the stack. This algorithm is

```
repeat with counter = 1 to the number of cards
```

By setting the start number at 1 and the stop number equal to the total number of cards, the loop to be repeated will always be applied to all of the cards in the stack.

The Next Repeat Command

Normally, you want all of the commands entered into a loop that is to be repeated to be executed. However, there may be times when you want all of the commands in a loop executed only when a particular condition exists. In such cases, you can use the Next Repeat command to tell HyperCard which commands are to be skipped when a particular condition exists.

The Next Repeat command is used with the If...Then construction. The program uses this construction to evaluate a true or false expression, and the Next Repeat command is entered as the <command> argument after the Then conjunction. Only when the expression is false will the program execute the commands in the loop that follows the If...Then construction. If the expression is true, the Next Repeat command instructs HyperCard to return to the top of the Repeat construction. If you are using the Repeat For or Repeat With construction, the counter is incremented by one at this time.

The Repeat Next command can be used with any Repeat construction. The general format of the construction is shown here with the Repeat With construction:

```
repeat with <variable> = <start number> to <stop number>
   <command>
   <command>
   if <true or false expression> then next repeat
   <command>
end repeat
```

Earlier, when discussing the Delete Card option on the Edit menu (way back in Chapter 2), you learned that you can use it to delete only one card at a time. However, you can get around this limitation by using the Repeat With construction with the Next Repeat command. Of course, for such applications, you have to have in mind a group characteristic that you can use as the <true or false expression> argument for this Repeat command.

For instance, assume that you have already sorted your address stack and copied all of the cards where the state is New York to a separate address stack. Now you want to delete all of the cards in the stack where the state (the State field) is New York (they are all redundant). To do that, you create a conditional delete button with this script:

```
on mouseUp
   ask "Enter the state code to delete for:"
   if it is not empty then
      repeat with counter = 1 to the number of cards
         go to next card
         if field "State" <> it then next repeat
            doMenu "Delete Card"
      end repeat
   end if
end mouseUp
```

When the mouseUp message is detected by the handler, the Ask command prompts you to enter the two-letter code of the state. In this particular example, you would enter *NY* into the dialog box to have all of the cards with the state code NY deleted from the stack.

The Ask command stores this response in the *it* memory variable. Because the first If...Then expression is true (it is not empty), the Repeat With construction is executed. It contains the algorithm (*counter = 1 to the number of cards*) to have all of the cards in the stack used. Therefore, the first command in this loop, *go to next card*, is executed for every card in the stack.

However, the second command, *doMenu "Delete Card"*, is executed conditionally. Only when the contents of the State field in the card is the same as NY (stored in the *it* variable) is this command carried out. This is because when the state code is not the same as NY, the <true or false expression> argument of the second If...Then construction is true. When this is the case, the Next Repeat command is carried out. This command returns control to the top of the loop and increases the counter by one, thereby bypassing the *doMenu "Delete Card"* command on the line below it.

This entire procedure is then repeated until the number stored in the counter variable is equal to the total number of cards. As the result, all of the cards where the state is NY will be deleted from the stack.

The Exit Commands

When you are working with HyperCard's control structures, there may be times when you want to have the program escape the control of the structure prematurely when a particular condition is met. To meet such a need, you can use one of the forms of the HyperTalk Exit command. If you are exiting from an If...Then or If...Then...Else construction, use the form Exit If. If you are exiting from a Repeat construction, use the form Exit Repeat. If you are exiting from a message handler, use the form

    exit <message>

where the <message> argument is the name of the message in the handler. For example, if you were using an Exit command to prematurely leave an *on mouseUp...end mouseUp* message handler, you would enter the Exit command as

```
exit mouseUp
```

in the script.

The Exit commands are normally used with an If...Then construction of their own. This construction determines when to terminate the control of the message handler, If...Then construction, or Repeat construction. Commonly, you will need to use the Exit command with a form of the Repeat construction, as in the following:

```
on mouseUp
    ask "How many cards do you want to add?"
    if it is not empty then
        repeat with counter = 1 to it
            if counter > 100 then exit repeat
            doMenu "New Card"
        end repeat
    end if
end mouseUp
```

As used in this example, the Exit Repeat limits the maximum number of cards that can be added with this button script to 100.

For example, if the user specifies a number of cards larger than 100 should be added, the loop with the *doMenu "New Card"* command will be faithfully executed only until the number of repetitions stored in the counter variable reaches 101 (exceeding 100 by one). At that time, the If...Then expression will become true, and the Exit Repeat command will be executed. This causes the program to stop processing the Repeat construction (so that no more cards will be added to the stack), and to begin executing the commands beyond the End Repeat statement. In this case, these commands include the End If and *end mouseUp* statements.

However, when the user specifies any number less than or equal to 100 in the Ask dialog box, the Exit Repeat command will not be executed before the stop number stored in the counter variable of the Repeat With construction is reached.

In a similar manner, when you use the Exit If command, the Exit command causes the program to break out of the If...Then or If...Then...Else construction when the true or false expression in its own If...Then construction becomes true. If you are using the Exit command with the <message> argument, it causes the program to break out of the message handler entirely when this is the case.

Summary

Learning Hyper-Talk is analogous to learning a foreign language. At this point, you have learned all of the basic grammar and now need to go on learning more vocabulary and special usages such as idioms. Beyond that, experience (practice!) is a key element in eventual fluency or mastery.

In this chapter, you examined the various control structures that you can add to scripts that should either be processed conditionally or repetitively. Congratulations are in order at this point. To have made it this far in your study of HyperTalk assures you that you will be able to go on to master specific HyperTalk commands and functions that are presented in the remaining chapters with little or no trouble. You have now been exposed to all of the basic structural elements involved in using HyperTalk. From this point, it is simply a matter of learning the arguments and uses of new commands and functions in the language as well as becoming more experienced in writing scripts of your own.

In the next chapter, you will look at creating scripts that perform common HyperCard commands such as printing, sorting, and browsing cards. By learning to incorporate many of the commands on the HyperCard menus into HyperTalk scripts, you can create buttons that perform these tasks, relieving you and your users of the need to use the menu options when working with your stacks.

Executing HyperCard
Menu Options

IN MANY OF THE STACKS YOU DEVELOP, YOU WILL want to create your own buttons that perform the various Hyper-Card operations that you, and your users, will need to use when working in them. In some applications, you can even dispense with the HyperCard menus while in the stack and rely entirely upon the buttons that you have created. In such cases, you should make sure that all routine operations such as adding new cards, deleting cards, or printing cards, and any specialized operations such as sorting cards are available through buttons added to the card background.

If you distribute your stack to others, you can't assume that they will know HyperCard as well as you do. For example, you can't take for granted that a user will know how to redisplay the HyperCard Menu bar (Command-Space bar) that your stack script has hidden. Therefore, if you remove the Menu bar from a stack, you should be absolutely certain that you have provided your user with buttons that will perform all of the menu options that they will need to use in the stack. Also, be sure that somewhere you explain how the stack works and what each button accomplishes. To do this, you can create a help button that takes the user to particular help cards that explain all of these matters quite clearly.

In this chapter you will examine scripts using commands that are normally executed from the HyperCard menu. These include such common operations as locating specific cards in the stack, flipping through the cards in a stack, editing their contents, and printing them out.

Scripts to Browse Cards

To create scripts that enable your users to browse through cards, you can use either the Go or Show HyperTalk command. The Go command takes you directly to a particular card, and the Show command flips through specified cards in a stack. Most of the time, you will use these commands to create scripts for buttons that take you or your users to various places in the stack.

Button Scripts Using the Go Command

You already have experience using the Go command in Hyper-Talk to have the program display a particular card on the screen. Up to now, your experience in using it has been limited to entering various Go commands in the Message box. Of course, any command that you enter there, you can also place in a button script. You have also seen that HyperCard creates a Go command for you when you use the LinkTo button in the Button Information dialog box and then indicate the card to go to when this button is used.

Remember that the Go command has the form

```
go [to] <destination>
```

When you use it, you must specify a destination of some kind. This can be in the form of the card name (if you have assigned one to the card) enclosed in a pair of quotation marks, as in

```
on mouseUp
  go to card "Buena Vista Winery"
end mouseUp
```

or in the form of the card number, as in

```
on mouseUp
  go to card 3
end mouseUp
```

or, more commonly, in the form of the card ID number, as in

```
on mouseUp
  go to card id 2834
end mouseUp
```

You can also use a memory variable as the <destination> argument of the Go command. For example, you could use the Ask command to prompt the user to enter the number of the card he or she wishes to see:

```
on mouseUp
    ask "Enter number of card to go to:"
    if it is not empty then
        go to card it
end mouseUp
```

The stack name is not required when you create a Home button that takes you to the Home Card. You can simply enter the button script as

```
on mouseUp
    go home
end mouseUp
```

There is no need to add *in stack "Home"* to this script.

When you use the Go command to display a card that is not in the current stack, you need to add the stack name as part of the destination. This is true whether you specify the card name, number, or ID. Remember that some of your buttons didn't work as planned when you copied them from the Wine Tour stack to the Wineries stack. This was because the stack name was required as part of the <destination> argument to make them work. Most often, you will want to add the stack name as part of the button script. That way, the button will always work, even when copied to a new companion stack.

To add the stack name, you enter *in stack* followed by the name of the stack enclosed in quotation marks, as in

```
on mouseUp
    go to card "Buena Vista Winery" in stack "Wineries"
end mouseUp
```

When creating a script that prompts the user to enter the card number or name of the card he or she wants to see, you can also prompt for the name of the stack:

```
on mouseUp
    push card
    ask "Enter name or number of card to see:"
    if it is not empty then
        put it into goCard
        get name of this stack
        put it into stackName
        ask "Which stack contains this card?" with stackName
```

```
    if it is not empty then
        go to card goCard in it
    end if
end if
end mouseUp
```

When the user clicks on this button, the program pushes the card for quick retrieval later on and then prompts him or her to enter the name or number of the card. It then stores this information in the *it* memory variable. Because this variable will be reused in the same script when the Get command is executed, the Put command is used to put this reply in a new memory variable called *goCard*.

Next, the Get command reinitializes the *it* memory variable with the name of the stack (in the form *stack "Wine Tour"*). The stack name is then put into a memory variable called *stackName*. This variable is used as the default reply of the second Ask question. The user can either accept it by clicking on the OK button (or by pressing Return or Enter) if the card is in the current stack, or edit the name of the stack in the dialog box, if the card is in another stack. Finally, the program stores the reply made in the dialog box in the *it* memory variable, and the Go command uses both the goCard and *it* variables in the <destination> argument.

For practice, you can create a new background button for the Wine Tour stack that contains this script. You can call the button Go Card and place it in the upper left corner of the card.

1. **Start HyperCard from the Home Card.**

2. **Click on the Wine Tour stack button.**

If you added the *Hide menubar* script to the background, you need to override it to display the HyperCard menu options.

3. **Press Command-Space bar.**

   The Menu bar will reappear.

4. **Select the Background option on the Edit menu (or press Command-B).**

   This button will be added to the background of the card.

5. **Select the New Button option on the Objects menu.**

Because the *get name of this stack* command returns the word *stack* as well as the name enclosed in quotation marks (as in *stack "Wine Tour"*), the Go command does not contain the word *stack* before the *it* memory variable in the last part of the <destination> argument. However, because the user is not required to enter the word *card* along with the card number or name in response to the first Ask command, *card* is added to this part of the <destination> argument.

6. **Select the Button Info option on the Objects menu (or double-click on the New Button).**

7. **Type** *Go Card* **as the button name.**

8. **Click on the Script button.**

9. **Enter the commands for this script between the** *on mouseUp* **and** *end mouseUp* **commands, as shown in Figure 12.1.**

   You can also refer to the previous example and type the commands from it.

When you press Return to enter the last End If statement for this script, the Script Editor will put a blank line into the script. To delete this, press the Backspace (Delete) key until the flashing text insertion pointer is right after the *f* in if. This brings up the *end mouseUp* statement that has already been added to this script.

10. **Click on the OK button.**

11. **Position the button in the upper left corner of the card (you can also shrink its length slightly, if you wish), as shown in Figure 12.2.**

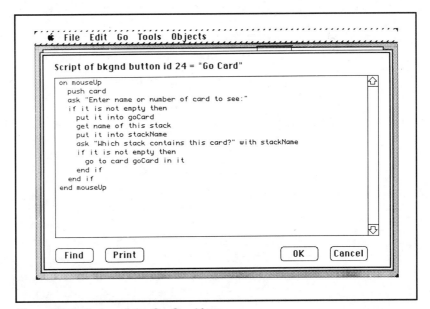

```
 File  Edit  Go  Tools  Objects

Script of bkgnd button id 24 = "Go Card"

on mouseUp
  push card
  ask "Enter name or number of card to see:"
  if it is not empty then
    put it into goCard
    get name of this stack
    put it into stackName
    ask "Which stack contains this card?" with stackName
    if it is not empty then
      go to card goCard in it
    end if
  end if
end mouseUp

 Find    Print                      OK    Cancel
```

Figure 12.1: Script of the Go Card button

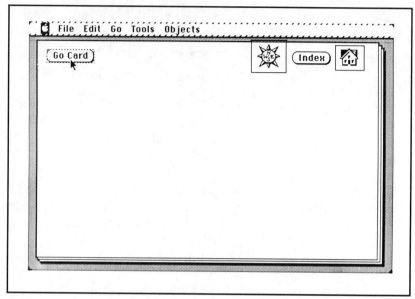

Figure 12.2: Locating the Go Card button in the Wine Tour stack

12. Select the Browse tool on the Tools menu.

Now test out the button by trying to go to different cards in this and the Wineries stack.

13. Click on the Go Card button.

14. Enter *2* and click on the OK button (or press Return or Enter).

15. Click on the OK button (press Return or Enter) to accept the default reply of *stack "Wine Tour"*.

Hopefully, your script worked and you are now looking at the map of the Valley of the Moon Wineries. If not, you received an error dialog box of some sort (perhaps *can't understand arguments...* came up). When HyperTalk encounters a command that it cannot execute, it displays a dialog box that contains Script and Cancel buttons. If you click on the Script button, which you will normally want to do, the program will bring up the button script and the Script Editor will locate the flashing text insertion pointer near the problem area. Always check the text immediately before and after this pointer for the source of this error.

The program will let you know when the script lacks an End If command or has too many End If statements. Although most of the error messages are self-explanatory, you may find some to be cryptic when you are still new to script writing. When hunting for nonspecific errors, always check for typos and incomplete arguments to the Hyper-Talk commands that you have used, and check your memory variables to make sure that they are initialized and used properly in commands and functions.

If your script has a problem, check the commands in each line against those in the example or shown in Figure 12.2. Once you have located and edited the error(s), click on the OK button and try steps 13 through 15 again.

Now try using the Go Card button to go to the Buena Vista Winery card in the Wineries stack.

16. Click on the Go Card button.

17. Type *Buena Vista Winery* **as the name of the card to go to, and click on the OK button (or press Return or Enter).**

18. Edit *"Wine Tour"* **to** *"Wineries"* **or type** *stack "Wineries"* **to indicate the name of the stack that contains this card, and click on the OK button (or press Return or Enter).**

This takes you to the Buena Vista Winery card in your Wineries stack.

If you want, you can copy the Go Card button from the Wine Tour stack to your Wineries stack. Be sure that you are in the background of the Wineries stack when you paste the copied button into it. You can locate the Go Card button after the Home button at the bottom of the winery cards.

Button Scripts Using the Show Command

The HyperTalk Show command has two uses. It can be used to display all or some of the cards in the current stack, or to show objects that have been hidden (with the Hide command). Let's look first at the more common use of the Show command to browse through the cards in a stack.

This form of the command is

```
show [<number> | all] cards
```

To create a button that displays all of the cards in the stack from the current card on, you can just enter the following:

```
on mouseUp
   show all cards
end mouseUp
```

You can also enter the command as just *show cards* if you wish, as the use of *all* is optional.

If you use the optional <number> argument, the program will display only the number of cards you enter for this argument. You can create a script that prompts the user for the number of cards using the Ask command, as follows:

```
on mouseUp
    ask "Enter number of cards or click OK to see all" with "all"
    if it is "all" then
        show all cards
    else
        if it is not empty then
            show it cards
        end if
    end if
end mouseUp
```

In this button script, the Ask command supplies *all* as the default reply. If the user clicks on the OK button (or presses Return or Enter), the *it* memory variable contains *all* and the *show all cards* command is used. If not, and the dialog box is not empty, then the number entered in reply is used as the <number> argument for the Show command.

When adding a browse button to your stack, you can use the Scan icon (icon ID 32670) to represent it. For practice, you can create a browse button for your Wineries stack. If you performed the last exercise, you are already at the Buena Vista Winery card in this stack.

1. **Select the Background option on the Edit menu (or press Command-B).**

2. **Select the New Button option on the Objects menu.**

3. **Select the Button Info option on the Objects menu.**

4. **Type** *Browse* **as the button name.**

5. **Click on the** *Show name* **check box to uncheck it.**

6. **Click on the transparent radio button.**

7. **Click on the Icon button.**

8. **Drag the scroll box down all the way to the bottom of the vertical scroll bar.**

9. **Click on the Scan icon.**

   This icon is located on the top row (refer to Figure 12.3) and has an icon ID of 32670.

10. **Click on the OK button.**

11. **Resize the button so that you can see the Scan icon, and it is square.**

12. **Position the button at the bottom of the card next to the Next button.**

   You will have to select the Prev and Next buttons and move them to the left to fit your Browse button between the Next and Home buttons.

13. **Hold down the Shift key and double-click the mouse.**

   This takes you directly to the Script Editor.

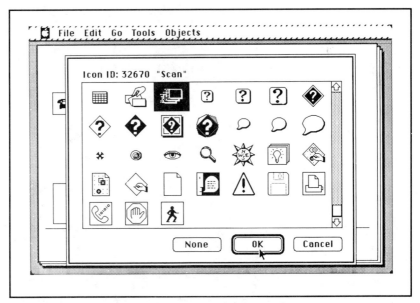

Figure 12.3: Selecting the Scan icon for the Browse button

14. **Enter the button script as shown in Figure 12.4, or refer to the text of the script shown earlier in this section.**

15. **Click on the OK button.**

16. **Select the Browse tool on the Tools menu.**

17. **Click on the Browse button.**

18. **Click on the OK button (or press Return or Enter).**

    The program will display all three cards in this stack.

19. **Click on the Browse button again.**

20. **Type *1* and click on the OK button (or press Return or Enter).**

    This time, the program displays the Hacienda Winery card, the next one in the stack.

Hiding and Showing Objects

You have already used the Show command in its second usage of redisplaying hidden objects when you created the background script

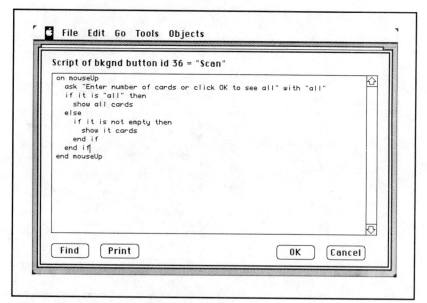

Figure 12.4: Script of the Browse button

that hides and redisplays the Menu bar in the Wine Tour stack. The form for this usage of the Show command is as follows:

```
show menubar | <window> | <button or field> [at <location>]
```

You use the <window> argument to have HyperCard display either the Message box, the Tools menu, or the Patterns menu on the screen. When you want the program to display the Message box, you can enter the <window> argument as *message box*, *message window*, *message*, or even *msg*. When you want the program to display the Tools menu or the Patterns menu, you must enter the <window> argument as *tool window* or *pattern window*, respectively.

You can also use the Show command to display buttons or fields on the screen. This allows you to hide fields or buttons in a stack that are made visible on the screen only when a button is selected or a particular system message activates a message handler in your scripts. This allows you to annotate information in a card or to include help messages in fields rather than on separate cards that appear only when needed (you will apply this technique to the Wineries stack, shortly). You can also add extra hidden buttons that appear only when a *More options* button is selected or when a particular message handler is activated.

When specifying the fields or buttons to be made visible on the screen, you can refer to them by name, number, or ID number. If the field or button is at the card level, you must enter the card before specifying its name, number, or ID number. For instance, if you enter the script

```
on mouseUp
    show field 5
end mouseUp
```

HyperCard will display the fifth field in the current card *background*. If you want the fifth card field to be displayed, you would have to enter the following

```
on mouseUp
    show card field 5
end mouseUp
```

If your stack uses more than one background and you want a field or button in a background different from the current background to be displayed, you must also specify the background of the field or card as part of the argument, as in

show card button 2 in background 2

You can also use containers, such as fields or memory variables, to supply the arguments for this usage of the Show command. For example, you could have the following script:

```
on mouseUp
    answer "Specify the window to display:" ¬
    with "Tools" or "Patterns" or ""Message box"
    if it is "Tools" then
        show tool window
    else
        if it is "Patterns" then
            show pattern window
        else
            show message box
        end if
    end if
end mouseUp
```

You cannot reposition the Menu bar by adding an [at <location>] argument to the Show command. HyperCard will only let you enter *show menubar*. It always remains at the top of the screen when displayed.

The optional [at <location>] argument allows you to position these windows where you want them to appear on the screen. When you enter this argument, you enter the horizontal and vertical screen coordinates separated by commas. When locating fields or buttons on the screen, these coordinates refer to the center of the field or button. When locating one of the windows, these refer to the upper left corner of the window.

When specifying the position, you must take care that the coordinates entered for the <location> argument allow all of the windows, fields, or buttons to be visible on the Macintosh screen. You will learn more about the coordinate system and specifying screen coordinates later on in this chapter, in the section on Scripts for Editing Text.

The HyperTalk Hide command is used in conjunction with the Show command when you use it to display objects such as windows, buttons, and fields. The Hide command takes this form:

hide menubar | <window> | <button or field>

You do not need to specify the location of the object used as the argument of the Hide command. As long as you specify the window, button, or field correctly, the program will hide it from view.

Using Hidden Fields and Buttons in the Wineries Stack

To show how you can use the Hide command to hide and display a hidden field and button, you are going to annotate the Tours field in the Buena Vista Winery card. You will do this by adding a Tour Message field that will remain hidden from view until you select a new button next to the Tours field. When you click on this button, the program will show the Tour Message field, which contains information about tours at this winery. This field will contain its own button. When you select it, the button will hide the Tour Message field and itself from view.

If you completed the last exercise and are still in HyperCard, the Hacienda Winery card will still be displayed on your screen. You should now click on the Prev button to go to the Buena Vista Winery card. If you are not currently in HyperCard, start the program from the Wineries stack. This will take you to the Buena Vista Winery card.

To begin, bring up the Message box and place the Tools menu on the screen.

You can quickly display the Tools menu on the screen by pressing Option-Tab. This key combination acts like a toggle switch. When you press Option-Tab a second time, the window containing the Tools menu is closed.

1. **Select the Message option on the Go menu (or press Command-M).**

   This displays the Message box at the bottom of your screen.

2. **Type** *show tool window* **in the Message box and press Return (or press Option-Tab).**

   This displays the Tools menu. Move it to the left side of your screen, if necessary.

Now create a new text field to contain additional information about the Buena Vista Winery tours. All of the objects that you are about to create (the field and buttons) will be added to the card level, so there is no need to use the Background option.

4. Select the **New Field** option on the Objects menu.

5. Select the **Field Info** option on the Objects menu.

6. Type *Tour Message* as the field name.

7. Click on the shadow radio button under Style.

8. Click on the **Font** button.

9. Click on the **Chicago** font.

10. Click on the **Center** radio button under Align.

11. Click on the **OK** button.

12. Reduce the length of this field until it contains only three lines of text.

13. Move the Tour Message field so that it is directly above the Tours heading and Tours field, and its right edge is in line with the right edge of the Tours field (Figure 12.5).

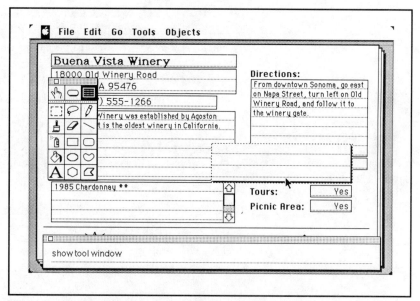

Figure 12.5: Positioning the Tour Message field on the card

14. Click on the Paint Text tool in the Tools menu.

To see how the buttons that you are about to create will work, experiment with the Hide and Show commands in the Message box before going on.

15. Type *hide card field "Tour Message"* **and press Return or Enter.**
The new shadow field disappears.

16. Use the I-Beam cursor to select the word *hide* **in the Message box.**

17. Type *show* **and press Return.**
This changes the command to *show card field "Tour Message"*. The Tour Message field reappears.

Before you create the Tours Info button that will show this field when it is selected, you will need to use the Paint Text tool to create a symbol that will mark its position on the card. This is because the Tours Info button will be transparent, meaning that you will not see its outline in the card.

18. Select the Text Style option on the Edit menu (or press Command-T), or double-click on the Paint Text tool.

19. Click on Chicago, click on the Bold check box under Style, and finally, click on the OK button in the dialog box.

20. Locate the I-Beam cursor in a blank area of the card and click the mouse.

21. Type * (asterisk, produced by pressing the Shift and 8 keys on the top row or the * in the upper right corner of the numeric pad).

22. Press Command-S to select the asterisk.

23. Move the asterisk so that it is located immediately to the right of the Yes in the Tours field.

24. Move the Lasso tool to a blank area of the card and click the mouse.

Now you will create the Tours Info button, a transparent button that will be located on this asterisk next to the Tours field.

25. Click on the Button tool in the Tools menu.

26. Select the New Button option on the Objects menu.

27. Select the Button Info option on the Objects menu.

28. Type *Tours Info* as the button name.

29. Click on the *Show name* check box to uncheck it.

30. Click on the transparent radio button under Style.

31. Click on the Script button.

    This takes you to the Script Editor.

The script for this button will show both the hidden Tour Message field and a hidden OK button that you will add next (this button will appear to be part of the Tour Message field when the Tours Info button is selected). Therefore, this button script will contain two Show commands.

32. Type *show card field "Tour Message"* and press Return.

33. Type *show card button "OK"* and click on the OK button in the Script Editor (Figure 12.6).

34. Resize the button so that it is a square that is large enough to cover the asterisk.

35. Move the button so that it encloses the asterisk to the right of the Tours field (Figure 12.7).

Now create the OK button that will hide the Tour Message field and itself when it is selected.

36. Select the New Button option on the Objects menu.

37. Select the Button Info option on the Objects menu.

38. Type *OK* as the button name.

39. Click on the Script button.

The script for this button will contain two Hide commands. The first one will hide the Tour Message field and the second will hide the OK button itself.

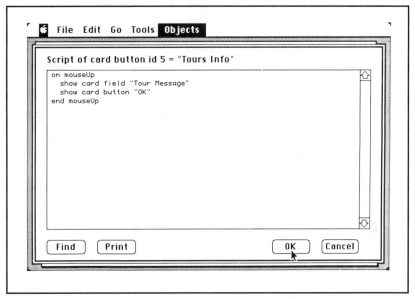

Figure 12.6: Script of the Tours Info button

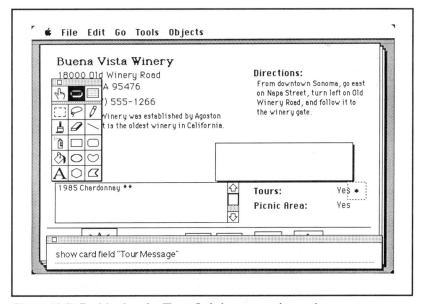

Figure 12.7: Positioning the Tours Info button on the card

40. Type *hide card field "Tour Message"* and press Return.

41. Type *hide card button "OK"* and click on the **OK** button in the Script Editor (Figure 12.8).

42. Resize the **OK** button so that its rounded rectangle just encloses **OK**.

43. Move the button so that it is located in the lower right corner of the Tour Message field (Figure 12.9).

44. Click on the Browse tool in the Tools menu.

Before you test out the Tours Info and OK buttons to make sure that everything works according to plan, you should enter the additional information in this field.

45. Move the I-Beam cursor to the top of the Tour Message field and click the mouse.

46. Type *All tours are self-guided.*

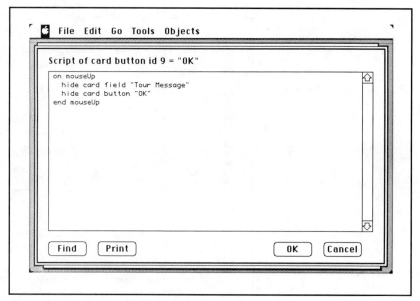

Figure 12.8: Script of the OK card button

Now, all that remains is to test out the buttons. Before you do, remove the Tools menu and the Message box.

47. Click on the Close box in the Tools menu and the Message box.

48. Move the Browse tool to the OK button.

49. With the Browse tool on the OK button, click the mouse.

The Tour Message field and OK button will disappear.

50. Move the Browse tool to the asterisk that marks the location of the Tours Info button and click the mouse.

The Tour Message field and OK button reappear (Figure 12.10).

51. Click on the OK button to remove the Tour Message field and this button.

From this exercise, you have a good idea of how you can use hidden fields and buttons to enhance the stacks that you create. If you wish, you can continue on and copy the Tour Message field and the Tours Info and OK buttons to the other cards in the Wineries stack.

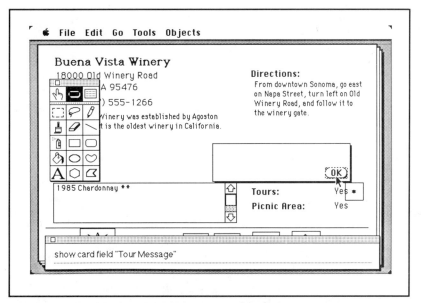

Figure 12.9: Positioning the OK button on the card

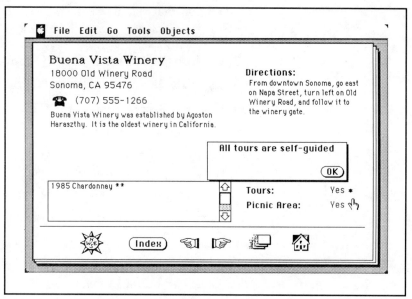

Figure 12.10: The Tour Message field and OK button that appear when you select the Tours Info button

Scripts to Find Cards

The Find command was one of the first HyperTalk commands that you learned. You have already used it to locate specific words and characters within text fields in the Address stack in the exercises in Chapter 2. You can enter similar Find commands in the scripts that you write. The forms of the Find command are as follows:

    find <source> [in field n]

    find chars | word <source> [in field n]

The <source> argument is the search text that you want the program to locate. As you know, it must be enclosed in a pair of double quotation marks. If you want to limit the text search to a particular field, you can add the optional [in field n] argument. The *n* in this argument is either the field name, number, ID number, or a Hyper-Card container that supplies one of these components. For example, you could create this Find button in a stack as follows:

```
on mouseUp
   ask "Enter text search for: "
   put it into searchText
   ask "Enter field name or number to search in:"
   put it into searchField
   if searchText is not empty and ¬
   searchField is empty then
      find searchText
   else
      if searchText is not empty and ¬
      searchField is not empty then
         find searchText in field searchField
      end if
   end if
end mouseUp
```

In this script, there are two Ask commands: the first prompts you to enter the text to be searched for with the Find command, and the second prompts you to enter the field to be searched in. If you do not enter a response to the second Ask question, the program searches all text fields in the stack. If you do enter a field, it then searches only that text field in the cards.

To limit the search to specific characters that are contained within a word (rather than begin a word), you add *chars* to the Find command. To limit the search to an entire word, you add *word* to the Find command. If you do not use either qualifier, the program considers a match to the <source> argument to be any characters that begin a word in the text, regardless of whether they make up an entire word. For example, to limit a search to the word *her*, you enter this Find command:

```
find word "her"
```

In this case, HyperCard would not consider text such as *here*, *her*self, and *here*with to be matches (as it would without the addition of *word* to the Find command). However, if you entered

```
find chars "her"
```

HyperCard does put the search text into the Message box when the Find command is executed from a script. Therefore, you can use the Find option on the Edit menu to locate subsequent matches as soon as the program locates the first match with the script.

the program would consider words such as *here, her*self, and *here*with to be matches as well as words like *there*, *with*er, and *where*as.

There is a drawback to using a Find command in a script as opposed to using the Find option on the Edit menu (Command-F). From a script, you cannot use Return to have the program locate subsequent matches to your search string, as is the case when using the Find option on the Edit menu. As you and users of your stacks become accustomed to this use of the Return key, you may find this difference to be frustrating. For that reason, you may want to think twice before adding a Find button to your stack, relying instead on the built-in command option.

Using the Result Function with the Find or Go Command

When you use the Find or Go command in HyperCard and the program does not find a matching text string or card, it lets you know by having the Macintosh beep at you. However, you can use a special function called *the result* to have your own error message displayed with the Ask command. To do this, you set up an If...Then construction that tests whether the result is empty. If it is not empty, this means that the Find or Go command has failed to locate the text or card searched for. In that case, the program will execute the Ask command you add as the <command> argument of the If...Then construction, thereby displaying the error message that you place in it.

For example, you could use the following script:

```
on mouseUp
   ask "Enter text search for: "
   find it
   if the result is not empty then
      ask "Could not find your text in the stack"  ¬
      with "Please try again!"
   end if
end mouseUp
```

This technique can also be applied to scripts that use the Go command to locate and display a particular card on the screen.

Scripts to Edit Cards

HyperTalk includes two commands that you can use in scripts to add text and delete text in particular fields. These commands are the Type and Delete commands. You can also use the Put command to put a particular message into a field. The Type command differs from the Put command in that with Type, the text is entered one character at a time (albeit at a very quick rate). The Type command has a simple form:

type <source>

The <source> argument is simply the text you want typed into a particular field or at a specific location in a card.

If you want the text to be typed in a field with the Browse tool, you use the Choose command to select the Browse tool and then use commands that position the I-Beam cursor in the field where you want the text entered. After positioning the cursor, you must use the Click command before your Type command if the I-Beam cursor has not already been changed to the flashing text insertion pointer (this point will made clearer shortly).

The Choose command has the form

choose <name of a tool>

You simply enter *choose* followed by the name of the tool you want used, as in *choose browse tool*, *choose text tool*, and so on.

Normally, to locate the I-Beam cursor at the beginning of a specific field of a card, you can use the Tab key. To enter it in a script, you simply enter *tabKey* on a line of its own. Placing this in a script is the same as pressing the Tab key to go to the beginning of the next field. Pressing the Tab key to go to a field in a stack does not require you to click the mouse before you begin entering your text. Therefore, you do not need to enter a Click command before your Type command.

To see how this works in practice, create a new example stack.

1. **Select the New Stack option on the File menu.**

2. **Type** *Edit Example* **as the stack name.**

3. Click on the *Copy current background* check box to uncheck it.

4. Click on the New Button (or press Return or Enter).

5. Tear off the Tools menu and locate it in the lower right corner of your screen.

6. Select the Background option on the Edit menu (or press Command-B).

7. Select New Field from the Objects menu.

8. Select Field Info from the Objects menu.

9. Click on the shadow radio button under Style.

10. Click on the Show Lines check box to select it.

11. Click on the OK button.

12. Move the field to the upper left corner of the card.

13. Hold down the Option and Shift keys and drag a copy of this field below it.

14. Select the New Button option on the Objects menu.

15. Drag the button so that it is positioned somewhere to the right of the first field.

16. Select the Button Info option on the Objects menu.

17. Enter *Type Text* as the button name.

18. Click on the Script button.

In this button script, you will enter an Ask question that prompts you to enter your name. Once you have entered it in the dialog box, the program will then type it into the first background field in the card.

19. Enter *choose browse tool* and press Return.

20. Enter *ask "Enter your name:"* and press Return.

21. Enter *tabKey* and press Return.

22. Enter *type it*.

23. Click on the OK button.

24. Click on the Browse tool.

Now test out your button.

25. Click on the Type Text button.

26. Enter your name in the dialog box and click on the OK button (or press Return).

Your name is typed very quickly on the first line of the first field. Although it is entered rapidly, you should be able to see that it is entered character by character instead of all at once. Contrast the effect of adding text to a field with the Type command to that of adding it with the Put command.

27. Click on the Button tool in the Tools menu.

28. Click on the Type Text button to select it.

29. Hold down the Shift and Option keys and drag a copy of this button down below it.

30. Select the Button Info option on the Objects menu.

31. Enter *Put Text* as the button name.

32. Click on the Script button.

33. Select the two lines that contain *tabKey* and *type it* and press the Backspace (Delete) key.

This deletes these lines from the script.

34. Press the Tab key and enter *put it into field 2* in the blank line.

35. Click on the OK button.

Now try out your new Put Text button.

36. Click on the Browse tool in the Tools menu.

37. Click on the Put Text button.

38. Enter your name in the dialog box and click on the OK button (or press Return).

This time, your name appeared all at once at the beginning of the first line of field 2. When you use the Put command, you do not need to use the Tab key to locate the cursor as you do with the Type command. Indicating the field that is to accept the text is all that is required.

Locating the Screen Position of the Cursor

You can also locate the position where text is to be typed by giving the screen coordinates of the place where you want the text to begin. In such a case, you must use the Click command to establish the cursor in this position before you use the Type command. The Click command has the form

click at <h,v> [with shiftKey | optionKey | commandKey]

The h argument represents the horizontal screen coordinate of the cursor, and the v argument represents the vertical screen coordinate.

Figure 12.11 shows the screen coordinate system used by Hyper-Card. As you can see, the coordinates at the top of the screen extend from 0,0 in the upper left corner to 512,0 in the upper right corner (because there are 512 pixels across the screen width). The coordinates at the bottom of the screen extend from 0,342 in the lower left corner to 512,342 in the lower right corner (because there are 342 pixels down the length of the screen). When specifying horizontal and vertical screen coordinates in HyperTalk commands, you can use any of these coordinate pairs.

> You can also click at a particular place with the Shift, Option, or Command key held down. You can combine the keys, as in
>
> click at 60,160
> with shiftKey, optionKey
>
> which is used when copying a field or button while restraining the motion to the horizontal or vertical axis. Normally, such a command would be followed by a Drag command, which you will learn about in the next chapter.

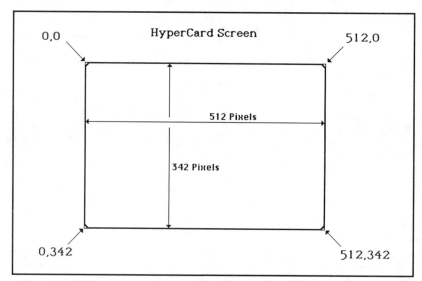

Figure 12.11: The system of screen coordinates in HyperCard

Entering the Click command with the horizontal and vertical screen coordinates is the same thing as moving the mouse to that position and physically clicking the mouse button, as in

click at 26,157

HyperTalk contains several functions that will return the screen coordinates of the position of the mouse. You can use these to get the coordinates that are supplied as the h,v arguments of the Click command. To get just the horizontal screen coordinate, you can use the MouseH command. To get just the vertical screen coordinate, you can use the MouseV command. To have the program return both the horizontal and vertical coordinates (required with the Click command), you can use the MouseLoc command.

There is even a function called the clickLoc that returns the horizontal and vertical screen coordinates of the most recent mouse click. To have the program return these coordinates, you just enter *the click-Loc* in the script.

You can also have the program get the screen coordinates of a particular window, field, or button. To do this, you use the Loc function. HyperCard returns the screen coordinates of the center of fields and buttons and those of the upper left corner of windows (the Message box, Tools menu, and Patterns menu mentioned earlier).

To see how you can use these functions to locate the position and then use the Click command to locate the cursor there, try making the following modifications to the script of the Type Text button. Here, you will change the Type Text button so that it types your name on the second line of the second field.

1. **Select the Message option on the Go menu (or press Command-M) to bring up the Message box.**

2. **Move the I-Beam cursor so that it is positioned at the beginning of line 2 in the second field.**

   Don't click the mouse!

3. **Type *the mouseLoc* in the Message box and press Return.**

   This gives you the horizontal and vertical coordinates of the I-Beam cursor.

4. **Select the Background option on the Edit menu (or press Command-B).**

5. **Click on the Button tool on the Tools menu.**

6. **Hold down the Shift key and double-click on the Type Text button.**

This takes you directly to the Script Editor.

7. **Drag the I-Beam over the line of the script that contains tab-Key until only this command is selected.**

8. **Type** *click at 28,158*.

Your coordinates will differ if you positioned the I-Beam in a slightly different place in the field or if you are using HyperCard with an external monitor. If they do, just type the coordinates you see in your Message box instead of 28,158.

9. **Click on the OK button.**

10. **Click on the Browse button in the Tools menu.**

11. **Click on the Type Text button, enter your name a second time, and click on the OK button (or press Return or Enter).**

This time, your name is typed at the beginning of the second line of the second field.

When you have a script enter some text in a field, either with the Type or Put commands, you can change the text style characteristics such as the font, font size, alignment, and so on. For example, you could get the program to type in your name in Chicago and center it in the first field by changing the button script as follows:

```
on mouseUp
   choose browse tool
   ask "Enter your name:"
   put it into msgText
   set textFont of field 1 to chicago
   set textAlign of field 1 to center
   get loc of field 1
   click at it
   type msgText
end mouseUp
```

In this script, the program stores your name in the memory variable called msgText, then uses the Set command to set the font of field 1 to Chicago and the alignment to center. The *get loc of field 1* statement returns the horizontal and vertical coordinates of the center of field 1. These are then used in the Click command to instruct the program where to position the flashing text insertion pointer. Finally, the Type command types your name as stored in the msgText variable, centered from the screen coordinates stored in the *it* memory variable, and supplied by the *get loc of field 1* statement.

If you want to see how this works, modify the script of the Type Text button to the one shown above on your own. Notice what happens to your name entered on the first line of this field when you use this revised button. It becomes centered and changes to the Chicago font because a text field can have only one set of text style characteristics. You must be mindful of this when you create scripts that modify the text style characteristics of a field.

Deleting Text Items in a Field

The Delete command in HyperTalk deletes only the text stored within a container such as a text field or memory variable. You cannot use this command to delete the container itself. If you want a script to delete a particular text field or button, you must use the doMenu command with the appropriate Edit menu option.

In addition to adding text to a field, you can also create scripts that will delete particular components of text in a field. Remember that you examined these components in Chapter 10. They include characters, words, items, and lines (defined by hard carriage returns). The HyperTalk Delete command has the form

```
delete <component>
```

To use Delete, you simply specify which items of text are to be deleted as part of the <component> argument. You also specify the container that holds the items to be deleted. Although this container will most often be a text field, it can also be a container such as a memory variable that you, or HyperCard, define. For example, you could have the program delete a particular word in a text field, as in

Remember that HyperCard recognizes both *words* and *items* as different text components. An item is any piece of text separated by commas or spaces. A word is any piece of text separated by spaces only.

```
delete word 2 of line 3 of field 1
```

or you could have something like

```
delete word 2 of it
```

In the first example, the second word of the third line of field 1 is deleted. In the second example, the second word is removed from the contents of the *it* memory variable.

You can see how the Delete command works by adding a Delete Text button to your Edit Example stack.

1. **Select the Background option on the Edit menu (or press Command-B).**

2. **Select the New Button option on the Objects menu.**

3. **Drag the button so that it is positioned under the Put Text button.**

4. **Select the Button Info option on the Objects menu.**

5. **Enter *Delete Text* as the button name.**

6. **Click on the Script button.**

7. **Enter the following commands between the *on mouseUp* and *end mouseUp* statements:**

```
ask "Enter number of field with text to delete:"
put it into delField
ask "Enter number of line to delete in field:" with 1
put it into delLine
if delField is not empty and delLine is not empty
then delete line delLine of field delField
```

8. **Click on the OK button.**

9. **Click on the Browse tool in the Tools menu.**

Now try using the Delete Text button to delete your name from the second line of the second field.

10. **Click on the Delete Text button.**

11. **Type *2* as the field number in reply to the first question, and click on the OK button (or press Return or Enter).**

12. **Type *2* as the line number in reply to the second question, and click on the OK button (or press Return or Enter).**

This deletes your name on the second line of the second field.

Try using this button to delete your name entered a second time in the center of the first field. Enter *1* as the number of the field to delete text in. Count the line number that holds the second occurrence of your name in this field and enter it as the number of the line to be deleted.

Scripts for Editing Scripts

HyperTalk even has an Edit Script command that takes you directly to the Script Editor window for any of the scripts that you have created for objects in the stack. Once you are there, you can edit the script the same as you do when creating a new script or revising an existing script. The form of the Edit Script command is

```
edit script of <target>
```

where the <target> argument consists of the object whose script you want to see. You can refer to the object by name, number, or ID number. Be sure to include the word *card* if you are referring to a button or a field that is not in the background.

To see how this works, add a Button Editor button to your Edit Example stack.

1. **Select the Background option on the Edit menu (or press Command-B).**

2. **Select the New Button option on the Objects menu.**

3. **Select the Button Info option on the Objects menu.**

4. **Type *Button Editor* as the button name.**

5. **Click on the Script button.**

6. **Enter the following commands between the *on mouseUp* and *end mouseUp* statements:**

```
ask "Edit which button?"
put it into buttonName
answer "Where is this button?" with "Card" or "Background"
if it is "Background" then
   edit script of background button buttonName
else
```

```
        edit script of card button buttonName
end if
```

7. **Click on the OK button.**

8. **Drag the Button Editor so that it is positioned beneath the Delete Text button.**

9. **Click on the Browse tool in the Tools menu.**

Test out the Button Editor by taking the following steps:

10. **Click on the Button Editor.**

11. **Enter *Type Text* as the name of the button to edit, and click on the OK button (or press Return or Enter).**

12. **Click on the Background button or press Return or Enter.**

    This takes you directly to the script of the Type Text button. If you receive an error message, try it again, this time clicking on the card option—you may have placed the Type Text button at the card level instead of the background.

13. **Click on the Cancel button in the Script Editor.**

Although this is not the kind of button that you will want to routinely add to stacks that you distribute to other people (thus allowing them easy access to all of your button scripts!), you can use it when you are developing a new stack and then delete it when you have completed the stack, before you distribute it.

Scripts to Print Cards

When you want to add a Print button to a stack, you can use the DoMenu "Print Card" or DoMenu "Print Stack..." command or some form of the HyperTalk Print command. The DoMenu "Print Card" command prints just the current card, and the DoMenu "Print Stack..." command allows you to print the entire stack (as well as specify the type of report format desired).

When you use the Print command, HyperCard actually sets up a print job that queues each card or group of cards that you add to it.

This allows you, or your users, to print individual cards from different stacks in one print job, something that is not possible when you use the DoMenu command with either of the print options.

The Print command uses these arguments:

print [all | <number> cards] | [this <card>]

To open the print job in the script, you use use the Open Printing and Close Printing commands. The Open Printing command follows this form:

open printing [with dialog]

When you add the [with dialog] optional argument, HyperCard opens up the Print Stack dialog box, just as it does when you select the Print Stack option on the File menu or use the DoMenu "Print Stack..." command in a script. From the dialog box, you can choose how many cards are to be printed per page as well as add a header to the printout, if you wish.

After you enter the Open Printing command, you can use the Print command as many times in your script as it takes to print all of the cards that you want included in one print job. If you want to print cards that are not located in the current stack, you must add an appropriate Go command to make the card current (or, at least, the stack that contains it) before the Print command that instructs HyperCard to add it to the print queue. After specifying all of the cards that are to be included in the job, you add the Close Printing command to your script.

To have the current card printed, enter

print this card

in the script.

To include a specific card in the print queue that is not the current card, you can refer to it by its name, number, or ID number as long as it is located in the current stack. For example, if the Wine Tour stack is the current stack, you can print the third card by entering "Index", 3, or ID 4853 (your ID number may be different) as the argument of the Print command.

To have all of the cards in the stack printed, enter

```
print all cards
```

You can also use the <number> argument to specify that the program print a particular group of cards in the current stack. These are printed in order, starting with the current card up to the number specified. You've already seen that you can supply this <number> argument either as a constant by entering the value in the script, or have it supplied by a memory variable. For example, you can enter

```
print 5 cards
```

which prints the next five cards in the stack (including the current card), or you can enter

```
print printNumber cards
```

where *printNumber* is a memory variable to which you have assigned an initial value either earlier in the text of the script or by prompting the user with an Ask or Answer command.

Consider the following example of a print button script that you could create for the Wine Tour stack:

```
on mouseUp
   open printing with dialog
   print this card
   print card "Index"
   go to stack "Wineries"
   print 3 cards
   close printing
end mouseUp
```

When you click on this Print button, the Print Stack dialog box appears on your screen. Here, you can select the number of cards you want printed on a page and add a header to the report. Say that you select the *Print half size cards* option on this dialog box, which allows you to print eight cards per page.

After clicking on the OK button, the script adds the first card (the Opening card) and the third card (the Index card) to the print queue.

It then goes to the Wineries stack and adds the next three cards to the queue. Finally, the *close printing* command instructs HyperCard to send these cards to the printer to print the page. Normally, when the the *Print half size cards* option is selected, HyperCard will wait until at least eight cards (a full page) have been sent to the printer before printing a page. In this case, however, the *close printing* command instructs it to print the selected cards even though there are only five in the queue, making a partial page.

Scripts That Use the Painting Program

Although less commonly required, you can create HyperTalk scripts that use the HyperCard painting program. For example, you might need to create a script that allows the user to add a particular graphic to each new card added to the stack, only if desired.

When you use the painting program in a script, the process and command used are similiar to those required when building a script to add text to a field with the Type command. However, instead of using the Browse tool, you have the script choose one of the Paint tools. For example, if you wanted the painting script to draw a line, you would enter

choose line tool

as one of the first command statements.

Remember that when painting with the Line tool—as well as with other Paint tools that create simple shapes, such as the Rectangle, Round Rectangle, Oval, and so on—you can vary the line thickness. To do this in a script, you use the Set command with the lineSize property and a value representing the number of pixels for the width (this number can be 1, 2, 3, 4, 6, or 8). For instance, to draw a line 3 pixels wide, you would add

set lineSize to 3

after the Choose command.

Once you select your Paint tool and make any desired modifications to its properties in the script, you need to position the cursor at the starting point and tell the program where to drag it to draw the line or shape.

There are many painting properties that can be set in drawing scripts that you create. Refer to Appendix C for a complete list of the painting properties that can be modified with the Set command or returned with the Get command.

To simulate physically dragging the cursor across the screen, you use the HyperTalk Drag command in the following form:

drag from <h,v> to <h,v> [with shiftKey | optionKey
  | commandKey]

As when using the Click command, you must give both the horizontal and vertical screen coordinates. However, with the Drag command you specify these screen coordinates for both the starting and ending points. For example, to draw a horizontal line across a card after choosing the Line tool, you could use this Drag command:

drag from 110,112 to 385,112

To draw a vertical line connected to the end of this line, enter

drag from 385,112 to 385,225

As you recall, the Line tool and the Paint tools that draw shapes can be used to draw the line or shape either from one of the ends or edges or from the center when the Draw Centered option on the Options menu is selected (exception: regular polygons can be drawn only from the center). In scripts, you can activate the Draw Centered option by using the Set command and setting the centered property to either true or false. For example, to draw a line from the center, you would add the statement

set centered to true

before you entered the Drag command to actually draw the line. To then turn this option off in the script before drawing other figures with other tools, you would enter

set centered to false

to turn it off.

Besides being able to draw figures and shapes from HyperTalk scripts, you can also add painted text to your cards with the Paint Text tool. Remember that text added with the Paint Text tool can't be edited like text entered into the fields. To add text to graphic images that your scripts draw, you choose the Paint Text tool with the command

> choose text tool

Then you use the Click command to position the starting point of the text and the Type command to enter the text, just as you do to have the program type standard text into fields.

When you create scripts to add text to your stacks with the Paint Text tool, you can then modify the text style by using the Set command and the specific attribute. For example, you could change the font to Chicago and the style to shadow by entering the following Set commands:

> set textFont to chicago
> set textStyle to shadow

To see how this works, you can add a new card to your Edit Example stack, then add a new card button that contains the following button script:

```
on mouseUp
    choose rectangle tool
    set lineSize to 4
    set centered to false
    drag from 110,112 to 385,225
    choose text tool
    set textAlign to center
    set textFont to New York
    set textSize to 14
    set textStyle to bold
    click at 244, 172
    type "Welcome to the machine!"
end mouseUp
```

When you've got this Draw button working with this script, experiment with making modifications to it. Try changing the tool selected, the drag coordinates, and the text style used to see what happens in the card. Remember that you can erase the rectangle and painted text by double-clicking on the Eraser tool.

Scripts That Use
Other HyperCard Menu Options

When you want a script to perform one of the options on the Hyper-Card or Apple menu that is not already covered by a specific HyperTalk command, you can always use the DoMenu command in the script. Remember that the argument for this command must be the name of the menu item you want used, in the form

doMenu <name of menu item>

When you enter the name of the menu option, you do not include the name of the menu it's located on and you must enter the name of the option enclosed in quotes exactly as it appears on the pull-down menu. For example, if the menu option uses an ellipsis (three periods), as does the New Stack... option on the File menu, then you must include the periods in the DoMenu command, as in

doMenu "New Stack..."

If the option does not use an ellipsis, you must not enter any trailing periods after the option name, as in

doMenu "Background"

Remember that the Cut, Copy, and Clear options on the Edit menu change depending upon the tool and object selected. For example, if you select a particular button in a card, these options are called Cut Button, Copy Button, and Clear Button. When using these options as arguments of the DoMenu command, you must word them correctly. Also, when specifying painting program options on the Paint and Options menus with the DoMenu command, make sure that your script has already chosen one of the Paint tools. These Paint and Options menu options are not available when one of the Object tools (Browse, Button, or Field) is selected.

The DoMenu command will work with Apple menu options. This means that your script will work with various desk accessories such as the Control Panel or Chooser. For example, you could create a script that prompts the user for his or her menu choice. If the user selects the Print Stack option, then the script will let him or her choose a new printer to use before printing the cards, as in the following:

```
if menuChoice is "Print Stack" then
    answer "Choose new printer?" with "Yes" or "No"
        if it is "Yes" then
            doMenu "Chooser"
            open printing with dialog
            print all cards
            close printing
        else
            open printing with dialog
            print all cards
            close printing
        end if
end if
```

Summary

In this chapter, you have examined how to create buttons that perform commands available from the HyperCard menus. In the next chapter, you will learn about writing scripts that perform operations not available on these menus. These operations include sorting cards, using special effects when going from one card to the next, and using sound in a stack.

Performing Special HyperCard Operations

NOW THAT YOU HAVE EXAMINED HOW TO WRITE
scripts that accomplish common HyperCard menu commands, it is
time to look at a few specialized operations that you can perform only
from scripts written in HyperTalk. The first of these operations is the
sorting of cards in a stack. You can sort cards in various orders
according to any field entry you wish. Even in those stacks where you
don't feel it's necessary to have a sort button, you may still need to
use the Sort command in the Message box to get the cards in a stack
into their final order before distribution.

In addition to sorting, you will look at the Visual command that is
used to produce a special visual effect when HyperCard goes from
one card to another in a stack. This command offers you many possibilities for enhancing your stacks, allowing you to make your transitions to new backgrounds and stacks much more exciting.

Finally, you will learn how you can add sound to a stack. Again,
sounds must be added to a stack with a HyperTalk script. Although
the voices available for sound production in HyperCard are limited,
the notes that you can have played are not. However, as you will learn,
sound production does not have to remain limited to the capabilities
of the HyperTalk Play command that you will learn about later in
this chapter.

Scripts to Sort Cards

Sorting the cards is commonly required in stacks that store a lot of
textual information. To give yourself, and your users, the ability to
sort cards in a stack, you need to create a sort button. The script of

this button will use the HyperTalk Sort command, which has the following form:

sort [ascending | descending] [text | numeric | international
| dateTime] by <field or expression>

When you use the Sort command in a script, you must specify at least the field that is to determine the sorting order. For example, if you just enter the Sort command as

sort by field "Name"

HyperCard will alphabetize the cards by the first word (usually a name or initial) in this field.

When you do not specify *ascending* or *descending* order in the command, HyperCard sorts the cards by the default of ascending order (from A to Z or lowest to highest). When you do not specify a type of order (text, numeric, international, dateTime), the program uses the text sort order. In this order, numbers are not sorted according their value, so that 120 would precede 79 because number 1 is ahead of number 7 in the sorting order.

Because the *text* sort order does not arrange numbers by their actual value, you want to reserve its use for sorting on fields that contain alphanumeric text, all text, or zip codes. Use the *numeric* type of order when you are sorting a field that contains actual values that you might perform calculations on, such as money fields.

The *international* order option is required only in the rare instances when the fields you are sorting contain words that use ligatures (letters that are tied together), such as æ and œ. In Germanic languages where these occur, they are sorted differently from separated vowels. You will seldom, if ever, need to use the international option if all of your stacks use modern English entries, as our language no longer uses ligatures.

HyperCard will accept the date and time in several formats. For a list of the permissible date and time formats, refer to the section on using the date and time functions in Chapter 14.

The *dateTime* order option is used when you are sorting a field that contains only dates or times that have been entered in one of the many permissible date or time formats. If you use this option with the ascending order, the program will sort cards by date from oldest to most recent. If you sort dates in descending order, they will be arranged from most recent to oldest.

When specifying the <field or expression> argument of the Sort command, you can specify an entire field or just a particular component (such as word, item, or line) of a field. For example, if you have a stack where the city, state, and zip code are always entered on the third line of the address field, you could sort the stack by city by entering

sort by first item of third line of field "Address"

By specifying *first item of third line* instead of just *third line* or *first word in third line*, you ensure that HyperCard will sort cities whose names consist of two words—New York, New Brunswick, San Diego, Santa Cruz, and so on—using both parts of the name rather than just the first part of the name.

If you wanted to sort the stack by the state entered in the Address field, you would change the Sort command to

sort by second item of third line of field "Address"

If you wanted to sort the stack by zip code, you would enter that sort command as

sort by last item of third line of field "Address"

You can also specify an expression that involves a calculation, such as the difference between the values in two fields of a card. For example, if you have a stack where you store the cost of an item in one field and its price in another field, you could sort the cards in descending order by the difference between the price and the cost by entering the Sort command as

sort descending numeric by field "Price" – field "Cost"

Creating a Sort Button for the Wineries Stack

To see how sorting works in action, go ahead and create a Sort button for your Wineries stack.

1. **Select the Open Stack option on the File menu (or press Command-O).**
   This brings up the standard file dialog box.

2. **Double-click on Wineries, or click on Wineries and then click on the Open button.**

   This takes you to the first card in the Wineries stack.

3. **Select the Background option on the Edit menu (or press Command-B).**

   You want to add the Sort button to the background.

4. **Select the New Button option on the Objects menu.**

5. **Select the Button Info option on the Objects menu.**

6. **Type *Sort* as the button name.**

7. **Click on the *Show name* check box to uncheck it.**

8. **Click on the transparent radio button under Style.**

9. **Click on the Icon button.**

10. **Drag the Scroll box down to the bottom of the vertical Scroll bar.**

11. **Click on the Sort icon (immediately left of the Scan icon on the top row).**

    Refer to Figure 13.1. The icon shows a hand reordering a card in a stack. This icon has an ID of 20186.

12. **Click on the OK button.**

13. **Resize the button so that you can see the Sort icon.**

14. **Select the Home button at the bottom of the screen, and move it to the right so that there is sufficient room for the Sort button.**

15. **Move the Sort button so that it is between the Browse and Home buttons.**

    Refer to Figure 13.2.

For the script of the Sort button, you should offer the user a choice between sorting in ascending or descending order by the winery name. You can do this with an Answer command that offers a choice between a descending and ascending sort order with ascending as the default. The reply to this Answer command is then used in an If...Then construction to determine which type of sort to perform.

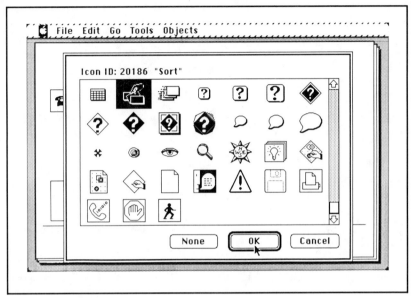

Figure 13.1: Selecting the Sort icon for your Sort button

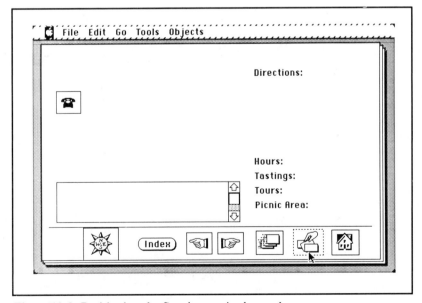

Figure 13.2: Positioning the Sort button in the card

16. Hold down the Shift key and double-click on the Sort button.

This takes you directly to the Script Editor.

17. Enter the following script for this button between the *on mouseUp* and *end mouseUp* statements:

```
answer "Sort cards by winery name in what order?" ¬
with "Descending" or "Ascending"
if it is "Ascending" then
   sort by first field
else
   sort descending by first field
end if
```

Figure 13.3 shows you the text of this script in the Script Editor.

18. Click on the OK button.

19. Click on the Browse tool in the Tools menu.

Now test out the button by sorting the cards in ascending order by the name of the winery.

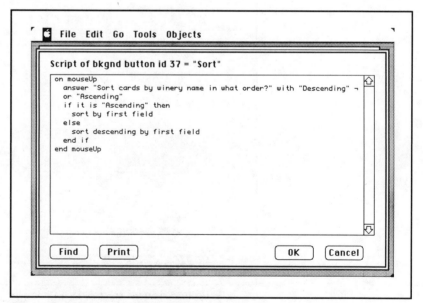

Figure 13.3: The script of the Sort button

20. Click on the Sort button.

21. Press Return or Enter (or click on the Ascending button).

When HyperCard is finished reordering the three cards in the stack, they should be in the order Buena Vista Winery, Gundlach-Bundschu Wine Co., and Hacienda Wine Cellars. Browse through them using the Next button to verify this. If that worked, now try sorting them in descending order by winery name.

22. Click on the Sort button.

23. Click on the Descending button.

This time the cards are in the order Hacienda Wine Cellars, Gundlach-Bundschu Wine Co., and Buena Vista Winery.

Scripts to Produce Special Screen Effects

HyperTalk includes a Visual command that can be used to produce a wide variety of visual effects when going from one card to another in a stack. The Visual command takes the following arguments:

```
visual [effect] <name of effect> [<speed>] [to black | white
| gray]
```

As you can see, the word *effect* is optional. There are many visual effects that you can specify when using this command:

- Dissolve: the card appears to dissolve into the next card.
- Checkerboard: the card dissolves in a block pattern like a checkerboard.
- Venetian blinds: the card dissolves in rows, like opening venetian blinds.
- Zoom open, zoom out, or zoom close: the transition from one card to the next is similar to the opening and closing of windows on the desktop with the Finder.

- Iris open or iris close: the movement of the transition is from the center outward or inward in a circle.

- Barn door open or barn door close: with the barn door open effect, the movement is from the center outward toward the left and right edges of the screen, like pulling open two sliding doors; the barn door close effect is just the opposite.

- Wipe left, wipe right, wipe up, or wipe down: the current card appears as though it is being erased or rolled up in the direction specified.

- Scroll left, scroll right, scroll up, or scroll down: it appears as though the card you are going to has been taken out of the stack and placed on the top of the current card (as in vaudeville, when the assistant took the card announcing the next act and placed it on top of the one describing the current act).

Although the names of the visual effects are descriptive, you have to experiment with them to get a good idea of what each does and which one is the most effective way to make the transition from one card to the next.

The optional [speed] argument of the Visual command controls the speed at which the visual effect specified is executed. For this argument, you can use the adverbs fast, very fast, slow or slowly, and very slow or very slowly. As you might expect, when you use the modifiers fast or very fast, the uniqueness of the visual effect is harder to discern than when you use the modifiers slow, slowly, very slow, or very slowly.

In addition to varying the speed, you can also specify that the visual effect is to go to a black, white, or gray background. You can add this argument to an effect such as wipe left in the first Visual command, and then follow it with a second Visual command that uses the opposite visual effect, wipe right, to simulate the use of a slide projector.

The Visual command can be used with either the Go or Find command in a script. The Visual command must precede the Go or Find command that it is to work on and be entered as part of the same message handler in which the Go or Find command is entered. HyperCard remembers the particular visual effect executed by the Visual command until a new Visual command is executed in the same handler or the handler is terminated with an *end message* statement.

Although you do not have to place the Visual command in the line immediately above the one that has the Go or Find command, it is a good idea to do so. That way, you will always know where to look if you want to modify the visual effect or remove it entirely.

Experimenting with Various Visual Effects

To see how the Visual command works and what some of the effects do, you can add several visual effects to the existing buttons in your Wine Tour and Wineries stacks. When choosing a visual effect, you will want to pick one that complements the graphic design of the cards involved.

For example, you have a button in the Opening card of the Wine Tour stack that takes you from the overview of the major wine-producing regions in Northern California to a detailed roadmap of the wineries in the Valley of the Moon. Because you are taking the user from a larger view to a close-up of part of the area, the iris open effect is appropriate. As you will see, it enhances the feeling of going from the macroscopic to the microscopic level.

When you use one effect to go to a particular card, you will often find it most appropriate to use the opposite visual effect for a button that returns you to your point of origin. For instance, if you use the iris open effect to go from the Opening card with the regional wine map to the Valley of the Moon Wineries map, you will want to use the iris close effect for the Opening card button that returns you to the Opening card.

You can start your examination of the various effects possible with the Visual command by adding the iris open and iris close effects to these buttons in the Wine Tour stack. If you have quit HyperCard since the last exercise, click on the Wine Tour stack button in the Home Card. If you are still in the Wineries stack where you just added the Sort button, open the Wine Tour stack with the Open Stack option on the File menu. You can also click on the Map button, which will take you to the Home Card (because you didn't go to one of the winery cards from the Valley of the Moon Wineries map) and from there you can get to the Opening card of the Wine Tour stack by clicking on the Wine Tour stack button.

1. **Press Command-Space bar if the HyperCard Menu bar is hidden.**

2. **Tear off the Tools menu and move it to the left side of the screen.**

3. **Click on the Button tool in the Tools menu.**

   You will see the outline of the Winery Map button on the regional map.

4. **Hold down the Shift key and double-click on the Winery Map button.**

   This takes you directly to the button script.

5. **Position the I-Beam cursor at the end of the first line of the script (after the *p* in mouseUp), click the mouse, and press Return (don't press Enter, which will take you out of the Script Editor).**

   This adds a blank line to the script and positions the flashing text insertion pointer at the first tab stop of this new line.

6. **Type *visual effect iris open slowly* as the command for the second line of the script.**

7. **Click on the OK button.**

8. **Select the Browse tool on the Tools menu.**

9. **Click on the Winery Map button (somewhere on the Valley of the Moon heading).**

Notice how the regional map seems to "open up" to reveal the detailed map containing the Valley of the Moon Wineries. Because the iris open effect proceeds from the center outward, it appears as though the map is opening up right from the Winery Map button.

Now that you are at the Valley of the Moon Wineries map, you can add a Visual command using the iris close effect to the Opening card button.

10. **Select the Button tool on the Tools menu.**

11. **Hold down the Shift key and double-click on the Opening card button (the one with the Compass icon at the top of the card).**

    This takes you directly to the Opening card button script.

12. **Position the I-Beam cursor at the end of the first line of the script (after the *p* in mouseUp), click the mouse, and press Return (don't press Enter or it will take you out of the Script Editor).**

13. **Type** *visual effect iris close slowly.*

14. **Click on the OK button.**

15. **Select the Browse tool on the Tools menu.**

16. **Click on the Opening card button.**

    This returns you to the Opening card, using the opposite iris effect.

When you tested this button, the Valley of the Moon Wineries map appeared to close up into the Valley of the Moon heading on the Opening card. Experiment going back and forth between these two cards, using the buttons with the new iris open and iris close commands. This should give you a good feel for how the two effects complement each other.

Next, add a different visual effect to the Index button. When you take the user to a new part of a stack that plays a different role, it's often a good idea to use a different type of visual effect. Doing this helps reinforce a transition to a new part of the stack, which functions differently. In this case, you will add the wipe visual effect. Make sure that you are at the Opening card before you add the Visual command.

17. **Select the Button tool on the Tools menu.**

18. **Hold down the Shift key and double-click on the Index button.**

19. **Position the I-Beam cursor at the end of the first line of the script (after the *p* in mouseUp), click the mouse, and press Return (don't press Enter, which will take you out of the Script Editor).**

20. **Type** *visual effect wipe right slowly.*

21. **Click on the OK button.**

22. Select the Browse tool on the Tools menu.

23. Click on the Index button to try the new visual effect.

When you test out this visual effect, you should see the Index card appear from underneath, as the current card appears to be wiped off the screen from left to right (you can also experiment by trying the directions left, up, or down in this script).

There are two more major transitions that occur in the Wine Tour stack. The first is when you go to one of the winery cards in the Wineries stack. The other is when you go to the Home Card. Let's add a different visual effect for each transition.

Begin by adding the zoom visual effect to the Home button. You are already familiar with this visual effect; it is the one that you see when you open and close a Macintosh application program from the desktop. It is most appropriate for opening and closing a stack from the Home Card, which acts as the HyperCard desktop.

24. Select the Button tool on the Tools menu.

25. Hold down the Shift key and double-click on the Home button.

26. Position the I-Beam cursor at the end of the first line of the script (after the *p* in mouseUp), click the mouse, and press Return (don't press Enter, which will take you out of the Script Editor).

27. Type *visual effect zoom close*.

28. Click on the OK button.

29. Select the Browse tool on the Tools menu.

30. Click on the Home button to try the new visual effect.

Although you can say *visual effect zoom in* instead of *visual effect zoom close*, it does not change the way the zoom effect works; the movement is still toward the center of the card you are going to.

Once you are at the Home Card, you will want to add the opposite zoom effect to the Wine Tour stack button. Although properly speaking, *zoom open* is the direct opposite of *zoom close*, you will use *zoom out* instead. By using *zoom out*, the opening of the Wine Tour stack will appear to happen directly from the Wine Tour stack button, rather than from the center of the Home Card.

31. Select the Button tool on the Tools menu.

32. **Hold down the Shift key and double-click on the Wine Tour stack button.**

33. **Position the I-Beam cursor at the end of the first line of the script (after the *p* in mouseUp), click the mouse, and press Return (don't press Enter, which will take you out of the Script Editor).**

34. **Type** *visual effect zoom out.*

35. **Click on the OK button.**

36. **Select the Browse tool on the Tools menu.**

37. **Click on the Wine Tour stack button to try the new visual effect.**

Next, add a visual effect to the Hacienda button on the Valley of the Moon Wineries map. For this transition to the winery cards in the Wineries stack, you can try combining two visual effects. The first will dissolve the Valley of the Moon Wineries map to gray (matching the background pattern of the card) and then use the iris open effect to open the new card from the center outward.

38. **Click on the Winery Map button.**

This takes you to the Valley of the Moon Wineries map.

39. **Select the Button tool on the Tools menu.**

40. **Hold down the Shift key and double-click on the Hacienda button.**

41. **Position the I-Beam cursor at the end of the second line of the script (after the *d* in card), click the mouse, and press Return (don't press Enter, which will take you out of the Script Editor).**

42. **Type** *visual effect dissolve to gray* **and press Return (not Enter).**

43. **Type** *visual effect iris open* **on the next line.**

44. **Click on the OK button.**

45. **Select the Browse tool on the Tools menu.**

46. **Click on the Hacienda button to try the new visual effect.**

Now, when you go to the Hacienda Winery card from the Valley of the Moon Wineries map, you are aware that a major transition is taking place. The screen dissolves briefly to a gray background, and then the winery card appears as the gray is wiped out from the center toward both sides of the card.

The Map button (using the Compass icon) in the Wineries stack now returns you to the previous card with the use of the *pop card* command. Even though this return is no longer accomplished with a Go command, you can add a visual effect to this transition. Here, you can add an opposite effect by dissolving to gray again and then using the iris close visual effect.

47. **Select the Button tool on the Tools menu.**

48. **Hold down the Shift key and double-click on the Map button.**

49. **Position the I-Beam cursor at the end of the first line of the script (after the *p* in mouseUp), click the mouse, and press Return (don't press Enter, which will take you out of the Script Editor).**

50. **Type *visual effect dissolve to gray* and press Return (not Enter).**

51. **Type *visual effect iris close* on the line above the *pop card* command.**

52. **Click on the OK button.**

53. **Select the Browse tool on the Tools menu.**

54. **Click on the Map button to try the new visual effect.**

If you like this effect for going to the cards in the Wineries stack, you will want to add the Visual commands that accomplish it to the Buena Vista and Gundlach-Bundschu buttons on the Valley of the Moon Wineries map.

Before leaving this practice session on adding visual effects to button scripts, you should try adding adding some visual effects to the Next and Prev buttons in the Wineries stack. For the Next button, you will add a visual effect that mimics the way a slide projector goes from one slide to the next. This is accomplished with the wipe left and wipe right visual effects, with the first Visual command going to gray.

55. Click on the Hacienda button to go to the Hacienda Winery card.

56. Select the Button tool on the Tools menu.

57. Hold down the Shift key and double-click on the Next button.

58. Position the I-Beam cursor at the end of the first line of the script (after the *p* in mouseUp), click the mouse, and press Return (don't press Enter, which will take you out of the Script Editor).

59. Type *visual effect wipe left very fast to gray* and press Return (not Enter).

60. Type *visual effect wipe right very fast* on the next line above the line with the *pop card* command.

61. Click on the OK button.

62. Select the Browse tool on the Tools menu.

63. Click on the Next button to try the new visual effect.

For the Prev button, try adding the scroll visual effect. This visual effect makes it appear as though the card you are going to is slipped in front of the current card.

64. Select the Button tool on the Tools menu.

65. Hold down the Shift key and double-click on the Prev button.

66. Position the I-Beam cursor at the end of the first line of the script (after the *p* in mouseUp), click the mouse, and press Return.

67. Type *visual effect scroll left*.

68. Click on the OK button.

69. Select the Browse tool on the Tools menu.

70. Click on the Prev button to try this visual effect.

Now that you know how to use the Visual command, you can continue on your own and experiment with other visual effects such as the checkerboard and venetian blinds visual effects. That way, you will have a good idea of all the visual effects you can use in your own stacks.

Scripts to Make Sounds

Digitized sounds must be in a Macintosh resource file available to the HyperCard resource stack in order to be used in the stacks you create. This requires the use of ResEdit or another utility for moving resources. Likewise, to use synthesized speech produced with MacinTalk (an Apple utility available on most electronic bulletin boards), the program file must be in the System folder and a utility must be used to install the commands in the Home stack or the actual stack where speech is used.

HyperCard gives you the ability to include sounds as part of the scripts you write for stacks. These sounds can include those recorded by a digitizer (a device that converts sound into electronic signals) and those produced with software such as MacinTalk (a Macintosh speech synthesizer), as well as those produced by HyperCard's own sound commands. By adding sound, you can add a third dimension to stacks that already incorporate a mix of text and graphics. The sounds can be used to warn, reinforce, or entertain the users. You can also create educational applications that rely on music (such as music theory or history) or language.

HyperCard comes equipped with two sound commands of its own. The simplest sound command is the Beep command. This command has only one argument, the number of times that the computer is to beep:

```
beep <number>
```

If you do not add the <number> argument to the Beep command, your Macintosh will beep only once. You can use the Beep command to get the user's attention. For example, you could have the computer beep to get the user's attention when he or she uses a delete button that will remove the current card, as follows:

```
on mouseUp
  beep 2
  answer "Delete this card?" with "Yes" or "No"
  if it is "Yes" then
    doMenu "Delete Card"
    put "There are now" && the number of cards – 1 && ¬
    "in this stack" into message box
    wait 2 seconds
    hide message box
  end if
end mouseUp
```

The only required argument is the name of the voice the Play command should use. The name of the voice must be enclosed in double quotation marks and must match the name of the resource installed in the stack.

HyperTalk also includes a Play command that enables you to reproduce sounds such as musical notes through the Macintosh's built-in speaker or a speaker attached to its audio port. The Play command has the following form:

play <voice> [tempo <tempo number>] [<notes>]

There are two voices included in HyperCard, the boing and the harpsichord, with the harpsichord being much more musical. When you enter the name of the voice, it must be enclosed in a pair of double quotations, as in *play "harpsichord"*.

The <tempo number> argument is optional. When you use it, you set a tempo by entering the word *tempo* followed by a number. This tempo number does not correspond to the traditional measurement of beats per minute. To set a normal andante tempo, use a tempo value of about 100. To increase the tempo, you enter a higher number. Once you have set the tempo, it remains in effect until the end of the Play command is reached or until you enter a new tempo number.

The <notes> argument allows you to enter the actual notes that you want played. You can also set the duration of the note, play it as a sharp or flat, and set the octave. When entering the notes to be played, you can use the traditional letters for the scale (C, D, E, F, G, A, and B). Just as with the <voice> argument, the <notes> argument must be enclosed in a pair of double quotation marks.

To add a sharp to the note, you follow its letter with the # (press Shift-3 on the top row), as in C#, F#, and the like. To make a note flat, you enter the letter *b* after the note letter, as in Eb, Bb, and so on.

The duration of the note is indicated by an abbreviation. You may assign a duration from a whole note to a thirty-second note by adding the following abbreviations:

w   whole note

h   half note

q   quarter note

e   eighth note

s   sixteenth note

t   thirty-second note

For example, to have the program play D as a whole note, then Eb as a half note, and A as an eighth note, you would enter "dw ebh ae" for the <notes> argument. To dot a note, you simply type a period after the abbreviation for its duration. For instance, entering "ge. es f#e" as the <notes> argument indicates that you want G played as a dotted eighth note followed by E as a sixteenth note and F# as an eighth note.

HyperCard allows you to play notes in different octaves. To specify the octave of a note, you enter an octave number after the note. Middle C is assigned 4 as its octave number. This octave, octave 3 below it, and octave 5 above are the ones with the best audio quality given the limitations of the built-in Macintosh speaker. The octave number is added to the note after you indicate its duration. To have HyperCard play G as a half note in the 3rd octave, C# as a quarter note in the fourth octave, followed by Bb as an eighth note in the fifth octave using the harpsichord voice, you would enter the following Play command:

play "harpsichord" "gh3 c#q4 bbe5"

Instead of entering the letter of the note and adding # and b to indicate sharps and flats, you can enter just a single value for the note. Middle C is given the value of 60. The note is increased or decreased one-half step for every number up or down. For example, to play C# in the middle octave, you could enter the note value 61; to play D in this octave, you would enter a note value of 62; and so on. For example, you could play the same three notes as indicated in the previous Play command example with note numbers by entering

play "harpsichord" "55h 618q 82e"

When you use the note number instead of the letter, you do not have to use any notation to indicate the presence of sharps or flats or a change in octave. You do, however, have to add the abbreviation to indicate the duration of the note.

Experimenting with the Play Command

To see how the Play command works, you can create a new stack that contains two octaves of the keyboard (the middle octave and the one above it—HyperCard octaves 4 and 5). You can use the painting

---

HyperCard uses octave 4 with middle C as its default setting. Therefore, you do not have to include the octave number unless you want the notes played in a different register. Also, once a new octave has been established, it affects all of the notes until a new octave number is given.

When you enter a Play command in a script, you cannot break the string of notes entered as the <notes> argument across two lines with a soft return (Option-Return). If you cannot fit all of the notes on a single line of the script, repeat the Play command on the following line, entering subsequent notes in the music for the <notes> argument of this new command.

program to draw the piano keys. To complete the keyboard, you can create buttons that play each note of the scale. You can then use the keyboard to play simple tunes.

1. **Select the New Stack option on the File menu.**

2. **Enter *Keyboard* as the stack name.**

3. **Click on the *Copy current background* check box to uncheck it.**

4. **Click on the New Button.**

5. **Tear off the Tools menu and locate it at the bottom of the screen.**

6. **Select the Rectangle tool on the Tools menu.**

7. **In the upper left corner of the screen, draw a long rectangle, representing a single piano key.**

8. **Type S to select the rectangle you just drew if the power keys are on; otherwise, press Command-S.**

9. **Hold down the Shift and Option keys, and drag a copy of the key to the right.**

    Drag it until its left edge is on top of the right edge of the original key.

10. **Continue to copy the key with the Shift and Option keys until you have seven contiguous (touching) rectangles drawn (Figure 13.4).**

11. **Select the Draw Filled option on the Options menu (or double-click on the Rectangle tool on the Tools menu).**

    Check the Patterns menu to make sure that the solid black pattern is selected. If not, click on it in the Patterns menu.

12. **Move the crossbar cursor to the top of the keys and position it slightly to the left of the line between the first and second keys.**

13. **Draw a thin solid rectangle representing the first black key. Drag it downward until it extends more than halfway down the length of the white keys (refer to Figure 13.5).**

14. **Hold down the Shift and Option keys and copy the black key, as shown in Figure 13.5.**

15. **Choose the Select tool and select the entire first octave.**

    Type S, if you have the power keys on, to have just the keys of the first octave selected.

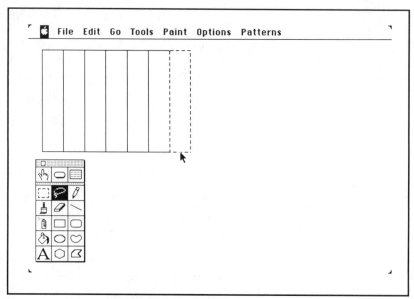

Figure 13.4: Drawing the white keys for the first octave of the keyboard

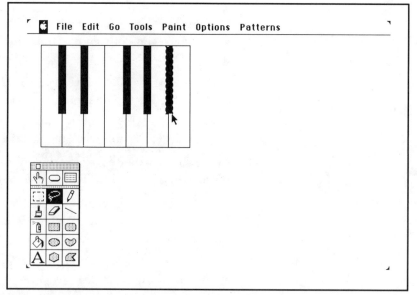

Figure 13.5: Adding the black keys to the first octave of the keyboard

16. **Hold down the Shift and Option keys and drag a copy of the first octave to the right so that it touches the first group of keys (Figure 13.6).**

Next, you need to add buttons to your keyboard that contain the Play commands to create the individual notes on the scale. The easiest way to do this is to create the first button and copy it to the other keys on the keyboard. Then, you can modify the button names and Play command <notes> arguments.

17. **Select the Button tool on the Tools menu.**

18. **Select the New Button option on the Objects menu.**

19. **Select the Button Info option on the Objects menu.**

20. **Type *C* as the button name.**

21. **Click on the transparent radio button under Style.**

22. **Click on the Script button.**

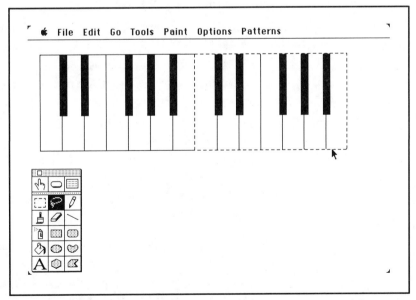

Figure 13.6: Copying the first octave to make the second octave of the keyboard

23. Change the handler from *on mouseUp* to *on mouseEnter*.

24. Enter *play "harpsichord" "c"* on the line below it.

25. Change *end mouseUp* to *end mouseEnter*.

26. Click on the **OK** button.

27. Resize the button so that is a rectangle that will fit at the bottom of the first key.

28. Position this button on the first key, as shown in Figure 13.7.

29. Hold down the **Option** and **Shift** keys, and copy this button to all of the white keys on the keyboard.

30. Double-click on the first copy of the button (on the second key). Change its name to **D**.

31. Click on the **Script** button and change the note from "c" to "d" in the Play command.

32. Continue in this way, changing the names and their notes in the Play command of the next five succeeding keys (to B of the middle octave).

    Refer to Figure 13.8 for the key names—change the notes to match these names in the Play commands.

33. When you reach the second C, the eighth note beginning the second octave, change the note in the Play command from "c" to "c5".

34. Go on and change the names of the last six buttons to match their notes. When modifying the Play command, change the "c" <note> argument to match the name of the key and add 5.

    For example, the next button (the ninth) will say *play "harpsichord" "d5"*.

Now that you have the buttons for the natural notes of the scale in two octaves, you have to create the buttons for the sharps (or flats). Do this by creating a single button for C#, the first sharp on the scale. Then copy this button and change its name and <notes> argument in the Play command to suit.

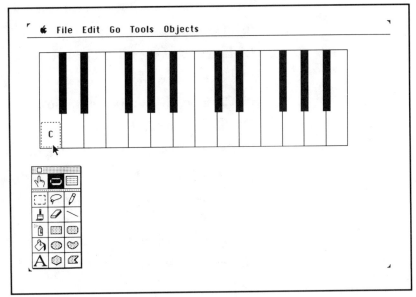

Figure 13.7: Positioning the C button on the first key of the keyboard

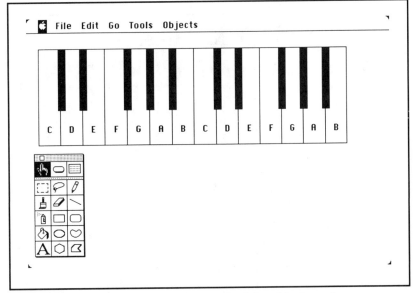

Figure 13.8: The keyboard with the names of the white keys shown

35. Select the New Button option on the Objects menu.

36. Select the Button Info option on the Objects menu.

37. Enter *C#* as the button name.

38. Click on the Show name check box to uncheck it.

39. Click on the transparent radio button under Style.

40. Click on the Script button.

41. Change the *on mouseUp* to *on mouseEnter* in the first line.

42. Enter *play "harpsichord" "C#"* as the second line of the script.

43. Change *end mouseUp* to *end mouseEnter* on the last line of the button script.

44. Click on the OK button.

45. Resize this button so that it will just enclose the black key shape (refer to Figure 13.9).

46. Move the button so that it is positioned over the first black key (Figure 13.9).

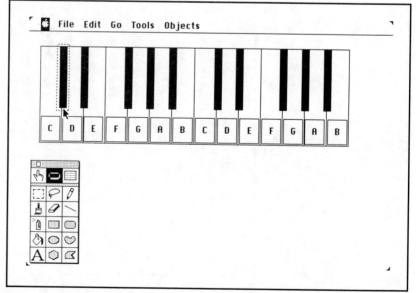

Figure 13.9: Positioning the C# button on the first black key of the keyboard

47. **Hold down the Shift and Option keys and copy this button to the remaining nine black keys.**

48. **Double-click on the second black key from the left. Change its name to D# and the Play command** <notes> **argument from** *"c#" to "d#".*

49. **Continue in this manner, changing the name and the** <notes> **argument for the next three black keys. Their names are F#, G#, and A#, respectively.**

The sharps repeat in the next octave. However, you must add 5 as the octave number when changing the <notes> argument in the Play command.

50. **Hold down the Shift key and double-click on the second C# key (the sixth black key from the left).**

51. **Change the** <notes> **argument for this Play command from "c#" to "c#5".**

52. **Continue editing the names and Play command arguments of the remaining sharps in the second octave. The** <notes> **arguments are "d#5", "f#5", "g#5", and "a#5", respectively.**

53. **Click on the Browse tool.**

Now you are ready to test out your keyboard. Position the Browse tool on the first C key and move it to the right to play the scale. If any of the notes fail to play or sound out of tune, check their button scripts. After testing the white keys, test the black keys, and then the white and black keys. If the notes are very soft, select the Control Panel option on the Apple menu. Then click on the Sound icon and increase the volume.

You can use your keyboard to play simple melodies. You can also experiment with changing the <voice> argument from "harpsichord" to "boing". After you have picked out a melody, you might want to note it down and add it to a new button using the Play command. Figure 13.10 shows you the note number associated with each key for these two octaves. You can use these in your musical button scripts instead of the standard letter notation, if you prefer.

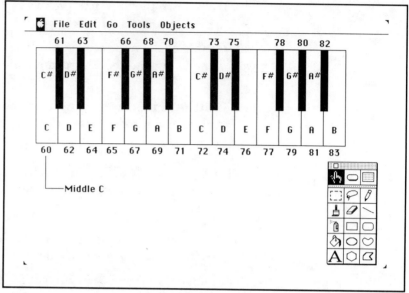

Figure 13.10: The keyboard with the note numbers assigned to all of the keys
in the fourth and fifth octaves

Summary

In this chapter, you have looked at special operations that are possible in HyperCard only when writing scripts in HyperTalk. These have included the Sort command, which allows you to sort cards in a stack by any component of a text field; the Visual command, which allows you to add special visual effects when going from one card to another; and the Beep and Play commands, which allow you to add sounds to a stack.

In the next chapter, you will look at HyperCard's ability to perform math calculations in cards. Along with the HyperTalk commands that allow you to perform simple arithmetic calculations such as addition, subtraction, multiplication, and division, you will look at its mathematical functions, including the special date and time functions.

CHAPTER 14

HYPERCARD CAN PERFORM MATHEMATICAL OPERA-
tions using arithmetic operators or the HyperTalk arithmetic commands or math functions. You can enter these operators, commands,
and functions either as part of scripts that you write or directly into
the Message box. When you enter a calculation directly into the
Message box, you are using it like an on-line calculator to obtain
results that may, or may not, have anything to do with the contents of
the current stack.

When you have the program perform math operations in the
scripts you write, you can have the results stored in fields. You can
also use memory variables to store intermediate results that are ultimately stored in fields of the cards in the current stack or other stacks.
Although the results of math calculations are stored as text with whatever precision is returned by the calculations, you can modify the
precision (the number of decimal places), the value, or the format by
the use of various HyperTalk functions.

Included as part of the math operations are those that deal with
dates and times. HyperCard allows you to store dates and times in a
variety of formats. It also allows you to perform arithmetic calculations between dates or times stored in various text fields.

Performing Arithmetic Calculations

HyperCard stores the contents of all containers such as fields and
memory variables as text. Because of this, you do not have to worry
about whether a particular field contains just values, just text, or a
mix of alphanumeric characters when issuing various HyperCard or

HyperTalk commands. However, in order for the program to perform math operations of any type, it must be dealing with numbers or containers that hold only numeric values.

There are two methods of performing the four arithmetic operations of addition, subtraction, multiplication, and division. You can use either the appropriate arithmetic operator or a special HyperTalk arithmetic command. You will first learn about the arithmetic operators before exploring the use of the corresponding HyperTalk commands.

Using the Arithmetic Operators

The arithmetic operators are + for addition, – for subtraction, * for multiplication, and / for division. In addition, you can raise one number to the power of a second number by using the ^ , and control the way any remainders in division are handled with the operators *div* and *mod*. Any of these operators can be used with values or containers that hold values entered directly in the Message box to calculate results. For example, you can enter

    30 * 5

which would give you the result of 150, or

    field 2 * .5

which would give you half of the value stored in field 2 of the current card. This assumes, of course, that field 2 contains a value or an expression that returns a bona fide value. If it does not, HyperCard will display an error dialog box informing you that it did not understand the use of *field*.

The results of calculations performed with the arithmetic operators can be, and often are, stored in memory variables. For example, if you enter

    get 30 * 5

in the Message box, the result of 150 will not appear there when you press Return or Enter. Instead, this result will be stored in the *it* memory variable (automatically used by the Get command). Only when you type *it* into the Message box and press Return will you see the result of 150 in this container.

You can also make use of the Put command to store results in a memory variable of your choosing. For instance, you could enter

   put field 2/2 into halfField

into the Message box. When you enter *halfField* and press Return, the Message box will display half of the value stored in the second field.

When you use the arithmetic operators to perform calculations in the scripts you write, you need to store the results either in a memory variable or some other HyperCard container, such as another field or the Message box itself. You would never just enter an expression such as 50 * 3 on a line of its script, for the program would not know where to store the result. You must specify some container that will hold the new value. Quite often, this container will be a new field in the card.

In stacks that deal with numbers, such as sales, inventory items, and the like, you can set up calculated fields whose contents are supplied from an arithmetic operation peformed between other fields in the card. For example, if you have a stack that inventories the items that you sell on each card, you could have calculated fields in each card that show the dollar amount tied up in stock as well as the margin of profit. The contents of these calculated fields would be determined by the values entered in the stock, cost, and price fields in the card.

The calculations would all take place as the result of arithmetic operations between fields defined by the arithmetic operators. If field 3 contains the number of items in stock and field 4 the cost, you could have HyperCard store the dollar amount in stock in field 7 by entering

   put field 3 * field 4 into field 7

in the background or stack script. Likewise, you could add a similar Put command to the script to determine the profit margin for each item and store it in the appropriate field.

Controlling Remainders in Division

When performing the arithmetic operation of division, you normally use the slash (/) as the operator, as in 9/2, which would result in the answer of 4.5. However, HyperCard gives you two additional operators for division, each of which control any remainder that results from the division in a slightly different way. If you want any remainder to be discarded, you use div as the operator, as in

   9 div 2

In this case, the program returns the answer of 4 because it drops the remainder of 1 and therefore does not include ½ or .5 in the answer.

If you want only the remainder to be used, you use mod as the operator. For example, entering

   9 mod 2

produces 1 as the answer because 1 is left over after 2 goes into 9 four times.

Using the Value Function

Although there is no problem with defining arithmetic operations beween fields that contain actual numbers, you can run into a problem if the field contains an unevaluated expression that you wish to use in a calculation. For example, assume that field 2 of a card contains the number 45 and field 3 contains the expression

   field 2 * 100

Instead of containing the result of 4500, field 3 contains the arithmetic operation that would return this answer. If you try to use the contents of this field in a new calculation, as in

   put field 3 * .25 into field 10

you will receive an error message, because HyperCard cannot multiply the text *field 2 * 100* by .25.

To obtain the desired result, you must use the HyperTalk Value function, which evaluates the contents of a container, thus converting

> You can use the mod operator to determine if a number is odd or even. All odd numbers have a remainder of 1 when divided by 2, and all even numbers do not have any remainder (2 goes into the number evenly). For example, to test if a number is even, you can enter something like this:
>
>   if testNumber mod 2 is 0 then ...
>
> The If...Then construction is true only when the value entered into the testNumber variable is even and therefore results in a zero remainder when divided with the mod operator.

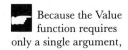 Because the Value
function requires
only a single argument,

value (<container or
expression>)

is also correct.

its text into a value that can be calculated. The Value function has
the form

> the value of <container or expression>

Therefore, you can obtain the desired result and have it stored in field
10 by entering

> put the value of field 3 * .25 into field 10

In this case, the program can calculate the answer of 1125 and put
this value into field 10 of the card.

You can use the Value function to convert any valid unevaluated
expression stored as text. This does not, however, apply to expressions that contain numbers written out as English words. For
instance, the Value function cannot convert expressions entered into
fields or memory variables such as *four hundred fifty*, *one half of field
"Subtotal"*, and the like. In addition, when the expression refers to
other fields or variables, they must also contain values for the Value
function to work.

Using the Arithmetic Commands

Although you can have calculations performed in scripts simply by
using the appropriate arithmetic operators between the containers
and values involved, HyperTalk also contains specific commands for
performing the four operations of addition, subtraction, multiplication, and division. When you use any of these arithmetic commands,
you are required to enter two arguments called the <source> and
the <destination>.

The <source> argument refers to the number, value, or container that the program gets information from in order to perform the
requested operation. It can be an actual value (27 or 1.023), an
expression (3.6/75 or field "Sum"/5), or a container (a memory
variable, a field, or the Message box) that contains such values
or expressions.

The <destination> argument refers to the HyperCard container
into which the program will put the result returned by the requested
operation. This container can be a memory variable, a field, or the

Message box. It, too, can contain numbers or expressions that are used in the calculation. However, its contents will necessarily be altered as a result of the arithmetic operation performed by HyperCard.

Each of the four arithmetic commands uses the <source> and <destination> arguments in a slightly different way. You will examine the form of each individually.

The Add Command

The form of the Add command used to perform addition is

add <source> to <container>

For example, to add the contents of field "Item 1" to field "Subtotal", you could enter

add field "Item 1" to field "Subtotal"

in a background script. If the Item 1 field of a card contains 105 and the Subtotal field is currently empty, the Subtotal field will contain 105 once this Add command is executed. Further, if the background script contains a subsequent Add command that says

add field "Item 2" to field "Subtotal"

Memory variables are often used as intermediate storage containers of calculated values. In this way, you might initialize a variable with zero, add several values to it, and then have the accumulated contents of the variable put into a particular field. If you make the memory variable global, you can then make the calculated total stored in it available to calculations performed by other scripts in the same, or a different, stack.

and the Item 2 field of the same card contains 25, the Subtotal field will contain 130 once this Add command is executed. In this manner, you could continue to add values stored in other fields of the card to the Subtotal field. Each time the value in a new field is added, the value of the Subtotal field will be recalculated.

Many times, however, you will want to use a memory variable as a temporary storage holder of the result returned by the Add command. This is the case when you are adding the values of fields and you wish to retain a record of the original values entered into each field. To avoid altering the values entered into two fields that are added together, their sum must be stored in a memory variable. You can place the memory variable in a third field of the card, if desired.

If you use the Add command to add values to a memory variable instead of a field, you must be sure to initialize the memory variable before you use the Add command. For example, if you enter

```
add 20 to sum
```

HyperCard will not understand the command if you have not previously assigned a value to the memory variable called *sum*. In many cases, you will find it necessary only to initialize the memory variable with a value of zero, as in

```
put 0 into sum
```

You can combine the use of the Add command with other math operations performed with arithmetic operators or math functions. For example, you could enter

```
put field 2/65 into newNumber
add field 7 – 15.45 to newNumber
put newNumber into field 8
```

The Subtract Command

The Subtract command is similar to the Add command. It is used to perform subtraction between numbers and containers that store numbers, and it has the following form:

```
subtract <source> from <destination>
```

The only difference between it and the Add command is that you use the operative word *from* instead of *to* with the command name and the <source> and <destination> arguments.

You will rarely, if ever, use the Subtract command to perform subtraction directly between two fields in a card. This is because the calculated difference is always stored in the container used as the <destination> argument. This means that the container will no longer hold its original value after the subtraction is performed.

Suppose that a card has a Cost field that contains 10.50 and a Price field that contains 45.00, and you want to know the difference between the cost and price of the item. If you enter

```
subtract field "Cost" from field "Price"
```

in the script, the Price field will contain the difference of 34.50 and no longer 45.00 when the Subtract command is executed. Assuming that you want this difference stored in a third field so that you can retain the price information, you would have to use a memory variable as a temporary storage container for the difference. Then you could enter this result into a third field using a Put command, as in

```
put field "Price" into temp
subtract field "Cost" from temp
put temp into field "Difference"
```

The Subtract command can also be combined with other arithmetic calculations performed with the arithmetic operators. For instance, to store twice the value of field 4 of a card in a memory variable called temp and then subtract 15 percent of the value in field 6 from it, you would enter

```
put field 4 * 2 into temp
subtract field 6 * .15 from temp
```

The Put command initializes the temp memory variable with twice the value of field 4. Then the Subtract command calculates the difference between this initial value and the 15 percent of the value in field 6, and puts the difference into this temp variable.

The Multiply Command

To perform multiplication between values stored in separate containers, you can use the Multiply command. This command has the form

```
multiply <destination> by <source>
```

Unlike the Add and Subtract commands, the <destination> argument precedes the <source> argument. Nevertheless, the product of the values found in these two containers is stored in the container specified as the <destination>.

For example, if the fifth field of a card currently contains 5 and you want to multiply the contents of the field by 12 with the Multiply command, you would enter

    multiply field 5 by 12

When this Multiply command is executed in the script, the fifth field of the card will then contain 60 as its value.

Just as with the Add and Subtract commands, you will often want to store the product of the Multiply command in a memory variable before entering it into another field of the card. That way, you can preserve the values used for the <source> and <destination> arguments in the card. For example, suppose the value in one field must be multiplied by a factor stored in another field. Once the program calculates the product of these two values, you will want to store it in yet a third field, as in

    put field "Sales" into monthlySales
    multiply monthlySales by field "Commission Rate"
    put monthlySales into field "Commission"

The Divide Command

The Divide command is similar to the Multiply command. The command divides the value placed in the <destination> argument by the value stored in the <source> argument. The result of this division is then stored in the <destination> container. The form of the Divide command is

    divide <destination> by <source>

For example, you can enter

    divide field "Total" by field "Number of Items"

In this case, the result of this division will be stored in the Total field. To keep the value in this field from being changed, you can use a memory variable that temporarily stores the result, which can then be placed into a new field, as in

    put field "Total" into totalAmount
    divide totalAmount by field "Number of Items"
    put totalAmount into field "Average"

Formatting the Results of Calculations

The calculated answers returned by all mathematical operations are stored as text with whatever precision results from the operation. For example, if you have the program mutliply 15 and .25, the answer of 3.75 will be stored as text in the designated container. If you divide 15 by 78, the value 0.192308 will be stored. If you add 15.00 and 25.00, the sum of 40 will be stored.

In those cases where you want to limit or control the decimal precision or format the result as currency, you must use one of Hyper-Talk's functions that either changes the value by rounding it off or dropping the decimal part of the number (truncates it), or formats it to display only a particular number of decimal places.

To round off a number, you use the Round function. It has the form

```
round(number)
```

For example, if you entered

```
put 15 into firstNumber
multiply firstNumber by .25
round(firstNumber)
put firstNumber into field 3
```

field 3 would contain 4 because 3.75 is rounded up to 4.

To drop any decimal values from a number, you use the Trunc function. It has the form

```
trunc(number)
```

If you apply the Trunc function to the previous example,

```
put 15 into firstNumber
multiply firstNumber by .25
trunc(firstNumber)
put firstNumber into field 3
```

field 3 will contain 3 as its new value because the Trunc function drops the .75 from the product of 3.75.

In addition to controlling the precision of a value by changing it with the Round or Trunc functions, you can just control the way the number is displayed by resetting the numberFormat property. This is a global property that follows the form

numberFormat <format string>

The <format string> argument is enclosed in a pair of double quotation marks and shows the number of decimal places to be displayed in the container. Use 0 in the <format string> argument for digits that you want held by zero when empty, rather than dropped from the number. Use # in <format string> for digits that should only be displayed when the digit in that place setting is not zero.

The numberFormat property is 0.###### until you change it with the Set command. This means that HyperCard will show up to six decimal places. However, it will not display any zeros that trail digits in the decimal part of the fraction. For example, the sum of 15.00 and 25.00 will be displayed as 40 and not 40.00 in this number format.

To always have two decimal places displayed in a number, as when working with currency, you would enter

set numberFormat to "0.00"

as part of the message handler before the command that performs the arithmetic calculation. With this format, all calculated values will have two decimal places even when they are zeros, as in 40.00. If any value is less than $1.00, as in .35, it will be formatted as 0.35.

If you want the result of a calculation to display a dollar sign as part of the value, you must use concatenation to join this symbol to the calculated result. For instance, you could have the following script:

```
on closeField
    set numberFormat to "0.00"
    put field 1 into tempNumber
    multiply tempNumber by field 2
    put "$" & tempNumber into field 4
end closeField
```

Because the numberFormat property is global, it affects all of the values returned by calculations in HyperCard. However, the program automatically resets the format to the default setting whenever an idle system message is sent. This means that you must reset it as part of a script of an object. You cannot change it from the Message box.

If you want a space between the dollar sign and the product in this example, use the double ampersand (&&) in the Put command:

```
put "$" && tempNumber
into field 4
```

Then, if the product is 100, it will be formatted as $ 100.00.

In this example, the program resets the numberFormat property for currency, then stores the value held in the first background field in a variable named tempNumber. This value is then multiplied by the value in the second field of the card, and the product is stored in tempNumber. When the program goes to put this product into the fourth field, it adds a dollar sign ("$") before it. For example, if the value in the first field is 25 and the value in the second field is 4, the product will appear in the fourth field as $100.00.

The Math Functions

HyperTalk includes a variety of predefined math functions that you can use in calculations. These functions include specialized scientific, statistical, and financial functions as well as more general mathematical functions such as Round and Trunc, which you have already encountered in the discussion of formatting the results of calculations. Table 14.1 lists these math functions and their purpose. You can also refer to Appendix B for more information on the arguments each requires and examples of their use.

In addition to the predefined math functions already in the Hyper-Talk vocabulary, the program allows you to define your own functions, which can then be applied to the calculations that you perform in scripts. Before you look at how you can define your own functions, let's look at how the predefined functions are used in scripts.

Using Functions in Calculations

Many math functions have alternate forms. Remember that functions requiring only a single argument can be entered with or without the argument in parentheses. For example, to have HyperCard return a random number between 1 and 10, you can enter either

```
random(10)
```

or

```
the random of 10
```

	Function	**Returns:**
Mathematical	Round(number)	The nearest whole number up or down
	Trunc(number)	The integer part of the number without fractions
Statistical	Average(number list)	The average (mean) of the values in the list
	Max(number list)	The highest value in the list
	Min(number list)	The lowest value in the list
	Random(number)	A random number between 1 and the number
Scientific	Abs(number)	The absolute value of the number
	Atan(angle in radians)	The arctangent of the angle
	Cos(angle in radians)	The cosine of the angle
	Exp(number)	The natural (base e) exponent of the number
	Exp1(number)	The natural exponent of the number minus 1
	Exp2(number)	The exponent of the number in base 2
	Ln(number)	The natural (base e) logarithm of the number
	Ln1(number)	The natural logarithm of the number plus 1

Table 14.1: The HyperTalk math functions

	Function	**Returns:**
Scientific (continued)	Sin(angle in radians)	The sine of the angle
	Sqrt(number)	The square root of the number
	Tan(angle in radians)	The tangent of the angle
Financial	Annuity (periodic rate, number of periods)	The present value of one payment
	Compound (periodic rate, number of periods)	The future value of one payment

Table 14.1: The HyperTalk math functions (continued)

However, when a function takes more than one argument—such as the Average, Max, and Min functions, all of which require a list of numbers separated by commas—you must enter their arguments within a pair of parentheses, as in

    max(23.4,17*2,25)

When using the trigonometric functions that return the sine, cosine, tangent, and cotangent of an angle measured in radians, you can use the constant π to convert an angle measured in degrees to radians. HyperCard stores an approximate value of π (pi). If you enter *pi* into a formula, the program uses the value

    3.14159265358979323846

in its calculations.

To convert an angle measured in degrees into radians so that it can be entered as the argument of one of the trigonometric functions, you multiply the number of degrees by pi/180. For example, if you want to know the sine of a 45-degree angle, you can have the program calculate it by entering

    sin(45 * pi/180)

which would return the value 0.707107.

The arguments of HyperTalk functions can be supplied from constants (by entering the number to be used) or from HyperCard containers such as fields or memory variables. For instance, as long as fields 1, 2, and 3 all contain values, you can calculate the average by entering

    put average(field 1, field 2, field 3) into avgValue

You can also use memory variables to supply the argument of a math function, as in

    put 49 into tempNumber
    put sqrt(tempNumber) into field 5

which would put 7 (the square root of 49) into the fifth background field of the card.

Many times, you will find it necessary to combine math functions with other arithmetic operators, commands, or functions. For example, you could modify the previous example to

    put 49 into tempNumber
    put 2 * sqrt(tempNumber) into field 5

which gives you 14 in field 5.

You can also combine functions. For instance, if you wanted to find the square root of the sine of 45 degrees, you would enter

    sqrt(sin(45 * pi/180))

Notice how the Sin function is nested within the Sqrt function. In this case, the entire Sin function is the argument of the Sqrt function.

When mixing simple arithmetic operations with functions, you will sometimes need to alter the order by which the calculations are

Be very careful, when combining math functions where the arguments are enclosed in parentheses, that the number of open (left) parentheses is equal to the number of close (right) parentheses. Each function's argument must be surrounded by a pair of parentheses. If often helps to count the number of open parentheses and then the number of close parentheses to make sure that they are balanced.

performed in order to get the desired calculated result. Table 14.2 shows you the order of operator precedence normally followed by the program when evaluating any kind of mathematical expression.

Any operator occurring in an expression that is on a higher level of this table is evaluated before those on a lower level of the table, regardless of the order in which they occur in that expression. Any operators on the same level in the table are equal in precedence and, in such a case, they are evaluated in a strict left-to-right order. For example, when the operators for addition and subtraction occur in the same expression, the addition is performed before the subtraction only if its operator occurs first in the expression (when going from left to right).

Order	Operators	Operation
1	Operators within parentheses are evaluated before those outside of parentheses	
2	– (signifying negative value), Not	
3	^	Raising a number by a power
4	*, /, div, mod	Multiplication and division
5	+, –	Addition and subtraction
6	&, &&	Concatenation
7	>, <, >=, <=, contains, is in	
8	=, <>	
9	And	
10	Or	

Table 14.2: The order of precedence followed by HyperCard

As you can see from Table 14.2, you can alter the order of operator precedence with the use of parentheses, which are always evaluated first. When several levels of nested parentheses are added to an expression, they are always evaluated from inside out. For example, in the expression

`10*2^2 + 3`

the ^ (exponent) operator is evaluated first, so that 2 is squared resulting in 4. Next, the * (multiplication) operator is evaluated, so that 10 is multiplied by 4 resulting in 40. Finally, the + (addition) operator is evaluated, so that 3 is added to 40 giving an answer of 43.

If the same expression is rephrased with the use of parentheses, you get quite a different result:

`10*(2^2 + 3)`

This time, the expression within the parentheses is evaluated first so that the 2 is squared and then is added to 3, resulting in 7. Then this result is multiplied by 10, giving you the answer of 70.

When HyperTalk math functions (see Table 4.1) are mixed in an expression with other arithmetic operations, they are always calculated first. In other words, they act like parentheses in altering the order of calculation in their favor. For example, in the expression

`sqrt(49)*5 + 2`

the Sqrt function is evaluated first and returns 7 as the result. Then 7 is multiplied by 5 and the product of 35 is added to 2, returning the answer of 37. However, you can still alter the order in which the multiplication and addition take place in this expression with the use of parentheses, as in

`sqrt(49)*(5 + 2)`

In this case, the square root of 49, or 7, is multiplied by the sum of (5 + 2), giving you the answer of 49 instead of 37.

Working with Dates and Times

You can use the HyperTalk Date and Time functions in those stacks that require you to keep track of time and even perform calculations between specific dates and times. These functions allow you to get the current date or time from the internal Macintosh clock and format them in a variety of ways. You can also enter other dates and times into HyperCard containers such as fields and memory variables, and then perform arithmetic calculations between these dates and the containers that hold the current date and time.

Let's begin looking at how you can use dates and times in the scripts you create by exploring the Date function.

The Date Functions

When you need the current date, you use the Date function. If the current date is January 11, 1988, and you enter

> the date

in the Message box, it will return 1/11/88 as the result.

You can also enter two variations on the Date function, each of which will return the current date in a slightly different format. If you enter

> the abbreviated date

into the Message box, it will return Mon, Jan 11, 1988, as the result, instead of 1/11/88. In this format, the day of the week and the name of the month are included in an abbreviated form. You can also enter the abbreviated date function as *the abbrev date* or even *the abbr date*.

If you want the full name of the day of the week and the month spelled out in the result, you use the function

> the long date

and place it into the appropriate HyperCard container. If today's date is 1/11/88, the result will formatted as Monday, January 11, 1988.

When entering your own dates in fields and memory variables, you can follow any of the formats used by the three date functions. The simplest way to enter a date is in the numeric form separated by slashes, as in 1/17/88, 2/15/88, or 3/5/88. Although the program always shows slashes as separators between the three parts of the date, you may use dashes, as in 1–17–88, 2–15–88, and 3–5–88. HyperCard will recognize this format as a valid date format for calculations involving date arithmetic. However, the program will not accept any date prior to January 1, 1904, regardless of the format used to enter it into a HyperCard container.

The Time Functions

The Time function returns the current time as stored by the internal Macintosh clock. There are two functions for returning the current time from the internal clock: the Time and the Long Time. If the time is 2:55 PM exactly when you enter

the time

into the Message box, HyperCard will show either 2:55 PM or 14:55. The result depends upon on whether the time is set to *12 hr.* or *24 hr.* in the Control Panel. You can change from a 12-hour clock to a 24-hour clock, and vice versa, at any time by selecting the Control Panel option on the Apple menu and then clicking on the appropriate radio button in the window.

If you want the number of seconds included in the date, you enter

the long time

and place it into the appropriate HyperCard container. In the earlier example, the time returned in the Message box will be either 2:55:00 PM or 14:55:00, depending upon how the time is set in the Control Panel, if the current time is exactly 2:55 PM.

When you enter your own times into fields and memory variables, you will want to follow one of the formats used by the Time or the Long Time function. For example, you can enter a departure time of 3:15 in the afternoon as 3:15 PM or 15:15 in a field or memory variable.

Performing Calculations between Dates and Times

The results of the Date, the Abbreviated Date, the Long Date, the Time, and the Long Time functions are all stored as text in the container you place them in. This means that you cannot perform calculations between them directly. For example, if you enter a departure date in one field and a return date in a second field and then try to obtain the difference, as with

```
put field "Return" into returnDate
subtract field "Depart" from returnDate
put returnDate into field "Trip Duration"
```

the program will tell you that it can't understand the arguments to the Subtract command.

To calculate between dates and times, you must first convert them into one of the HyperCard date and time formats. The form of the Convert command used for this purpose is

```
convert <container> to <format>
```

The container can be any HyperCard container that holds a valid date or time, such as a field or memory variable. The formats are as follows:

Name of Format	Example
seconds	265472640
short date	2/15/88
abbreviated date	Mon, Feb 15, 1988
long date	Monday, February 15, 1988
short time	4:15 PM or 16:15
long time	4:15:05 PM or 16:15:05
dateItems	1988,2,15,16,15,5,2

You can use any of these formats as the argument of the Convert command. Most often, you will find it convenient to convert the date or time in question to seconds using the seconds format. The number of seconds returned when you use this format in the Convert command is the number of seconds between the date and time you are converting and 12:00:00 AM on January 1, 1904, which represents base date and time used by the program in all such calculations.

The other formats used as arguments in the Convert command are identical to the date and time functions, except that they are not preceded by *the* (you use *short date* as the <format> argument instead of *the short date*). The only format that is new is called dateItems. When you convert a date or time using the dateItems format, HyperCard lists each component of the date and time as an equivalent number. These items are, from left to right in the list, the year, the month, the day, the hour, the minutes, the seconds, and the day of the week (with Sunday equal to 1 and Saturday equal to 7).

You can add and subtract individual items in the list as long as the results are not negative. Most of the time when performing date arithmetic, you should convert the dates to seconds, have the program perform the desired calculation between them, and then convert the dates in seconds back into a recognizable date format.

For example, an earlier example said you could not just subtract a date stored in the departure field from another stored in the return field to get the number of days that has elapsed. Instead of directly calculating the difference, you have to use the Convert command. You use it first to convert the dates to be subtracted into equivalent seconds and then later on in the same handler to convert the seconds back into the short date format, as in the following:

```
on closeField
    convert field "Depart" to seconds
    convert field "Return" to seconds
    put field "Return" into returnDate
    subtract field "Depart" from returnDate
    put returnDate/(24*60*60) into field "Trip Duration"
    convert field "Depart" to short date
    convert field "Return" to short date
end closeField
```

Notice in this field script that the difference between the dates in seconds put into the returnDate memory variable is divided by 24*60*60 (the number of hours in a day, times the number of minutes in an hour, times the number of seconds in a minute) to obtain the answer in days instead of seconds before it is put into the Trip Duration field of the card. After the difference has been calculated and the number of days has been placed in the Trip Duration field, the dates converted to seconds in the Depart and Return fields are converted back to the short date format.

When performing date and time arithmetic between HyperCard containers using the Convert command with the seconds format, you will often have to use a similar factor to convert the resulting seconds into the appropriate units of measurement, such as days, weeks, minutes, and so on.

Calculating Elapsed Time

HyperTalk also includes two functions that can be used when you need to calculate the elapsed time within a HyperCard application. The first one is called the Seconds. It stores the number of seconds that have elapsed since the first second of January 1, 1904. It can be entered into a script as

    the seconds

or

    the secs

You can use the Seconds function to keep an accurate account of the time that has elapsed between two separate events that take place in an application. For example, you can tell the user how long it has taken to browse through all of the cards in a stack by adding the following script to the Browse button:

```
on mouseUp
    put the secs into startBrowse
    show all cards
    put "Total browsing time is" && the secs – startBrowse ¬
    && "seconds" into the Message box
end mouseUp
```

As soon as the user clicks on the Browse button, HyperCard stores two items: the number of seconds that have elapsed since January 1,

1904, and the moment that you click the mouse. It stores this number in a local memory variable called startBrowse. Then, after it displays all of the cards in the stack, it subtracts the number of seconds from that moment and subtracts the beginning of the year 1904 from the number of seconds stored in the startBrowse variable. The difference is concatenated with the text that is placed in the Message box. For example, if the difference is 10, the user will see the message

Total browsing time is 10 seconds.

in the Message box.

In addition to the Seconds function, HyperTalk has a function that stores the number of ticks (each tick is equivalent to one-sixtieth of a second) since the Macintosh was last started up. To get the number of ticks since startup, you enter

the ticks

into a HyperCard container. Each time you start the Macintosh, the number of ticks is reset to zero and the system begins counting them.

The Ticks function can be used to determined elapsed time in much the same way as the Seconds function. However, the Macintosh may skip a tick or two in operation (especially during a disk drive access), so it is often more reliable to use the Seconds function, which relies upon the system clock instead.

Creating Your Own Functions

HyperCard enables you to create functions of your own in the scripts that you write. These functions can include those that perform mathematical calculations or those that perform other functions, such as returning part of the date or time. When you define your own function, you follow this form:

```
function <function name> [parameter]
   <command>
   <command>
   return <value>
end <function name>
```

This use of *return* to have the program perform a designated calculation as part of a user-defined function is limited strictly to this usage. Normally, Hyper-Card interprets the return in a script as a constant that substitutes for pressing the Return key on the keyboard.

When entering commands in the new function that calculate results, you use *return* as the operative word. For example, to calculate the monthly payment due for a loan amortized at a set rate of interest, you can create a Payment function. In the card or background script of the stack, you would enter the following commands that define the Payment function:

```
function payment x, y, z
    return x*(y/(1 – (1 + y) ^ – z))
end payment
```

Then you can apply the Payment function as you would any other HyperTalk function. For example, you could add it to a button script like this:

```
on mouseUp
    ask "Enter the amount of the loan:"
    put it into x
    ask "Enter yearly interest rate:"
    put it/12 into y
    ask "Enter term of the loan in years:"
    put it*12 into z
    put payment (x,y,z) into field "Monthly Payment"
end mouseUp
```

You can also create functions that return just part of a date or time. For instance, you could create Year and Month functions that return just the year or month part of the date. For the Year function, you could enter the following commands to the stack or background script:

```
function year date
    get date
    convert it to dateItems
    return item 1 of it
end year
```

After defining it, you can use it in a button script like this:

```
on closeField
    put Year(the date) into field 5
end closeField
```

To define the Month function that returns just the name of the month, you could enter these commands in the stack or background script:

```
function month date
    get date
    convert it to long date
    return word 1 of item 2 of it
end month
```

You can then use the newly defined Month function in the stack as you would any other in HyperCard.

Summary

In this chapter, you have looked at all of the ways you can perform calculations in a HyperCard stack. As you have seen, HyperTalk provides you with many ways to perform simple arithmetic calculations between values stored in a variety of containers. In addition to performing simple arithmetic with the arithmetic operators or commands, you will also find use for the built-in math functions that HyperTalk provides. Remember that you can also define your own functions for situations where you repeatedly use a prescribed set of calculations in a stack. Creating your own function for performing these calculations can be most efficient, because you can quickly copy the scripts that perform them to the background or stack scripts of other stacks that require similar calculations.

In the next, and final, chapter on HyperTalk, you will examine how you can interface HyperCard stacks with the other application programs that you use on the Macintosh. Here, you will find out how you can open other applications from HyperCard and print documents created by these applications, as well as import and export information between HyperCard stacks and the documents created with other Macintosh programs.

Interfacing HyperCard
with Other Applications

AT THIS POINT, YOU HAVE A GOOD IDEA OF THE capabilities of HyperCard as a tool for creating information systems. You can extend these capabilities by interfacing HyperCard with the other Macintosh application programs and the documents created with them. In this chapter, you will explore how you can open and use other application programs from within HyperCard. As soon as you close the application opened in this way, you are immediately returned to the place in HyperCard from which you launched this program. You will learn how you can use this ability in HyperCard to create your own Finder stack.

The discussion in this chapter on importing and exporting information between HyperCard and other applications is limited to text-based information. If you want information on how to transfer graphic images between Hyper-Card and other graphics programs, see the discussion on importing and exporting graphics at the end of Chapter 8.

You will also look at how you can transfer information to and from HyperCard stacks. This allows you to share information with application programs such as database managers and spreadsheets. For example, you may already have a database of clients' names and addresses in Microsoft Works that you want to bring into a HyperCard stack so that you can use its fast retrieval and automatic dialing capabilities. Conversely, you may create a HyperCard stack to track sales information that you want to bring into an Excel spreadsheet, where you can graph the data as well as subject them to further analysis.

Opening Applications from HyperCard

To start an external application program from HyperCard, you use the HyperTalk Open command. This command has the following form:

```
open [<document> with] <application>
```

As you can see from the arguments, you have the option of opening a specific document with the application, or opening the application program alone.

Opening a document with an application is analogous to positioning the cursor on the file icon in its folder and double-clicking on it. This opens the application at the same time as the document. Just opening an application with the Open command is analogous to positioning the cursor on the application icon in its folder and double-clicking on it. This takes you to the startup screen of the application, from which you can use the appropriate options on the File menu to either start a new document or open an existing one.

When specifying the <document> argument, you must enter the document name exactly as it appears on the file icon and enclose it in a pair of double quotation marks. The same is true of the <application> argument.

Although capitalization of the application name is not important, the addition of any version numbers, spaces between words, or special characters—such as the trademark (^{TM}), registered trademark ($^{®}$), and the like—is crucial. If the application name in the Finder uses one of these special symbols, you must reproduce it as part of the <application> argument for the Open command. The alternative to reproducing special symbols as part of the application name is to rename it. You do this by clicking on the icon in its folder to select it and then typing a new name. In most (although not all) cases, this will not affect your ability to start the application.

When you open an application program from HyperCard with the Open command, HyperCard sends a *suspend* message to the current card, which clears HyperCard from the computer's memory. However, when you finish work in the application and quit it, the System restarts HyperCard, at which time HyperCard sends a *resume* message, which brings you back to the card from which you started the application.

Naturally, in order for the Open command to work, it must be able to locate the application and/or document that you specify. You can indicate where the application programs and documents are located by typing their path name in the *Look for Applications in* and *Look for Documents in* cards in the Home stack. If you do not enter their path names in these cards, HyperCard will present you with the standard

To produce the trademark symbol (^{TM}) from the keyboard, press Option-2. To produce the registered trademark symbol ($^{®}$), press Option-R. To produce the copyright symbol ($^{©}$), press Option-G.

If you are using MultiFinder instead of the standard Finder, the System will not restart HyperCard, and you will not be taken back to the card from which you launched the application. Of course, when using MultiFinder with sufficient memory (at least 2 megabytes), you can have HyperCard and other application programs running simultaneously and only need to click on the appropriate window to go from one application to another.

file dialog box when it is unable to locate an application or document specified in the Open command. You can then point out where the application or document is by clicking on the apppropriate folder name and document name. HyperCard will record the path name that you point out in one or the other of these cards in the Home stack. Thereafter, you will not be prompted for the application's or document's location when you use the Open command.

Creating a HyperCard Finder Stack

The HyperCard Finder stack is only an effective means for starting applications from HyperCard on a hard disk. If you are using HyperCard on 3½-inch disks, you will have to perform a great deal of disk switching between your HyperCard disk and the application disk. Nevertheless, you might want to try this exercise just to see how the Target function and Open command work. Just click the Cancel button when HyperCard asks you where the application is located.

To see how the Open command can work for you, you can create a HyperCard Finder stack that will allow you to start any application you want from HyperCard just by clicking on the appropriate button. Because the applications that I run on my Macintosh may not be the same as the ones you use, you will have to adapt this exercise to your own situation, substituting the names of the applications you have for the ones indicated, where they differ.

To begin the new stack, start HyperCard from the Home Card. Make sure the user level is set to Scripting before you begin work on this stack.

1. **Select the New Stack option on the File menu.**

2. **Enter** *HyperCard Finder* **for the new stack name.**

   Leave the *Copy current background* button checked.

3. **Click on the New Button.**

4. **Select the Background option on the Edit menu (or press Command-B).**

5. **Tear off a copy of the Tools menu, and position it in the lower right corner of the screen.**

6. **Select the Paint Text tool by clicking on the A icon in the palette.**

7. **Select the Text Style option on the Edit menu (or press Command-T).**

8. **Click on the Chicago font and then the OK button.**

9. **Move the I-Beam cursor to the top of the card, and click the mouse.**

10. Type *HyperCard Finder*.

11. **Press Command-S.**

    This selects the text that you just typed.

12. **Move the text so that it is centered at the top of the card (Figure 15.1).**

    You can use the Next and Prev arrows at the bottom of the card as a guide.

13. **Click the Browse button on the Tools menu.**

14. **Select the Open Stack option on the File menu.**

15. **Click on Art Ideas and then the OK button.**

16. **Click on the Disk icon marked Disks, Diskette Library in the lower left corner of the first card of the Art Ideas stack.**

    This takes you to this card in the Art Ideas stack.

17. **Select the Lasso tool in the Tools menu.**

18. **Drag the end of the lasso to completely outline the drawing showing two disks lying on top of each other immediately to the left of the Tools menu (Figure 15.2).**

19. **Select the Copy Picture option on the Edit menu (or press Command-C).**

20. **Select the Recent option on the Go menu (or press Command-R) and click on the first (almost blank) card miniature.**

    This returns you to your HyperCard Finder stack.

21. **Select the Background option on the Edit menu (or press Command-B).**

22. **Select the Paste Picture option on the Edit menu (or press Command-V).**

23. **Position the selected drawing of the disks so that it is located after the HyperCard Finder title.**

24. **Hold down the Shift and Option keys, and drag a copy of this drawing so that it is located immediately before the HyperCard Finder title (Figure 15.3).**

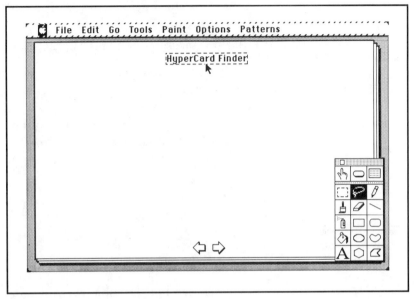

Figure 15.1: Positioning the title of the card

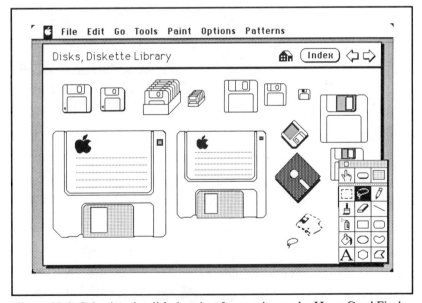

Figure 15.2: Selecting the disk drawing for copying to the HyperCard Finder
stack

25. **Select the Background option on the Edit menu (or press Command-B).**

This takes you out of the background into the card level.

To open various application programs from this card, you must create buttons for each application. These buttons will display the name of the application (exactly as it appears on the file icon). The script containing the Opening command to launch each application need not be attached to each button. You can get around having to enter individual scripts for each button by using the Target function placed in the card script.

The Target function returns the ID number and name of the last object to receive a message sent up the HyperCard message hierarchy. For example, if you enter

   get the target

in a script and the last object receiving a message was a card button named Home, the *it* memory variable will contain

   card button "Home"

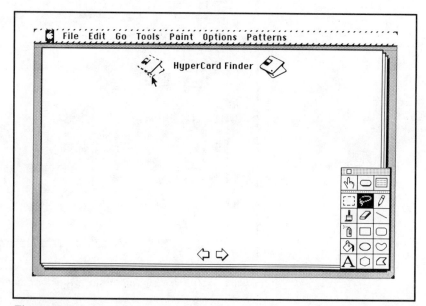

Figure 15.3: Positioning a copy of the disk drawing in front of the card title

However, if you enter

get the short name of the target

in the script and the same message was last received, the *it* memory variable will only contain

Home

You can use the short name of the target to have HyperCard store just the button name that is displayed along with a button icon in the finder card. As long as this button name exactly matches the file name of the application to be launched from HyperCard, you use the Get command and the short name of the Target function to store the application name in the *it* memory variable and have it used by the Open command. This is accomplished by adding the following script to the background of the stack:

```
on mouseUp
    get short name of the target
    open it
end mouseUp
```

Whatever button you click on will be the last receiver of the mouseUp message. Therefore, the program will store the short name of that button (that is, just the application name) in the *it* memory variable that is then used as the argument of the Open command. That way, you can continue to add new application buttons to the finder card without having to add a script to them. All that is required is that the name you give the button match the name of the application to be started from HyperCard.

To see how the Target function works, you should first add a script to the background that just displays the name of the target in the Message box. Later on, you will edit this script so that it displays only the short name (that is, the application name given to the button). Once you have ascertained that this is working correctly, you can edit the background script so that it contains the Open command to launch your applications.

26. Select the Bkgnd Info option on the Objects menu.

27. Click on the Script button.

28. Drag the cursor over all of the existing background script so that all of its lines are highlighted.

29. Type *on mouseUp* and press Return.

30. Type *get name of the target* and press Return.

31. Type *put it into the message box* and press Return.

32. Type *end mouseUp* and press Return.

Your script should now match the one shown in Figure 15.4.

33. Click on the OK button (or press the Enter key).

34. Select the New Button option on the Objects menu.

35. Select the Button Info option on the Objects menu.

36. Type *Microsoft Word* as the button name.

If you don't have Microsoft Word but use MacWrite or some other word processor, enter its file name as the button name instead.

37. Click on the transparent radio button under Style.

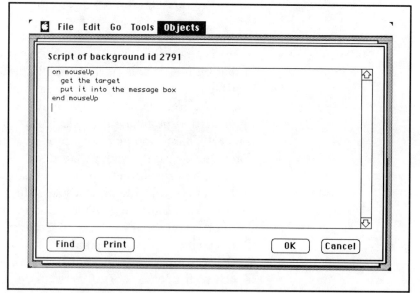

Figure 15.4: The background script for the HyperCard finder stack

38. Click on the Icon button.

39. Click on the MacWrite icon (icon ID 1005) located at the very end of the first row of icons and click the OK button (Figure 15.5).

40. Resize the button so that you can see the button name.

41. Move the button so that it is located at the left edge of the card below the card title (refer to Figure 15.6).

42. Click on the Browse tool in the Tools menu.

Now see what appears in the Message box when you click on the Microsoft Word button. You should see

    card button "Microsoft Word"

in the Message box.

Next, edit the background script so that the Get command just gets the short name when it executes the Target function.

43. Select Bkgnd Info on the Objects menu.

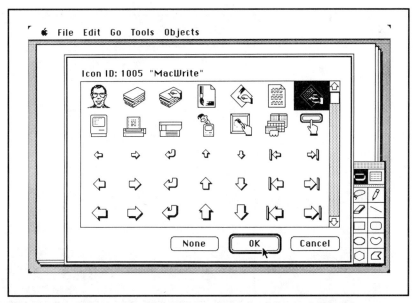

Figure 15.5: Selecting the MacWrite icon for the Microsoft Word button

44. **Click on the Script button.**

45. **Move the I-Beam cursor right before the *n* in name, and click the mouse.**

46. **Type *short* and press the Space bar.**

47. **Click on the OK button (or press the Enter key).**

48. **Click on the Microsoft Word button in the finder card.**

This time the Message box contains only the name *Microsoft Word*, which is the short name of the object that is stored in the *it* memory variable. By using the contents of the *it* variable as the argument of the Open command, you should be able to have HyperCard open this application.

49. **Select Bkgnd Info on the Objects menu.**

50. **Click on the Script button.**

51. **Drag the I-Beam cursor across the third line of the script that contains the Put command, and type *open it*.**

52. **Click on the OK button (or press Enter).**

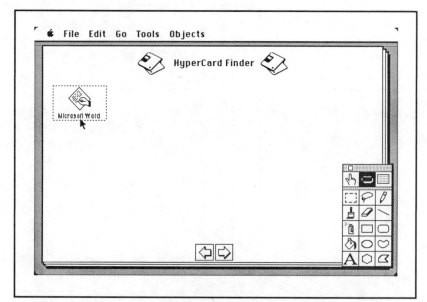

Figure 15.6: Positioning the Microsoft Word button in the card

53. Click on the Microsoft Word button in the finder card a second time.

This time, you are probably looking at a dialog box that asks you where Microsoft Word (or MacWrite) is located. If you want, you can go ahead and open the word processor. Otherwise, click on the Cancel button in the dialog box.

To open the word processor, you must indicate where this application is located. Click on the folder at the top and drag down until you highlight the name of the folder that contains the word processor. Then perform this same procedure to open that folder and click on the name of the application. HyperCard will record the path name in the *Look for Applications in* card in the Home stack so that you do not have to repeat this procedure more than once. After the word processor is opened, select the Quit option on the File menu (or press Command-Q). This will return you to the finder card in the HyperCard Finder stack.

You can now continue on your own, adding buttons for the other application programs you use to the first card in your HyperCard Finder stack. Be sure that each button you add is given the name of the application exactly as it appears in its file folder. Also, change the style of each button to transparent. Figure 15.7 shows you my completed HyperCard Finder. Notice that the buttons for applications such as the 4th Dimension and GraphicWorks use the trademark symbol in their file names, and these have been added to their buttons. Also notice that applications such as PageMaker and MORE require the addition of version numbers to their buttons because these version numbers are part of their file names.

If you use so many applications that you fill up the first card with buttons, just add a new card to the stack. The background script will still be operative, and you can use the Next and Prev buttons to go back and forth between finder cards. As usual, you will want to add a Home button to the stack so that you can easily get to the Home button to open new HyperCard stacks.

Importing and Exporting Information

You can import information in documents created with other applications into HyperCard stacks or export information to other documents.

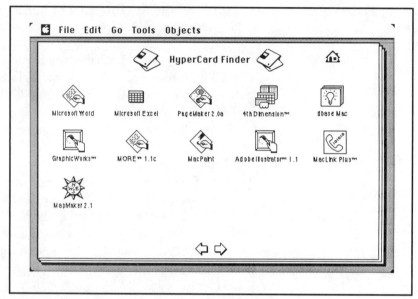

Figure 15.7: Completed HyperCard Finder

When you bring data from other documents into a HyperCard stack, this operation is referred to as a *read* operation because the program reads information in the external file and copies it into the cards in a stack. When you export HyperCard data to other files, this is referred to as a *write* operation because HyperCard writes the data copied from the stack into the new document.

Before your scripts can commence either a read or write operation, you must use an Open File command. This command always precedes Read or Write commands that perform the actual importing or exporting. The Open File command prepares the program for the data transfer that is about to take place. It has the form

> **open file <fileName>**

If the file entered as the <fileName> argument is not located on the disk, HyperCard will create it. If the file is located on the disk, the program merely opens it so that it can be read or written to.

When specifying the <fileName> argument, you must enclose the file name in double quotation marks. If you are opening an existing file that is not located at the topmost (root) level of the disk or topmost folder, you must include the path name as part of the <fileName> argument. For example, if a file named Accounts 1988 is located in a folder named Regional Sales within your Excel folder on the hard disk, you would enter

```
open file ":Excel:Regional Sales:Accounts 1988"
```

After transferring data with either the Read or Write command, your script must contain a Close File command. This command closes the file that has been read from or written to. Do not forget to add a Close File command using the same file name as the earlier Open File command before the end of the message handler. The Close File command has an almost identical form to the Open File command:

```
close file <fileName>
```

Using the Read Command to Import Data into HyperCard

To bring in data created with other application programs, you must use the Read command after the Open File command in the script. The Read command has two alternate forms:

```
read from <fileName> until <character>
```

```
read from <fileName> for <number of bytes>
```

In both forms, the <fileName> argument must be enclosed in a pair of double quotation marks. Again, specify the path name if the file is not located at the topmost level of the current disk or folder. When you use the Read command, you will be working with existing files that contain the data you want brought into a HyperCard stack. You should be sure where the file is located and how to enter its path name before you execute the script.

You can always have the program prompt you to enter the file name to read from by entering something like the following:

```
on mouseUp
  ask "Enter name of file to import data from?"
```

```
    put it into readFrom
    if it is not empty then
        open file readFrom
        .
        read from file readFrom until tab
        .
        .
        close file readFrom
    end mouseUp
```

In this case, the Ask command allows you to enter the file name (including the path) in a dialog box. Once you enter the the file name, it is stored in the *it* memory variable and then placed in a variable called readFrom that is used in the Open File, Read, and Close File commands.

⊙ The Read command stores the imported text in the *it* memory variable. Thus, if you prompt the user to enter the file name with an Ask command, make sure that you follow this command statement with a Put command that places the file name in a memory variable with another name. Remember the Ask command also uses the *it* memory variable to store the user's reply.

As you can see from the alternate forms, you can specify that the Read command read data until it reaches a particular character or for a specific number of bytes (1 byte being equal to one character of text). Most often, you will use the first form whereby you specify a character that limits the text to be imported. Depending upon the program that produced the file to be imported, this delimiting character will be either a tab or a return. Regardless of the form you use, HyperCard stores the text read in the *it* local memory variable.

HyperCard has several reserved words that simplify the use of keyboard characters such as tab and return in scripts that use the *read from* <*fileName*> *until* <*character*> form of the Read command. These values are referred to as *constants* (a full list of HyperCard's constants is included at the end of Appendix C). Instead of having to specify the code number of the tab or return characters, HyperCard allows you to enter the word *tab* or *return* for these values.

Whether you use the tab character as opposed to the return character as the delmiting character in a Read command depends upon the type of file you are importing. It is important to note that all files you import must be saved in a text file format. Spreadsheet, database management, and word processing programs allow you to save the files you create in them in a text file format. This is done by specifying the Text format when you use their equivalent of an Export or Save As command.

Some database management programs, such as dBASE Mac, do not have a Text format option. However, they allow you to specify the characters to be used to delimit fields and records of the exported database. In such a case, you will want to specify the tab character as the delimiter for field information and the return character as the delimiter for records.

For example, if you save a spreadsheet created in Excel in the text file format, the information entered into each column will be delimited by a tab character, and the end of each row will be delimited with a return character. When you save a database created in the 4th Dimension, each field of information is delimited by a tab and each record in the database is delimited by a return. When you save a word processed document created in Microsoft Word or MacWrite, each paragraph of information is delimited by a return.

If the information in the text file you want to import into a HyperCard stack is delimited by tabs, as is the case with most spreadsheets and databases, you will use the form

    read from <fileName> **until tab**

in your import script. If the information in the text file is delimited by returns, as is the case with word processed documents, you will use the form

    read from <fileName> **until return**

When importing databases, consider the database field as the counterpart of an individual HyperCard text field and the record the counterpart of each card in the stack. When importing spreadsheets, consider the column as the counterpart of a HyperCard text field and the row of data as the counterpart of an individual card.

instead.

Because the data read into HyperCard is stored in the *it* memory variable, you need to use a Repeat construction in the script to have the program place the data in *it* into the appropriate text field in the card stack and then repeat this procedure until all of the data is imported. This means that you must first create a stack whose cards have a text field for each item of information in the text file to be imported.

For example, if you are importing data from a database that has six fields in each record, each card in the stack that is to receive this information must also have six text fields in it. Then you can create an Import button, whose script contains the necessary commands to bring all of the data items into each card. A typical Import button script for taking in data delimited by a tab character follows.

```
on mouseUp
    ask "File to import text from?"
    if it is empty then exit mouseUp
```

The double dashes (--) are used in this button script to add comments to the script. You can, and should, add short comments explaining the purpose of the command line to your more complex scripts. As long as you separate the comment from the commands with a double dash, HyperCard will not intepret your comments as HyperTalk commands to be executed.

```
put it into readFrom
open file readFrom
repeat
   doMenu "New Card"
   repeat with fieldCount = 1 to the number of fields
      read from file readFrom until tab  -- use tab as delimiter
      if it is empty then  -- end of file reached
         if fieldCount = 1 then doMenu "Delete Card"
         close file readFrom
         exit mouseUp
      end if
      put it into field fieldCount
   end repeat
end repeat
end mouseUp
```

When the Import button that contains this script is clicked on, it prompts you for the file name that contains the data to be imported. The program takes the name you enter (including path name) out of the *it* memory variable and places it in a variable called readFrom. As long as the contents of readFrom is not empty, it opens this file with the Open File command.

Next, the script begins a Repeat construction where it adds a new card to the stack. Remember that your stack should already contain at least one card that has background text fields for each item of data to be imported (that is, data up to the tab character). After adding the new card to accept the imported data, the script performs a second Repeat construction, which is repeated as many times as there are fields in this card (repeat with fieldCount = 1 to the number of fields).

You may run into a problem when using this script with spreadsheet or database text files, whereby the first data item at the beginning of a new row or record is skipped. If this happens, you need to edit the text file with your word processor and add a tab at the beginning of each line of text right before the first data item.

As part of this repeated loop, the program reads the data in the text file up to the tab character. This data is stored in the *it* memory variable. Next, the program examines the contents of this variable. If *it* is empty, then you assume that the program has reached the end of the file. At that point, the program deletes the current card (it will not be used because you have run out of data to import), closes the open file, and exits from this message handler.

However, if *it* is not empty, the script puts the contents of the *it* variable into the current field (fieldCount) and repeats the repeat loop that adds a new card (doMenu "New Card") and the counter loop.

If you are importing text from a word processed document, you need to change the Read command in this script so that it reads from the file until it reaches a return:

```
read from file readFrom until return
```

If you are preparing a document form to import into a HyperCard stack, be sure to press Return after you have typed each data item that is to go into an individual HyperCard text field. That way, each data item will be on its own line of the document.

If you want a paragraph of information to be imported into a single HyperCard text field, don't press Return at the end of each line; press Return only when you come to the end of the paragraph. However, in such cases, make sure that the text field or fields to receive this information can accommodate all of the text in the paragraph. The best way to ensure that this is the case is to make the receiving field or fields scrolling text fields.

Using the Write Command to Export Data from HyperCard

The Write command, used to export information stored in a HyperCard stack to a text file, is the reverse of the Read command. It has only one form:

```
write <source> to file <fileName>
```

The <source> argument is the field or character that you want written into the resulting text file. Again, the <fileName> argument must be enclosed in a pair of double quotation marks.

When writing HyperCard text field information to a new file, you must decide what character you want to use to delimit each data item stored in a separate field. If the new file is to be used with a spreadsheet or database management program, you will want to use the tab character, as in the following button script:

```
on mouseUp
  ask "Name of file to write text to?"
```

```
            if it is empty then exit mouseUp
            put it into writeTo
            open file writeTo
            go to first card
            repeat for the number of cards
               repeat with fieldCount = 1 to the number of fields
                  write field fieldCount to file writeTo
                  write tab to file writeTo
               end repeat
               go to next card
            end repeat
            close file writeTo
         end mouseUp
```

In this script, the program repeats the Write command for all of the fields in all of the cards. First, it writes the contents of the field into the new text file, and then it writes a tab character to the file (with the second Write command). After the data in the fields of all of the cards has been written into the new text file, the Close File command closes it, preventing any other information from being written in it by mistake.

If you want to use the new file with a word processor, you may want to have a space character entered after the data written in from each field. In such a case, you would enter these Write commands after the second Repeat construction that sets up the counter loop (repeat with fieldCount = 1 to the number of fields):

```
      write field fieldCount to file writeTo
      write space to file writeTo
```

If want each item of information in the HyperCard fields stored on a separate line of the text file, you would substitute the *return* constant for the *space* constant in the second Write command.

Summary

As you have seen, you can extend the power of HyperCard by interfacing it with the other software programs you use. If you are not using MultiFinder (the multiuser version of the Finder) on your

Macintosh, you can create a HyperCard Finder card that allows you to start up other applications and then return to your original place in HyperCard once you have finished working with them. Remember that in addition to being able to launch new applications from Hyper-Card, you can also open the specific document that you want to work on at the same time as the application program that runs it.

Part of interfacing HyperCard with other software involves importing and exporting information between HyperCard and the other programs you use. When you import information from a file created with other programs, you must first save a copy of this file in the text file format. Also, before you import the data from this file, you must have already created a HyperCard stack that will receive the information. This stack should have a text field for each data item in the text file to be brought in.

Individual data items in the text file are most often marked by either a tab or a return character. In spreadsheets and databases, the tab is used to delimit the data in individual fields and the return is used to mark the end of each record. In word processing documents, the return is used to mark the end of each paragraph or separate text item on a line. The <character> argument of the Read command you use in the script of the import button will depend upon the character that delimits each data item in the text. When you are importing text information where individual data items are not an issue, you can just specify the number of bytes to be imported. In such a case, be sure that the text field in the HyperCard stack where you place this information is large enough to accommodate all of the incoming information.

When you want to copy data stored in one of your HyperCard stacks into a file that can be used by other application programs you use, you can export the information to a new text file. This involves the use of the Write command (the reverse of the Read command). Remember that before importing information with the HyperTalk Read command or exporting information with the Write command, you must use the Open File command in the script. Also, after the data transfer has taken place, you must have a Close File command in the script to protect the file from further manipulation.

APPENDIX A

THIS APPENDIX GIVES YOU AN ALPHABETICAL LISTING of all the HyperTalk commands. Each command entry contains a short description of what the command does; the form it takes, including all required and optional arguments; and examples of the command's usage in a script.

Arguments that are required are entered in a pair of angle brackets, as in

convert <container> to <format>

where both the <container> and <format> arguments are required to make this command work.

Arguments that are optional are entered in a pair of square brackets, as in

ask <question> [with <default>]

where [with <default>] is an optional argument in the command. You can get the command to work simply by using the form

ask <question>

Some HyperTalk commands give a choice between arguments. These are presented in a list separated by a vertical bar (|). These argument choices can be required or optional. For example, when you use the Show command to redisplay an object that has been previously hidden, it has the form

show menubar | <window> | <field or button>

where you have a choice between entering *menubar* or the name of a window, field, or button as the argument of Show, but must enter at least one of these objects. When you use the Show command to browse through cards in a stack, it has the form

> show [all | <number>] cards

In this usage, the choice between entering *all* or *<number>* as the argument of *show* is optional. You can simply enter

> show cards

which is the same thing as entering the command

> show all cards

However, if you want to have the program browse through a set number of cards, you must enter a value for the <number> argument.

Add

Adds the contents of the <source> to the <destination> and puts the answer in the container specified as the <destination> argument.

Form

> add <source> to <destination>

Examples

> add 5 to field 1
> add field "Cost" to temp

Answer

Prompts the user to choose up to three possible replies that are displayed in a dialog box along with the prompt. The reply chosen is stored in the *it* memory variable.

Form

> answer <question> [with <reply> [or <reply> [or <reply>]]]

Examples

> answer "Delete this card?" with "Yes" or "No"
> answer "Go to which card?" with "First" or "Last" or "Home"

Ask

Prompts the user to answer a question with a default reply or a reply of his or her own presented in a dialog box along with the question. The response chosen is stored in the *it* memory variable. If used in the *ask password* form, the reply entered by the user is stored as an encrypted number in the *it* memory variable.

Forms

```
ask <question> [with <default>]
ask password <question>
```

Examples

```
ask "How many cards to print?" with 1
ask "What is your name?" with userName
ask password "Please enter your password."
```

Beep

Sounds the bell the number of times specified.

Form

```
beep [<number>]
```

Examples

```
beep 3
beep beepNumber
```

where beepNumber is a memory variable containing a value.

Choose

Selects a new tool from the Tools menu.

Form

```
choose <tool>
```

Examples

> choose browse tool
> choose text tool

Click

Clicks the mouse at a specified location in the screen.

Form

> click at <location> [with shiftKey | optionKey | commandKey]

Examples

> click at 26,160
> click at 15,100 with shiftKey

Close File

Closes the file after importing or exporting data to and from Hyper-Card and another application program (see Open, Read, and Write).

Form

> close file <fileName>

Examples

> close file "Client List"
> close file transferFile

where transferFile is a local memory variable.

Convert

Converts the date or time in a container to a specified format.

Form

> convert <container> to <format>

The formats include:

- *seconds*, which are the seconds since 1904
- *long date*, as in Friday, December 25, 1987
- *short date*, as in 12/25/87
- *abbreviated date*, as in Fri, Dec 25, 1987
- *long time*, as in 3:15:20 PM
- *short time*, as in 3:15 PM
- *dateItems*, which are integers representing the year, month, and day in a date, as in 1987,12,25, or those representing the hour, minute, and seconds in the time, as in 03,15,20

Examples

```
convert field 1 to the abbreviated date
convert returnTime to seconds
```

where returnTime is a local memory variable.

Delete

Deletes text in a specific component of a container, such as a field or memory variable.

Form

```
delete <component>
```

Examples

```
delete word 2 of line 3 of field 2
delete last item of field "Street Address"
```

Dial

Dials a telephone number through a modem or an audio device that can send tones generated by the Dial command over the telephone lines.

Form

> dial <source> [with modem [<modemParameters>]]

The <modemParameters> argument can include modem commands, often referred to as AT commands because they are preceded by *AT*. These commands are used to set up tone or pulse dialing, control the volume of the speaker, or tell the modem how long to stay on the line after the number has been dialed. Refer to your modem documentation for the specific AT commands used by your modem.

Examples

> dial "(312) 555–7896" with modem "ATDTS7 = 1"
> dial line 2 of field "Telephone"

Divide

Divides the number in the <destination> by the number in the <source> and puts the answer in the <destination> argument.

Form

> divide <destination> by <source>

Examples

> divide field 1 by field 2
> divide yearlyInt by 12

where yearlyInt is a local memory variable.

Do

Executes the lines of text in the <source> argument as though they were entered as a script with the Script Editor.

Form

> do <source>

Examples

do line 3 of field 2
do card field 3

DoMenu

Performs one of the menu options on the HyperCard menus. You must enter the option name exactly as it appears on the menu. If it includes an ellipsis (...), it must be entered.

Form

doMenu <name of menu item>

Examples

doMenu "Delete Card"
doMenu "Print Stack..."

Drag

Drags the mouse from one location on the screen to another. You don't have to include the Click command when using the Drag command.

Form

drag from <h,v> to <h,v> [with shiftKey | optionKey
| commandKey]

Example

choose rectangle tool
drag from 35,100 to 70,200

Edit Script

Opens the Script Editor of an object to allow you to edit the script.

Form

edit script of <object>

Examples

edit script of button id 3456
edit script of card "Opening"

Find

Finds characters specified as the <source> argument in the stack. If you use the *find chars* form, the program does not limit the characters to the initial characters of words, but will match the characters in the <source> argument no matter where they occur in the word. If you use the *find word* form, the program will limit the search to whole words that match the characters in the <source> argument.

Forms

find <source> [in field <n>]
find chars <source> [in field <n>]
find word <source> [in field <n>]

Examples

find "Smith" in field "Name"
find chars "start" in field 3
find word "start" in field 3

Get

Puts the value of the <expression> argument into the *it* memory variable.

Form

get <expression>

Examples

```
get name of this stack
get textFont of field "State"
get loc of card button 4
```

Global

Declares a local memory variable to be a global memory variable that can be used in other scripts in the same and new stacks until you open another application from HyperCard or quit HyperCard. You must declare a variable to be global each time you use it in a script.

Form

```
global <variable name>
```

Example

```
global total, grandTotal
```

Go

Takes you to the card specified in the <destination> argument. If no stack is specified, HyperCard uses the current stack. The Go command can be used with the Visual command.

Form

```
go [to] <destination>
```

Examples

```
go home
go to next card
go to card 3 of stack "New Accounts"
go to next card of this background
```

Help

Goes to the HyperCard Help stack. Putting help in a script is equivalent to selecting the Help option on the Go menu or typing Command-? when using a stack.

Form

help

Hide

Version 1.1 allows you to hide the entire card window (HyperCard screen).

Hides the HyperCard menus, a window (message, tool, or pattern), or a specified field or button from view. They are redisplayed with the Show command.

Form

hide menubar | <window> | <field or button>
| <card window>

The <card window> argument occurs only in version 1.1.

Examples

hide menubar
hide card button 2
hide tool window
hide message

Multiply

Calculates the product of the <destination> and <source> arguments and puts the answer in the <destination> argument.

Form

multiply <destination> by <source>

Examples

```
put field 1 into term
multiply term by 12
put term into field "Number of Payments"
```

Open

Opens a new application from HyperCard. If you don't specify a file name for the <document> argument, the application opens a new file. You can also open a document or application entered in a field.

The command form *open file* is used before a Read or Write command when transferring data between HyperCard and an external file. Be sure to enter a Close File command with the name of the document file after the Read or Write command (see Read and Write).

Forms

```
open [<document> with] <application>
open file <document>
```

Examples

```
open Microsoft Word
open "Franklin Letter of 9/28" with Microsoft Word
open file "Client Data"  -- before a Read statement
```

Open Printing

Starts a print job. All of the cards that you specify for printing are put in a print queue for this job. When the program reaches a Close Printing statement, the print queue is closed and the job is sent to the printer.

Form

```
open printing [with dialog]
print...
close printing
```

Example

```
open printing with dialog
go to card "Opening"
print card
go to stack "Wineries"
print 3 cards
close printing
```

Pass

Used to pass the original message to the next object in the message inheritance path.

Form

```
pass <message>
```

Example

```
ask "Enter menu option to perform?"
put it into menuChoice
    .
    .
    .
on doMenu menuChoice
   if menuChoice is "Delete Stack..." then
      ask "Sorry, can't allow that!"
      pass doMenu
   end if
end doMenu
```

Play

Plays musical notes through the Macintosh built-in speaker or an external speaker connected to the computer in either the "boing" or "harpsichord" voice. To use other voices, you must include their resources in the Home stack or the stack that contains the Play command.

Form

play <voice> [tempo <tempo number>] [<notes>]

Examples

play "harpsichord" tempo 250 "c g# eb3 bb"
play "boing" "d e f# a"

Pop

Goes to the card most recently marked for retrieval with the Push command.

Form

pop card [into <container>]

Examples

pop card −− takes you to last card pushed in stack
pop card into field 5

This line stores the long name of the last card pushed in the stack in field 5 without taking you to this card.

Print

Prints the current card, a set number of cards, or all cards in the stack. When used with the Open Printing and Close Printing commands (see Open Printing), adds specified cards to the print queue of the print job.

The Print command can also be used to print a document created with another application program.

Forms

print [all | <number> cards | this card]
print <document> with <application>

Examples

```
print this card
print 10 cards
print all cards
print "Cost Estimate 4" with Excel
print field 7 with Microsoft Word
```

where field 7 holds the name of the document to be printed.

Push

Marks the current card for later retrieval with the Pop command. The last card pushed is the first retrieved by the Pop command.

Form

```
push [this | recent] card
```

Example

```
on mouseUp
   push this card
   go to card ID 4567 in stack "Clients"
end mouseUp
```

Put

Puts the contents of the <source> argument before, into, or after the container specified as the <destination>. If the <destination> argument is omitted, HyperCard puts the contents into the Message box.

Form

```
put <source> before | into | after <destination>
```

Examples

```
put sum into field "Total"
put it into field 4
put "See you later!"  -- puts text into Message box
```

Read

Imports data from an external file into a HyperCard stack and stores the data in the *it* memory variable. The Read command must be preceded by a Open File command and followed with a Close File command, which specify the name of the file whose text is to be imported.

Forms

read from file <fileName> until <character>
read from file <fileName> for <number of bytes>

Example

```
on mouseUp
  ask "Enter name of file to import text from?"
  if it is empty then exit mouseUp
    put it into importDoc
    open file importDoc
    repeat
      doMenu "New Card"
      repeat with field# = 1 to the number of fields
        read from file importDoc until tab
        if it is empty then  -- end of file
          close file importDoc
          exit mouseUp
        end if
      end repeat
    end repeat
end mouseUp
```

Reset Paint

Resets the options in the painting program's Options menu and the characteristics of the paint text back to their default settings:

Setting	Default
Grid	False
LineSize	1

Filled	False
Centered	False
Multiple	False
MultiSpace	1
Pattern	12 (black)
Brush	8 (medium dot)
PolySides	4 (square)
TextAlign	Left
TextFont	Geneva
TextSize	12
TextHeight	16
TextStyle	Plain

Form

reset paint

Send

Sends a message to an object not in the regular message hierarchy of the current script.

Form

send <message> to <target>

Examples

send "mouseup" to card button 3
send "close field" to button "Next"
send "doMenu Quit" to HyperCard

Set

Sets the property of an object to a new value (see Appendix C for a list of HyperCard properties).

Form

> set <property> of <object> to <value>

Examples

> set textFont of field 1 to Chicago
> set style of card button 3 to shadow
> set visible of tool window to true
> set icon of button 2 to "Sort"

Show

Redisplays the Menu bar, window, field, or button that has been previously hidden with the Hide command.

This command can also be used to have HyperCard browse through a set number of cards or all of the cards in the current stack.

Forms

Version 1.1 allows you to redisplay the entire card window if it has been hidden. It also allows you to change the location of the card window on an external monitor. The <h,v> coordinates are those of the upper left corner of the HyperCard screen.

> show [<number> | all] cards
> show menubar | <window> | <field or button>
> [at <location>] | <card window> [at <h,v>]

The <card window> [at <h,v>] argument occurs only in version 1.1.

Examples

> show menubar
> show tool window
> show message
> show field "Notes"
> show 10 cards
> show all cards

Sort

Sorts the cards in a stack in ascending or descending order by the field or the expression specified. If the field contains only values, specify sorting with the numeric option. If the field contains only dates or times, specify sorting with the dateTime option. Text sorting is the default used when the field contains alphanumeric text or numbers such as zip codes that are not calculated.

Form

sort [ascending | descending] [text | numeric
| international | dateTime] by <field or expression>

Examples

sort by field 2
sort by last item of line 4 of field "Address"
sort numeric by field "Cost"
sort descending dateTime by field "Date Entered"

Subtract

Subtracts the value in the <source> argument from the value in the <destination> and places the answer in the <destination> argument.

Form

subtract <source> from <destination>

Example

put field 1 into newNumber
subtract field 2 from newNumber
put newNumber into field 3

Type

Types the text that you enter as the <source> argument into a container such as a field or memory variable.

Form

type <source> [with shiftKey | optionKey | commandKey]

Example

```
choose browse tool
click at loc field 3
type "Check calendar and schedule meeting."
```

Visual

Specifies a particular visual effect to be used at the next Go or Find command. You can specify a speed at which the visual effect is to occur and can use multiple visual effects one after the other.

Form

```
visual [effect] <name of effect> [<speed>] [to black
  | white | gray]
```

Examples

```
visual effect wipe left slowly
visual effect iris open fast
visual effect checkerboard very slowly
visual effect scroll right
visual dissolve slowly to black
```

Wait

Pauses the execution of the commands in a script for a set period of time or until a particular condition is met or ceases to exist.

Forms

```
wait [for] <number of ticks>
wait [for] <number> seconds
wait until <true or false expression>
wait while <true or false expression>
```

Examples

```
wait for 30  -- 30 clicks equals 30/60 or ½ second
wait 3 seconds
```

```
wait until mouse is down
wait while mouse is up
```

Write

Writes the text specified in the <source> argument into a Macintosh text (ASCII) file. The Write command must be preceded by an Open File command and followed by a Close File command.

Form

```
write <source> to file <fileName>
```

Examples

```
open file "Clients"
write field 1 to file "Clients"
write tab to file "Clients"
close file "Clients"
```

APPENDIX *B*

THIS APPENDIX CONTAINS AN ALPHABETICAL LISTING of all the HyperTalk functions, arranged into two groups: general and math functions. Each function entry gives you a short description of what the function calculates, the form or forms it takes, and examples of the function's usage in a script.

General Functions

CharToNum

Converts the character specified as the function argument into its ASCII code decimal number.

Forms

```
charToNum(<character>)
the charToNum of <character>
```

Examples

```
charToNum("A") -- returns ASCII code 65
the charToNum of "a" -- returns ASCII code 97
```

ClickLoc

Returns the location of the most recent click of the mouse. This location is given by the horizontal and vertical screen coordinates.

Form

the clickLoc

Example

```
if the item 2 of the clickLoc > 100 then
    show message box at 20,50
end if
```

CommandKey

Returns *up* or *down*, depending upon whether the Command key is depressed when the function is executed.

Forms

the commandKey
the cmndKey

Example

```
on mouseUp
    if the commandKey is down then exit mouseUp
    .
    .
    .
end mouseUp
```

Date

Returns the current date in a variety of formats, depending upon the form specified.

Forms

```
the date  -- 12/28/87
the long date  -- Monday, December 28, 1987
the abbreviated date  -- Mon, Dec 28, 1987
or the abbrev date
or the abbr date
```

Length

Returns the number of characters in the <source> specified as the function argument.

Forms

the length of <source>
length(<source>)

Examples

the length of line 2 of field "Address"
the length of temp – – temp is local memory variable
length(second word of last item of field 4)

Mouse

Returns *down* if the mouse button is being pressed at the time the function is executed. Returns *up* if the mouse button is not being pressed.

Form

the mouse

Examples

wait until the mouse is down
if the mouse is down then show message box

MouseClick

Returns *true* if the mouse has been clicked since the message began. Returns *false* if the mouse has not been clicked.

Form

the mouseClick

Examples

wait until the mouseClick
repeat until the mouseClick

MouseH

Returns the current horizontal screen coordinate of the cursor.

Form

the mouseH

Example

if the mouseH > 250 then show tool window at 15,100

MouseV

Returns the current vertical screen coordinate of the cursor.

Form

the mouseV

Example

if the mouseV > = 200 then hide message box

Number

Returns the number of cards, buttons, or fields in the stack. When using this function to find out the number of background buttons or fields in a stack (as opposed to card buttons and fields), you need to add *background* to the buttons or fields argument. You can also use the number function to find out the number of components in a particular HyperCard container such as a field or memory variable.

Forms

[the] number of cards | buttons | fields
[the] number [of] <components> in <container>

Examples

the number of cards
the number of buttons in stack "Clients"
the number of background fields
the number of lines of field "Address"
the number of items of field 3

NumToChar

Returns the character equivalent of the ASCII decimal code number specified as the function argument.

Forms

numToChar(<number>)
the numToChar of <number>

Examples

numToChar(65) –– returns A
the numToChar of 97 –– returns a

Offset

Returns the starting position of a text string (the <text1> argument) within a second text string (the <text2> argument).

Form

offset(<text1>,<text2>)

Examples

If field 3 contains the text string *San Francisco, CA* and you enter

put offset("San",field 3)into startPos

the memory variable startPos will contain 1 because *San* begins at the first position in the text string *San Francisco, CA*. If you enter

> put offset("Fran",field 3)into startPos

the startPos variable will contain 5 because the text string *Fran* begins at the fifth position in field 3. If you enter

> put offset("o",field 3)into startPos

the variable will contain 13 because the *o* in *Francisco* occurs in the 13th position in field 3.

OptionKey

Returns *down* if the Option key is depressed when the function is executed, and *up* if it is not.

Form

> the optionKey

Example

> if the optionKey is down then
>   choose rectangle tool
> end if

Param

Gets a single parameter of an argument by position. Enter 0 as the <number> argument to get the command word itself. Enter 1 as the argument to get the first word after the command word, and so on.

Forms

> the param of <number>
> param(<number>)

Examples

    put the param of 0 into paramMsg
    if param(1) is empty then go Home

where paramMsg is a local memory variable.

ParamCount

Returns the total number of parameters in the current message.

Form

    the paramCount

Examples

    if the paramCount is 0 then go to stack "Stack Help"
    put the paramCount into paramNumber

where paramNumber is a local memory variable.

Params

Returns the entire current message along with the command word.

Form

    the params

Example

    if the params is "mouseUp" then go to stack "Help"

Result

Holds the text of an error message explaining what went wrong in the previous command. Normally, *the result* is empty.

Form

the result

Example

find "George" in field 1
if the result < > empty then
   ask "You have not yet made an entry for George"
end if

Seconds

Returns the number of seconds since the first second of the year
1904 (0:00:00 hour on January 1, 1904), the reference point used in
HyperCard date calculations.

Forms

the seconds
the secs

Example

on mouseUp
   ask "Enter number of cards to print:" with 1
   put the seconds into startPrint
   open printing
   print it cards
   close printing
   put "Elapsed printing time is" ¬
   && the seconds − startPrint && "seconds." ¬
   into the message box
end mouseUp

ShiftKey

Returns *down* if the Shift key is pressed or *up* if it is not pressed.

Form

the shiftKey

Example

```
if the shiftKey is down then
    hide the message box
end if
```

Sound

Returns the name of the voice that is playing, or *done* if no sound is being produced with the Play command.

Form

the sound

Example

```
if the sound is "done" then
    go to stack "New Music"
end if
```

Target

Returns the ID number and name of the object that received the last message sent up the message hierarchy. If you get the short name of Target, it returns only the name of the object that received the last message.

Form

the target

Examples

```
send "mouseUp" to the target
get the name of the target
```

If Target is the Help button, returns *card button "Help"*.

>   get the short name of the target

If Target is the Help button, returns *Help*.

>   put the target into targetID

where targetID is a local memory variable.

Ticks

Returns the number of ticks (each tick is equal to one-sixtieth of a second) since the Macintosh was started up.

Form

>   the ticks

Example

```
on mouseUp
   put the ticks into tickNumber
   show all cards
   put the ticks – tickNumber && "ticks have elapsed" ¬
   into the message box
end mouseUp
```

Time

Returns the current time from the Macintosh internal clock. You can get the time (or the short time) or the long time. The long time includes seconds. To use the time in calculations, convert it to seconds or ticks (see Convert command or Ticks function).

Forms

```
the time  – –  2:15 PM or 14:15
the short time  – –  2:15 PM or 14:15
the long time  – –  2:15:25 PM or 14:15:25
```

Example

```
put the long time into field 2

on mouseUp
    put the time into now
    convert now to seconds
    convert field 1 to seconds
    subtract field 1 from now
    convert now to short time
    put now into field 3
end mouseUp
```

where *now* is a local memory variable.

Tool

Returns the name of the tool currently chosen. The tool names are as follows:

browse tool	spray tool
button tool	rectangle tool
field tool	round rect tool
select tool	bucket tool
lasso tool	oval tool
pencil tool	curve tool
brush tool	text tool
eraser tool	regular polygon tool
line tool	polygon tool

Form

the tool

Example

```
if the tool < > "browse tool" then
    choose "browse tool"
    .
    .
    .
end if
```

Value

Converts a string of text into an expression that can be evaluated.

Forms

```
the value of <expression>
value(<expression>)
```

Example

If the first line of field 5 in the card contains the text 4 + (10 * 2) and you enter the Put command as

```
put the value of card field 5 into field 7
```

field 7 will contain 24.

Math Functions

Abs

Returns the absolute value of the number entered as the argument.

Forms

```
abs(<number>)
the abs of <number>
```

Examples

abs(– 17)
the abs of temp

where temp is a local memory variable.

Annuity

Returns the present value of an annuity.

Form

annuity(<periodic rate>, <number of periods>)

Examples

annuity(.12,36)
annuity(field "Rate",field "Term")

Atan

Returns the arctangent of the angle specified.

Forms

atan(<angle in radians>)
the atan of <angle in radians>

Examples

atan(35*pi/180)
atan(acuteAngle)

where acuteAngle is a local memory variable.

Average

Returns the average (mean) of the list of numbers entered as the argument of the function.

Form

average(<number list>)

Examples

average(15,23.2,7*5.12,56)
average(field 1,field 3, field 5)

Compound

Returns the compound interest of an annuity.

Form

compound(<periodic rate>, <number of periods>)

Examples

compound(.09,48)
compound(field "Rate",field "Term")

Cos

Returns the cosine of the angle specified.

Forms

cos(<angle in radians>)
the cos of <angle in radians>

Examples

cos(25.5*pi/180)
cos(acuteAngle)

where acuteAngle is a local memory variable.

Exp

Returns the natural exponent—that is, the exponent in base e—of the number specified.

Forms

exp(number)
the exp of <number>

Examples

exp(3.5)
the exp of temp

where temp is a local memory variable.

Exp1

Returns the natural exponent—that is, the exponent of base e—of the number specified minus 1.

Forms

exp1(<number>)
the exp1 of <number>

Examples

exp1(5)
the exp1 of temp

where temp is a local memory variable.

Exp2

Returns the base-2 exponent of the argument.

Forms

exp2(<number>)
the exp2 of <number>

Examples

exp2(6)
the exp2 of temp

Ln

Returns the natural logarithm of the number specified.

Forms

```
ln(<number>)
the ln of <number>
```

Examples

```
ln(10)
ln(logNumber)
```

where logNumber is a local memory variable.

Ln1

Returns the natural logarithm of 1 plus the number specified.

Forms

```
ln1(<number>)
the ln1 of <number>
```

Examples

```
ln1(9)
the ln1 of logNumber
```

where logNumber is a local memory variable.

Max

Returns the highest number in the list of numbers specified.

Form

```
max(<number list>)
```

Examples

```
max(5*4, 16, 300/12)
max(field 1, field 2, field 3)
```

Min

Returns the lowest number in the list of numbers specified.

Form

```
min(<number list>)
```

Examples

```
min(16, 23, 40*.66)
min(field 5, field 10, field 7)
```

Random

Returns a random number between 1 and the number specified. The number specified in the argument is used as the upper limit of the random function.

Forms

```
random(<number>)
the random of <number>
```

Examples

```
random(5)
```

returns a number between 1 and 5.

```
the random of highNumber
```

where highNumber is a local memory variable.

Round

Rounds the number specified up or down to the nearest whole number. If the fraction is .5 or less, the number is rounded down. If the fraction is greater than .5, the number is rounded up.

Forms

```
round(<number>)
the round of <number>
```

Examples

```
round(4.5)  –– returns 4
round(4.51)  –– returns 5
```

Sin

Returns the sine of the angle specified in radians.

Forms

```
sin(<angle in radians>)
the sin of <angle in radians>
```

Examples

```
sin(45*pi/180)
sin(acuteAngle)
```

where acuteAngle is a local memory variable.

Sqrt

Returns the square root of the number specified as the function argument.

Forms

```
sqrt(<number>)
the sqrt of <number>
```

Examples

sqrt(45*7 – 2.5)
sqrt(temp)

where temp is a local memory variable.

Tan

Returns the tangent of the angle specified in radians.

Forms

tan(<angle in radians>)
the tan of <angle in radians>

Examples

tan(32.5*pi/180)
tan(angleB)

where angleB is a local memory variable.

Trunc

Drops the fractional part of any decimal number specified as the function argument and returns the whole number.

Forms

trunc(<number>)
the trunc of <number>

Examples

trunc(56.345) –– returns 56
the trunc of 0.456 –– returns 0

HyperCard Properties
and Constants

APPENDIX C

ALL HYPERCARD OBJECTS HAVE CHARACTERISTICS referred to as *properties* that you can retrieve information about and reset. When operating HyperCard from the menus, you can reset these properties by clicking on new settings that appear in dialog boxes. In HyperTalk scripts, you retrieve information about the current settings with the Get command and make changes to the settings of these properties with the Set command.

Remember that the Get command has the form

    get <expression>

When you want to retrieve information about a specific property, you enter the name of the property along with the object it describes as the <expression> argument. For instance, to obtain the name of a stack in your script, you enter

    get the name of this stack

Remember that the Get command always places the information that it retrieves into the *it* local memory variable.

The Set command has the form

    set <property> of <object> to <value>

To set a new characteristic for a particular property with the Set command, you enter the name of the property for the <property> argument, the ID or name of the object for the <object> argument, and the new setting for the <value> argument. For example, to change the style of a button from the round rectangle to the transparent type, you enter

    set style of bkgnd button 3 to transparent

Not all HyperCard properties can be changed with the Set command. For example, although you can use the Get command to retrieve the ID number of an object such as a field or button, you can't change this number with the Set command. Those properties that cannot be reset are clearly indicated in this appendix.

With the Get and Set commands, the word *the* before the property is always optional. With other commands, such as Put, *the* is required only if there are no parameters.

HyperCard properties are divided into eight categories: global, window, stack, background, card, painting, field, and button properties. In this appendix, you will find the properties alphabetically listed according to these categories. However, because of the similarity between the stack, background, and card properties, you will find these listed under one heading.

After the listing of the HyperCard properties, this appendix contains an alphabetical listing of the constants used by HyperTalk. These constants provide a means to initialize and test variables as well as to enter keyboard characters directly into scripts without having to use their numerical code equivalents (see the Read and Write commands in Chapter 15).

Global Properties

Global properties apply to all stacks in HyperCard. They can be thought of as the properties of HyperCard itself.

BlindTyping

If blindTyping is set to true, you can type HyperCard commands into the Message box even when it is hidden. If blindTyping is set to false, the Message box must be displayed on the screen before you can enter HyperTalk commands into it.

Form

blindTyping <true or false>

Examples

get the blindTyping
set blindTyping to true

Cursor

Controls the shape of the cursor during the execution of a script.

Form

cursor <id number>

There are four cursor shapes that you can set by entering their ID numbers:

The cursor returns to its normal shape as soon as the script ends. You cannot use the Get command with the cursor property. You can change its shape only with the Set command.

ID Number	Cursor Shape
1	I-Beam cursor
2	Standard crossbar
3	Thick version of the crossbar
4	Wristwatch (typically denoting that HyperCard is busy and you must wait)

Examples

set the cursor to 1 −− I-Beam cursor
set cursor to 4 −− Wristwatch icon for wait cursor

DragSpeed

Controls the speed at which the Drag command operates.

Form

dragSpeed <number>

The <number> argument represents pixels per second. Entering 0 as the dragSpeed <number> argument sets the drag speed to the fastest speed that the Macintosh is capable of. A comfortable speed for watching a drawing appear on the screen is about 150.

Examples

get the dragSpeed
set dragSpeed to 75

EditBkgnd

Takes you from the background of a stack to the card level and vice versa. Setting the editBkgnd property to true is the same as selecting the Background option on the Edit menu when you are at the card level. Setting editBkgnd to false is the same as selecting the Background option when you are in the background.

Form

editBkgnd <true or false>

Examples

get editBkgnd
set the editBkgnd to false
set editBkgnd to true

LockScreen

When the lockScreen property is set to true, HyperCard freezes the screen display during the execution of the HyperTalk commands that follow the Set command in the script. When lockScreen is set to false, the user sees all updates on the screen as the program executes the HyperTalk commands that follow the Set command in the script.

Form

lockScreen <true or false>

Examples

get the lockScreen
set lockScreen to true
set the lockScreen to false

NumberFormat

Sets the display format for all numerical results calculated by HyperTalk's math operators and commands.

Form

numberFormat <format string>

The <format string> argument must be enclosed in a pair of double quotation marks.

Examples

get the numberFormat
set numberFormat to "0.00"

This second example sets 2 decimal places; 0 before the decimal point, as well as trailing zeros, are retained.

set the numberFormat to "0.######"

sets 6 decimal places; 0 before the decimal point is retained, and any trailing zeros are dropped.

PowerKeys

Turns the painting program's power keys on and off. When you set the powerKeys property to true, the power keys are activated. When you set powerKeys to false, the power keys are deactivated.

Form

powerKeys <true or false>

Examples

get the powerKeys
set powerKeys to true
set the powerKeys to false

TextArrows (Version 1.1 Only)

When the textArrows property is set to true, the arrow keys can be used to move the cursor within text fields and the Message box. When the textArrows property is set to false, the arrow keys move you to new cards in the stack. When the textArrows property is set to true, you can navigate through the cards in the stack by pressing the Option key and an arrow key. Resetting this property in a script is the same as checking or unchecking the Text Arrows check box in the User Preferences card.

Form

textArrows <true or false>

Examples

get the textArrows
set textArrows to true
set the textArrows to false

UserLevel

Sets the user level from a script.

Form

userLevel <1 to 5>

The user levels and their numeric equivalents are as follows:

User Level	Number
Browsing	1
Typing	2
Painting	3
Authoring	4
Scripting	5

Example

get userLevel
if it > 2 then
    set userLevel to 2
end if

Window Properties

There are three windows in HyperCard: the tool window (the Tools menu), the pattern window (the Patterns menu), and the message window (the Message box). There are three window properties that affect the use of these windows.

Location

Sets the location of the upper left corner of the window.

Forms

```
loc <top left h,v>
location <top left h,v>
```

Examples

```
get the loc of tool window
set loc of message window to 30,250
set the location of pattern window to 225,100
```

Rectangle

Gets the location of the upper left and lower right corner of the window.

Forms

```
rect <top left h,v and bottom right h,v>
rectangle <top left h,v and bottom right h,v>
```

The rect property cannot be changed with the Set command.

Examples

```
get rect of message window
get the rect of tool window
get the rectangle of pattern window
```

Visible

When the visible property is set to true, the window is displayed on the screen. When the visible property is set to false, the window is hidden from view.

Form

visible <true or false>

Examples

get the visible of the message window
set the visible of the tool window to true
set the visible of the pattern window to false

Stack, Background, and Card Properties —

The properties of the stack, background, and cards are similar. However, the stack does not use the number property, as in the number of the card or background, and backgrounds and cards do not share the size and freeSize properties used by the stack.

FreeSize

Returns the amount of space freed up in a stack by the deletion of objects such as buttons, fields, and cards from the stack. Free space in a stack is unusable and can be removed only by using the Compact Stack option on the File menu. The freeSize property cannot be changed with the Set command.

Form

freeSize of <stack>

Example

get the freeSize of this stack
if it is > 500 then doMenu "Compact Stack"

ID

Returns the ID number of the stack, background, or card. The ID number cannot be changed with the Set command.

Form

id of <property>

Examples

get id of this stack
get the id of card
get the id of background

Name

Returns or changes the name of the stack, background, or card. When you specify *short name*, HyperCard returns only the name of the object. If you specify *name* or *long name*, it returns the type of object, its ID number, and name (if any is assigned).

Form

name of <property>

Examples

get name of stack – – stack "Home"
get the short name of stack – – Home
set the name of this card to "Anderson Engineering"
get the name of this background

Number

Returns the number of the card or background in the stack (the number property is not used with the stack). The card and background number cannot be changed with the Set command.

Form

number of <property>

Examples

get the number of this card
get number of background id 3001

Script

Returns the text of the script of a stack, background, or card to the *it* memory variable. Can also be used with the Set command to modify or add to the script of one of these objects.

Form

script of <object>

Examples

get the script of this background
get script of stack "Address"
set the script of card 1 to empty
set the script of card 1 to newScript

where newScript is a local memory variable that contains the message handler and HyperTalk commands of the new card script.

Size

Returns the size in bytes of the stack (not used with the card or background). The size property cannot be changed with the Set command.

Form

size of <stack>

Examples

get size of this stack
get the size of stack "Home"

Painting Properties

The painting properties allow you to control many of the painting program attributes from the scripts you write.

Brush

Sets the brush shape for the Brush tool. This is the same as clicking on one of the brush shapes in the Brush Shape dialog box.

Form

    brush <brush number 1–32>

Numbers are assigned to the brush shapes in the Brush Shape dialog box starting with 1 for the brush shape in the upper left corner of the dialog box, and increasing as you go down the first column and subsequent columns.

Examples

    get the brush
    set the brush to 5
    set brush to 10

Centered

Turns on and off the Draw Centered option. When the centered property is set to true, the Draw Centered option on the Options menu is turned on. When the centered property is set to false, the Draw Centered option is turned off.

Form

    centered <true or false>

Examples

    get the centered
    set centered to true
    set the centered to false

Filled

Turns on and off the Draw Filled option. When the filled property is set to true, the Draw Filled option on the Options menu is turned on. When the filled property is set to false, the Draw Filled option is turned off.

Form

filled <true or false>

Examples

get the filled
set the filled to true
set filled to false

Grid

Turns on and off the painting grid. When the grid property is set to true, the painting grid is turned on. When grid is set to false, the painting grid is turned off.

Form

grid <true or false>

Examples

get the grid
set the grid to true
set grid to false

LineSize

Sets the thickness of the line size used by various painting tools. The line size is set by entering the number of pixels. You can set the pixel width to 1, 2, 3, 4, 6, or 8 pixels.

Form

lineSize <pixel number 1, 2, 3, 4, 6, or 8>

Examples

get lineSize
set the lineSize to 2
set the lineSize to 4

Multiple

Turns on and off the Draw Multiple option on the Options menu. When the multiple property is set to true, the Draw Multiple option is activated. When the multiple property is set to false, the Draw Multiple option is deactivated.

Form

multiple <true or false>

Examples

get the multiple
set multiple to true
set the multiple to false

MultiSpace

Sets the spacing between multiple images when the Draw Multiple option is active.

Form

multiSpace <1 to 9>

The lower the number assigned to the multiSpace property, the closer the spacing between images.

Examples

    set the multiSpace to 1
    set the multiSpace to 4
    set multiSpace to 9

Pattern

Sets the current pattern from the Patterns menu.

Form

    pattern <1 to 40>

The palette containing the 40 different patterns is arranged in four columns of ten patterns each. The numbers start at 1 for the pattern in the upper left corner and increase down each column and across the palette.

Examples

    get the pattern
    set pattern to 5
    set the pattern to 25

PolySides

Sets the number of sides drawn by the Regular Polygon tool.

Form

    polySides <number of polygon sides>

You can set the polySides property to 3, 4, 5, 6, or 8. Three (the triangle) is the default setting for the Regular Polygon tool.

Examples

    get the polySides
    set the polySides to 4
    set polySides to 6

TextAlign

Sets the alignment of the text entered with the Paint Text tool.

Form

textAlign <left | right | centered>

Left alignment is the program default.

Examples

set textAlign to centered
set the textAlign to right
set textAlign to left

TextFont

Sets the font of the text entered with the Paint Text tool.

Form

textFont <font name>

Typical font choices include Chicago, Courier, Geneva, Helvetica, Monaco, New York, and Times.

Examples

get the textFont
set textFont to Chicago
set textFont to New York
set the textFont to Monaco

TextHeight

Sets the spacing (leading) between text that is entered with the Paint Text tool.

Form

textHeight <leading>

The <leading> argument is specified by a number representing point size.

Examples

```
get the textHeight
set the textHeight to 16
set the textHeight to 18
```

TextSize

Returns or sets the size of the font (in points) entered with the Paint Text tool.

Form

```
textSize <font size>
```

The <font size> argument is specified by the point size. The choice of font sizes varies according to the font specified.

Examples

```
get the textSize
set the textSize to 10
set textSize to 18
```

TextStyle

Sets the style of the text entered with the Paint Text tool.

Form

```
textStyle <bold | italic | outline | shadow | condense
| extend | plain>
```

Examples

```
get the textStyle
set the textStyle to bold
set textStyle to condense
```

Field Properties

The field properties apply to both background and card fields in a stack. When retrieving or setting the property of a background field, you must use the word *background* or *bkgnd* when referring to that field (when you just enter *field*, HyperCard assumes that you are referring to a card field).

ID

Returns the ID number of the field. You cannot use the Set command to change the ID number assigned by HyperCard to a field.

Form

id <id number>

Examples

get the id of the bkgnd field "Address"
get id of field 5

Location

Returns and sets the location of a field by the screen coordinates at its center.

Form

loc <center h,v>
location <center h,v>

Examples

get the loc of bkgnd field 3
set the loc of field "Address" to 25,150
set location of field 7 to 130,200

LockText

When the lockText property is set to true, the user cannot modify the contents of a field. When it is set to false, its contents can be edited at any time.

Form

lockText <true or false>

Examples

get the lockText of field "Name"
set lockText of bkgnd field "Password" to true
set the lockText of field 10 to false

Name

Returns or sets the name of the field.

Form

name <field name>

Examples

get the name of field 2
set name of bkgnd field 3 to "City"

Number

Returns the number of the field. You cannot change the field number with the Set command. The only way to change a field's number is to use the Bring Closer or Send Farther option on the Objects menu.

Form

number <bkgnd or card field number>

Examples

get the number of field "State"
get the number of bkgnd field 5

Rectangle

You can use the rectangle property to move or resize a field in a card or just to retrieve its location. The property returns the horizontal and vertical screen coordinates of the upper left and lower right corner.

Forms

rect <top left h,v and bottom right h,v>
rectangle <top left h,v and bottom right h,v>

Examples

get rect of field "State"

set the rectangle of bkgnd field 4 ¬
to 174,117,323,157

Script

Returns or sets the field script.

Form

script of <field>

Examples

get the script of field "Total"
set the script of bkgnd field 2 to empty
set script of bkgnd field 2 to newScript

where newScript is a memory variable that contains the message handler and HyperTalk commands for the field script.

Scroll

Sets the number of pixels that the program scrolls the text in a scrolling field.

Form

scroll <number of pixels from top of text>

Examples

set the scroll of bkgnd field 1 to 50
set scroll of field "Comments" to scrollPixels

where scrollPixels is a local memory variable.

ShowLines

When the showLines property is set to true, the lines in a field are visible in a card. When the showLines property is set to false, the lines in a field are invisible.

Form

showLines <true or false>

Examples

get the showLines of field "Address"
set showLines of bkgnd field 3 to true
set showLines of field id 3456 to false

Style

Returns or sets the style of the field.

Form

style <transparent | opaque | rectangle | shadow
| scrolling>

Examples

get the style of field "City"
set the style of field 4 to scrolling
set the style of bkgnd field "Last Name" to transparent

TextAlign

Returns or sets the alignment of text on each line of a field.

Form

textAlign <left | right | center>

Left alignment is the default setting.

Examples

get textAlign of bkgnd field "Telephone"
set the textAlign of field 2 to center
set the textAlign of bkgnd field 3 to right

TextFont

Returns or sets the font of the field.

Form

textFont <font name>

Typical font choices include Chicago, Courier, Geneva, Helvetica, Monaco, New York, and Times.

Examples

get the textFont of field 1 to Courier
set textFont of bkgnd field "City" to Chicago
set the textFont of field id 2345 to New York
set the textFont of bkgnd field 5 to Monaco

TextHeight

Returns or sets the spacing (leading) between the lines of text in a field.

Form

```
textHeight <leading>
```

The <leading> argument is specified by a number representing point size.

Examples

```
get the textHeight of bkgnd field 3
set textHeight of field "Address" to 16
set the textHeight of field id 1267 to 18
```

TextSize

Returns or sets the size of the text (in points) of the field.

Form

```
textSize <font size>
```

The <font size> argument is specified by the point size. The choice of point sizes varies according to the font specified.

Examples

```
get the textSize of field 2
set textSize of bkgnd field "Name" to 10
set the textSize of field id 7854 to 18
```

TextStyle

Returns or sets the text style attributes assigned to the font used in the field.

Form

textStyle <bold | italic | underline | outline | shadow
| condense | extend | plain>

Examples

get the textStyle of bkgnd field 5
set the textStyle of field "Comments" to italic
set textStyle of field id 4598 to bold

Visible

When the visible property of a field is set to true, the field is visible in the card. When the visible property of a field is set to false, the field is hidden.

Form

visible <true or false>

Examples

get the visible of bkgnd field 7
set visible of bkgnd field "Notes" to false
set visible of field id 5643 to true

WideMargins

When the wideMargins property is set to true, the field uses wide margins, which allows you to enter more text on each line. When the wideMargins property is set to false, the field uses standard margins.

Form

wideMargins <true or false>

Examples

get the wideMargins of bkgnd field 5
set wideMargins of bkgnd field "Company" to true
set the wideMargins of field id 4398 to false

Button Properties

The button properties apply to both background and card buttons in a stack. When retrieving or setting the property of a background button, you must use the word *background* or *bkgnd* when referring to that button (when you just enter *button*, HyperCard assumes that you are referring to a card button).

AutoHilite

When the autoHilite property is set to true, the button is momentarily highlighted when you click on it (the autoHilite property does not work with check box or radio button styles). When the autoHilite property is set to false, this highlighting does not take place when the button is clicked.

Form

autoHilite <true or false>

Examples

get the autoHilite of bkgnd button 3
set autoHilite of button "OK" to true

Hilite

When the hilite property is set to true, the button is highlighted (most often signifying it as the default choice). When the hilite property is set to false, the button does not appear highlighted.

Form

hilite <true or false>

Examples

get the hilite of bkgnd button 3
set hilite of field button "Delete" to false

Icon

Returns or sets the icon of the button.

Form

icon <icon number or name>

Examples

get the icon of bkgnd button 3
set icon of button "MacWrite" to "MacWrite"
set the icon of bkgnd button 5 to 3835

ID

Returns the ID number of the button. You cannot change the button ID with the Set command.

Form

id <button id number>

Examples

get the id of button 5
get id of bkgnd button 5
get the id of button "Next"

Location

Returns or sets the location of the button on the screen by the horizontal and vertical coordinates of its center.

Forms

loc <center h,v>
location <center h,v>

Examples

get the loc of bkgnd button id 4567
set the location of button 3 to 320,175
set loc of bkgnd button "Prev" to 250,330

Name

Returns or sets the name of the button.

Form

name <button name>

Examples

get the name of bkgnd button 3
set the name of button 5 to "Next"
set name of bkgnd button 16 to "Home"

Number

Returns the number of the button. You cannot use the Set command to change the button number. The only way to change the number of a button is to use the Bring Closer or Send Farther command on the Objects menu.

Form

number <button number>

Examples

get number of bkgnd button "Home"
get the number of button "Add"
get the number of bkgnd button id 6789

Rectangle

You can use the rectangle property to move or resize a button in a card or just to retrieve its location. The property returns the horizontal and vertical screen coordinates of the upper left and lower right corners.

Forms

rect <top left h,v and bottom right h,v>
rectangle <top left h,v and bottom right h,v>

Examples

get the rectangle of bkgnd button 3
set rect of button "Comments" to 20,250,27,280

Script

Returns or sets the button script.

Form

script of <button>

Examples

get the script of button 12
set script of bkgnd button 2 to empty
set script of bkgnd button 2 to newScript

where newScript is a memory variable that contains the message handler and HyperTalk commands for the button script.

ShowName

If the showName property is set to true, the name of the button is displayed. If the showName property is set to false, the name is not displayed within the button.

Form

> showName <true or false>

Examples

> get the showName of bkgnd button 2
> set the showName of button "Next" to false
> set showName of bkgnd button "More Buttons" to true

Style

Returns or sets the style of button.

Form

> style <transparent | opaque | rectangle | shadow
> | roundRect | checkBox | radioButton>

Examples

> get the style of bkgnd button id 5678
> set style of button "Home" to opaque
> set style of bkgnd button 3 to shadow

TextAlign

Returns or sets the alignment of the button name in the button.

Form

> textAlign <left | right | center>

Center alignment is the default setting.

Examples

> get the textAlign of bkgnd button "Phone"
> set the textAlign of button 2 to left
> set textAlign of bkgnd button 3 to right

TextFont

Returns or sets the font of the button name.

Form

textFont <font name>

Typical font choices include Chicago, Courier, Geneva, Helvetica, Monaco, New York, and Times.

Examples

set textFont of bkgnd button "Delete" to Courier
set the textFont of button id 2345 to New York
set the textFont of bkgnd button 5 to Monaco

TextSize

Returns or sets the size of the text (in points) of the button name.

Form

textSize <font size>

The <font size> argument is specified by the point size. The choice of point sizes varies according to the font specified.

Examples

set textSize of bkgnd button "Find" to 10
set the textSize of button id 7854 to 18

TextStyle

Returns or sets the text style attributes assigned to the font used for the button name.

Form

textStyle <bold | italic | underline | outline | shadow
| condense | extend | plain>

Examples

set the textStyle of button "Delete" to italic
set textStyle of button id 4598 to bold

Visible

When the visible property of a button is set to true, the button is visible in the card. When the visible property of a button is set to false, the button is hidden.

Form

visible <true or false>

Examples

get visible of bkgnd button 7
set visible of bkgnd button "Notes" to false
set the visible of button id 5643 to true

Constants

HyperCard has several constants that can be used in scripts to test for a particular condition or to enter characters such as tab, space, and return without having to know their code numbers.

Down

Used to test the result of the Shift key, Option key, Command key, and mouse.

Examples

if shiftKey is down then exit mouseUp
if the commandKey is down then go to stack "Help"
if the mouse is down then go home

Empty

Used to test if a HyperCard object is empty. (This is not the same as testing if the object has a value of zero.)

Examples

```
put empty into field 1  -- clears out current contents

if bkgnd field "Name" is empty then
   ask "What is your name?"
   put it into field "Name"
end if
```

False

Stores false to memory variables that are tested later in the script.

Example

```
put false into testVar  -- testVar is local memory variable
.
.
.
repeat while testVar  -- same as repeat while false
```

FormFeed

Enters a form feed character (ASCII code 012).

Example

```
open file "Text3"
write field 1 to "Text 3"
write formFeed to file "Text3
close file "Text3"
```

LineFeed

Enters a line feed character (ASCII code 010).

Example

```
open file "Stock Quotes"
write field 1 to "Stock Quotes"
write return & lineFeed to file "Stock Quotes"
close file "Stock Quotes"
```

Quote

Enters a quotation mark within text that is already enclosed within quotation marks.

Example

```
Put "She says," & quote & "Never!" & quote into field 2
```

Thus, field 2 contains *She says, "Never!"*

Return

Enters a single return character (ASCII code 013).

Examples

```
put return after word 4 of line 1 of field 2

open file readFrom  -- readFrom is memory variable
read from file readFrom until return
close file readFrom
```

Space

Enters a single space character (same as entering " ").

Examples

```
put space before word 1 of field 4
put space & space after word 3 of field 7
```

Tab

Enters a single tab character (ASCII code number 009).

Example

```
open file readFrom  –– readFrom is memory variable
read from file readFrom until tab
close file readFrom
```

True

Stores true to memory variables that are tested later in the script.

Example

```
put true into testVar  –– testVar is a local memory variable
.
.
.
if testVar then beep 3  –– same as if true then beep 3
```

Up

Used to test the result of the Shift key, Option key, Command key, and mouse.

Examples

```
if shiftKey is up then exit mouseUp
if the commandKey is up then go to stack "Help"
if the mouse is up then beep
```

INDEX

with calculation results, 451
changing text style with, 408–409
memory variables with, 331–332, 384
Type command vs., 403

Q

Quitting HyperCard, 44–45
Quotation marks (" "), as delimiters, 33–34
Quote constant, 568

R

Radians, converting from degrees, 462–463
Radio buttons, 23
Random function, 460–461, 533
Read command, 486–491, 509
  Open/Close File and, 505
Recent command, 25–26
Rectangle property
  for a button, 563
  for a field, 555
  for a window, 543
Rectangle/Round Rectangle tools, 263–264, 285–286
Reduce or Enlarge box, 71
Reduction, Precision Bitmap Alignment and, 73
Regular Polygon tool, 267–268, 284–286
  PolySides property, 550
Repeat commands, 368–377
  Boolean operators, 346–347
  format of, 369
  for importing data, 489
  for modifying order of execution, 345
  Next Repeat command with, 375–377
  number argument, 370–371
  Repeat For, 368, 370–372
  Repeat While/Repeat Until, 368, 372–373
  Repeat With, 368, 373–375
Reports
  columnar, 86–87
  HyperCard vs. database manager, 8
  mailing labels, 85–86
  printing, 80–90
Resedit, 248
Reserved words, with Read command, 488
Reset Paint command, 509–510
Result function, 402, 523–524

Resume message, 315–316, 476
Return, as constant, 488, 492, 568
Return key
  as line indicator (hard return), 328
  with Paint Text tool, 266
  system messages, 309–310
  for terminating command statement (soft return), 300
  with user-defined functions, 472
Revert option, in Paint menu, 278
Rotate Left/Rotate Right options, 275
Round function, 458, 461, 534
  with Repeat construction, 371
Round Rectangle tool. *See* Rectangle/Round Rectangle tools
Rows, reports arranged by, 89–91

S

Saving, automatic, 47
Scrapbook. *See* Clipboard
Screen coordinates, 406–409
  with Drag command, 416
  Location property and, 561–562
Screen display
  card design concerns, 133–134
  field attributes for, 105–106
  locating cursor on, 403, 405–409
  pixels on, 253
  printing card from, 74
  saving as MacPaint file, 287
  special effects scripts, 427–436
  startup screen, 13
Script button, 106
  editing, 239–241
  Script Editor selected with, 295
Script Editor, 295–299
  automatic formatting in, 300
  Do command and, 500–501
Scripting level, 11–12
  for Finder stack, 477
  Objects menu role, 123
Script option, 213
Script property
  for a button, 563
  for a field, 555
  for a stack, background, or card, 546
Scripts, 294–306
  attaching, 303
  background vs. card fields in, 341
  for browsing, 382–400
  comments in, 490

constant vs. variable information in, 326–327
defining information in, 319–330
for deleting, 409–411
DoMenu command in, 418–419
editing, 295–299, 411–412
for editing cards, 403–412
for exporting data, 491–492
for finding cards, 400–402
for importing data, 489–490
for making sounds, 436–446
for menu options, 381–419
message handlers in, 300–301, 308–309
message inheritance hierarchy, 302–306
with painting program, 415–417
for printing cards, 412–415
printing text of, 298–299
searching in, 298–299
with Show command, 387–400
for sorting, 421–427
for special screen effects, 427–436
structure of, 299–306
system messages in, 306–316
visual effects in, 428–436
See also specific scripts
Scrolling
  in Script Editor, 297–298
  in text fields, 2
Scroll left/right/up/down (visual effect), 428, 435
Scroll property, 556
Searching
  field references in, 104–105
  inserting text into search string, 39
  limiting, 35–43
  in Script Editor, 298–299
  scripts for, 400–402
  See also Find command
Seconds function, 470–471, 524
Select All option, 270–271
Selected background fields option, 87
Selection memory variable, 342
Selection tool, 161, 255–258
  Fill option and, 272
  Lasso tool vs., 161
  for moving paint text, 267
  for positioning captions, 179–182
Select option, 270
Send command, 510
  for modifying order of execution, 345
Send Farther option, 146
Set command, 510–511
  for changing properties, 340, 537

Wine Tour Stack: Disk Offer

For readers who would like to obtain the complete Wine Tour stack introduced in the exercises in this book, a companion disk is available. This disk contains all the linked cards describing the wineries in the Valley of the Moon, Sonoma Valley, and Napa Valley.

The disk is in 3½-inch Mac format. To obtain the disk, complete the order form and return it with a check or money order for $30.00 (U.S. dollars), payable to Greg Harvey.

Greg Harvey
P.O. Box 1175
Point Reyes Station, CA 94956–1175

Name _____

Address _____

City/State/Zip _____

Enclosed is my check or money order (in U.S. dollars) for $30.00.

SYBEX is not affiliated with Greg Harvey and assumes no responsibility for any defect in the disk.

SYBEX Computer Books
are different.

Here is why . . .

At SYBEX, each book is designed with you in mind. Every manuscript is carefully selected and supervised by our editors, who are themselves computer experts. We publish the best authors, whose technical expertise is matched by an ability to write clearly and to communicate effectively. Programs are thoroughly tested for accuracy by our technical staff. Our computerized production department goes to great lengths to make sure that each book is well-designed.

In the pursuit of timeliness, SYBEX has achieved many publishing firsts. SYBEX was among the first to integrate personal computers used by authors and staff into the publishing process. SYBEX was the first to publish books on the CP/M operating system, microprocessor interfacing techniques, word processing, and many more topics.

Expertise in computers and dedication to the highest quality product have made SYBEX a world leader in computer book publishing. Translated into fourteen languages, SYBEX books have helped millions of people around the world to get the most from their computers. We hope we have helped you, too.

For a complete catalog of our publications:

SYBEX, Inc. 2021 Challenger Drive, #100, Alameda, CA 94501
Tel: (415) 523-8233/(800) 227-2346   Telex: 336311
Fax: (415) 523-2373

KEYBOARD SHORTCUTS FOR CHANGING THE TEXT STYLE OF A FIELD

Keys	Result
Command-T	Displays Text Style dialog box
Command->	Selects next larger text size in the font
Command-<	Selects next smaller text size in the font
Command-Shift->	Selects next font in system
Command-Shift-<	Selects previous font in system
Command-Option->	Increases the number of points between lines
Command-Option-<	Decreases the number of points between lines

THE POWER KEYS FOR THE PAINTING PROGRAM

Menu	Key	Command	Menu	Key	Command
Paint	**A**	Select All (Command-A)	Options	**C**	Draw Centered (on/off)
	D	Darken		**G**	Grid (on/off)
	E	Trace Edges		**M**	Draw Multiple (on/off)
	F	Fill		**1, 2, 3, 4, 6, 8**	Line Size (number of pixels)
	H	Flip Horizontal			
	I	Invert			
	L	Lighten	Patterns	**B**	Black Pattern
	O	Opaque		**W**	White Pattern
	P	Pickup			
	R	Revert			
	S	Select (Command-S)			
	T	Transparent			
	V	Flip Vertical			
	[	Rotate Left			
	]	Rotate Right			